BEHIND the POSTMODERN FACADE

BEHIND the POSTMODERN FACADE

Architectural Change in Late Twentieth-Century America

Magali Sarfatti Larson

UNIVERSITY OF CALIFORNIA PRESS
Berkeley • *Los Angeles* • *London*

University of California Press
Berkeley and Los Angeles, California

University of California Press, Ltd.
London, England

© 1993 by
The Regents of the University of California

Library of Congress Cataloging-in-Publication Data

Larson, Magali Sarfatti.
    Behind the postmodern facade : architectural change in late twentieth-century
America / Magali Sarfatti Larson.
        p.   cm.
    Includes bibliographical references and index.
    ISBN 0-520-08135-8 (alk. paper)
    1. Architectural practice—United States.   2. Architectural services marketing—
United States.   3. Architecture—United States—Technological
innovations.   4. Architects—United States—Psychology.   I. Title.
    NA1996.L37   1993
    720'.68—dc20   92-25694
                                                                                        CIP

Printed in the United States of America

9   8   7   6   5   4   3   2   1

The paper used in this publication meets the minimum requirements of American National
Standard for Information Sciences—Permanence of Paper for Printed Library Materials,
ANSI Z39.48-1984. ⊗

*For Charlie, who has read it
and Tony, who someday might*

Contents

Illustrations

Foreword

In the last decade or two, contradictions and conflicts have arisen between what we architects conceive as our goals and purposes and what we accept from project developers as *their* goals. These growing complexities in the production of architecture constitute a dramatic shift that many either failed to notice or became resigned to. The changes in the environment in which architects work (and worked for the better part of this century) have transformed both what architects do and how they do it, in everything from architecture as idea to architecture as built fact. That sea change in architecture as object and architecture as process is addressed with authority and insight in this book.

No architect needs to be told that the process of producing architecture is complex. But architects rarely have time to study the nature or causes of that complexity. Fragmentary explanations exist, but they assume that each element in the complex task is an autonomous unit, separate and uncontaminated. In *Behind the Postmodern Facade* Magali Sarfatti Larson examines both the outer complexities and the inner struggles of architecture; nothing so complete or so penetrating has been undertaken before.

No architect can realistically believe in anything approaching complete autonomy. Even such autonomy as does exist is being eroded by complexities and conflicts arriving from new quarters. Dealing with these largely external changes by traditional responses or with traditional perceptions and ideas can hardly work. To begin again, to move forward responsibly, will require a full understanding of the environment in which architects work as well as an understanding of our habits of discourse, of the ways architects perceive the world and deal with it.

This study, revealing as it does the extraordinary changes in the inner and outer forces central to the production of architecture, should encourage genuine dialogue and debate about possible futures, of perhaps different "architectures." Such a debate cannot assume a tabula rasa. In this century we have seen post–World War I European "modern" architecture, an architecture of strong social purpose and commitment, transformed, on its arrival in this country, to an architecture of form and style and, after World War II, to a worldwide means of aggressive development. We need to revisit and to understand the history of these transformations of architecture.

History, good history, informs us about what happened but also about why, in all its complexity. Architectural history, much of it growing from the traditions of German art history, has been preoccupied with the *what* of events and—since events in architecture are visible—with what things look like, often with little regard to intentions, foreground, or background, temporal or physical. Similarly, current architectural criticism tends to be preoccupied with the *what,* ignoring settings, focusing on fragments and ornaments—shells of ideas—and failing to explain in any useful way how things came to be as they are. Architectural history and much of the discourse about architecture have become a limiting diversion, a presetting of our perceptions and expectations.

Architecture as it is practiced, taught, and talked about generally assumes an autonomy that is in conflict with the notion of architecture as a service profession, integral to the society and culture, embedded in everyday life. There are, indeed, responsibilities that are particularly architectural, but those responsibilities are deeply implanted in our society and culture. Architects are fortunate to be in a profession that is inherently *not* isolated, *not* pure or narcissistic, one that has to be integrated into the surrounding society and culture to exist. It is only in the polemics of current discourse that architecture becomes esoteric and isolated.

Much of architectural discourse and criticism today resembles missiles fired randomly in all directions. This book lays the foundation for a new beginning, a new debate. Architectural books are, too often, the end of the affair. This one suggests movement and a progression of events; rather than driving for finality, it looks forward to a needed open-endedness.

Debate would be welcome on what architects *can* control and what is beyond our control; that is, What are the particular and specific responsibilities of architecture? To answer this is to decide in which direction to move; toward autonomy over a smaller slice or toward cooperation and integration with the larger society and culture. It has never been an either/ or situation—the reality is more fragmented. The great value of this book is as a beginning; it should be widely read by architects and anyone concerned about the future of our society and culture.

It is entirely possible that to understand this foreword one will have to read the book. So much the better: do it.

Joe Esherick
San Francisco, September 1992

Acknowledgments

I have incurred many debts in writing this book. I started working on architects at the Shelby Cullom Davis Center for Historical Studies of Princeton University in the spring of 1980. It is therefore appropriate to repeat my gratitude and admiration for the Center and its founder and first director, Lawrence Stone. Judith Blau, the author of an exemplary study of architects, encouraged me to publish those first pieces of work; I am grateful for her advice and support over the years. I also owe much to the work and encouragement of Robert Gutman.

In 1987–88, the National Science Foundation awarded me a Visiting Professorship for Women Scientists, which I spent at New York University. Barbara Heyns and Wolf Heydebrand of NYU's Department of Sociology made it possible institutionally; Patricia Hartman made dealing with the bureaucracy almost easy; the faculty and students in sociology and elsewhere made the "interactive" part of the Visiting Professorship exactly what it was supposed to be. I am grateful to all these people and to the Department of Sociology. Last but not least, Eliot Freidson provided generous intellectual mentorship then and later. I cannot even begin to thank him for his mentorship, for his very close reading of the final manuscript, for his excellent suggestions, and for reading crucial chapters a second time.

The VPWS did for me what it does for many women, rescuing me from the agony of rejection by other funding sources, giving me generous financial support, and making me very proud of being a woman scientist. I am grateful to the Director of VPWS, Dr. Gretchen Klein, and to NSF for this great program. Without that year almost entirely devoted to research, this book would not have been written.

Over fourteen years, Temple University has given me a fair share of its always scarce resources, wonderful colleagues, interesting and endearing students, quite a few headaches, and pride in its "urban mission." I gladly record here some more specific debts: a 1988–89 study leave, which allowed me to finish the research and start writing; a 1991–92 grant-in-aid, which subsidized the photographs and the index of this book; finally, a month's summer salary and medical benefits, which I owe to the support of Dean Lois Cronholm, made it possible for me to accept the invitation of the Swedish Collegium for Advanced Study in the Social Sciences (SCASSS) in the fall of 1990.

The three and a half months I spent at SCASSS in Uppsala came as close to perfect freedom as I have known recently. I finished the first draft of the manuscript thanks to SCASSS, and I shall be forever grateful to its directors, Bö Gustafsson and Björn Wittrock, and to their staff—Gunilla Backström, Catarina Nilsson, Kit Nylhem, Merrick Tabor, and Boris Kahn. However, my preeminent debt is with Rolf Torstendahl, founder and former director of SCASSS, who invited me to Sweden for the first time in 1986. Rolf's probing questions reoriented me theoretically and empirically toward the professional aspects of architecture. It has been an honor to collaborate with him over the years.

I am grateful to the Fine Arts Library of the University of Pennsylvania for its hospitality and its collections, which would have been inaccessible without the help of the librarian, Mr. Alan Morrisson, and his assistants Ed Deegan and Kurt Winkelman. Like most students who have used the Furness Library before Bela Zichy's untimely death, I remember the helpfulness of this generous and unforgettable man.

This is a book about architects and architecture. Logically, my foremost debt is with over thirty-five architects who accepted invitations to talk with me (sometimes repeatedly) and gave generously of their time, insights, and wisdom. Their names are recorded throughout the pages of this book, which is in many ways *their* book. They are obviously not responsible for what I have done with what they told me.

Besides the architects themselves, many people have helped me with their knowledge of architects and their work, with key introductions, or with both. I thank Jerry Bragstad, Philip Cannistraro, Weld Coxe, Dana Cuff, Joseph Denny, John Morris Dixon, Nan Ellin, Timur Galen, David Gracie, Jack Heinz, Carol Krinsky, Hélène Lipstadt, Loren Leatherbarrow,

Walter Molesky, John Mollenkopf, Gail Radford, Miles Ritter, Joseph Rykwert, Tony Schumann, Philip Siller, Suzanne Stephens, Friedrike Taylor, Carol Willis, Stuart Wrede of the Museum of Modern Art, Gwendolyn Wright, John Zuccotti, and Mathilda McQuaid of the Museum of Modern Art, who was particularly helpful in my search for photographs. I am very much indebted to Philip Johnson. He has supported my research since the beginning by his great knowledge and wit, by many authorizations to use his name, and even by refusing to believe it would ever become a book. It has been a rare pleasure to get to know him.

All my friends have made life worth living, but some have participated more closely than others in the writing of this book. In Sweden, I am grateful to Göran and Marianne Ahrne, Margareta Bertilsson, Tom Burns, Barbara Czarniawska-Joerges and Bernwald Joerges, Jim and Renate Fernandez, Anita Jacobsson-Widding, Walter Karsnaes, Uskali Maki, Sandra Mardones, Païvi Oinas, Hilary Rose, Bö Rothstein, and Kerstin Sahlins-Andersson for their warmth and intellectual camaraderie. In addition, I thank Göran, Tom, Barbara, Hilary, and Kerstin for their penetrating reading of chapters 1, 4, and 5.

Especially (though not exclusively) during my stay at NYU, Yasmin Ergas and Leonard Groopman, Kathleen Gerson and John Mollenkopf, Molly Nolan, and Ingrid and George Rothbart have offered me generous hospitality and intelligent interest in my work. The encouragement of Renate and Umberto Eco, Carole Joffe, Alcira Kreimer, Margaret Levi, Lynn Mally, Tim Mason, Simonetta Piccone Stella, Eliseo Verón, and Bob Wood was particularly welcome in the beginning, as were a conversation with Amy Shuman and the approval of Helen Giambruni at the very end. My friends and former students, Michael Blim, Nancy Kleniewski, and Douglas Porpora, gave me incisive readings of particular chapters. Carolyn Adams took the time to read chapter 3 and to make important suggestions. Sue Wells made helpful comments on early versions of chapters 7 and 8. Evelyn Tribble listened and offered invaluable editorial help, as did Peter Salomon. Roland Schevsky took for me the photographs of the Berlin housing projects. Diana Crane and David Leatherbarrow gave me invaluable support, advice, and information throughout the writing. I am grateful to all of them.

Susan Stewart has believed in this project to the point of organizing a session of the Modern Language Association around it. Her presence and support at Temple, as also those of Sherri Grasmuck, make Temple much more than a place of work. They know how much feeling goes into saying this. Fred Block read many chapters and in the end gave a generous but critical reading to the entire manuscript. There cannot be sufficient words of thanks for the brotherliness and the intellectual comradeship he has given me during the past seventeen years.

I received cogent suggestions from the reviewers for the University of California Press. I thank Howard Becker, Diana Crane, Harvey Molotch, and Roger Montgomery, who identified themselves to me after the fact. Naomi Schneider, my editor at the Press, had confidence in the project from the outset and steered it through many hurdles. Tony Hicks produced the book with great skill, resolving many problems that he had not created. Above all, he showed sympathy for the chronic anguish of the author. David Severtson was a demanding, intelligent, interested, and therefore excellent copy editor. I am grateful to all three.

My students Douglas Eaves and Lynette Manteau gave me competent (and Doug, especially dedicated) assistance in the library. Elinor Bernal made a crucial contribution in transcribing the tapes. Gloria Basmajian rushed several printings through with unfailing good grace. Ruth Smith of Research and Program Development at Temple University was always helpful. Cynthia Barnett came to work as my department's head secretary in time to help with the copyrights and the bills for the photographs. Selma Pastor produced an intelligent and competent index in record time. My thanks to all and each of them.

We usually wait until the end to thank the ones we love most. I do not believe they necessarily help us the most in the selfish and demanding task of writing. Yet my husband's participation in the making of this book has gone far beyond noninterference and even beyond his usual exceptional helpfulness. Some things stand out within a stream of constant and assiduous support: He has taken entire responsibility for our Tony for long stretches of time; he has read the book chapter by chapter and sometimes page by page; he has made special efforts to take pictures for the book; he developed the original concepts for the cover and the display of the photographs. Above all, he has been enthusiastic and enlightening, sharing his knowledge of construction, his love for architecture, his austere good taste, and his strong sense of priorities. My son has been gracious enough to recognize that "Mommy's book" was important. This book is dedicated to my husband and my son. Their love graces my life and makes my work both possible and worthwhile.

PART ONE

The Background
of Architectural Change

CHAPTER ONE

Architecture as Art and Profession

Building is the activity by which human beings make their shelter and their mark upon the earth. It is as closely associated with the celebration of power and the sacred as with humble everyday uses. Although beautiful and significant buildings have been produced in every society since ancient times, architects first laid a lasting claim to the responsibility for designing them during the Italian Renaissance.

The patronage of the new city-states and a wealthy merchant class encouraged the expression of a new sense of monumentality and a new style. Beginning in the late fourteenth century, patrons who wanted to sponsor special buildings looked for talent among craftsmen who were trained in design and experienced in managing large workshops. Most architects of the early Renaissance, therefore, came from the ranks of stonecutters (on their way to becoming sculptors), goldsmiths, cabinet-makers, and painters. The fifteenth century brought new requirements: State architects were frequently involved in civil engineering projects, notably hydraulic works; more important, improvements in artillery compelled cities to build new and more complex fortifications.[1] Neither civic nor military buildings required new construction methods, but they did require design skills only rarely found among master masons.

Because they could rely on the established competence of workers in the building crafts, the designers of buildings were able to appropriate for themselves the intellectual task of conceiving the entire project. The first

3

architects were not only freed from the stigma of manual work, they gained prestige from the complexity, the civic importance, and the ancient aesthetic lineage claimed for the new style of building. Assisted by humanist theoreticians like Leon Battista Alberti, able to respond to central concerns of the state, and supported by the keen interest of amateur patrons, architects became the first artists to move closer to the ruling class, into an intermediate social status inaccessible to mere craftsmen.

As the new style consolidated into conventions of design, the architects gave a disciplinary foundation to their field, based on two-dimensional abstract representations of buildings, on built exemplars, and on the theoretical work of men like Alberti and Antonio Filarete. With design as their specific competence and a theoretical foundation for their art, architects increased the distance between themselves and traditional builders, for design, theoretical discourse, and practical treatises could be studied. Training in the skills and the discourse of architectural design increasingly became the hallmark of the architects for the elite and, later on, the central element of professionalization.

In capitalist societies, architecture emerged as a profession that possesses artistic, technical, and social dimensions. The emphasis placed on each varied in different times and places. However, the existence of engineering as a separate profession precluded almost everywhere a strictly technical concentration.[2] In the face of engineering's more-established position, it was strategically easier for architects to base their professional claims on the aesthetics of construction than on technological mastery or scientific methods. Thus, the image and identity of modern architecture remained centered on the subordination of technology to design.

Design gives the purpose of building a form. It defines the *telos*, the building's reason for being, which transcends technique and utility. For the eminent historian and critic Reyner Banham, the specific characteristic of Western architecture is "the persistence of drawing—*disegno*—as a kind of meta-pattern that subsumes all other patterns. . . . Being unable to think without drawing," he says, with some exaggeration, "became the true mark of one fully socialised into the profession of architecture."[3]

Beyond what Banham argues, design did make architecture an academic subject, and the new style of the Renaissance was important in the social ascent of architects. A sociologist, David Brain, underscores the persistent significance of style in the nineteenth-century professionalization of architecture. Now as then, style is a principal way in which buildings claim the status of architecture. The rhetorical aspects of style introduce buildings into a system of interpretation and justification that is at the core of professional discourse.[4]

From a sociological point of view, discourse includes all that a particular category of agents say (or write) in a specific capacity and in a definable thematic area. Discourse commonly invites dialogue. However, in architecture (as in all professions), discourse is not open to everyone but based on social appropriation and a principle of exclusion. Laypersons are not entitled to participate in the production of the profession as a discipline.[5]

The discourse of architecture is based on a contested premise that it must always seek to prove. Critics, historians, and practitioners of architecture operate on the assumption that only what legitimate architects do deserves to be treated as art and included in architectural discourse. I call this basic exclusionary principle the ideological syllogism of architecture: "Only architects produce architecture. Architecture is an art. Architects are necessary to produce art."

Although the syllogism is necessary to found the discipline's discourse, it is compromised by a contradiction characteristic of this profession. The discourse of architecture is constructed autonomously, by experts who are accountable only to other experts. However, in order to continue "formulating fresh propositions," disciplines need to show how their rules become embodied in a canon, and the canon of architecture consists of beautiful or innovative *built exemplars.* These buildings are not and cannot be exemplars of the architect's autonomous application of knowledge and talent alone. They are also striking manifestations of the architect's dependence on clients and the other specialists of building, be they rival professionals or humbler executants. I call this dependence *heteronomy,* because it contrasts radically with the autonomy that is always considered a defining attribute of professional work.

In sum, because the discourse of architecture is ultimately based on its practice, and because this practice points to a fundamental heteronomy, the basic syllogism is as much an ideological position as a functioning principle of exclusion. The dialectics of discourse and practice (or of autonomy and heteronomy) are salient in architecture. They are particularly significant in the analysis of its discursive shifts.

Twice in our century, Western architecture has gone through significant changes in both discourse and realizations. In the orthodox historiographic accounts, submerged currents of stylistic change seem to have produced both times the architectural conceptions of elite designers. Indeed, despite architecture's characteristic dependence on patrons or clients for its work, the histories of architecture locate the origins of change within the discursive field itself, in the theories and ideas of architects.

The first and most radical shift in the discourse of architecture culminated in the Modern Movement of the 1920s in Europe. An adapted European modernism became *the* architectural style of international capitalism after World War II. The second shift originated in reaction to the debased architecture that, however unwanted, derived from modernism. Arising against the latter's universalistic claims, the postmodern revision refuses formal and ideological unity (and indeed does not appear to have any).

The subject of my study is postmodernism as it occurred in the United States roughly from 1966 to 1985. On the one hand, postmodernism is undeniably connected to architectural discourse: What became of European modernism in the United States (and spread from here to the whole world) was both the target of postmodern attacks and the antithesis that gave postmodernism much of its substance. Thus, I shall deal at some length with the discourse of architectural postmodernism itself.

On the other hand, I hold the general hypothesis that changes in ideas and styles correspond to (and attempt to make sense of) structural changes lived through and perceived by strategically located groups of people. In ways that should not be prejudged but always explored empirically, cultural change may also correspond to broad changes in social structure. Given this hypothesis, I take changes in aesthetic preference and taste among architects not as signs of whim or trendiness, nor as indications of idealist reorientation, but as symptoms of changes in architects' conceptions of their professional role and in the conditions of their practice. In postmodern discourse, the model of European modernism is related as much to practical conceptions of the architect's role and to changes in the way architects must make a living as to their formal imagination.[6]

ELITES, ART, AND PROFESSION

In any profession, the elites play a crucial part in the elaboration of discourse; their important position in the discursive field is precisely what makes them *professional* elites. This implies theoretically that elite standing depends on the perceived discursive capacity of particular producers in specialized areas of the production of culture. At the same time, elite standing in the field is what entitles its beneficiaries to make and continue making authoritative contributions.

In architecture, historians assign to a handful of noted designers a privileged position in the making of discourse. The architectural elite is anointed in relative autonomy, yet my postulate about the fundamental heteronomy of architectural practice requires me to examine the connections between the elite and other sectors of the profession. The importance of built exemplars in architectural discourse suggests a situation more complicated than the (increasingly blurred) dichotomy of "high" and "popular" forms in other art media.[7]

The expansion of a market for architectural services did not happen on any substantial scale until our century. In this market (which licensing is intended to protect) the vast majority of clients need relatively standardized competence from their architects. It is true that the site, if nothing else, makes each architectural commission to some extent unique; but other requirements (including the budget) are relatively standardized for most types of buildings. Besides respecting the budget, the primary demand of the program (the mandate that the architect receives from the client) is that the building be adequate for the social functions it must serve.

Adequacy implies a notion of at least minimal comfort and efficiency. Distinctiveness and pleasantness (let alone beauty) are secondary considerations for the typical client. The resulting standardization of architectural requirements creates a distinction between ordinary and extraordinary projects. The standard project can be ordinary, but when a project has cultural significance, the projected buildings must look and feel extraordinary. Under such circumstances, clients tend to seek designers noted for their artistic talent.

The elite of noted designers comprises varied abilities and different kinds of practices. Yet their number is very small and they often travel in the same circles—with each other, with "cultivated clients," and with the cognoscenti. Even for this select group, the first requirements of the architectural task are couched in terms of professional service: to satisfy the client by a design that is technically sound, serves the program well, and respects the budget.

Large architectural firms (an American invention dating from the late nineteenth century) are known, sought after, and handsomely paid for providing this kind of service efficiently in very large and very costly projects.[8] These complex firms assemble and organize many of the other professions involved in production of the built environment (engineers, landscape architects, planners, interior decorators, construction managers, and the like), with architects occupying the top position in the hierarchy. From the practical professional point of view, these firms offer clients unmatched guarantees of competence, efficiency, reliability, and technical support. To employed architects, they offer the prospect of regular career advancement. Yet public fame, the aura of architecture as art, and the creator's aspirations to immortality are seldom, if ever, attached to the rationalized "corporate" form of professional practice.[9]

Indeed, the persistent claim of architects to a special role in the process of construction (against and, in fact, *above* the rival claims and encroachments of other specialties) depends on implicit ideological appeals to the *telos*, the cultural significance, and the noble tradition of architecture. Not merely adequate building but culturally significant building is the lasting confirmation of architecture's professional claims. It follows that the charismatic authors of these buildings and their extraordinary practice serve as ideological warrant for the normal or routine practice of the profession as a whole. The obvious distance between these two segments of architecture is not so great as to be atypical among professions.

In all professions, in fact, there is a "discursive center," an ideal place where knowledge and discourse are produced. The social and intellectual distance between the discursive centers of the knowledge-producing professions and their underlying ranks is so considerable, in fact, that we may legitimately wonder whether any of these apparently well-delimited fields has any unity beyond its name.

And what is in a name? The reciprocal indifference of the various strata of specialists suggests that the unity of specialized fields of knowledge is illusory. In addition, the different strata frequently regard one another with contempt, animosity, and resentment, suggesting an antagonistic concern with the disciplinary frame that binds them nominally together.

In architecture, distance and indifference (and at times resentment) are perceptible in the different orientations of architectural schools.[10] These qualities are visible in the different conceptions, promoted by professional organizations of different level and scope, of what makes good architecture, and they are present as well in the distinct and unreconciled concerns contained within the major professional associations. Irritation toward the professional publications and awards that emphasize "design" is often and openly expressed by both ordinary practitioners and heads of large firms. Distance (though not ill feelings) reflects the realities of a clearly segmented market, in which architectural firms specialize in the provision of services that are, in fact, quite substantially different.

In this profession, the charismatic bias of the ideology of art, exalting and mystifying the centrality of the "masters of design," may intensify resentment. At the center, there is Art, Architecture, Immortality; away from the center, there is service, building, business, and money if one is lucky.

Clients' demands tend to divide the field of architecture into specialized segments. In most segments and for most clients, aesthetic concerns have no place. The more pragmatic architects resent the "unbusinesslike" reputation of their noted confreres. And yet, if they heed, even subliminally, the "art" in the profession's discourse, this constitutes an assertion (however unconscious) of professional autonomy against the clients, or the market. Historians, critics, and the cultivated public uncritically take the work of the elite designers as representing the whole field. However maddening, this usurpation of the *telos* of construction shows that *there is a telos*. The work of artist-architects, which easily seems superfluous or frivolous from the standpoint of commercial and corporate practice, argues tacitly against the superfluity of any architect's service. Thus, the pragmatic majority derives professional legitimacy from the presence in the same field of the very small elite of artist-architects.

That "art" contributes ideological legitimacy to "service" still does not mean that this profession has any unity beyond its name. Even minimal unity implies a relationship (to some extent reciprocal) between the elite of artist-architects and the other sectors of the profession.

INSTITUTIONAL BRIDGES IN IDEOLOGY
AND PRACTICE

The professional *service* that architects provide coordinates the different dimensions of construction. This coordination subordinates "firmness, commodity and delight" to the economic imperative of the budget and to the formal imperatives of the design. One critic suggests that elite designers cultivate the distinction between "ordinary" and "extraordinary" design. Indeed, in the relational system of architectural objects, artistic and innovative architecture stands out against the necessary background of *ordinary* design.[11]

Ideological benefits may go both ways, but the architectural field is made up of more than just ideology. The "pure" designers need the technical competence and economic efficiency of service-oriented professionals, not least to assuage the client's fear of the artist's unpredictable, headstrong, and profligate reputation. The "designer" firms benefit directly from the competent firms whose work seldom gets published and never gets awards. In the United States, where a period of apprenticeship is obligatory for professional registration, design firms benefit from hiring technically proficient personnel trained by the others.[12]

Contact and communication among professional segments occur through the labor market and also directly—in schools, professional organizations, publications, and awards programs. I have mentioned them in relation to the divisions and conflicts they incorporate, yet, by the same token, *professional* institutions, which pretend to some autonomy from uncontrollable market forces, can also bridge differences.

In the United States, architectural societies, like all professional organizations, perform corporative functions for the profession as a whole at the national, regional, and local level. Professional organizations confer recognition by bestowing office, awards, and other honors. Especially at the local level, these official accolades do two things: First, they identify deserving practitioners to their peers; second, they give them authority vis-à-vis potential clients.

Schools, of course, are central institutions for all fields that claim to produce and transmit specialized theoretical and applied knowledge. Besides teaching standard technical competence, architecture schools teach conceptions of design, relying less on abstract theory than on the analysis of great exemplars, on the studio, and on the critical evaluation of students' work. The studio simulates practical problems for which apprentice architects must find realistic solutions; the use of critics and juries may be seen as a proxy for the fact that real architectural work is always submitted to the ultimate judgment of outsiders.

These distinctive pedagogies introduce a fantasized and idealized notion of architectural practice, perhaps an inevitable result of the abstract approach of schools. But they also bring students into direct contact with real practitioners. Designers of local or national fame are the most desirable visitors, for their presence gives luster to the students, their teachers, and the school, even in the institutions that care little about artistic design. In turn, designers' willing participation in the juries offers them a chance to influence the formation of future architects. Being known and respected in local or national schools has other, more practical implications: Students fight for the honor to help out in the noted architects' rush jobs and peak work periods (the famous "charrettes" of architectural jargon), and, after graduation, they apply to their offices in numbers large enough to keep elite firms well supplied with "the best" at low wages.

Schools, then, are both an audience of choice and a recruiting pool, especially for practitioners with design reputations. Moreover, ambitious artist-architects have always sought (and increasingly found, since the 1950s) the support of academic positions. These provide prestige, a complement to the income from an always uncertain profession and contacts useful in building their practices. In architecture, as in all other disciplines, future professional ties and networks are formed to a large degree in schools.

The autonomous discourse of a profession—the knowledge and justifications it produces by and for itself—is articulated, transmitted, and, above all, received in schools. This is so in architecture, even though the pivotal place of built exemplars in architectural discourse gives practice inescapable primacy.[13] Schools broadcast architecture's canon, its standards of evaluation, its judgments of taste, and the challenges that arise to future practitioners and to others who shall never practice. Students are the main readers of professional journals and the main audience for the profession's system of awards and rewards. Therefore, different architectural tendencies and orientations find their followers primarily in schools.

Publications are the third important bridge across professional segments. Schools provide audiences and followings for new ideas, which can rapidly become trends, but architectural journals promote imitation itself. Important, innovative, or just fashionable designs are repeatedly published in practically all the professional journals of the world. Because of the unmoveable nature of architectural objects, illustrated journals and "picture books" (even more than serious and long treatises) perform an essential discursive function: They constitute what I would call, after André Malraux, the imaginary museum of world architecture. They provide tangible raw material for the canon, the system of interpretation and justification that consecrates buildings as architecture.

Architects in commercial or service-oriented practices do not ignore "beautiful pictures." Whatever they think of architecture as art, they still must provide their clients with designs—that is to say, buildings with forms and looks. Even in the less design-oriented segments of the profession, illustrated publications become a "research tool," a catalog of solutions and ideas.[14]

The rapid inclusion and widespread circulation of design innovations in the repertory of the architectural profession generalize elements of its discourse, linking the form-givers, the architects "with ideas," with the rest. The effect is bilateral, however: Publication spurs on the rapid formation of trends, to which innovators, in turn, must react if they want to preserve their leadership and their distinctiveness in design.

In sum, the institutional bridges that connect different segments of this profession are also centers for the production and reproduction of discourse. Schools, professional societies, foundations, institutes, editorial boards, specialized publishers, and (because architecture is an art) muse-

ums and art galleries all concur in reinforcing the special place of the elite
form-givers, creating, through this elite, a measure of ideological and practical unity in this divided profession.[15]

AUTONOMY AND HETERONOMY
IN THE DISCOURSE OF ARCHITECTURE

Every profession that claims to be based on knowledge produces and reproduces culture: not in its specialized body of knowledge and its canon only
but also in its codified practices, its explicit and implicit norms, its ways of
making sense of rules and legitimizing practices. All these components
constitute a discursive field.[16] Specific categories of specialists *profess* in
specific discursive fields, in which and by means of which they act with
authority. By virtue of the expertise they require, all professions and all
disciplines claim the right to create their discourse autonomously. They
respect, that is, the outside boundaries set by nonexpert authorities; yet, in
principle, they brook no interference from the latter.

In architecture, despite its stark differentiation and stratification, disciplinary legitimacy is founded on the aesthetics of design, a situation that
gives elite designers a privileged position in the field. Elite standing is
further aggrandized by the charismatic ideology of art. Yet, outside the
delimited discursive field of professional architecture, even the elites'
authority is undermined by their inescapable dependence on clients and
on other technical experts. The ideological autonomy that our society
accords to professionals and, even more so, to artists cannot hide the fundamental heteronomy of architectural work.

I have repeatedly mentioned how important it is that exemplars be built.
Even the specialists' most autonomous creation—the canon produced for
their own use and the systems of justification to which it gives rise—implicitly acknowledges the heteronomous conditions of architecture's existence.
The discourse of architecture is autonomous as long as it is on paper: drawings, words, ideas, but not buildings. At the heart of the profession's identity
there is a radical and deeply felt distinction between what is imagined and
what is realized, between "paper architecture" and architecture that is
built. Hear, for instance, Michael Graves, a world-renowned American
architect of the postmodern period, known for his buildings as well as for
his exquisite drawings, which sell dearly to art collectors:

> I was known as the "Cubist Kitchen King," the painter and the architect, all
> kinds of things that would say "Good here, but he hasn't built." . . . My life has
> been changed so dramatically by virtue of the fact that I had no work for so

long! I can say to you that I did a lot of work, and I *did* work night and day every day. . . . Not very much was built of significance, of any size, and that fear that you will never work again, or that you will *never* get proper work, adequate work, is with you. And as we have said in the office for the last few years, it is very, very difficult how to learn to say "no" to somebody who calls.[17]

Being a "real" architect depends on making architecture, and this depends on a crucial factor that no architect controls, unless he (more rarely she) builds for himself. Clients—their wills, their tastes, their money—control commissions. And commissions are not only the livelihood for which architects must compete; they are what allow architectural exemplars to exist. Architecture must be built precisely because the claim to be an art privileges sensory experience, which goes beyond mere form and plan. Once architectural ideas have been built, the task of historians and critics is to organize them *discursively,* transforming a collection of separate finished buildings into a system of architectural exemplars.

The client always influences the completed exemplar through a program, which represents not only economic constraints but the building's *social* reason for being. The program is the principal sociological reason that architectural objects are not only stylized but typed. Architectural judgment cannot avoid considerations of type or implicit judgments of propriety, which is a composite of size, plan, looks, and materials, all of which should be historically and locally adequate to the building's social function. Thus, the client's program places conditions upon the kind of symbolic capital architects accumulate in the discursive field just as directly as the client's initial selection of a designer.[18]

Much more than the idiosyncrasies of the clients, it is the nature of their programs and the types of buildings that constitute different areas of *normal* architectural practice. Because satisfied clients repeat their choices, their architects tend to concentrate on *types* of design and to be specialized by clients' needs. The specialization induced by clients creates special market niches, which have the well-known effect of containing competition. In architecture, the lines of containment correspond broadly with building types.

But then, does not the segmentation of practice make short shrift of the ideological and material links that I have described between artist-architects and other professionals? If specialization lines tend to harden into structural barriers, if most architects cannot realistically expect to stray very far from their usual kinds of clients and types of design, if exemplars introduce the dictates of the market within the discursive field, in what sense are the "master designers" a professional elite?

The answer must be that insofar as architects consider themselves architects, they are implicitly participants in a common discursive field. In other
words, when architects talk or think about architecture, they have primarily
other architects in mind or across the table (even if only to curse what the
"worthless rascals" are doing to the art, the profession, or the business).
The common discursive field holds autonomy and heteronomy together in
a permanent and constitutive contradiction. Some critics call this basic
contradiction the "double coding" of architecture (speaking to the client,
or to the public, *and* to other architects); some architects call it a duty to
deceive: They must satisfy the client, but they must "make architecture,"
even despite the client's wishes.

Because of this duplicity, because architects take the discursive field of
architecture as their frame of reference, clients' wills cannot account for
the development of new concepts of architecture nor even entirely for their
consolidation into styles. Innovation depends on new ideas, and the significance of the latter depends on the problems they address and claim to
resolve in the discursive field.

Since dependence on the client is inescapable, I will briefly outline how
it works in relation to architectural change. First, clients have the power
to choose architectural innovators and thus help their reputations in the
delimited field of architecture. They also have the power to lift the barriers
of specialized practice and look for architects across market segments.
Today, the increasing popularity of architectural competitions as methods
of selection indicates a willingness to do precisely this.

Second, more significant than the client's choice of designer is the identity of the client or of the building's prospective users. If there arise new
kinds of clients who have the means of commissioning architecture, they
are likely to generate new programs that express new or different outlooks.
This is even truer where new needs or new users must be served. In turn,
new programs are more likely than the usual ones to present architects
with new problems in both the social and the aesthetic aspects of design.
New problems open up opportunities for innovative solutions. It follows
that the combination of new clients with new social needs should present
the best conditions for architectural change. Yet these are still external or
heteronomous factors: They may help explain the *context* of architectural
innovation, but they do not directly explain its substance or evolution,
which depend on the evolution of the discursive field itself.

The autonomous pursuit of architecture and the heteronomous conditions
of its making insert a permanent contradiction into the heart of the profession's practice and even of its discourse. We can expect from the professional
ideology tacit attempts to reduce or deny this tension. The cultural signifi-

cance of building is an ideological theme that serves as a bridge between the contradictory terms: It provides many of the important reasons that make clients want to buy architecture, rather than merely shelter, and that lead them to go for this to experts in the design of beautiful and significant artifacts. Not surprisingly, the discourse of the experts is organized around the axiom that architectural beauty (as they define it) has extraordinary cultural importance.

From the fifteenth century to the present day, the learned discourse of architecture has intended to educate potential clients in this axiom. Alberti encouraged patrons of the new style of the Renaissance in these terms: "Since all agree that we should endeavor to leave a reputation behind us, not only for our wisdom but for our power too, for this reason we erect great structures, that our posterity may suppose us to have been great persons."[19] Important buildings, whether for private or collective use, are usually erected because powerful individuals want them. Alberti suggests that architecture may be delightful to enjoy in private but is much more important to the patron's glory for all to see in public, now and in the distant future. The axiom of cultural significance is founded on the public existence and visibility of architecture.

The new architecture of fifteenth-century Florence was meant to celebrate that city's emergence as a major Italian state and to convey the sense that the new state transcended fragmented feudal power.[20] Closer to our age, Marshall Berman's childhood reminiscence of the glorious apartment buildings of the Bronx's Grand Concourse also confirms the public essence of architecture: "We couldn't afford to live in them," he says, "but they could be admired for free, like the rows of glamorous ocean liners in port downtown."[21]

For the philosopher Suzanne Langer, the essence of architecture is also public and collective. In Langer's aesthetics, each art symbolizes human feeling through forms that spin a distinctive primary illusion. The plastic arts use "visual substitutes for the non-visible ingredients of space experience . . . in order to present at once, with complete authority, the primary illusion of a perfectly visible and perfectly intelligible total space." Architecture converts an actual place into a *virtual* place, one that exists only as artistic illusion. Langer calls this specific architectural illusion an "ethnic domain," because public architecture, being inseparable from ritual, abstracts "the total pattern of life" from all the physical, mental, and behavioral fragments that signify a culture to those who live in it.[22]

Alberti's encouragement hinted at something else, something transhistorical in the desire that powerful but mortal men (it is, indeed, mostly men who are powerful) have for lasting buildings. Modern clients are far from even knowing that they want the public symbols of glory that the Malatesta or the Medici wanted. Yet architects, either in their dutiful deception of the client or in the elaboration of autonomous discourse for their own use, cannot fail to invoke and articulate the *public* properties of architecture.

Indeed, it is the public face of buildings that detaches them from the personal and private requirements of their owners' programs. Significant buildings can express the ethnic domain or acquire cultural significance only in public. Besides, *all* buildings participate in the making of urban fabric. In cities, buildings present to anonymous viewers, now and for many years to come, a system of relationships in which the sponsors' ambitions and the designers' aspirations implicitly counterpose cultural significance to crass utilitarianism, with results that vary in their critical openness or in their sensitivity to the manifest culture.

Thus, the peculiarity of architecture among the arts and the professions is that it contributes to culture not through discourse and codified practices alone but also, and crucially, through *artifacts* that are useful and can be beautiful. The artist's imagination labors here not with representation but, as Langer says, "by exemplifying the laws of gravity, statics and dynamics." [23] Architecture is a public and useful art, an art that cannot disguise its social and collective origins, for it must convince a client, mobilize the complex enterprise of building, inspire the public (and not offend it), and work with the culture, visual skills, and symbolic vocabulary not of the client only but of its time.[24] The contradiction of autonomy and heteronomy inherent in making architecture and architecture's eminently public character give it emblematic sociological significance.

THE RELEVANCE OF DISCURSIVE BATTLES

Architectural schools and distinctive pedagogies, professional organizations and journals, market-induced specialization and associations, the public interest piqued by the general press, all serve as channels for the circulation and the reproduction of architectural ideas, inducing imitation and promoting stylistic trends. But this is not all. The occupational identity formed and nourished by these means can include a deeper attention to the idea of architecture as art.

Normal architectural practice is oriented to service and commercial interests, inevitably heteronomous, and often subordinate and alienating. To compensate for these disadvantages, it may prompt broad attention among architects to the discourse that exalts the artistic dimension of their trade. It does not have to be conscious attention: it may well be only distracted, or nostalgic, or resentful. Appropriately, a Philadelphia architect with a "normal" practice quips that the annual design awards of the journal *Progressive Architecture* are *"True Confessions* for architects." Awards for "pure" design (and "pure" design itself) are pipe dreams, this architect thinks; nonetheless, these dreams engage deep and unspoken yearnings and thus offer architects a fantasy, one that supports their ideological claim to be artists, not mere crafts-people. Technological advances, after all, are the province of engineers and manufacturers; and being a commercial hack or a good employee is nothing to fantasize about. Art and celebrity are the stuff of which individual dreams are made in this profession.

Two kinds of struggle in the discursive field of architecture are able to elicit at least the unconscious attention of ordinary professionals. Neither is unique to architecture, but they both appear repeatedly in the modern politics of culture.

The first kind of struggle is framed in specialized terms, even though it may implicate several art media in an aesthetic movement and exceed the boundaries of a delimited "art world." Specialized cultural debates matter most of all to the producers and other specialists of the field rather than to clients. The reason, as Pierre Bourdieu has argued for scientific fields, is not purely intellectual and disinterested. Rather, there are special interests at stake: The outcomes of disputes among experts affect each field's internal hierarchy, rankings, networks of influence, and personal standing—all the strategic positions by means of which symbolic capital is formed and resources of wealth and power claimed.[25]

When "purely" aesthetic challenges reverberate through the medium of discourse in the professional field of architecture, they can evoke support or opposition from heterogeneous sources. Debates that originate among different factions of the design elite can thus become (as in other specialized fields) the occasion for conflicts and alliances of another sort. What is distinctive in architecture is the role that clients' choices can play in the resolution of the debate. Controversy is fierce, but where a project reaches the stage of realization, controversy must normally be tempered at least enough to assuage the clients' fears (if not quite to accommodate their wishes).

The second kind of cultural struggle draws the first into a broader (and hazier) frame, but it is a different phenomenon analytically. The impulse for the first kind of struggle comes from within the field, picking up steam from possible coalitions with insiders or related outsiders as it unfolds. The second kind of struggle has its own specific language and objectives, but the impulse comes from the outside: In specific historical circumstances, the modern politics of culture are played out against the background of larger social conflicts, from which delimited fields borrow intensity and substance. These are the distinctive moments of the Western art avant-gardes. On the one hand, formal aesthetic challenges are infused with the resonance of political and moral struggle. On the other hand, debates that are still couched in esoteric language and concerned with specialized issues may come to move along with larger movements: The dissenters, not content with challenging discourse alone, may attempt to renegotiate the power relationships within and around their special field of practice and may, in fact, attack its established protective boundaries.[26]

The modernist phase of twentieth-century architecture, distinguished by an ideological moment of birth, clearly illustrates the struggle of a political-aesthetic avant-garde. In the 1920s, new visions of architecture inflamed the profession's discourse by seeking to transcend the internal divisions and to forge anew the institutions of practice. My study will show that political fervor was not characteristic of the postmodern transformation yet not entirely absent from its early phases.

Battles in the discursive field of architecture are as narrow and specialized as in any other field. However, the utility, the visibility, and the public character of architecture tend to give to its battles a metaphorical significance greater than in other arts and even other professions. Indeed, I believe that the ideas of architectural innovators have shaped the distinctive public face of our modernity.

Architecture has provided potent symbols for our century, and its evolution has been taken as a mirror for the discontinuities in the substance and quality of our collective experience. Recent philosophers and critics, in particular, have taken the vehement reaction to modernism in architectural discourse as a starting point and a central metaphor in the debate on postmodernism.[27] I, too, believe that architecture engages the sociology of culture in broader and deeper ways.

From the last century on, architects have retreated from the aspiration of "building cities" and instead have moved toward the design of single objects, however gigantic or prototypical. While there are exceptions to this trend, design is still a most significant public function.[28] Architecture has lost the connection with the organization of state power, a connection it had in the age of the baroque, but it still provides the most effective symbolic expression of the state's presence. Second, it remains the most visible image of magnificence that private or corporate wealth can buy. Third, it has descended into social reality and entered the domain of mass consumption. Fourth, utility and a new vocation called some of the leading modern architects of the 1920s to revise architecture's connection with mass housing. Modern architecture intervenes, therefore, in dense fields of social relations, expressing social needs in both standard programs and in its vocabulary of forms, symbolizing social relations, channeling our movements through space, and providing our lives with a stage and a physical code.

It is evident from my approach and from the attention I pay to the modernist background that I plan to participate in the present debate regarding the transformation of modernism. I believe, however, that probing the conditions of work and the orientations toward design of an elite of cultural producers will yield a great deal more insight than any consideration of cultural change in the abstract. Accordingly, a large part of my investigation is based on in-depth interviews conducted in 1988–90, primarily with the members of a loose, heterogeneous, and eclectic elite: the architects identified by peers and critics as significant protagonists in the transformation of modernism in the United States from 1966 to 1985.[29]

The first part of this book serves as background. It consists of this chapter and of an analytical overview of twentieth-century architectural history, which acquaints the nonspecialist with the substance and scope of architectural change and with the cast of characters it involved. I pay special attention to architectural modernism in Weimar Germany as the tacit model (or the explicit foil) of the subsequent transformation.

In the second part, I examine the structural underpinnings of the recent phase of architectural change. Chapter 3 concentrates on postindustrial restructuring and its urban effects, suggesting some links between postmodern revisionism in architecture and the larger process with which it has roughly coincided. In chapter 4, I turn to the structure of architectural practice and how elite architects perceive it at present. I conclude with an analysis of different types of elite careers or, more precisely, different paths to elite standing in the profession.

The third part is directly concerned with the emergence, adoption, and meaning of postmodernism in American architecture. As the title ("The Revision of the Modern") indicates, I understand postmodernism more broadly than architects usually do, as a revisionist movement that includes many different tendencies. Chapters 5 and 6 are also based on my extended conversations with architects and on their published writings: I describe, first, how these noted architects think and talk about their work. Second,

I analyze how they view design, the architects' common competence, and its recent evolution.

Finally, in chapters 7 and 8 I extend the roster of elite architects to all the noted designers who participated as jurors in the Design Awards Program of the journal *Progressive Architecture* from 1966 to 1985. Based on the awards and, especially, on published transcripts of the proceedings, my analysis composes a narrative of the postmodern transformation viewed from the most autonomous level of the discursive field: For, indeed, the awards are given for "paper architecture," a stage at which the client has provided only a program but no other restrictions. In chapter 7, the analysis of these twenty years of debate takes one building type (the private house) as its point of departure. The changes discovered by holding the type of building constant are followed in chapter 8 across the whole spectrum of the juries' discussions.

These chapters result from related but differently based empirical probes. Their unity comes from the guiding themes of the investigation: art and profession, aesthetics and utility, discourse and building, extraordinary and ordinary design, autonomy and heteronomy. Even for a recognized elite, these are essential dilemmas, rooted in the contradictions of architectural practice.

CHAPTER TWO

Architectural Change
in the Twentieth Century

The search for a new architecture started with the theoretical quest and visionary projects of French rationalist architects in the late eighteenth century. Working during the French Revolution, the generation of architects born about 1760 sought to express the reign of Reason in a way that included a new "respect for the properties of the material" and a preference for the elementary geometries of an abstracted classicism.[1]

Later, in the nineteenth century, restoration and reaction attempted to contain both the spirit of the French Revolution and the social consequences of industrialization. The ascendant bourgeoisie, without lineage and uncertain of its position in a reactionary and monarchic Europe, favored for its new buildings and newly acquired mansions the picturesque and romantic associations of historical revivals. Thus, in Europe and the colonies, bourgeois architects built the elegant side of the new capitalist world in the eclectic image of an invented past and transformed the architecture of the colonized into different brands of exoticism.

Italicist, Grecist, Orientalist, and neo-Gothic styles had this in common: They all sharply differed from the utilitarian yet often striking forms that the revolution in production and transportation had erected without the help of any architect. Experiments with new materials and technologies, with new building types and kinds of architectural commissions, prompted deeper changes in the conception of architecture than did all the formal novelties. After World War I, in the revulsion against an old order and the

21

convulsions of a new birth, multiple experiments converged toward the new architecture.

The new form of building (das neue Bauen, as it was called in what seemed its German stronghold before Hitler banned it) was a minority position in a very conservative profession. But during a brief moment in the 1920s, it appeared to have both forged the century's architecture and given the architect a new social identity. In the words of one architectural historian, "between 1925 and 1928, in only three years, there emerged in Europe the idea that in the field of architecture an 'irreversible' transformation had taken place, one that no longer concerned only small avant-garde groups but had actually taken shape in the public mind in numerous countries."[2] This idea was a wild exaggeration. And yet, the ones to give this new movement credence were not the historiographers of the new movement, nor its patrons alone, but above all its enemies. Barbara Miller Lane's masterful study suggests, in fact, that Adolf Hitler's persecution of the Modern Movement achieved two things: One, it gave the modernists' minority position more importance than it had had and an aura of progressivism that not all the victimized artists deserved; and, two, the diaspora caused by Hitler's persecution of the Modern Movement was ultimately responsible for the belated triumph of the new aesthetics.[3]

In the 1930s, then, the Modern Movement was faltering under the blows of cultural policy in Nazi Germany. Elsewhere, modern architecture was in retreat. In the Soviet Union, the Russian constructivists, whose aesthetic ideas had been essential for the West European artists (especially the architects), were silenced by Stalinism. Architecture was suffering everywhere from the effects of the depression. Parts of the modernist experiment continued timidly through the 1930s—in the Netherlands, in Scandinavia, sporadically in England, and in the United States, where some German émigrés had taken refuge. But a mellower attitude toward tradition and the vernacular became perceptible almost everywhere, even in the work of Le Corbusier, the apostle of modernism. In public commissions, the end of the 1930s saw a return to monumental classicism, not only in the totalitarian states but even in Holland; it was prevalent in France, where the Modern Movement had never been widely accepted, as also in the United States.[4]

War engulfed the world at the beginning of the next decade. But, even before the deluge, the heroic phase of architectural modernism was over. What happened, and what did it mean? These are questions not only for us; contemporaries sought answers to them as well. In fact, the historiographic reconstruction started very soon, with the result that the discursive power of the modernists within the profession of architecture was multiplied.

Many publications on the national and international dimensions of the Modern Movement had accompanied its ascendancy.[5] But two historical interpretations that appeared in the stagnant climate of the 1930s became standard works: The 1936 work by Nikolaus Pevsner, *Pioneers of the Modern Movement from William Morris to Walter Gropius,* traced the origins of the Modern Movement until 1914; the 1938–39 Harvard lectures by Siegfried Giedion, the former secretary of the International Congress for Modern Architecture (or CIAM), were published in 1940 under the title *Space, Time, and Architecture: Growth of a New Tradition.*[6] The titles themselves are telling. Pevsner's reference to William Morris suggests that for Pevsner the movement was not only an aesthetic response to industrial production but a deeply critical one. In Giedion's "new tradition" the Modern Movement crowns, as a new beginning, the long chain of Western architectural history.[7] For both men, the fundamental event in the history of modern architecture is capitalist industrialization.

I begin this analytical survey of modern architecture by looking at its industrial background and, more briefly, at some architectural responses to the effects of industrialization. Second, I introduce the canonic cast of characters of the Modern Movement, such as one finds it in architectural history books. Third, I consider the ideas, achievements, and architectural language of the Modern Movement, focusing for detail on Weimar Germany, the epicenter of architectural modernism before World War II.

The story resumes after the war: I briefly cover the transformation of modernism into an American yet truly "International Style" in order to introduce the theoretical "antifunctionalism" of the 1960s, mainly through the work of Robert Venturi. Finally, I look at the gradual passage of revisionist (or postmodern) architects into the "establishment," concluding with some of the questions that inform my study of postmodernism.

THE INDUSTRIAL MATRIX
OF ARCHITECTURAL MODERNISM

In nineteenth-century Europe and America, urbanization and the slow democratization of social life created new social functions and needs. Work, commerce, transportation, schooling, health, and pleasure demanded buildings for which there were no direct precedents. In the sphere of production, as in that of leisure, the predominant needs were those of the industrial bourgeoisie and of a middle class with enough money to spend.

Thus, on one side of industrial capitalism, there were the factories and warehouses that served production most directly. In the second part of the century, the railways called for the iron bridges and the magnificent stations that are the true monuments of the industrial revolution, while grandiose ports, piers, and storage facilities followed the development of the world economy. In the 1890s, the first "tall office buildings" of Chicago and New York added still another building type to the modern metropolis. Banks and stock exchanges belonged by their appearance to a separate domain.

On the other side of industrial capitalism, there were theaters and opera houses, concert halls and museums, libraries and city halls and post offices, and also elegant apartment buildings and department stores, in which the new civilization displayed and marketed an undreamed-of profusion of commodities. Sharp distinctions of appearance—of construction too, but above all of style—separated the world of work, where the bourgeoisie faced its class antagonist (the industrial working class), from the world of culture, where it still confronted the social ascendancy of the old aristocracy.

The first effect of the industrial revolution was therefore to relegate architecture to the domain of pomp, affluence, and leisure, sharply dividing it from work and capitalist production. Second, modern industry produced cast iron, steel (in large quantities after 1870), reinforced concrete, and glass—the new construction materials required by the expansion of capitalism. By the second half of the century, skeletons of cast and wrought iron (later on of steel and ferroconcrete), often used in conjunction with modular glazing, had displaced the massive supporting walls of the past in all large utilitarian structures.[8] From the 1890s on, electricity and mechanical ventilation freed construction from natural light and air circulation, making it possible for architecture to seem immaterial.[9] Electricity opened the unprecedented, magical vision of buildings fully lighted and floating, like ocean liners, in the night. Innovative architects were prompted to exploit the potential of new technologies and new materials that had been used for the first times in the new industrial and utilitarian buildings.

Indeed, the mechanization and rationalization of manufacturing served architects and everyone else as a permanent reminder of the enormous potential of mass production and standardized components. The world fairs, with their demand for huge covered spaces and rapid construction, helped fix international attention on the new methods of building. Two extraordinary technological achievements are worth mentioning, for they excited the enthusiasm of large publics. The first is the Crystal Palace, built for the first great exhibition of 1851 in London: 800,000 square feet covered with glass, four times the area of St. Peter's in Rome. Its designer, Joseph Paxton, a gardener and estate manager, took from the construction of greenhouses the idea of entirely prefabricated units. A contemporary considered it "a revolution in architecture from which a new style will date."[10]

The second unprecedented achievement is the 1,000-foot iron tower designed for the 1889 exhibition in Paris. The Eiffel Tower immortalized the name of one of the greatest constructors of iron bridges of his time, but it did much more than that: In itself and through the work of painters like Robert Delaunay, it gave modernity its urban icon. In 1925, Le Corbusier wrote:

> The Eiffel Tower has been accepted as architecture.
> In 1889 it was seen as the aggressive expression of mathematical calculation.
> In 1900 the aesthetes wanted to demolish it.
> In 1925 it dominated the Exhibition of Modern Decorative Arts. Above the plaster palaces writhing with decoration, it stood out as pure crystal.[11]

Third, the Crystal Palace and the Eiffel Tower illustrate some less direct but no less important implications of the industrial revolution: Its technological feats did not signify a gain in either intellectual or social status for nineteenth-century architects. Engineers and other technical devisers, including the industrial entrepreneurs themselves, were the mythical protagonists of capitalist industrialization and the beneficiaries of the middle class's enthusiasm for technology.

Henceforth, a central part of the modernist architects' task of redefining their field would deal with the machine (representing the whole of technology and industry) and with the rival figure of the engineer, the machine's symbolic master. One ideological strategy had been evolving since the beginning of the century: It took the industrial builder and the engineer as the "noble savages" of the new age. Later, Le Corbusier learned from Walter Gropius to admire American industrial building and to pronounce engineers as naïve form-givers who have "retained a natural feeling for large compact forms fresh and intact." But the engineer's naïveté about artistic traditions implies that aesthetic leadership properly belongs elsewhere: to the architects, obviously, who must move to reappropriate it.[12]

A fourth consequence of industrial modernity for artists (and ambitious architects considered themselves artists) was kitsch, the peculiarly modern form of a bad taste that is always expressed in consumption. Capitalist industrialization was directly and indirectly responsible for the flowering of kitsch. Given that the working class's capacity to spend was limited throughout the nineteenth and a good part of the twentieth century, kitsch appeared as a distinctive taste of the expanding middle class. In Clement Greenberg's words, kitsch "is vicarious experience and fake sensations. Kitsch changes according to style, but always remains the same. Kitsch pretends to demand nothing of its customers, except their money—not even their time."[13] From William Morris on, modern artists opposed the kitsch of industrial capitalism, while at the same time many took the incipient mass culture for their subject. Painting, especially, represented the vulgarity of new forms of urban leisure (repulsive and fascinating at the same time) for an elite audience, which for the most part supported capitalist society in all but its standards of taste.

The sense of estrangement of the progressive artist is to be found in the objective duplicity of producing art that is critical of the class for whom one works. It is compounded by knowing that this class's system of production is always looking to seize, after domestication, the forms that the avant-garde produces. For the historian Thomas Crow, the essence of modernism lies in responding to this estrangement: "In search of raw material, mass culture strips traditional art of its marketable qualities, and leaves as the only remaining path to authenticity a ceaseless alertness against the stereotyped and the pre-processed. The name of this path is modernism, which is . . . vulnerable to the same kind of appropriation. . . . *Mass culture is prior and determining; modernism is its effect.*"[14]

If, as Hermann Broch suggests, kitsch is always a system of imitation, then the architecture of exotic medleys and historicist revivals was a full participant in the production of kitsch.[15] But for the architects the central problem cannot only be to find a way out of kitsch while still accepting the advantages of the machine age.

From 1842 (the date of Edwin Chadwick's report entitled *Sanitary Conditions of the Labouring Population in England*), it was official that the ugliness and banality of the industrial city were merely ancillary to the appalling living conditions of the urban poor. If visual and decorative artists could define their problem as keeping one step ahead of middle-class kitsch, architects of good conscience could not. Because of the utilitarian essence of building, even the purest and most radical architecture was a silent reminder of its opposites: the absence of decent shelter for the working poor and uncontrolled urban growth.

Neither the most influential idea of nineteenth-century urbanism (Ebenezer Howard's Garden City, of which a minimal example was raised at Letchworth in 1905) nor the bureaucratic measures passed before World War I in France, Italy, the Netherlands, Britain, and Germany involved architects in conceptual or actual work on new dwelling types. It took a world war to change the parameters of the housing question.[16]

In sum, capitalist industrialization and the countermovements it awakened were the moving forces of modernity. Perhaps no one has expressed with more power than Marx the entwining of the objective and the subjective, the negative and the affirmative, in this staggering experience:

> Constant revolutionizing of production, uninterrupted disturbance of all social conditions, everlasting uncertainty and agitation, distinguish the bourgeois epoch from all earlier ones. All fixed, fast-frozen relations, with their train of ancient and venerable prejudices and opinions, are swept away, all new-formed ones become antiquated before they can ossify. All that is solid melts into air, all that is holy is profaned, and man is at last compelled to face with sober senses his real conditions of life and his relations with his kind.[17]

To instate a protective separation between civilization (the German *Kultur*) and the economy, the bourgeoisie sought the security of "ancient and venerable prejudices." In art and architecture, it looked to the traditional embellishments of life to display its wealth and legitimize its rule. Even when some educated bourgeois began to follow modern art in their taste, the narrow bourgeois democracies (just like the fascist and bureaucratic socialist regimes of the 1930s) held tight to the giant buildings in baroque or neoclassic style and the vast empty spaces that symbolized the state.

Thus, the majority of elite nineteenth-century architects went on as in the *ancien régime*, lavishing their imagination on the better commissions—those that employed "noble" materials like stone and marble and conventional methods of masonry building, at least for their decorated facades. Yet, to more searching minds, the revivals and the eclectic medleys seemed painfully unadapted both to modern technology and to the problems of modern social life. But for architecture to change in purpose and content, for architects to tackle the question of mass housing, social policy (indeed, social relations) had to change. Meanwhile, architectural progressivism was perforce limited to mounting formal attacks and advancing either purely formal or utopian alternatives.

FORMAL AND IDEOLOGICAL RESPONSES

In the 1890s, decorative artists began searching for unity in a novel approach to decoration. Art nouveau made its appearance at the Paris exhibition of 1900, giving a European reputation to the Belgian architect Henry van de Velde. Retrospectively, Le Corbusier wrote a sarcastic comment:

A dazzling handful of those works was displayed in which nature, giving geometry time off for a rest cure, twists the life out of those building and craft materials which normally suffer from it. . . . People began then to talk about Decorative Art. And skirmishes broke out. . . . Houses were dreamed up with the rhythm of the living stem of wild clematis (Gallé). . . . Water, earth and sky, the Botanic Gardens and the Natural History Museum—they were all there to be explored with ineffable love for the creatures of the Good Lord. Ruskin had softened our hearts.[18]

Art Nouveau architecture gave a new formal expression to iron and cement construction, spreading a profusion of natural motifs in harmony with the severe structure of its buildings, or converting structural members into decoration, as in Hector Guimard's famous iron gates for the Paris Metro.

Furniture had been prominent in the development of Art Nouveau. Furniture is not only something that architects without building projects can design but also something that workers can hope to buy sooner than a house. Yet the furniture revealed where the movement was retrograde, for it required craft production. The more lasting design innovations moved soon, and resolutely, to purify forms in anticipation of mass production.[19] Architecture also began to move further away from decoration before the war: the design of furniture and household objects was in some cases a direct inspiration, but a strong impulse came both from fine arts and from the economics of industrial building. This double impulse pushed architects to look in geometric form for a symbolic reconciliation of their art with technology and science.

On the one hand, modern art was attempting on its own to come to terms with scientific discoveries.[20] With the rise of abstraction, visual artists based their work on "lines, planes, surfaces, volumes, the interpenetration of figures and geometric solids, in sum, on categories of pure visibility which until then had been considered especially relevant for architecture."[21] The experiments of the Russian supremacists, the cubists, and the De Stijl group in Holland suggested entirely new conceptions of space to architects, who were often members of the same avant-garde circles.

On the other hand, some architects had been looking for the "truth of building" in the styleless architectonics of industrial builders.[22] In 1908, the Viennese Adolf Loos, distilling his American experience of fifteen years before, castigated Europe's cultural "stragglers and marauders" in the famous pamphlet "Ornament and Crime." There was no need "to discover the style of our age," he proclaimed against the German Werkbund—the organization of artists, craftsmen, manufacturers, and intellectuals formed in 1907: "We already have the style of our age. . . . The evolution of culture

is synonymous with the removal of ornament from utilitarian objects. . . .
Ornament is wasted labor power and hence wasted health."[23]

The German Werkbund, however, harbored advanced principles of
design among its different factions. The architect and Prussian official Hermann Muthesius, one of the Werkbund's founders and its moving force,
represented most coherently the nationalist and rationalizing vision of the
prewar Werkbund. The central objectives were to raise the average quality
of German products; to develop an aesthetically valid style for machine-
produced goods; to insure industrial positions for artists, who would direct
themselves to design prototypes (*Typisierung*), as would architects, fully
aware of the need for workers' housing; to rely on proportions and, in
architecture, on the abstracted neoclassicism of Schinkel and Semper. In
the words of one historian, "exactness, simplicity and regularity of form
were seen not simply as functional requirements of the machine, but
expressive and even symbolic desiderata, in themselves expressions of the
power, economy and efficiency of modern social and economic organization; hence their value lay beyond the mode of execution."[24] The affinity
of this section of the Werkbund with modern industry was supported by
the presence of Peter Behrens among its founding members. Architect,
graphic artist, and director of the Düsseldorf School of Applied Arts, Behrens occupied from 1907 to 1914 the post of artistic director of the AEG
(Allgemeine Elektricitats Gesellschaft) and was charged with the responsibility for redesigning "the company's buildings, products and publicity
material, from the celebrated turbine hall [of 1909] right down to tiny
publicity seals."[25]

Two principles, which we must keep distinct, fused in the modernist
rejection of applied ornament. On the one hand, rationalization was invoked
by Loos as a principle of industrial and *economic* efficiency, against the
Werkbund's purified and classicizing notions of style. On the other hand,
the rejection of ornament and the purification of forms was held to have
moral connotations, a principle that aligned progressive architects with an
artistic and ideological movement.

Because they represented Platonic solids and were easier to produce by
machine, simple geometric forms and volumes made it possible to assim-
ilate designed artifacts (including buildings) with machine production,
hence technology, hence science. A new poetry of form thus signaled architects' ambitions to change their role from the embellishment of leisure to
the equipment of production.

Purified form harmonized with the potential of the new industrial materials, especially glass. Together, form and materials opened the way toward

a new conception of built space. In the United States, Frank Lloyd Wright had not only formed, before the German Werkbund, the idea of transforming industry through art; by 1908, he had already carried to maturity principles of architectural composition that so impressed the Europeans.[26] His work was published and exhibited in Berlin in 1910 and 1911. Ludwig Hilberseimer, the uncompromising planner of the Bauhaus, remembers its effect:

> This exhibition was a big event. It was surprising to observe how Wright, starting from the traditional house, had succeeded in creating something radically new. He was already at the point of perfecting what others were still looking for: his projects expressed and demonstrated a new sense of space. . . . It was as if someone had suddenly opened the shutters in a dark room, flooding it with air and light.[27]

The signs of a new architecture had therefore emerged before the war, not in the work of Wright only but in Holland, in the industrial architecture of Germany and Italy, in France, England, Austria, and Belgium. And, as is always the case with innovative architecture, there had also been more manifestoes and drawings than buildings of a revolutionary stamp.[28]

The experience of war and revolution was the dividing line between modern tendencies and a Modern Movement. The diverse tendencies did not coalesce into one after the war, as some histories would pretend, but the war imparted to the progressive architects born in the 1880s a new urgency and a new hope in their work. Like many of their generation, they were convinced that Europe had been given "a second chance." And architecture would necessarily occupy an important place in the new order.

In the revolutionary Berlin of 1919, the Work Council for Art proclaimed with the quasi-religious fervor of expressionism the need for a democratic art. Yet it was clear that utility would have to be a component in the artists' move toward "the people." The decisive role of architects in the Council (from Walter Gropius and the noted critic Adolf Behne, who directed it, to Bruno Taut, who chaired the architecture committee) insured recognition of architecture's primary ideological place:

> Art and people must form a unity.
> Art shall no longer be the enjoyment of the few but the life and happiness of the masses.
> The aim is alliance of the arts under the wing of a great architecture.

Foreshadowing its architects' involvement with the democratic government, the Council advanced six preliminary demands. Demand 1 read,

"Recognition of the public character of all building activity, both State and private. . . . People's housing as a means of bringing all the arts to the people. Permanent experimental sites for testing and perfecting new architectural effects." Demands 2 to 4 asked for "the dissolution of the Academy of Arts, the Academy of Building and the Prussian Provincial Art Commission in their existing form"; freedom from all state interference in the new institutions and radical transformation of training in architecture, arts, and handicrafts and revitalization of the museums. The provocative fifth demand called for "destruction of artistically valueless monuments as well as of buildings whose artistic value is out of proportion to the value of their material, which could be put to other uses. Prevention of prematurely planned war memorials." The manifesto closed by demanding "a national centre to ensure the fostering of the arts."[29]

The next year was Le Corbusier's turn. Yet the tone of his series for *L'Esprit nouveau,* the journal he had founded, was different. First, Le Corbusier asserts, "It is a question of building which is at the root of the social unrest of today: Architecture or Revolution. Then, he goes on to explain this surprising alternative:

> If we eliminate from our hearts and minds all dead concepts with regard to the houses and look at the question from a critical and objective point of view, we shall arrive at the "House-Machine," the mass production house, healthy (and morally so too) and beautiful in the same way that the working tools and instruments which accompany our existence are beautiful. Beautiful also with all the animation that the artist's sensibility can add to severe and pure functioning elements. If existing property arrangements were changed, and they are changing, it would be possible to build. . . . The morality of industry has been transformed: big business is today a healthy and moral organism . . . we have Revolution in method and in the scale of the adventure. . . . There has been Revolution in methods of construction. . . . Architecture or Revolution. Revolution can be avoided.[30]

Even though Le Corbusier implicitly addresses himself to industry rather than to the state, the texts of the period are consistent about the place of architecture. Their ideology *is* architecture, and it is married to a general confusion about the rationalization of production and the conciliation of class conflict. Architecture as ideology could admit opposite political tendencies, as long as the state was in favor of massive building programs and of the new forms that the architects took for proxies of truth, goodness, justice, and progress.

Before introducing the main protagonists of this movement in which architecture became ideology, we must consider what they had in common.

The first and most important thing that modernist architects shared was the experience of World War I. Certainly, the war had been different for the victors and the vanquished, for the countries that were battlefields and those that were not. Yet the war gave a tragic urgency to the rejection of the bourgeois past, animating the intellectuals' romantic identification with the revolutionary movements of postwar years.

The only total break with the past had been realized, so it seemed, by the Russian Revolution. During the 1920s the USSR hovered in the background of architectural modernism (especially for the Germans) as an open alternative to the restoration of the bourgeoisie and the frustrations of architects' hopes.[31]

From the first months of the war, the shortage of credit, materials, and labor had stopped civilian construction, exacerbating the already severe housing conditions faced by the poor. In Britain, rent control was introduced early, in 1915, and later in France and Germany. In Germany, where average rents had quadrupled since 1914, housing legislation was passed in the final months of the Reich and incorporated into the republican constitution of August 1919. The stage was set for the immense efforts in social housing of the Weimar Republic, a program hailed by contemporaries (and others since) as the foundation of modernist architecture.[32]

A second element that progressive architects shared was their prewar contacts with the avant-gardes. Fired by fervent belief in the transformative capacity of art, the contacts continued after the war, yielding in part to the more deliberate organization of new centers and new networks in the 1920s. The desire to help construct a new society and a new way of life transformed the former avant-gardists into *artistes engagés*.

Dutch architects, their country having been spared the devastation of the war, had continued working; many progressives among them had already passed from the avant-garde into the service of the government before the war. Later, the Scandinavian, the Austrian, and the German architects followed the same path to work in town planning and in the design of mass housing for democratic governments.

Last but not least, modernist architects had in common with other intellectuals of both the left and the right an ideological faith in technology and industrial rationalization that can be summed up by "the idea of technology as a social arbiter."[33] After the war, the belief required extra faith, for the demonstrated potency of modern industry would have to be turned from destructive to (literally) constructive use. The model for modernity came from America, symbolized by Taylorism and Fordism. Social democrats, with some confusion, saw in Frederick Taylor's ideas of scientific management the means for overcoming scarcity through increased productivity and for submitting the capitalist entrepreneur to the objective dictates of "science." The capitalist would thus become an industrial expert, like his engineers, with no special rights of control attached to his property claims.

Rationalization seemed to promise architects an especially important role. The historian Mary Nolan has followed the concerted efforts of philanthropic and state agencies to "Taylorize" the housewife's work in Weimar Germany, but, she says, the "effort to create modern, scientific homes and efficient homemakers" was international. The decade of the 1920s saw the formation of a modern *female* working class and, in consequence, middle-class "reformist" efforts to create "a new woman," neither independent nor sexually liberated but capable of rationally organizing her home and her family.[34]

The Weimar architects, imagining everything, from the *existenz minimum* dwelling, to the kitchen as the housewife's laboratory, to the design of appliances no German working-class family could yet afford, were much ahead of Le Corbusier in realizing the "machine tool" house, which he only projected. In the general enthusiasm about rationalization, the way things *looked* was important. By proclaiming the unification of the life of work and the life of leisure under the sign of rationality and ever-increasing productivity, the appearance of houses and objects symbolized modern technology.

The rationalization of production along Taylorist lines promised an ever-expanding national product that could therefore bypass the need for income redistribution policies by the government. Conflicts would be resolved, in this technocratic dream, by an expert elite, to which progressive architects quite logically wanted to belong. The vision could appeal, the historian Charles Maier points out, to Italian fascists, German or Scandinavian social democrats, or even Lenin in Russia—the latter because the issue of class conflict supposedly had not been denied but decided. Analogously, both left- and right-wing artists in Germany could adopt the *Neue Sachlichkeit* (the new objectivity), pretending to have superseded the expressionism from which they still derived impetus and form.[35]

Maier interprets the shift toward Fordism in the late 1920s as the reinstatement of entrepreneurial power over technocratic ambitions. Extensive cartelization and centralization of the economy had been achieved, yet the domestic markets remained very narrow, precisely because no redistribution had taken place. In most European countries, industrialists feared the saturation of internal markets and the loss of competitiveness abroad. Fordism, to them, was not primarily a Model-T in every home but a way of

cutting labor costs and standardizing production. Ultimately, "rationalization in Europe ... served a conservative business community seeking to
exploit, first, the transition to overall non-inflationary monetary conditions,
then the prosperous but increasingly saturated market of the later 1920s."[36]

Whether modernist architects had been able to realize part of their vast
dreams or not, they remained close to the productive and technocratic
vision of rationalization. By their choice of a style and by their conception
of collective and individual dwellings, they hoped to influence—even more,
to compel—the inhabitants' choice of a rational and a communal life. Modernist architects lived the change of architecture as a thoroughly objective
and rational way to insure their place in a reconstructed social order.
Almost inevitably, as the depression deepened and hope disappeared, they
once again subconsciously took architectural aesthetics for a new social
order and their own new vision as the only radically new form that had
taken root in postwar society.

MODERNISM'S INTERNATIONAL CAST OF CHARACTERS

The canonical account of the cast of characters can be kept brief. Five men
are the recognized masters of twentieth-century architecture: the American
Frank Lloyd Wright, born in 1869, well before the Europeans of the 1880s
generation; the Germans Walter Gropius (1883–1969) and Ludwig Mies
van der Rohe (1886–1969); the Swiss-born Parisian Charles Edouard Jeanneret, alias Le Corbusier (1887–1965); and the Finn Alvar Aalto (1898–
1976). But geniuses, no matter how extraordinary, do not make a movement, nor do they effect a cultural change. The incomplete roster that
follows still suffers from the emphasis on charismatic individuals typical of
art history books. I can only say in apology that it is only intended to
acquaint the reader with names that recur in architectural discourse.

In France, after having worked briefly in Peter Behrens's Berlin office
and in Paris for Auguste Perret (known for his mastery of innovative construction in concrete), Le Corbusier founded with the painter Amédée
Ozenfant the review *L'Esprit nouveau* in 1920. There were other modernist architects in France, but their often important work practically disappears in the presence of Le Corbusier's influence.[37] Le Corbusier the
artist—architect, painter, sculptor—has so dominated twentieth-century
architecture by his command of form and the diversity of his achievements
as to evoke Michelangelo. Le Corbusier the writer and publicist gave to
the Modern Movement its most inspiring manifestoes as well as concrete
methodologies of urban planning and design.

France did not have the practical legislation in favor of mass housing that Germany had, nor did it experience the latter's political upheavals. Le Corbusier found neither a large audience for his experiments in the design of prototype housing nor a large following among architects.[38] His plans for the contemporary city were first shown in 1922, elaborated in the 1925 Plan Voisin for the center of Paris, and formed into doctrine in the "Athens Charter," which he signed for the CIAM meeting of 1933. His plans were to have a lasting and powerful impact on urban planning after World War II. Le Corbusier's early leadership was therefore based on his projects, his theoretical work, and his role in CIAM.[39]

The Modern Movement's true epicenters were Holland and Germany. In Holland, a group of artists gathered since 1917 around the review *De Stijl*, from which they took its name, put into practice the uncompromising abstraction learned from the painters Piet Mondrian and Theo van Doesburg, the group's tireless propagandist. De Stijl was an avant-garde response to the young architects grouped around H. P. Berlage in Amsterdam, who sought, instead, to reconcile the new architecture with tradition.

The major figures of Dutch architectural modernism were the De Stijl members J. J. P. Oud, Cor Van Eesteren, Gerrit Rietveld (for his formal inventions), and Willem Dudok, who came from the Berlage group tendency to work in the planning office of Hilversum, Holland, in 1915. For all their advocacy of abstract decomposition and systematic contrast of adjacent elements, the De Stijl architects (with the exception of Gerrit Rietveld, known especially for his work in small houses and furniture) had to temper their approach as soon as they started building. It was as Rotterdam's city architect from 1918 on that Jacob Oud produced some of the most remarkable housing districts of the Modern Movement. Cor Van Eesteren, Amsterdam's planner, was with Le Corbusier a major influence in CIAM's approach to urbanism after 1930. These and younger architects—like J. A. Brinkmann and A. C. Van der Vlugt, designers of the 1927 Van Nelle factory (which, for Le Corbusier, "removed all the former connotation of despair from that word 'proletarian' ")[40]—continued to advance modernist architecture in Holland when it had been silenced in Germany.

In the 1930s and 1940s, modernism managed to survive in Sweden and Denmark. In Sweden, young architects were struggling to adapt modernist principles to the incipient social democratic housing program. Despite the conversion to modernism of the noted architect of the romantic school, Erik Gunnar Asplund, the most remarkable monuments were still identified with the romantic revival, in particular Ragnar Ostberg's masterpiece, the Stockholm City Hall. Danish modernism of the 1930s followed that of

Sweden, with the exemplary work of Arne Jacobsen. But the most original talent, Alvar Aalto, was in Finland, whose most famous architect, Eliel Saarinen, had left for America in 1923. Aalto, an early member of CIAM, had started building along strict modernist lines; but in 1933, with the competition for the sanatorium at Paimio, and in 1935, with the library at Viipuri, Aalto came into his stride, achieving rapid renown. Early on, his work was hailed with that of Frank Lloyd Wright as a distinctively modern correction to the excesses of modernist dogma.

A word should be said about Italy because of three things: the presence of futurism and its visionary architect, Antonio Sant'Elia, before World War I; the Fiat-Lingotto factory (which was finished in 1926 and captured the imagination of contemporaries); and the international significance its architecture would gain after World War II. Italy's Modern Movement worked under fascism; in 1931, the short-lived Italian Movement for a Rational Architecture opened its exhibition with a deliberate attempt to put itself at the service of the fascist government and enlist its support. From 1930 until his death in 1936, Edoardo Persico, in the journal *Casabella,* provided a lucid international perspective on the Modern Movement. Individual architects (among whom the most gifted was Giuseppe Terragni, who died in 1942) obtained several commissions, notably Rome's projected Universal Exhibition, but architectural work became increasingly politicized in the late 1930s. The "moderns" veered definitively toward the clean neoclassicism for which the regime is known.

In Germany, examples of the new architecture blossomed in smaller towns where the younger architects found municipal appointments or commissions: in Celle with Otto Haesler, in Dessau with Walter Gropius, in Stuttgart with the Weissenhof housing exhibition of the Deutsche Werkbund. The Bauhaus, the school for the applied arts reorganized by Gropius in Weimar from 1919 to 1925, then in Dessau, was the movement's foremost training institution in art and theory. Occupying a special position, Eric Mendelsohn's modernist expressionism reached great commercial success when construction resumed after 1924. With the stabilization of the currency, Berlin and Frankfurt became the vital centers of the Modern Movement, demonstrating the shift that had been taking place from a still vigorous expressionism toward the colder geometries and rationalizing ideas of the *Neue Sachlichkeit.*

In Berlin, modernist architects of different tendencies—Bruno and Max Taut, Hugo Häring, Otto Bartning, Fred Forbat, Hans Henning, Hans Scharoun, Ludwig Hilberseimer, Ludwig Mies van der Rohe, and Walter Gropius (after leaving the Bauhaus in 1928)—became involved in the remarkable program of public housing organized by Martin Wagner, appointed director of planning for the Greater Berlin in 1926. In Frankfurt, the progressive mayor Ludwig Landmann appointed Wagner's counterpart, Ernst May, in 1924 and supported him unfailingly until he decided to leave for the Soviet Union in 1930 with part of his team.

In the 1920s, German modernist architects produced striking isolated masterpieces (such as Mendelsohn's department store in Chemnitz, the rich villas by Wassili and Hans Luckhardt in Berlin, Gropius's building for the Bauhaus school at Dessau, Mies van der Rohe's 1926 monument to Karl Liebknecht and Rosa Luxemburg, his German pavilion for the Barcelona exhibition of 1929, or the Villa Tugendat at Brno in 1930), even though they did not obtain a single large commission.

The monument of German modernism was mass housing: During the brief years between 1924 and 1930, Wagner and May's organizing talents assured Germany's international leadership in the Modern Movement. The innovations of Germany's radical architects made up in controversy for the small part they actually designed of what was built.[41] The American housing expert Catherine Bauer recalls the European movement's original principles:

> At that time the new architecture was wedded to a pair of principles which gave the word "functional" a double meaning: (1) The full use of modern technology and its honest expression in design; and (2) a scientific approach to human needs and uses in programming, planning and design. . . . For a brief period, much of the resulting architecture fulfilled the principles of both movements [the professional and the social democratic movement] to a very considerable extent. What I saw in Europe in 1930 was so exciting that it transformed me from an aesthete into a housing reformer.[42]

The depression interrupted the most ambitious construction projects, until they were resumed as public works. In Germany, the Nazis were as interested as the social democrats in continuing with the housing programs, but they were vehemently opposed to the Modern Movement for aesthetic and symbolic reasons. Their opposition contributed in large part to giving German modernists their prominent position in twentieth-century architectural discourse. Because of the enormous international resonance of its architects, Germany merits special consideration.

GERMANY: SOCIAL ARCHITECTURE AS MONUMENT

During the period of hyperinflation, little was built in Germany. Most modernist works recorded by history books before 1924 were isolated projects, such as Erich Mendelsohn's expressionist Einstein observatory tower at Potsdam in 1920 and Gropius's forceful Municipal Theater in Jena of 1922. Older or less radical architects, like Hans Poelzig, Paul Bonatz, and Fritz Höger, got important commissions in the 1920s and after. Yet, at Gropius's new school for the applied arts (the Bauhaus) in Weimar, around the avant-garde groups in Berlin, and around the pivotal figure of Martin Wagner, planning director for the borough of Schöneberg since 1919, the new concepts of functional building and planning were widely discussed.[43]

Attacked early on by the conservatives and the Nazis, the radical architects relied on their social democratic sponsors; after 1924, they organized themselves in a nationwide group, Der Ring, in which Mies van der Rohe played an important part. For its historian, Barbara Miller Lane, the battle between modern and traditional design was definitely centered on housing: "The distinction between the new architecture and other buildings was . . . most clearly apparent in dwelling design. And although many of the most famous buildings executed in the new style were institutional structures like the Bauhaus or commercial buildings like Mendelsohn's department stores, the radical architects received the largest proportion of their commissions in public housing."[44] The state's housing function was therefore the foundation of the Modern Movement in Germany, as it had been in Holland.

The crucial factors for success in Germany were cheap land (permitting a remarkably generous ratio of covered floor area to sites) and low-cost financing, funded by the house equity tax, which Martin Wagner had conceived. The *Hauszinsteuer* was redistributive: It taxed existing buildings whose outstanding mortgages had been swept away by the tremendous inflation to finance new construction at very low interest. The housing program depended directly and crucially on these funds.

The active core of the German program was the public-interest organizations, the regulations of which barred public-housing participants from trading their dwelling on the market or making profits on resale. The non-profit corporations set up by the trade unions and other organizations (including the Bauhutten, self-help construction cooperatives that Wagner started in Berlin) acted as the clients for the government-financed housing projects.[45] The modern German Siedlungen (the outlying housing projects and, more specifically, Bruno Taut's famous project in Berlin-Britz) prompted a British observer to write: "If the new movement in the arts is going to produce a Utopia, that utopia will be found in Germany and the centre of it in Berlin. All the forward-looking ideas, ideals, enthusiasms, and tendencies of the century have found a home there."[46]

"Utopia" indeed, for the harsh living conditions and the terrible scarcity of housing in the dense German cities were modified only for a minority. The Berlin projects had common features, which one scholar describes as follows: "An outlying site; public transit linkage to the urban center; a clear, identifiable image and sense of containment; shops, meeting rooms, day-care centers and other facilities; subtle arrangements of buildings and streets to create outdoor community areas and nodal points; concentration of dwellings on one-tenth of the site; and a careful integration of trees, gardens and other landscape features."[47] Site plans, dwelling plans, and communal facilities were required by the municipal governments' housing offices; room sizes, full exposure to the sun in at least one room, cross-ventilation, and minimal numbers of windows were similarly required. In Berlin as in Frankfurt, the new flats contained unheard-of luxuries: a water closet, a bathtub, and central heating. In Frankfurt, May's team had developed a new system of construction and even mass-produced kitchen equipment that was sold in packages. The escalation of costs had forced May's designers to research the minimum ratio of "space, air, light and warmth that man needs." These were minimal standards of "spartan oversimplification," as Catherine Bauer says, but they were important and new, and they were augmented, as in Berlin, by communal facilities for washing and drying, "schools, shops, guest houses, churches . . . a theatre . . . and large areas of open space."[48]

When planning and building standards decided so much, what, then, did architecture contribute? First of all, the architects were not separate from the planners: To mention but a few of the most noted designers, Gropius at the Bauhaus, his successor in Dessau, Hannes Meyer, Bruno Taut, and Häring participated directly in the research that was going on everywhere. May's *existenz minimum*, while minimal indeed, was conceived as a right and hence as a tool for political organization.

Second, the Modern Movement was not monolithic. The still impressive 1929 achievement of Siemenstadt in Berlin (the work of Bartning, Forbat, Häring, Gropius, Scharoun, and others) exhibits its remarkable variety. The influential expressionist Hugo Häring, for instance, rejected the cost-effective conceptions of the predominant *Sachlichkeit* for an organic understanding of functionalism. He wrote in 1927, "the important thing is to envision a house by starting from the inside, from the actual processes of living. . . . The spaces will be attuned to their purpose." In a personal reply, Mies not only pointed back to the tyranny of cost but also to that of overdesign: "You keep torturing yourself to find out exactly what people want. Just build a large enough shed and let them do inside what they want to!"[49]

Third, neither economic nor technical efficiency can resolve problems of plan and form, even if the parameters are fixed. A designer's intervention is therefore decisive in determining a project's appearance. In the heated political climate of Europe between the two world wars, forms, appearance, and symbols were important as signals of political and ideological identity. If this was so for most citizens, it must have been particularly important for architects.[50]

Indeed, for decades, architects had been trained to take conflicts about style and form as a proxy for the battles they were not able to fight. To many in the generation of modernist architects, the war had rendered all things from the past meaningless and repulsive. As Bruno Taut calmly remembered in 1929: "It was not possible for anyone to make use of any pre-war traditions, for that period was perforce regarded as the cause of the misfortunes of the past, and because every achievement of those days seemed more or less to hang together with the origins of the war."[51] Nine years earlier, in his brand new journal *Urban Architecture Ancient and Modern,* Taut had rhapsodized:

> Down with the respectability of sandstone and plate-glass, in fragments with the rubbish of marble and precious wood, to the garbage heap with all that junk! . . . "Oh, our concepts: space, home, style!" Ugh, how these concepts stink! Destroy them, put an end to them! Let nothing remain! . . . Death to everything stuffy! Down to everything called title, dignity, authority! Down with everything serious! . . . In the distance shines our tomorrow. Hurray, three times hurray for our kingdom without force! . . . Hurray and again hurray for the fluid, the graceful, the angular, the sparkling, the flashing, the light—hurray for everlasting architecture![52]

Reality has a sobering effect on architects; yet these statements suggest the spirit Taut brought to his task as the principal architect for the Gehag (the building cooperative for the federation of industrial unions in Berlin) and for Berlin's Planning Office, under Martin Wagner's directorship. What architecture stood for was clearly spelled out in Taut's famous Hufheisen Siedlung in Berlin-Britz (the "horseshoe" project, for the shape of the main apartment complex surrounding ample gardens), which, with about one thousand units, was Gehag's first major project.

Except for the horseshoe, the other half of the Siedlung, designed for the civil servants' building society by two traditional architects, was not different in site plan or function—row houses and apartment buildings, structures only two rooms deep. The buildings, however, sported pitched roofs, traditional garb, and dull color against Taut's clean, perfectly flat roofs, square windows and openings, and pure white (or pure red) walls:

"the unmistakable signs of truly collective building," as Taut explained in writing. And to make it lastingly clear, the band of apartments he designed facing the Degewo project "was the most uncompromisingly geometric of all, almost fortress-like, and painted a deep red. The message . . . required as little interpretation as the raised fist salute of the communists."[53]

Not all the modernist Siedlungen were as extreme, nor as deliberately provocative. But these buildings either stood outside the dense, wretched life of the city or appeared within it as a fragment of utopia. In Germany, architecture became embodied ideology.

It was in Germany, too, that the Modern Movement first presented itself to the public as an international force. In 1927, on the occasion of the exhibition of the German Werkbund for the applied arts, the city of Stuttgart agreed to let Mies van der Rohe organize a district of permanent houses for the upper middle class. On the outskirts of town, Mies devised the plan for the sloping Weissenhof site and invited some of the best modern architects to design prototype houses: Le Corbusier, the Austrian Josef Frank, the Dutchmen Jacob Oud and Mart Stam (Ernst May's collaborator), and twelve Germans—among whom were Mies himself, Walter Gropius, Ludwig Hilberseimer, Hans Scharoun, Bruno and Max Taut, as well as Peter Behrens and Hans Poelzig (two representatives of the older generation). Twenty thousand people a day visited the Weissenhof. It was at the Weissenhof, too, that the idea of forming a permanent international congress of modern architects emerged: The next year, the CIAM met and took root.[54]

For the promoters, the Weissenhof had successfully demonstrated the international unity and the rational quality of the new architecture. According to its most exhaustive historians, the Weissenhof "so hardened the opposition of modernist and antimodernist architectural styles that they came to be widely read as political signs of nationalism versus internationalism."[55] After 1927, while observers spoke of an international movement, the opposition closed its ranks against a "betrayal" of German patriotism.

For the most political of the modernists, the Siedlungen demonstrated that the tasks of architecture go beyond form yet also that form inevitably comes to represent a hierarchy of values. In the new monuments of a new age, architecture had demonstrated that style means more than style itself.

The Americans Henry Russell Hitchcock and Philip Johnson were among those who came to Germany to observe the new style. In the 1932 exhibition at the Museum of Modern Art, they introduced the Modern Movement to the United States *as a style*, giving its American name of "International Style" to the new architecture. Their reading of the movement fell far short of its intentions and its depth, while their forced reduction of many formal tendencies to one—the Weissenhof's *Sachlichkeit*—was clearly wrong. But their emphasis on style and form pointed to the essential and specific means by which architecture goes beyond itself.

THE REVOLUTION IN STYLE AND PURPOSE

The new architecture was rooted in the extraordinary conditions of optimism and despair of the postwar years. Its spirit was that of a movement. But what were its properly architectural foundations? In the almost prescriptive catalog for the 1932 Museum of Modern Art exhibition, Hitchcock and Johnson summarized its *stylistic* principles in these words: "There is, first, a new conception as volume rather than as mass. Secondly, regularity rather than axial symmetry serves as the chief means of ordering design. These two principles, with a third proscribing arbitrary applied decoration, mark the productions of the international style."[56]

The modernist conceptions of space and plan were self-consciously founded on a constructional fact: The structural cage of steel or ferroconcrete had eliminated the wall's function of providing support. Walls could therefore be reduced to a membrane (of which glass gave the most literal expression), fitted between the columns of the cage or placed in advance of it like a screen. The interior planes, similarly freed of all supports but the skeleton, could become open geometries. In these the designer could place partition walls, stairs, and other service elements without disturbing the immateriality of three-dimensional space but, on the contrary, articulating it and composing it. On the facade, the openings (always the most important elements of the boundary between inside and outside) could fade into the skintight walls: The characteristic windows became a strip reaching toward the edges, sometimes turning them; or sometimes, as in Gropius's Fagus factory of 1914, the window became a vertical pane of glass, showing off the sculptural form of the spiral staircase inside.

In the architecture of the 1920s, wrote Hitchcock and Johnson, "the prime architectural symbol is no longer the dense brick but the open box. . . . The great majority of buildings are in reality, as well as in effect, mere planes surrounding a volume."[57] Geometry and standardization unified the composition enough to make the hallowed principle of axial symmetry unnecessary. The new buildings could be articulated less compactly, over a larger expanse, displaying the different functions served by each part.

The purified geometry and the architectonic strictness of the Modern Movement's aesthetics were perfectly compatible with the call for standardized constructional units. The call was born of necessity, and, in their ambition to play a significant role in the expected social reconstruction, the architects heeded it. Transforming architecture implied transforming the architect, and this, indeed, went beyond constructional efficiency. If the functionalist principles had been truly followed, the architect would have faded into a team—not (or not only) a team of artists and craftsmen, as Gropius wanted in the first Bauhaus period, but a research and experimental team of engineers, planners, and social scientists. This simply did not happen. In Germany, for instance, the pressures of cost, politics, and ideology hardened May's approach into dogma. Catherine Bauer Wurster reports that in 1930 "Ernst May and his architects decided they had achieved the perfect site-plan, the ultimate, universal solution. It was a rigidly geometrical scheme . . . solely geared to a narrow system of standardized solar orientation."[58] After the brutal interruption of the depression and an even more terrible war, modernism resurrected, indeed, as an architectural style. The famous innovators reverted to the charismatic prima donna role of the architect for whom aesthetic expression comes before function and urbanity.

The responsibility commonly attributed to Hitchcock and Johnson for this involution is as unlikely, given the pressure of circumstances, as it is immaterial. Their stylistic reading subtracted desire and technocratic will from the formal choices: the desire to be modern and the will to deliver social engineering by means of art.[59] Yet, by highlighting choices that were neither architectonic nor social but aesthetic, their interpretation uncovers something that was already incipient in 1932.

The surface, they say, *had to look* smooth and continuous even if large plates of stone or metal sheathing were unavailable or too expensive. To avoid the suggestion of mass or weight, small glazed tiles or very smooth stucco were the next best thing.[60] White was chosen for aesthetic reasons as a unifying agent (it looked precisely like snow). The distinctive and controversial flat roof, despite Le Corbusier's attempts to borrow technical justifications from the Mediterranean vernacular, was also an aesthetic choice. While gabled roofs looked heavy to the American critics, to the Europeans they symbolized the past; instead, the flat slab of the modern roof underlined the continuity and the weightlessness of the interior volume it bounded. Extremely impractical in rain and snow, the flat roof perfected a form whose geometry alluded both to the eternal and to the "man-made" industrial world.

To a certain extent the stylistic principles that Hitchcock and Johnson outlined followed Le Corbusier's "Five Points of a New Architecture" of 1926. Le Corbusier and his partner Jeanneret stayed clear of philosophical justifications in this text, prescribing form in almost exclusively technical terms. We already know the flat roof, the free plan, the long window, the skinlike facade. The fifth is unique to Le Corbusier: the "pilotis," tall foundation columns of reinforced concrete that elevate the house, making it seem like an object that has landed there, not risen from the ground up. "The house is in the air," Le Corbusier says, "away from the ground; the garden runs under the house, and it is also above the house, on the roof."[61] Here, nature is reintroduced into the built environment, but within a single building. The urbanistic principle (in which Hitchcock and Johnson had no interest) became Le Corbusier's guide in his approach to the city, which he articulated for CIAM in the Athens Charter of 1933. The coherence between the unit and the city, the part and the whole, signals the architect's intention to claim a total role involving both construction and planning.

In the Plan Voisin for the reconstruction of Paris, presented by Le Corbusier at the exhibition of 1925, the green zones (what is left to "nature" in his strictly zoned modern city) become like the unifying tissue, devoted to human recreation, on the skeleton of free-standing buildings. The skyscrapers of the business districts and the residential slabs, "about a hundred and fifty feet high, with glass walls, standing on pillars," are disposed in zigzag over green areas like towers in a park. The residential districts and their communal amenities are clearly separated from the downtown, as are motorways from pedestrian ways. The motorways, classified by the type of traffic they serve, organize the whole: In the Algiers plan, for instance, a curvilinear roadway tops a rounded "viaduct slab" of dwellings designed by the inhabitants in different styles.[62]

In the best new districts of Holland, Germany, and Scandinavia, the Modern Movement created distinctiveness and variety, forming enclosures, establishing hierarchies of spaces, breaking blocks of houses, even using symmetrical arrangements. The standards, as we have seen, were preestablished: cross-ventilation, no more than two units per landing, an ideal height of three to four stories, collective amenities, and green spaces compensating for the exiguity of *existenz minimum* units. A favorite plan, which the German Siedlungen inherited from prewar projects, was the courtyard-type, with buildings located on the perimeter of the block and open space inside. Under real and ideological pressures, planners like May and Ludwig Hilberseimer replaced it with the rigidly parallel rows familiar to us since the end of World War II. Efficiency was becoming dogma and pushing out architecture.[63]

Le Corbusier's Plan Voisin and his Radiant City were ideal applications of the Athens Charter; they worried little about implementation or cost. Based on a decisively technocratic attitude, instating the strict separation of the "four key functions: residence, work, recreation (during free time) and circulation," the Charter contemplated a new city within a comprehensive regional plan. Green spaces, parks, woods, sports fields, stadiums, and beaches occupied a much larger place than that occupied by the cities' historical patrimonies.

> Historical and architectural monuments, the Charter declared, shall be preserved . . . if they are the expression of a preexisting culture and if they are in the general interest . . . if conserving them does not require that populations be kept at a sacrifice in unsanitary conditions . . . if it is possible to correct the disadvantages of their presence by radical measures: for instance, by detouring vital circulation arteries or even by moving centers heretofore considered unchangeable. . . . The destruction of the slums around the historical monuments will allow the creation of green spaces. . . . *To use . . . styles of the past for new building constructions in historical areas has nefarious consequences.* To continue with such usage or to introduce such initiatives will not be tolerated in any way.[64]

The Charter's rigid and dogmatic abstraction still echoes a common attitude of 1920s modernity: a desire to open the city up, to lighten its fabric, to decentralize. Thus, despite the enormous distance between the militant utopia of the Plan Voisin and the plans realized by the German and the Dutch, a new aesthetic conception of space informs them both.

"Space perception," writes the psychologist Rudolf Arnheim, "occurs only in the presence of perceivable things."[65] In the streets of an old city, we are aware of space that is carved out, packed in the recesses of the houses, spreading out and surging high in the piazzas like water contained in a pool. The architect Steven Peterson points out that this kind of space "is perceived as the *form* of the 'in-between' itself."[66] This is profoundly different from the space experienced in any expanse punctuated by separate objects, which appear to generate space and nail it down around them. There is too much space there for us to feel that space is *itself being formed:* The objects have forms that animate the space around them, but they concentrate attention upon themselves. The conspicuous forms of the Plan Voisin, like the office buildings and shopping malls of suburban America or the Las Vegas strip, impart to their unbounded backgrounds a vibrant but abstract life. Space around them *appears* empty: "It is perceived as the tension and direction in between things," says Peterson, who calls it "anti-space."

In practice, the wide and asymmetric spacing of the modernist buildings requires more space than the old streets; in turn, the zigzagged apartment slabs permit both population density and the circulation of air and light on all sides. Free-standing buildings, moreover, have no "backside," which in nineteenth-century tenements or even in the back alleys of bourgeois neighborhoods hid ugliness and decay behind decorated facades. On the one hand, the modernists' social engineering demanded air, light, trees, green spaces—health and hygiene, as Le Corbusier repeated—for the new districts. Much open space was needed for their ideal housing and the roads they imagined (built, as in America, for workers' automobiles). On the other hand, indefinite and formless space had the aesthetic merit of accenting the pure geometrical forms of the self-standing canonical buildings. In the modernist monument of Brasilia, most strikingly, space becomes something natural, like ether, organized by the geometrical grid, fluid and dynamic like the highway.[67]

The notion of space as a positive entity in which architecture *occurs* had transformed architectural thought at the turn of the century. "Henceforth," says the historian Alan Colquhoun, "architects would think of space as something preexistent and unlimited, giving a new value to ideas of continuity, transparency and indeterminacy."[68] Technology, which made it possible to eliminate the load-bearing wall, had also enabled architects not only to think but to build *in* space and *with* space rather than hollow out sequences of rooms in a masonry mass. Much later, a contemporary American architect, James Ingo Freed, recalled what it felt like to learn the new conception of space from Mies van der Rohe at the Illinois Institute of Technology in the 1950s: "At that time, we were made to feel the tangibility of space; we could swim in it like a fish swims in water. Space was a metaphysical solid. You didn't have to confine yourself to the surface of a wall to imbue a building with symbolism; space itself had iconic and symbolic value."[69] In modernist interiors, open space seems to reject turn-of-the-century bourgeois clutter, which a 1906 Berliner described in this manner:

> An endless, narrow and totally obscure corridor stretches out ahead. . . . Then we enter the front room. . . . Harshly painted ceilings, admittedly senseless, hideous and foolish, but "rich." An elaborately over-decorated tiled stove, smeared with gilt-bronze paint and huge double doors crowned right up to the ceiling . . . made of a wood so poorly treated that the resin of the knotholes seeps through the layers of oil paint. The leftover wall space is covered with glossy gold wallpaper.[70]

Can we not understand that the modernists displaced and condensed political and architectural meanings? Half a century after the Weissenhof, the Museum of Modern Art revived in a controversial exhibition the architectural drawings of the French École des Beaux-Arts. An American architect, William Conklin, gave an important explanation of what the modernist revolution had meant:

> The violence of the revolution speaks of something which the modernists saw in the Beaux-Arts as incredibly antagonistic, alien, morally wrong and personally hateful ... Gropius, Corbu, Mies saw banishment of historical imagery as a prerequisite for the new free world they were fighting for. ... The inner heart of the modernists' revolution was [a] reversal in the rank order of human activities, totally upsetting what they saw as the topsy-turvy values of the Beaux-Arts.[71]

Le Corbusier's powerful icons of modernity—the silos, ocean liners, airplanes, and automobiles that so often inspired the free sculptural parts of his buildings—evoke the unbounded space of their "natural habitat." But the free, fluid space of 1920s modernism can also evoke in the viewer the desire to defeat its opposite: the knickknacks, the dense, disorderly old streets, even the closed world of late nineteenth-century geopolitics.

After a war marked by the clash of imperialist powers over colonial territory, could these radical manipulators of space, these resolute internationalists, these technocratic remakers of cities have chosen except by compromise the cramped, full spaces of the past? The best buildings and projects of modernism created tense, symbolically charged space, which ideally penetrated the physical mass of architecture and made it seem ethereal. But after the polemical phase, after the diaspora that separated the Central Europeans from the soil and the ideas in which they had been formed, after another world war, as modernist buildings frequently turned bland or dogmatic, the space in which they happened also lost its dynamic qualities. Blank space paralleled barren buildings.

The German émigrés who were to change the course of American architecture arrived in the late 1930s, well after the closing of the Modern Movement's heroic phase.[72] Many critics concur with the assessment of the historian William Jordy that, in America, "the efforts of assimilation and popularization, together with the profusion and variety of commissions ... did little to counter the relaxation that customarily accompanies the success of any radical venture."[73] It was in a "relaxed" American version that architectural modernism, after World War II, set out to become hegemonic.

After all the commercialization, the rigidification, the variations, the regressions, the excesses, and even the achievements, the critique of the

modern style followed many tracks. Besides the important reconsideration
of historicism and eclecticism, the specific revision of the modernist conception of space followed two significant lines: It returned to formal experiments with abstract space, albeit in singular buildings; and, conversely, it
rejected the abstract and rigidly zoned urban spaces of modernism, in the
name of the density and continuity of city fabric.

THE AMERICANIZATION OF MODERNISM

William Jordy gives a vivid description of the cityscape that spread from
America to the world during the long building boom after the end of World
War II:[74] "Overnight, it seemed, the skyscraper silhouette of brick and
stone at the heart of large American cities gave way to highly polished
reticulated metal and glass walls nearby. In the suburbs and countryside,
a comparable style appeared in low, spreading shopping centers, schools and
industrial complexes. From the United States, the style spread throughout
the world."[75] The most characteristic buildings of the second half of the
twentieth century are undoubtedly American. From the American suburbs,
depending on region and income category, came either the model Cape
Cod cottage of the Levittowns or the flat California-style ranch house.
From the cities came the glass tower, exhibiting a reticulated structure
tightly draped in a "curtain wall," geometrical panels, preferably of glass,
leaving little place to architectural fancy.

Ludwig Mies van der Rohe perfected the model in the American phase
of his work. It had structural precedents in the Chicago commercial buildings of the end of the nineteenth century, in the best industrial architecture
of America, and in Mies's theoretical thinking of the 1920s and 1930s. His
greatest American victory, his perfect archetype, one of the great canonical
buildings of the twentieth century, is a glass tower: the Seagram building
in New York, which he designed with the collaboration of Philip Johnson
from 1954 to 1958.

Sybil Moholy-Nagy's harsh evaluation of the diaspora architects in
America is worth quoting at some length. Their hope (and that of their
U.S. sponsors) that they would revolutionize architecture by "science and
technology" fizzled rapidly. Instead, the United States got an academic
revolution:

> Architectural school programs were reformed in the Bauhaus image. This was
> such an improvement over what the watered down Beaux-Arts education had
> offered, that the lack of distinguished building design by the imported architect
> educators was gladly overlooked. . . . Mies van der Rohe seemed to be wholly a

part of that slow death when he finally arrived in this country in 1937. . . . Yet he was the only one of the diaspora architects capable of starting a new life as a creative designer following World War II, because to him technology was not a romantic catchword, as it had been for the Bauhaus program, but a workable tool and an inescapable truth.[76]

Mies started bringing the structural frame to the surface in his work at the Illinois Institute of Technology in 1939. Architectural historians see a direct line between the IIT and America's first glass tower, Pietro Belluschi's Equitable building in Portland (1944–47). By the early 1950s, there were three more: the United Nations Secretariat in New York (which, under the coordination of Wallace Harrison, the architect of the Rockefeller Center, had taken and botched Le Corbusier's ideas); Mies van der Rohe's twin towers on Lake Shore Drive in Chicago; and the Lever House by Gordon Bunshaft of SOM-New York (Skidmore Owings and Merrill, America's largest architectural firm and leading provider of towers for the corporate world). The Lever House and Eero Saarinen's General Motors Technical Center at Warren, the one standing, the other lying down, became the models for corporate America's ubiquitous glass and steel presence.[77]

Indeed, at the end of the Korean War it became economically feasible to replace reinforced concrete cages by steel frames, which could be rapidly assembled and welded into place. In the hands of developers, Mies's severe dictum "less is more" became a practical program of cheap construction covering the world with "cost-accountant buildings that bear no trace of human imagination: three-dimensional graphs of optimal efficiency, seemingly designed by computers for insects."[78]

What spread all over the world in the 1950s and 1960s was *a style*, which the critic Michael Sorkin aptly calls "*Multi*national," implying the connection (which a younger generation would often try to make) between the end of American hegemony and the demise of the Inter- (or Multi-) national Style:

> The period of expansion and corporate wealth of the fifties and sixties demanded a truly imperial building program . . . overweaning government buildings, opulent palaces of culture, majestic corporate headquarters in urban and suburban versions (the same building done either vertically or horizontally), giant retail complexes, vast highways and sprawling pseudo-Georgian suburbs were thrown up in the heavy ersatz classicism of the Multinational Style. . . . The multinational mentality, unlike the modernist, had a profound sense of the symbolic utility of architecture, subscribing as it did not to the philosopher's truth, but to the sophist's.[79]

Architectural critics have retrospectively discovered how difficult it was for the premier American architects of the 1950s, trained in the modernist

doctrine or influenced by it, to find a convincing language. Suzanne Stephens, considering the work of five important (and eclectic) architects,
shows their work caught between the axiomatic interdiction of applied
ornament and the desire of giving at least *visual* interest to the dull uniformity of standardized structures: Their historicist or expressionist design
tendencies surface either as monolithic sculptural forms or in decoration
disguised as structure. The exception is Louis Kahn, the most profound
influence and the only teacher of the group. Only in his work does Stephens
see the revival of a centuries-old monumental conception of "space and
light and a molding of space with mass."[80]

Other critics blamed the superficiality of Gropius's and Breuer's teaching at Harvard for the lack of passion and the superficiality of modernism
in America. A sophisticated architectural analysis by Klaus Herdeg starts
with the observation that the most influential American architects of the
1950s and 1960s graduated from Harvard during Gropius's tenure from
1937 to 1953—I. M. Pei had his first (and brief) teaching job there after
the war. With the exception of Pei (the only American architect to be taken
right out of the academy to head the architectural office of the legendary
developer William Zeckendorf), the careers of these men followed similar
patterns of development, from small residential to larger institutional commissions. What matters to Herdeg, however, is their approach: a frozen
division between a design's *formal* qualities and the underlying solution,
pragmatic and tending to the standardized. Reading Gropius's teaching
methods back into these men's works, Herdeg detects a design attitude
that leads to formalism in the pejorative sense: "that is, connoting the
employment of forms for purely literal or superficial reasons such *as visual
variety*. Formalism in this sense implies a total non-recognition of the mul-
tiplicity of meanings a form may have: intrinsically, as part of a structure
or system of forms or a fragment of imagined or real wholes; iconograph-
ically, as a cultural symbol; and empirically, as a functional clue."[81] More
interesting, however, are the examples Herdeg gives of Gropius's teaching
at Harvard. Gropius's master class exercises ask students to reconcile the
modernist emphasis on "the mass production of standardized building
parts" with "man's desire for individuality," suggesting the master's own
effort to get attuned to the road taken in postwar America: individualist
over collectivist values, variety and choice over uniformity, distinction
(however superficial) over standardization, and, far in the future, a postindustrial over an industrial economy.[82]

The modernism of Europe in the 1920s had sought to merge aesthetic
innovation with economic rationality, signifying how architects rejected

their subaltern and constricted role in bourgeois culture. The industrial source of the new architectural language stridently proclaimed the abolition of coded barriers between collective work and private life. The modernists had translated the myth of rationalization "above the class struggle" into a symbolism of machine productivity, reading into both the essence of modernity: Their architecture was thus a metaphorical conduit from the surface of bourgeois life to the rational and instrumental core of capitalist production. But now, in a thoroughly rationalized capitalist system, the metaphor was lost: The new language became only an accessory to the expression of corporate power, and the architect turned into an expert in aesthetics, struggling with a role more prestigious, yet less integral, to capitalist production than that of the industrial designer. Compared to the excessive hopes of the heroic phase, the fate of modern architects seemed to have become the superficial celebration of the new prosperity. A frozen style seemed to echo the self-satisfied conformism of the culture. Here and there, the heroic monumentality of some achievements (in particular the new Third World city centers of Brasilia, Chandigarh, or Dacca) contradicted the architects' fate, if not quite yet their official style—only to prove their inadequacy vis-à-vis urban problems that hardly waited for the cement to set before cropping up to destroy the best projects' intentions.

The most intractable and urgent problem, indeed, was not form (as architects are always prone to believe) but, once again, the city. What suburbanization meant for cities in the United States has been analyzed, studied, and many times described, though no urbanist had on the American architectural profession an impact comparable to that of the journalist Jane Jacobs. In her 1961 bestseller *The Death and Life of Great American Cities* (parts of which had previously appeared in *Architectural Forum*), Jacobs used social science studies and her own observations to denounce the destruction of old and viable neighborhoods.[83]

Highways headed for the suburbs and the corporate and speculative towers of the "Multinational Style" had committed indiscriminate "unslumming" against populations that were left behind. Stable city dwellers, who had never been offered a chance for gradual improvement of their habitat, were forced instead into rapidly "reslummed" public-housing projects. The city of megalithic structures that had taken shape was like another world, meant to be seen from a speeding car on a circling freeway. Jacobs celebrated instead the diversity, the spontaneity, and vital disorder of the pedestrian's city, its *public* life—the "collage city," where human beings can work in *and* live in *and* see whole buildings rather than only their bottoms or their tops.

American architects in the early 1960s may have harbored a utopian sense of what architecture should do, but they did not have the power to reverse the course of urban planning and building. Moreover, the architects trained in the modernist spirit often saw a technocratic promise in urban renewal, something vaguely reminiscent of Le Corbusier's dictum "Architecture or Revolution." The young men and women who rushed into advocacy work in the late 1960s reversed the dictum: Architecture in their mind could *cause* revolution. In consequence, they interpreted Jane Jacobs as calling for the kind of architecture that does not do too much harm.

Read in this light, Jacobs's book is a fitting prelude to the almost simultaneous work of Robert Venturi, *Complexity and Contradiction in Architecture,* which he wrote in the early 1960s.[84] Venturi's book can be taken as the beginning of the story of American postmodernism, a story analogous to (but also very different from) that which was simultaneously unfolding in Europe.[85]

While young American architects were directly confronted with ghetto revolts, Vittorio Gregotti recalls that CIAM ended in a crisis provoked by a more distant "other": Starting in 1952, the young South American architects burst on the scene attacking not only Josep Luis Sert (Le Corbusier's disciple and Gropius's successor at Harvard) but even the sacred figure of Le Corbusier himself. They mounted a counterexhibition "to demonstrate that architectural functionalism had become merely an instrument of capitalist profit."

In Europe, functionalism and CIAM were buried together by the deliberate reintegration of architecture with history and regionalism. The reinterpretation of the Modern Movement, says Gregotti, was not a historicist search for its "purest forms" but historical: Architectural modernism took its proper place, as one expression of a complex, now exhausted phase in the "history of modernity." Similarly, the German historian of postmodernism Heinrich Klotz sees it "as primarily a designation for a break of continuity, pinpointing the fact that the tradition of the Modern Movement in architecture has ceased to be a continuum."[86] From this perspective, it is not possible to *resuscitate* either modernism or what preceded it through formal gestures but only to provide *images* of a discontinuous past.

COMPLEXITY AND CONTRADICTION

In postmodernism, as in all architectural movements, words and drawings came before buildings. Philip Johnson, the historian who introduced the International Style to the United States, the architect who collaborated with Mies, the patron of architecture par excellence, the propagandist of all architectural novelties, has repeatedly declared that Robert Venturi "revolutionized architecture in 1966 with his book." He considers "the freedom that Venturi gave us" as the first factor in the 1970s revision of modernism.[87]

Although *Complexity and Contradiction* stays clear of contemporary urban issues, it can be taken as the architectural counterpart of Jacobs's defense of the city as it already exists. The affinities with Jacobs's urbanism emerge in Venturi's loving attention to history, in the preference he shows for urban examples, in his eclectic and inclusive taste, in the obvious effects that Rome had on his culture and his theory. It is a theory attentive to sixteenth-century mannerism, the exaggeration of architectural elements for aesthetic or dramatic effect. Venturi sees mannerism as an expression of the resurgent desire for complexity and the tolerance of contradictions, both of which have followed reductive periods of Western architectural history. Here is how Venturi declares himself against "orthodox modern architecture":

> I am for messy vitality over obvious unity. . . . I am for richness of meaning rather than clarity of meaning. . . . I prefer "both-and" to "either-or," black and white, and sometimes gray, to black or white. . . . But an architecture of complexity and contradiction has a special obligation toward the whole. . . . It must embody the difficult unity of inclusion rather than the easy unity of exclusion. More is not less.[88]

Venturi's sources are mostly Italian, in the Renaissance, mannerist, and baroque periods, extending to the English and French eighteenth century, and rescuing from neglect the early twentieth-century work of Sir Edwin Lutyens, the architect of imperial New Delhi, the Philadelphian Frank Furness, and Louis Sullivan. Le Corbusier, Alvar Aalto, and Louis Kahn complete Venturi's "canon": This critical detachment vis-à-vis the Modern Movement indicates that, for Venturi, it can already be treated as "a source," like any other period of architectural history.

History was a subject excised from Gropius's Bauhaus program and paid only superficial attention in American architectural schools in the 1950s and 1960s. Therefore, Venturi's careful recovery of historical tradition and his treatment of parts of the Modern Movement as history signal a double break with the still-reigning pedagogy.

As in all documents that have influenced modern architecture, the subtext of *Complexity and Contradiction* is the renegotiation of the architect's role with self, profession, and society. From this sociological point of view, these are the most salient points of Venturi's "gentle manifesto" (see also table 1):

1. "Unorthodox" architects must design in terms adequate to the complexity of the client's programs. The increasing complexity of the architectural program is a fact of contemporary life. The concern with formal purity of orthodox modernist architects is better suited to single-function buildings than to complex programs. The office building with its repetitive modular units is therefore the fitting archetype of American modernism.

While Venturi seems to indulge rhetorically in the conceit that *some* architects get to choose what they do, he is also implicitly comparing other architects' situations to his own at the time. The great majority of architects who work as independent or self-employed professionals are likely to encounter small projects and very modest budgets, which nonetheless can have programs as complex as the larger ones. Venturi's implicit insistence that architects must be committed to the client's needs simply restates the principle of architecture's *professional* morality.

2. Despite all the dogmatic declarations of the Modern Movement, form does not follow function: Venturi asserts that there are no good *architectural* reasons (as against economic or constructional ones) why it should. If exclusions of nonstructural elements (decoration, eclectic details, etc.) are not justified by functionality but by ideology, that ideology ought to be rejected as aesthetically irrelevant—as an encumbrance that often conceals the *aesthetic* preferences and choices of the modernist masters.[89]

In reaction to the nineteenth-century nostalgic appropriation of many pasts, the Modern Movement has chosen to create unity and order by classification—namely, the separation and specialization of elements at all levels of the built environment. This rigorous emphasis on order reflected the heroic and utopian vision of an architecture that was going to remake the world. Now that the urban world has been remade, the exclusionary principles—unity, order, purity—have become a totalizing ideology that excludes the *projection and communication of all meaning but one:* the implacable and impersonal order of the machine (or, more precisely, as the South American architects told CIAM, the implacable order of profit).

3. Architecture has multiple meanings (it is polysemic, as we would say today), and the elements by which it projects meaning may be "contradictory to the form, structure and program with which they combine." In the extremely controversial book of 1972, *Learning from Las Vegas,* Venturi, Denise Scott Brown, and Steven Izenour extended to mass culture the problem of signification in architecture. Orthodox architects, they argued, are

TABLE 1.   VENTURI'S COMPLEXITY AND
CONTRADICTION IN ARCHITECTURE

Modernist Orthodoxy	Venturi's Postmodernism
Basic Principles	
Exclusion: either/or	Inclusion: both/and
Aims for unity/purity/order	Aims for the complex order of the whole
Prefers simple or simplified programs; separation and specialization of materials, structure, programs, and space.	Prefers complex programs; multifunctional buildings, elements, materials
Excludes symbolism (except industrial or mechanical)	Uses conventional symbolism (vestigial vernacular, popular, commercial culture)
Inside/Outside Relations	
The outside flows from the inside	Inside can contrast with the outside
Space is flowing	Space is enclosed
Architecture of related and intersecting horizontal and vertical planes	Architecture of containment and intricacy within defined boundaries
Emphasis on continuity	Emphasis on wall and facade
Parts are hierarchically arranged, held together by dominant binder (like the color white)	Parts are equal but inflected
Results	
Isolated, freestanding buildings	Implicit accommodation to street ("infill")
Finished buildings	Unresolved buildings, changing programs
Architect's Role	
Heroic, utopian visions	Criticizes social priorities by means of irony
Searches for a grand role	Admits a modest role
Recommends innovative technology	Prefers existing conventions and unobtrusive technology

dissatisfied with the monotonous and unexpressive rigor of the dominant
code but still imprisoned by the dogmatic exclusion of ornament. Therefore, they veer toward monumental expressionism. But the study of architectural history teaches that there are two basic types of "signifiers"—"the
duck" and "the decorated shed":

> Where the architectural systems of space, structure, and program are submerged
> and distorted by an overall symbolic form, this kind of building-becoming-sculp-
> ture we call the *duck*, in honor of the duck-shaped drive-in . . . illustrated in
> *God's Own Junkyard* by Peter Blake. Where systems of space and structure are
> directly at the service of program, and ornament is applied independently of
> them. This we call the *decorated shed*. The duck is the special building that *is*
> a symbol; the decorated shed is the conventional shelter that *applies* symbols. . . .
> We think that the duck is seldom relevant today, although it pervades Modern
> architecture.[90]

4. The unorthodox architect rededicates him- or herself to the creation
of meanings that are ambiguous, complex, and contradictory—like modernity itself. A contemporary architecture is therefore *realistic;* it should adapt
itself modestly to what exists, using conventions to create the unconven-
tional. Throughout history, decoration has been (and should be again) an
important way of creating meaning through image.

In his book, Venturi offered the Pop painter, "who gives uncommon
meaning to common elements by changing their context or increasing their
scale," as a role model: "The architect who would accept his role as com-
biner of significant old clichés—valid banalities—in new contexts as his
condition within a society that directs its best efforts, its big money and its
elegant technologies elsewhere, *can ironically express in this indirect way
a true concern for society's inverted scale of values.*"[91]

5. Decoration is now permissible. Other means available to the unorthodox architect for generating form include:

• Inflection, the art of the fragment, the achievement of a difficult unity
through inclusion: Inflected parts are partial elements that maintain their
identity and diversity yet are more integral to the whole than uninflected
parts. They correspond to *formed* space (as opposed to fluid and continuous
space).

• Emphasis on the wall: a boundary, between two spaces, to which decoration and symbols are attached. It induces simultaneous awareness of
what is significant on either side.

• Emphasis on the facade: It allows urbanity and leads to revaluation
of the street. In *Learning from Las Vegas*, the facade becomes the locus

of permissible ornament, the essential part of the decorated shed, which itself is the cheap and meaningful architecture for our time.

• The unresolved building: It can accommodate growth and changing programs. Venturi legitimizes it by reference to literature: Poets and playwrights acknowledge dilemmas without solutions.

• The vast symbolic repertories of history and popular culture: American vernacular *is* commercial culture, which can be adopted in earnest with a view to making it "all right."

Concerning this last point, Venturi has been maligned enough to be quoted exactly: "In *God's Own Junkyard,* Peter Blake has compared the chaos of commercial Main Street with the orderliness of the University of Virginia. Besides the irrelevancy of the comparison, is not Main Street almost all right? Indeed, is not the commercial strip of Route 66 almost all right? As I have said, our question is what slight twist of context will make them all right? Perhaps more signs, more contained."[92] In sum, Venturi responded to the Miesian dictum "Less is more" with the playful populism of "Less is a bore!" His realism about the contemporary conditions of architecture in America corrected Mies's naïveté about speculative building;[93] His challenge was directed against an architecture that, having become commercial and corporate in the image of American postwar power, still pretended to the aspirations of peaceful internationalism, unity, and universality of another era.

To understand the liberating effects of the first manifesto of postmodernism, we must understand several points. First, we must not omit the fact that Venturi, with a teaching job at an elite university, a small office, and little work, enjoyed a total though unwanted freedom from corporate dictates. While perhaps not original nor too scholarly, Venturi's wide-ranging and intelligent explication of his own taste provided serious intellectual legitimation for the repressed components of architectural delight.

Second, Venturi complemented the admission of ornament with an emphasis on symbolism, making it easier for architects to achieve originality and variety in small-scale, nonmonumental (and relatively cheap) architecture.

Third, the insistence on the relation of the part to the whole and of structure to use merged with the keen practical awareness that buildings seldom have ideal sites. This amounted to giving the context primacy. In *Learning from Las Vegas,* Venturi, Scott Brown, and Izenour would recommend an architecture of urban infill: The ugly and ordinary building, when artfully and carefully designed, is the truly extraordinary one in an urban fabric torn asunder by monumental and original "ducks." It is important to point out that "ugly and ordinary" and "infill" are the only kinds of commissions at which most architects can get a crack.

Fourth, in *Learning from Las Vegas,* Venturi and his associates made good on the promise to reveal the communicative potential of clichés. Under the acknowledged influence of the sociologist Herbert Gans, they were in fact consciously erasing the high modernist barrier between high and low culture. Last but not least, *because* of their love for European cities and buildings (not *despite* it), Venturi, Scott Brown, and Izenour (like Gans and Jacobs) managed to find possibilities for complexity and contradiction, enjoyment and diversity, collages and layers of meaning in an American environment.

Taken together, Venturi's two books draw an optimistic picture of the potential of American cities, most evident in the deliberately shocking comparison of private and public spaces in eighteenth-century Rome with the Las Vegas Strip. Venturi's theoretical work is essentially a critique *of* modernist architecture, calling it pompous, humorless, ugly, and harmful. For an architect, there is nothing wrong with concentrating on modest, small-scale architecture.

Venturi's challenge clearly has liberating aspects: the unsentimental recovery of history, the respect for the context, the desire to communicate, the openness to many cultural codes or, in the words of the movement's popularizer, Charles Jencks, a characteristic *double-coding.* On the one hand, postmodern work displays modern technology and expresses the modern purposes of the buildings (if necessary with esoteric means that only architects understand); on the other hand, it expresses the desire to communicate with a larger audience through conventional signs.[94] Modernity is embedded *ironically* in the past, which gives modernity meaning and which only arrogance can presume to leave forever. Yet, as one critic observes, the liberating message is totally professional—addressed to other architects, safely contained within architectural discourse: "The oppositional pose Venturi strikes primarily guarantees one thing—that the architect remains safely insulated from all those "complexities and contradictions" outside the boundaries of the discipline, a discipline increasingly defined precisely by such insulation. His later juggling with the terms *form* and *symbolism* only thickens the walls."[95] A large and growing segment of the American architectural profession was ready for Venturi's iconoclastic message. Tongue-in-cheek, Hugh Hardy, the principal of the very successful "young" New York firm Hardy Holzman Pfeiffer, described the mood: "We rejected the fifties, we rejected the AIA, we rejected midtown, we rejected contracts, we rejected working drawings, we rejected design, we rejected everything but clients."[96]

THE INCORPORATION OF POSTMODERNISM

If the new principles of design were to pass from books, or the pages of student journals, or even the award pages of *Progressive Architecture* into the built environment, clients had to be found. For architects inspired by Venturi's call, it would seem that only openness to new kinds of clients could allow the momentous passage. Thus, the early postmodern commissions tended to come from clients who demanded to approve the project by absolute majority vote (as happened to Charles Moore for a church near Santa Monica), clients in the antipoverty projects, clients in community development, friends with some or little money, academics who wanted to renovate their suburban houses, and so on. Few such commissions are noted by the established profession, unless they launch their architects toward more prestigious undertakings. The exhibitions of "new" architects' work (built or unbuilt, big or small), such as those organized by the Architectural League of New York City or by the Museum of Modern Art, were intended to have that amplifying effect.[97]

Up to this point, the new architecture was largely consonant with what Andreas Huyssen considers the emancipatory phase of postmodernism in the 1960s. Architectural imagination seemed to divide itself between an elaboration of a futuristic technological symbolism, prevalent in the work of European architects like Norman Foster, Richard Rogers, and Renzo Piano, and a return to either historical sources or abstract formalism. Nevertheless, there was in the architectural *discourse* of the late 1960s a sense "of rupture and discontinuity, of crisis and generational conflict." In the work of Venturi, Charles Moore, and many other known and unknown architects, there is a populist attack on the idea of "architecture as art," a "vigorous, though . . . largely uncritical attempt to validate popular culture" and become at last organically attached to a client of democratic origins.[98]

I emphasize "architectural *discourse*": Postmodernism in the 1960s and 1970s was still largely a change "on paper." Given the scale of what the new architects were building, the spotlight turned only on their published or exhibited work. Important and novel in this respect was the foundation, in 1967, of the New York Institute for Architecture and Urban Affairs, of which Peter Eisenman was the guiding spirit and intellectual leader until 1983. With the publication of the journal *Oppositions* in 1973, the Institute adopted an ambitious "European model"; the main objective was to give

American architecture the theoretical analysis that neither its schools nor its professional journals provided.[99]

A series of colloquia at the Museum of Modern Art and a book called *Five Architects* created a revisionist group where there was none. The press made "the New York Five"—Peter Eisenman, Michael Graves, Richard Meier, Charles Gwathmey, and John Hejduk—into a media event, followed by controversies about the "gray" architecture of historicist and vernacular inspiration (Venturi, Charles Moore, Robert Stern, Alan Greenberg, among others) and the "white" tendency. The latter (of whom Richard Meier is the most consistent representative) preferred abstract formalism and turned for inspiration to early modernist work (always and above all Le Corbusier, the Italian Terragni, or the Russians Tatlin and Melnikov). The moment of enthusiasm and emancipation seemed to be fading gradually into discourse—picture books, some drawings, a great deal of esoteric writing.

In 1977, Charles Jencks's influential book, *The Language of Post-Modern Architecture,* in a sense tried to do for postmodernism what Giedion had done for the Modern Movement. Bringing together architectural works from all over the world, Jencks offered an evolutionary tree of architecture from 1960 to 1980 which recognized six major tendencies: historicism; straight revivalism; neo-vernacular; ad hoc urbanist; metaphor metaphysical; and postmodern space. Twenty-four subtendencies straddle the main boundaries, while some major figures appear in different periods all across the tree (casting great doubt on its "evolutionary" accuracy).[100]

Robert Stern's grouping of revisionist trends is simpler and therefore more useful to the lay reader. Stern groups stylistic manifestations according to the predominance of a "schismatic" or a "traditional" sensibility. Schismatic revisionism attempts to continue "modernism's aspiration toward a clean break with the Western Humanist tradition." But in its most radical form, it rejects even modernism's faith in art; it falls then into the paradox of the avant-gardes, which proclaim the dissolution of art while continuing to produce new work with artistic aspirations. Traditional revisionism accepts "the cultural tradition of Western Humanism of which it holds modernism to be a part"; in particular, it seeks reintegration "with the Romanticism which flourished between 1750 and 1850." These tendencies, which we should more properly call *pre*modern, correspond to the eclectic historicism for which architects reserve the label of "postmodernism." Venturi, whose intentions were in part to make an architecture of invented or reconstructed "American vernacular," marks yet a different path.[101]

However, an indirect advantage of Jencks's work is that it symbolizes by its exaggeration the formalist mood. The year that Nixon was reelected to his second term, 1972, is for Jencks the year that the Modern Movement died (and *not* because Jencks pays any attention to the forthcoming moratorium on new public housing). On July 15, at 3:32 P.M., the Pruitt-Igoe housing project in St. Louis was finally put out of its misery by dynamite. Designed by Minoru Yamasaki according to the most progressive ideals of CIAM, it had received an award by the AIA in 1951. It died a long, agonizing death under the coercive management and the rage of its poor black residents.[102] For Dolores Hayden, a progressive historian and designer, this was a signal: "Architects long frustrated by the conditions of work in the profession rushed to follow [the] new aesthetic adventures and abandon their sense of guilt and frustration about the larger problems of patronage for housing."[103]

Hayden exaggerated too, focusing only on the elite of architects who make stylistic changes. In fact, there was little to show for the new architecture. In 1972, Venturi had a residence for old people and his mother's house as major built works. Charles Moore, chairman of the Department of Architecture at Yale since 1965, had made larger contributions: in partnership with Donlyn Lyndon, William Turnbull, and John Whitaker, Moore had produced a much-noted "postmodern" Faculty Club for the University of California at Santa Barbara and a condominium for Sea Ranch on the northern California coast in a vernacular style that Joseph Esherick, also a Sea Ranch architect, had been practicing since the 1940s.

Regionalism in the late 1960s was still largely confined to the West Coast. Soon Frank Gehry was to develop an abrasively original "new vernacular" that flaunted its Los Angeles roots. But the achievements of the new regionalisms of the early 1970s, in California, Illinois, New England, New Mexico, like those of the East Coast historicist "grays" and abstract "whites," were, with few exceptions, small, suburban, isolated, and residential.

Architects who design visible public projects or high rise buildings are not necessarily more influential with their peers than those who innovate in small and private buildings, but the former group's work is inherently more public. Architectural change becomes a public matter only when it exceeds the bounds of discourse and the sphere of the cognoscenti. This means that the new forms must either be widely used or widely viewed.

Public awareness of postmodernism required visible changes in International Style's archetypical creations. With some exaggeration we can say that, to be visible, architectural revisionism demanded the demise of the glass box. Nobody outside architecture schools or art galleries would have cared to derive the practical implications of Venturi's *Complexity and Contradiction in Architecture* or noticed the architecture of Charles Moore, Joseph Esherick, or Chicago's Stanley Tigerman. Something else had to happen. And since American Siedlungen are produced by Mr. Levitt, not Martin Wagner, the larger firms or the architects who design for corporations and developers had to get involved in the new design modes.

The first large-scale realization was the reflective glass Pacific Design Center, designed by Cesar Pelli for Victor Gruen Associates in 1970 and dubbed the Blue Whale by the locals. For Heinrich Klotz, this strongly defined irregular shape was like "a gigantic fragment" that stands "as an anti-monument" in the middle of Los Angeles's urban "nowhere."[104]

John Portman, the Atlanta architect and developer, showed the way to countless followers with his monumental atrium hotels—odd-shaped fortresses of glass or concrete on the outside, domesticated pseudo-nature inside. In the early 1970s, Atlanta's Hyatt Regency and the San Francisco Embarcadero Center proved that the transformation of the glass box could attract crowds just to *see* the inside of a building. In 1974, Philip Johnson and his partner John Burgee cut the tops and the sides of their twin glass boxes at Pennzoil Place in Houston and rotated them around a low triangular atrium: The box was going out of style.

With Michael Graves's winning design for the 1979 Municipal Services Building Competition in Portland, Oregon, and the mounting publicity around Johnson and Burgee's design for the AT&T headquarters in New York, traditional postmodernism—inspired by classical motifs and composition—had its first monuments. In 1984, the AT&T building appeared on the skyline, coiffed with a broken pediment of clear mannerist inspiration, meeting the street on a monumental classical arch, symmetrical lower porticoes, and a glass arcade on the back. The art historian Vincent Scully commented:

> AT&T's stance has the effect of making the other new buildings around it look obsolete. Why do they have flat tops, we ask? Why is the corner of one of them cut away and the lower floors of another slanted outward? In a way, they don't look like buildings at all, and in an urbanistic sense they are not. *They are objects, scaleless, which happen to be large and are set down in a city. . . .* Johnson . . . has clearly looked at older urbanistic models, at Rockefeller Center, for example. But it is here, in fact, that his design gives pause, insofar as it is thinner, less generous, more brittle than that of his models. Is this a matter of economics as Cesar Pelli claims it to be?[105]

The AT&T, followed by Graves's building for the Humana Corporation in Louisville in 1982, ushered in the boom in office building of the 1980s.

Aware that design "made news," the press gave increasing space to the new looks of buildings, providing the architects with free glamor and the developers with free publicity.[106]

By the mid-1980s, neotraditionalism in various guises had become a favorite dress of corporate headquarters and "upscale" new developments. The rising firm of the 1980s—Kohn Pedersen Fox of New York—tried hard to "design for the street" and to impart architectural dignity to objects whose mass and scale are objectively antiurban in any city except New York. KPF is appropriately known for the extraordinarily adroit marketing of designs that carefully revalue the contextual gestures and vocabularies of the 1920s and 1930s.[107] In New York's Battery Park City development, the different architects of Rector Place, its residential crown jewel, look to older New York models to create a rentable and much more massive scenography. The "anchor" of the project, Cesar Pelli's 1981–85 office complex, gives 1930s' sculpted tops to twin towers much more thickset than their models. Vincent Scully, like many other critics, noted the contradiction between the sources to which postmodern design alludes and the constrictions of contemporary construction:

> The thin curtain wall, which Pelli insists is the only viable cladding under present economic circumstances, creates an insubstantial and transparent effect consorting strangely with the mountainous massing of the buildings as a whole and very different from the densely articulated surfaces of the earlier skyscrapers. But . . . the buildings do seem to stretch and loom, creating a great landing place off the Hudson, ringed by vast, magical beings, mediators with the World Trade towers behind them.[108]

The feeling of standing in the middle of a fantastic scenography (massive, yet thin-skinned; looking solid, yet clad in granite sheets thin as glass; looking profusely decorated, through painted-on, vaguely "traditional" details) becomes a common effect of postmodern designs. In fact, the designers often seek to create estrangement through the deliberate contrast between the formal evocation of the urban past and its impossible restoration in the present. Other postmodern designs (which Klotz calls "container architecture") deliberately look unfinished, presenting themselves as giant fragments of a whole that is nowhere.

The designs of Helmut Jahn for the old Chicago firm of C. F. Murphy (which Jahn now owns) are fantastic examples of both things. Jahn's most distinguished work is probably the 1988 United Airlines Terminal at O'Hare Airport. The structure is remarkable both for its efficiency and for the tall, airy space created by a "technical" vocabulary of light metal arches, glass, and neon. Like an airplane, it suggests the impossible: solid lightness and simple grandeur. Yet Jahn's skyscrapers and public buildings are more striking: In Chicago, the cut-out cone of his Illinois State Center (1983) "appears to be a whittled-down leftover from a previous environment";[109] while the Board of Trade expansion and the Northwestern Station tower form glass and "cold" materials into evocations of the 1920s with a powerful but estranging effect. In Philadelphia, Jahn's 1986 Liberty Place alludes to William Van Alen's 1930s Chrysler building in New York in a wondrously reflective glass cladding, recalling a softened-down fantasy by the futurist Antonio Sant'Elia as much as Van Alen's model.

Finally, in the 1980s, the historicizing approach of Adrian Smith, partner at SOM-Chicago, and of David Childs, partner at SOM-New York, brought to the new style an accolade from the premier modernist bastion. Postmodernism had developed into a style that American business and real estate could live with.

Postmodernism started as a movement within architectural discourse, but many charged it with broader resonance. Toward the mid-1980s, new forms of architectural design appeared to have become closely integrated into a new phase of capitalist production and consumption.

There are two directing lines to this story. One is the development of dissenting ideas and new conceptions of design, against a dominant but weakened paradigm. The other is the conditions of practice, on which architects depend to realize new ideas and which, in turn, depend on social forces that architects do not control. The last part, and its connections with opportunity and constraint in architectural work, can be described objectively. For the details of the story, and for insights into the meaning of change, I turn mainly to the protagonists themselves.

Architects draw ideas from the internal evolution of their discipline. For them to realize these ideas, autonomy and heteronomy, the two opposite and conflicting terms, must somehow be reconciled. The visibility of architectural change—and therefore the marks it may leave on our culture—depend on this compromise. It is my contention that architectural change primarily reflects the architects' interpretations of their own situations and possibilities in a changing society. The social and political environment creates opportunities and constraints for the work of these peculiar experts. In a society devoted to profit, their specialty includes the possibility of creating delight or memorable experiences through the complex medium of usable buildings.

PART TWO

The Postindustrial Matrix of American Architecture

CHAPTER THREE

Architecture in the Political Economy of Cities

The triumph of architectural modernism as a style is synonymous with the reconstruction of the capitalist world economy after World War II. Accepted by American corporate leaders as a symbol of progress, this truly International Style became the architectural expression of modernization in the age of American hegemony.

The postmodern transformation of architecture has coincided chronologically with a different phase of capitalist development. In advanced capitalist countries, and particularly in the United States, the economic crisis of the 1970s accentuated structural trends that had been at work for a long time.

The rough correspondences that one may discern between the forms of architectural postmodernism and the general characteristics of the new phase of international economic restructuring do not tell us much about the process of architectural change.[1] Architecture, like all other socially constructed activities and beliefs, occurs locally, in specific contexts. These local settings are connected to much broader economic, political, and cultural developments by linkages so complex that they defy summary. On the one hand, we have architects, putting into practice ideas that make up the discourse of the discipline. On the other hand, we have external forces—economic, political, social, and cultural movements—bearing down with more and more specific effects upon the practice of architecture.

In the short run, architecture, like construction, is most directly and potently affected by local conditions and contingent economic factors—interest rates, government policy and expenditures at all levels, tax laws and tax revenues, labor laws, public debt, average per capita income, and other tangible and intangible factors that make up a locality's "business climate." Dealing in detail with these fluctuating variables would far exceed the scope of my study. Moreover, they are not depersonalized forces but the result of political responses by actors who attempt to cope with systemic developments. Among the latter, two are most significant for the cities in which architecture is practiced: spatial restructuring and the growth of a "professional managerial class," the two of which are interrelated by their common dependence upon deindustrialization.

The term *deindustrialization* suggests the effect of different movements of capital in search of higher profits. It refers to the "runaway shop" phenomenon—the decision by industrial firms to leave the nation's more mature industrial regions for domestic or foreign areas that offer cheaper facilities, cheaper labor, lower unionization rates, and more complacent local governments. But it also refers to investment shifts across economic branches and sectors: First, within the manufacturing sector, capital seeks high-technology industries; second, it moves from the transformative sector as a whole to services. Both intra- and intersectoral shifts favor economic activities that employ higher proportions of technical and professional personnel than the old basic industries like textile, steel, and automobile.[2]

Deindustrialization implies the hegemonic presence of large "multilocal" firms. No longer tied to any special place by the advantages of regional specialization, these firms are able to shirk the efforts local governments may want to make on behalf of the livelihood and the quality of life of their constituents. Thus, the "multilocality" of big firms pushes the task of regulating them from local and regional governments to the federal level, but the development of exceptionally powerful transnational corporations threatens to exceed even the latter's regulatory capacity. The presence of transnational headquarters in a city ties its fortunes directly to the world economy and ranks it in an urban hierarchy that is not just national but worldwide.[3]

"Postindustrial" restructuring and the widened scope of business activity affect architecture mainly through changes in the prospects of cities and in the structure of the labor force. On the one hand, population shifts toward newer geographic areas increase the demand for architectural services. Architects design some of the office buildings where the newcomers work, as well as some of the commercial and institutional (more often than the residential) facilities they and their families need.[4]

On the other hand, even in older areas (especially in "headquarter" cities), the presence of large-scale employers of "professional, managerial, and technical" workers is correlated to the massive construction of office and institutional buildings that occurred, with some interruptions, from the 1960s through the unprecedented speculative boom of the 1980s. The architects' expertise in design and style serves not only the needs for space and image of corporate employers and local governments but also the distinctive consumption patterns of the "baby boom's" highly educated cohorts.

In the postindustrial city, the presence of professional and managerial groups (in which women play an increasingly important role) tends to blur the classic distinctions between productive and nonproductive investments. The corporate organizations that employ large numbers of urban professionals are normally interested in minimizing turnover among their high-level personnel, partly for reasons of productivity. According to specialized surveys, this was "the largest single reason that owners went into the new building market."[5] Since productivity is notoriously hard to measure in skilled and often indeterminate services, managers may reasonably consider a well-designed environment, compatible with the consumption patterns of their highly skilled employees, as a necessary "factor of production."

Some of these elite employees engage in urban gentrification, a distinctive (though far from predominant) form of consumption that I shall consider in conclusion. The loss of jobs and the consequent abandonment and decline of traditional working-class neighborhoods link gentrification to deindustrialization and restructuring. However, for many of the affluent "symbolic analysts," the complex of buildings where they work may well be most of what they see in the city.[6]

Philip Siller is a former New Yorker, a vice president of the Canadian Olympia and York Properties, responsible for New York's Battery Park City and London's Canary Wharf. He describes, unwittingly perhaps, how the built forms of the new economic order drain life out of the city:

> People used to define themselves by their home, and they worked wherever they had to work. It didn't matter if it was a nice building or not, a park-like setting or not. . . . But as the dichotomy between their home and their city widens, either because they live further away from it or they skip over the city when they go to work . . . the place where they work becomes an important part of

their self-image. . . . The amenities offered to them at the places where they work have to replace all the organic amenities that neighborhoods automatically provided. You get your dry cleaning done at the American Express Building and you carry it home. You buy your dinner at some gourmet takeout where you work and you carry it home. It used to be that "Pick something up on the way home" meant when you get out of the subway, while you're walking to the house.[7]

Trends more widespread than those that affect only the local business scene thus have direct and indirect effects on architectural work. General economic conditions and expectations about the economy are directly related to investments in real estate.[8] The level of personal income (and its concentration in the hands of those who can afford to spend it on design) affect architectural practices geared not only to the work and recreational settings of the upper middle class but also to its mostly suburban residences, its holiday retreats, and even its quality furniture.

Cities and their fortunes are the most important connecting link between vast structural forces and the making of architecture. This is not only because a majority of architects work in cities but also because it is in cities that architecture, in theory, becomes public—a public space, a public good, and publicly visible. At city level, architecture becomes implicated, usually on the side of the powerful, in the class and race conflicts "over the assignment of certain goals to certain spatial forms."[9]

Politics, indeed, is the fourth component of architecture's structural background. Regardless of international economic trends, the largest part of what people need and buy—housing, health care, education, prepared meals, transportation, and the like—is produced and consumed domestically. The resources devoted to these services and the decision to subsidize them as public goods are clearly not an automatic effect of global economic forces but the results of political choice.[10] Notably, in the United States, federal investment policies in housing and community facilities and federal tax legislation are crucial intermediaries between needs and their satisfaction.

Tax policy, for instance, subsidizes large mortgages more generously than smaller ones (and therefore, presumably, the minority of architect-designed homes). Tax credits encouraged historic preservation in the 1970s and 1980s. Before being sharply curtailed in 1984 and 1986, the generous depreciation allowances of the 1981 Economic Recovery Tax Act spurred the boom in office construction (as did considerable tax abatements at the local level). Overall, since the 1970s, federal tax concessions have replaced direct grants as the most important form of support for public or public–private urban projects.

Here, the distinction between "social overhead capital," which serves community needs (housing, schools, fire and police stations, libraries, recreational and health facilities), and "economic overhead capital," which supports private sector economic activity (not only roads, bridges, airports, sewers and water systems but also convention centers, stadiums, private–public investments in large retail centers, and the like), is important. It suggests, among other things, different kinds of demands for professional design services.

Many students of the urban scene have argued that local progrowth coalitions, in which business is the best organized actor, have enough power to systematically bend urban renewal efforts toward economic overhead capital and downtown projects. Seeing the city primarily as a "growth machine," private interests overtly oppose capital expenditures that serve poorer neighborhoods and poorer people or best them in the competition for funds. In this view, the urban priorities of the federal government act as either a major constraint or a major encouragement for local progrowth coalitions.

While there can be little doubt about the influence of progrowth forces, other scholars question whether the business community even needs to put direct pressure on city governments. Their argument is that the latter are forced to choose economic over social capital expenditures by the need to compete with other cities in the national urban system. As Carolyn Adams writes, "developmental policies are essential to sustaining a city's market position. That is why city officials so consistently favor them over community programs, especially those in low income communities."[11]

The subject of real estate investment and urban politics is too complex and vast for me to review in detail. I believe, however, that significant modern architecture is almost inevitably urban, and I am particularly interested in experts' opportunities to play a *public* role. It is therefore necessary for me to sketch the broad connections (or disconnections) between background forces, mediated by urban policy and politics, and changes in American architecture since the end of World War II.

THE ARTICULATION OF URBAN LIBERALISM

In the United States, the articulation of liberal urban policies is a signal achievement of the New Deal. But, in contrast with social democratic Germany, the great public works of the New Deal did not establish a particular affinity with avant-garde aesthetics. Let us consider first the dynamic historical context within which the Democratic party created a new urban role for the federal government.

Spatial mobility and decentralization have been constant and primary forces in the shaping of American life. Suburbanization has only been the most striking recent incarnation of this centrifugal tendency. Its early start and enormous scale have made its impact on cities far more devastating than elsewhere in the capitalist world. Spatial segregation and confinement have always served everywhere to classify and separate different groups of people and, pointedly, to contain "the rabble" and insulate the "respectable" citizens. But in America the effects of spatial segregation have been magnified and intensified by racism.

Racial and xenophobic prejudice has often sought the cover of a deeply antiurban ideology, which looks to the small town and later to the suburbs for a socially homogeneous Arcadian myth. Yet, antiurban sentiment has never challenged the "growth machine" ideology, for which urban growth automatically results in collective benefits, despite the disproportionate profits it brings to real estate interests.[12] Rather, from the Progressive era on, the boosterism of progrowth coalitions has been ideologically reinforced by what Carolyn Adams calls "positive environmentalism." Analyzing the renewal of Philadelphia's Society Hill (the brainchild of Edmund Bacon, Philadelphia's noted director of city planning in the 1950s), Adams observes: "In emphasizing the physical dimensions of renewal, [Bacon and his small group of reformers] believed they were directly addressing the city's social and economic problems. Far from separating the two aspects of development, they, like the earlier Progressives, saw the solution of social and economic problems as dependent upon physical reconstruction."[13] The conviction that a better physical environment not only directly improves the wretched lives of the poor but also changes their self-concept, their attitudes, and their civic behavior thus establishes a direct line of communication between urban reformism and a cherished belief of architectural modernism. It is important to keep this affinity in mind when we examine later attempts to reverse urban decline.

American capital continued to concentrate rapidly during and after World War I. The big corporations took advantage of truck freight to move their productive plants to the suburbs while clustering their administrative headquarters in a few regional and national centers.[14] In the years of turmoil before 1914, some industrialists had explicitly expressed the hope that a suburban location would protect their workers from the "infection" of strikes and labor organizing. Many affluent families also sought an early suburban escape from the consequences of industrial density. The white collar middle class, prompted by streetcars and cheap housing, started early on to follow the elites out of town.[15] Commercial establishments sprung up around the new markets, while the presence of a labor force and the relative cheapness of automobiles amplified the trend.

Starting with the 1930 census, the population of metropolitan areas was growing faster in the suburbs than at the center. The depression and World War II stymied the migration to the suburbs, but big business took full advantage of wartime federal financing to reindustrialize along the spatial lines prefigured in the 1920s. The influence of corporate leaders in the War Production Board allowed them to opt for a location policy that placed "their new facilities largely beyond the reach of the unions, New Deal-leaning mayors, and the other constituencies which had fueled urban liberalism in the 1930s."[16] Indeed, the political relationship between cities and the federal government had been transformed by the New Deal.

John Mollenkopf argues in a compelling study that the economic collapse of the 1930s provided national and local political entrepreneurs with a platform on which they were able to formulate progressive programs, pass them against conservative opposition, implement them in part, and use them to create a new constituency for the Democratic party among urban workers of ethnic origin.[17] The political base of urban liberalism was, in his term, the "iron triangles" that federal programs had forged between state managers, congressional Democrats, and local beneficiaries or ideological supporters of the programs. The Democratic party tried to preserve or to reconstruct this base almost until the 1980s. Mollenkopf observes that "the great physical accomplishments of the New Deal programs pointed the way to future directions in urban land use. The slum clearance projects, the parkways, the new public buildings, and publicly subsidized private housing construction all showed how government could accelerate and direct market forces."[18]

Many architects and planners participated in the New Deal programs, if for no other reason than that the government had become not only one of the most important but also one of the few employers. In the new technocratic positions that the New Deal was making available, American architects were able to play a role not that different from the public role of their European colleagues, applying, for instance, their long experience with prefabrication to the large-scale projects of the New Deal. The Italian historian Leonardo Benevolo assesses the experience of the 1930s as follows: "A new class of technicians was growing up, aware of the demands of collaboration and used to contact with political and administrative authorities, while the architect became ever less an independent technician and ever more a coordinator of the works of other technicians."[19] Benevolo tends to exaggerate (without evidence) the influence of the Modern Movement and, after 1933, the role of the European émigrés. On the whole, the technocratic role that the New Deal offered to American architects was not at all ideologically identified, as it was in parts of Europe for a time, with the new architecture.

Richard Pommer has documented the limited influence of European modernism on American urban housing in the early 1930s. Confronted with the new task of designing large-scale projects (fifty-nine were built or financed by the government from 1932 to 1934), "a few younger architects succeeded in introducing designs from European housing of the Modern Movement. . . . These methods of site planning and ideals of architectural form collided, however, with the vaguer and more timid traditions of American housing design; and the social and political implications of Continental housing became caught in the American shift from private initiatives to bureaucratic control." For Pommer, both architects and critics missed the modernist lesson "of the inseparability of housing, planning and architecture."[20] In America, aesthetics and social purpose remained divorced. One illustration is the 1932 exhibition at the Museum of Modern Art, which introduced the Modern Movement to the cultivated public. It was clearly split between, on the one hand, Philip Johnson and Henry Russell Hitchcock's formal emphasis on International Style architecture and, on the other hand, housing. The latter part was curated by Clarence Stein, Henry Wright, and Catherine Bauer, with a catalog introduction by Lewis Mumford.[21]

The reception of the work of Clarence Stein and Henry Wright, the United States' most distinguished housing experts of the period, is another illustration of the divorce between aesthetics and social purpose. In the first place, their notable achievements set more a *suburban* than an urban model of development.[22] Second, their aesthetics stood in the way of recognition by many architects of the younger generation. Robert Stern has noted that Harvard's central role in introducing the European movement to America was deeply marked by the school's traditional emphasis on aesthetics. Holmes Perkins remembers that Harvard students in the 1930s

> thought of [Stein, Mumford, and Henry Wright] as planners. The distinction they were making in their mind was that these men were concerned with program, with social responsibility, with the need for creating a decent environment. . . . The architects, who had always been concerned with aesthetics, were not much inclined to pay attention because, frankly, Stein's architecture was

damn dull! But when you looked at Gropius's architecture or Mies's or Le Corbusier's . . . it was exciting, because it was absolutely different. There was no
precedent for it in this country.[23]

Modernism, therefore, did not give its typical architectural face to the
New Deal's progressive urban movement.[24] A much more conservative
progrowth coalition was to sponsor its hegemonic rise in the postwar
period.

SUBURBS, FREEWAYS, AND URBAN RENEWAL

During the extraordinary economic expansion of the war years and the
prosperous 1950s, many experts concluded that the central cities had
become obsolete.[25] Despite Truman's narrow victory, conservative opponents of the New Deal had reorganized and regained strength in Congress.
Their influence bent the bulk of Truman's housing program to the benefit
of the private sector and away from the Democrats' urban strongholds. In
the older industrial cities, fate appeared to be sealed, first, by continuing
suburbanization and, second, by the movement of business and people to
the new cities of the Southwest. The immediacy of urban blight and growing worries about the cities' tax revenues spurred efforts to "save downtown
for business," with "positive environmentalism" for ideological justification.
Modernist architecture played a very visible part in the undemocratic and
unpopular attempts to stem the tide.

Federal policies that favored suburbs, private homeownership, and the
automobile subsidized one of the great migrations in American history.
Federally insured mortgages enabled a new industry of residential builders
to take full advantage of cheap suburban land. After 1956, the Interstate
and the Revenue Highway Acts, cheap cars, and cheap gasoline encouraged
commuting to the detriment of urban transportation. Returning veterans,
workers with wartime savings, and the emergent professional-managerial
class left in droves for the lily-white new suburbs to start the baby boom.[26]
By 1950, writes Patrick Ashton, "the population of suburbs was growing
ten times as fast as that of central cities; nearly one in four Americans was
a suburbanite. . . . By 1970, 76 million Americans lived in suburbs. They
represented 57 percent of the total metropolitan population and a plurality
(37.6 percent) of the . . . nation as a whole."[27]

With time, the disparity of incomes and political clout increased the
heterogeneity of the suburbs and their inequality of resources.[28] Yet, for
the mostly white middle class and skilled working class, who participated
in the exodus, the gains (like the achievements of the housing industry)
had been impressive indeed. In 1946, it had been estimated that a mini-

mum of five million units were needed immediately and twelve and a half million over the next decade. After the Housing Act of 1949 was passed, almost a million and a half units were started, most of them by the private sector; from 1950 to 1959, *over fifteen million* new units of housing were provided. In two decades, "the suburban boom produced about 30 million new housing units . . . increasing homeownership from about 40 percent at the end of the war to over 60 percent by the 1960s."[29] The look of suburban developments was undoubtedly influenced by the 1930s innovations in planning and by the wartime workers' villages, many of which had been designed by architects, including such noted names as Gropius, Breuer, Neutra, Eero Saarinen, George Howe, William Wurster, and Oscar Stonorov.[30] The radical separation of housing, work, recreation, and traffic advocated by Le Corbusier and the CIAM in the Athens Charter was unwittingly (or ineluctably) re-created in the suburbs. Similarly, features such as Frank Lloyd Wright's centrally located fireplaces, the small kitchens adjacent to the dining areas, and, above all, the open plan of modernist housing were adapted by the developers' "in house" architects and incorporated into the new prototypes of American homes, to be repeated in both modest and more luxurious versions throughout the land.

Yet, in general, independent architects had a very small *direct* role in building the suburbs.[31] And while they had nothing but contempt for the builders' aesthetics ("an inebriate lot of criminals," Frank Lloyd Wright called them), developers paid them in kind. New York's David Rose quipped to Martin Mayer, "I would not give a famous architect a dog house to build. . . . When I build a dog house I'm interested in the dog. He is not." As Mayer explains, "the architect's fee is the element of expense that the builder can most easily eliminate, turning instead to floor plans and elevations in books and catalogues."[32] In the inner cities, architects' intervention was both more difficult to avoid and much more controversial than whatever influence they had in the suburbs.

The population left behind in the old inner cities consisted disproportionately of those barred from suburban homeownership by their income, the inconvertibility of their assets (homes that could not be sold, experience that could not be transferred, low-level skills), and, conspicuously, their race. If the population vacuum of the inner city was filled at all, it was mostly by more poor and more minorities from the South and Latin America (Asia came later, in the 1980s).[33] Their occupational prospects were bleak and worsening. In the 1960s, the inner cities of the fifteen largest metropolitan areas lost almost one million jobs, while the suburbs gained three million.[34]

The Republican administrations in the 1950s and 1970s favored the suburbs and the newer metropolitan areas of the South and the West. Moreover, the urban redevelopment programs destined to rescue the older cities were clearly oriented toward slum clearance and the sanitization of downtown.

Eisenhower's Housing Advisory Committee had recommended in 1953 that "overemphasis on housing for reuse should be avoided and the land should be put to industrial, commercial, institutional, public or residential use or any combination thereof."[35] The Housing Act of 1954 required advisory citizen committees. Predictably, most of their members came from the progrowth associations of downtown businessmen that had been forming since the war in major cities, in coalition with developers, building trade unions, newspaper editors, and urban professionals. Large architectural firms, in particular, had always been part of the urban "growth machines."

On the one hand, city governments were determined to favor in every way the businesses and the middle-class constituencies who had not yet fled the city. On the other hand, urban renewal legislation allowed technocratic planners to circumvent much of the elected local government's supervision. Thus, during the 1950s, assisted only by small civic elites, planners had free rein.

Two observers sympathetic to developers note that neither planners nor businessmen made any "serious attempt to look at the city through the eyes of average people who needed homes, jobs, and recreation. They spoke more as guardians of the cultural values that the cities represented, now threatened by suburban growth." The image of the "obsolete city" convinced them that "in order to save downtown, it was going to be necessary to destroy it."[36] And destroy they did. Their instruments were the highway and the renewal programs, which provided enormous funds.

Armed with the right of eminent domain and high-handed methods of eviction, urban renewal authorities managed to clear expanses of land so large that they would have been impossible to assemble through normal market operations. But federal legislation excluded developers from taking part in preliminary planning, and many decaying cities found themselves with no takers for their acres and acres of vacant lots:

> St. Louis had its "Hiroshima Flats" and St. Paul its "Superhole." Vacant lots littered with junked cars, piles of garbage and rats' nests were the most visible results of thirteen years of work on the ambitious Ellicott project in Buffalo. . . . As late as 1971, more than half the projects begun between 1960 and 1964 still had land unsold and only the very earliest projects—those begun between 1950 and 1959—had completed two-thirds or more of their land sales.[37]

The vastness of the vacated sites called for large projects, working to the advantage of the large architectural firms capable of handling them. In place of the often spurious "blight" it had cleared, urban renewal too often put upscale apartment buildings, office towers, and institutional complexes like New York's Lincoln Center. The modernist planning and aesthetics the large firms espoused were well suited to the enormity of the sites.

For the historian Vincent Scully, all types of large-scale projects in post-war America followed the principles of Le Corbusier's visionary 1925 Plan Voisin for Paris. Here is how Scully describes the revolutionary impact of this never-realized utopia:

> The old streets and blocks of Paris were to be destroyed in favor of towers standing in super-blocks with tremendous throughways flashing between them. . . . By the 1960's, it was the striking visual effect of the *ville radieuse*, not its social intent, which came to dominate the conceptions of urban redevelopers. It constituted their preconceived formal image, which they discovered could be as appropriate for luxury apartments or for office buildings as for the proletarian army that Le Corbusier had paraded. Despite their protestations of functional objectivity, they tended simply to reproduce it for all functions, except that now the gardens between the towers were normally filled with parked automobiles.[38]

Typically, urban renewal projects were conceived for a single social function, separated from their surroundings by wide avenues or expressways and made of boxy towers, looming over ubiquitous parking lots and vast barren plazas where no one liked to sit.

In the three decades after the war, headquarter cities (most notably, Chicago and New York) and university towns like Cambridge and New Haven had acquired some modernist buildings of great distinction. But in most cities, urban renewal spread both aggressive urban design and an impoverished version of modernist architecture. For dozens of serious or spurious followers in the 1950s and 1960s, the main source of inspiration was the "laconic splendor" of Mies van der Rohe's steel structures.[39]

Mies used the steel frame for the first time in 1948–51 in the twin towers on Chicago's Lake Shore Drive. The perfection of Mies's modular compositions gave architects a model for the controlled design of large-scale units; the use of steel contributed to the solution of some of the industry's overproduction problems; and his conception of the high rise building proffered great profits to developers. Indeed, as William Jordy emphasizes, the Lake Shore towers had cost from 5 to 10 percent less than comparable apartment buildings: "Inevitably, the purely technological aspect of Mies's work and the profits to be made from it accounted for the tremendous influence of the Miesian example. In most of the offshoots by other architects and builders, however, neither the 'less' nor the 'more' had much to do with Mies's teaching, except to prove that The Building was as much a prototype as he had intended it to be."⁴⁰ Mies's much-copied steel-and-glass tower became the monumental signature of corporate modernization. Monumentality, however, was less important sociologically than the association of modern architecture with urban renewal and public housing.

In the late 1950s and 1960s, a simplistic and reductionist version of modernism became the expression of urban redevelopment, its frozen looks indelibly tied to the large-scale demolition that had preceded it. For working class and especially minority neighborhoods, urban renewal and freeway construction meant the equivalent of wartime destruction. Expressways divided their neighborhoods and cut them off from the rest of the city; like redevelopment, these expressways displaced with little or no compensation thousands of residents, who were then left on their own to cope with rising rents, substandard housing, and racial discrimination. Thousands of small businesses were evicted and a large proportion condemned to failure. The people displaced were disproportionately nonwhite; if they received priority for relocation in public housing, their presence there helped to discredit the projects and to silently justify their subsequent abandonment by the authorities.⁴¹

The revolt against the freeways started in San Francisco in 1959 and spread in the early 1960s to other parts of the country. In New York's Greenwich Village, seasoned middle-class activists (among whom Jane Jacobs played a prominent role) stopped the West Village project and advised the opponents of the Lower Manhattan Expressway. Before meeting its political doom, the demolition phase ushered in among middle-class urban constituencies a strong movement for the preservation of historical landmarks (or just nice old buildings). Even more than the strength of the movement, its ideology of urban permanence, focused on buildings and not on people, had a profound influence on architectural postmodernism.

More tragically and more significantly, highways and urban renewal paved the way in many cities for the black insurrections that started with Watts in 1965. As a first response, the Housing and Urban Development Acts of 1965 and 1968 stopped the worse "Negro removal" aspects of urban redevelopment while still keeping its focus on downtown areas. But Lyndon Johnson's landslide victory went farther: Johnson's War on Poverty attempted to contain urban conflict and reabsorb black mobilization within the folds of a revamped New Deal coalition.

The tragic irony is that urban liberalism, having solved neither the problems of the Democratic party nor those of the cities, accelerated instead the flight of business toward the safer political areas of the South and the West.[42] At the national level, the wreck of the Great Society on the shoals of Vietnam and the ghetto revolts opened the long reaction that brought Nixon to power in 1968 and has not been reversed since then, despite the Carter interlude.

At the end of the 1960s, the improvements in highway access and the major increase in office construction allowed the thirty largest metropolitan areas to hold on to a 20 percent share of new office construction, against the strong competition of newer cities and the suburbs.[43] The results, however, offered nothing to endear the public to technocratic planning or modernist architecture. The latter's triumph in the postwar period could not be separated from what urban renewal had done to the poorest and most powerless inhabitants of the cities. Neither could it be disassociated from the bulldozing of cherished landmarks that so offended the educated public. Finally, the new and growing professional-managerial strata did not even seem to like the glass-box derivations of Miesian exemplars, set in dreary Corbusian plans, where they were supposed to work, live, and entertain themselves.[44]

Yet, during the years of the Community Action and the Model Cities programs, young designers mobilized by "the Sixties" had been practicing in the neighborhoods an architecture of community centers, district clinics, and modest renovations. Within schools and professional organizations, they battled to have their elders recognize their modest work as architecture and, beyond that, as the counterhegemonic dimension of the architect's mandate. The first phase of architectural postmodernism belonged to them. They opened it self-consciously on a stage strewn with the rubble of the 1950s and 1960s. On this stage, aesthetic critique merged for a moment with social indignation and political strife.

COMPETITION BETWEEN THE CITIES

During the 1970s, the population loss of "snowbelt" cities went beyond simple transfer to the suburbs. After a century of steady growth, the largest metropolitan *regions* themselves began to contract, as migration of firms and people toward the new cities of the Southwest gathered increasing strength.[45]

The long recession that started at the end of 1973 (after the steep rise in oil prices) and lasted until 1975 was the worst the United States had experienced since the depression. Architecture, which so closely depends on the volume of construction, seemed particularly threatened. Housing starts fell from over 2 million per year to 1.34 million in 1974. In January 1973, the Nixon administration suspended all federal subsidies to housing; and while the full impact was not felt until 1976–78, the moratorium stopped $12 billion in appropriated funds from flowing.[46] The crisis in construction ended toward the end of the decade, thanks to the spectacular recovery of the private sector.

I will review first the politics of urban investment, as the primary context for the public practice of architecture, and then turn to the extraordinary real estate boom of the late 1970s and early 1980s. Finally, I will sketch some speculative connections between background factors and the reception of architecture, taking gentrification as my empirical stepping stone.

The cities of the Northeast and Midwest bore the brunt of the long recession (as also during the shorter one of 1969–70) in terms of job, population, and income loss. They also paid a heavy price under Nixon's "New Federalism." The federal government's retreat from direct subsidies to the cities did not actually take effect until the late 1970s, but its tendency to withdraw from urban spending was clear in Nixon's reversal of the Great Society programs. Policies like general revenue sharing, new employment and training programs, and the Community Development Block Grants (which replaced the Model Cities program in 1974) engaged the older and largely Democratic cities in keen and uneven competition for federal funds with both Southern and Southwestern cities and smaller towns.[47]

Experts disagree on the exact contribution of federal policy shifts and urban strife to the economic decline of the older urban areas in the 1970s. But there is little doubt about the fact of decline or the effects of the shift on urban capital programs. In the "stagflation" of the 1970s, major cities like New York, Boston, Detroit, Cleveland, and Philadelphia hovered on the edge of bankruptcy. Big city mayors faced growing social expenditures, a heavy burden of tax-supported general obligation debt, and the impossibility of increasing local taxes without provoking more middle-class flight—all this against growing federal indifference to their endemic fiscal crisis. The response of most city governments was "to refocus the city's activities on economic growth rather than on social programs."[48] It is instructive to consider how they went about it.

For cities strapped by their stagnating or declining tax base, the first priority was to reconstruct it. But city governments have no effective means of reversing regional or national economic trends. Unable for a long time to hold on to industrial jobs, the governments of older cities were compelled to go with the postindustrial shift. The first part of their strategy was to keep and attract businesses and middle-class people downtown. Richard

Hill has described the "corporate center" strategy for Detroit (where it has failed):

> Overall investment priorities are to transform this aging industrial city into . . . a financial, administrative and professional services center for auto and related industries; a research and development site for new growth industries . . . [with] an emphasis upon recommercialization rather than reindustrialization; and an orientation toward luxury consumption that is appealing to young corporate managers, educated professionals, convention goers and the tourist trade.[49]

Cities engaged in this path to recovery with different physical, social, cultural, and economic endowments. Yet, regardless of how these affected the outcome, adopting the same strategy was bound to increase competition among cities at all levels of the hierarchical urban system. And while downtown projects are more visible and therefore more significant for both politicians and architects, their importance should not be exaggerated. The silent second part of the strategy was to continue creating for capital—and also for people—the city-wide infrastructures that they required.[50]

The fiscal situation forced many cities into another form of competition as well. In the late 1970s, it had become compulsory for most U.S. cities to find sources of financing other than tax appropriations or tax-supported bonds for *any* project—neighborhood, downtown, or city-wide. The federal government was always the cities' first resort, but, as Washington started to withdraw from direct financing, urban administrations increasingly turned to the capital market for funds. Both Carter and Reagan promoted public–private ventures enthusiastically, offering them financial complements through Urban Development Action Grants. The market's demands for a stable return on investments, combined with the often dismal record of recent urban renewal projects, subjected the new municipal ventures to the imperative of efficiency. To pay for themselves, they would have to be built with minimum delay and managed efficiently. In general, this meant two things: turning over the new undertakings (with tax abatements and cheap credit) to the private sector; and slowly doing away with the concessions to low-income housing (if any had been won), to preserve the new projects for financial and service centers and for an upper middle-class residential clientele.[51]

In "public" ventures, competition for funds in the capital market pushed the cities to establish special authorities and quasi-public corporations at the same time that city managers increasingly relied on off-budget financial techniques for the public part of the deal. The resulting autonomy from the budgetary authority of elected officials encouraged appointed technocrats or city mayors to act as real entrepreneurs in their dealings with private developers.[52] The centralization of decision making in the hands of special-purpose authorities and a financial elite may have improved economic and commercial efficiency, but it also increased the opportunities for corruption and "sweetheart deals" with the private sector. Moreover, as Adams notes in her Philadelphia study, independent special-purpose authorities centralized decision making but fostered fragmentation, making it much harder to devise and coordinate an overall strategy for urban redevelopment.

With this background, the question of direct concern to us is what the private sector and the privatized public agencies wanted to have built. City authorities could not afford a repeat of urban renewal and much less the near insurrection it often had fired. The competition among cities, few of which could pursue much else than the same floundering "postindustrial" strategies, meant that downtown projects would be chosen in largely similar ways. A very sympathetic study of the new forms of urban redevelopment sums up the municipal acquisitions of the 1970s and early 1980s: "By now most cities have *the basic equipment to attract development: a new office district, good hotels and restaurants, a shopping mall, a convention center, a historic neighborhood or two.* They have projects that keep downtown competitive as a place for business, as well as ornaments that make it enjoyable *for the public.*"[53]

It is important to note the mystifying use of the concept "public" next to a list of mostly private facilities. Architectural receipts from public and institutional clients declined substantially in the 1970s, proportionally less, however, than the increase in receipts from commercial work.[54] The urban projects of this period, primed with public funds and based on public land, accelerated the privatization of public space. To the cheers of city authorities, new forms of hybrid "private public space" appeared in the postindustrial city: "Routinely . . . public areas, paid for with private funds, furnish private redevelopment projects with the amenities necessary to maximize profits. In other cases, city regulations require corporations, in exchange for increased density allowances, to build privately owned atriums or plazas. The resulting locations are designated 'public spaces.' "[55] Within the new "postindustrial" projects, "the public" ideally consists of those who can pay their way.

The competition among cities to each build its own "architectural spectacle" has had obvious implications for architectural practice. An exhaustive study of downtown shopping malls emphasizes the role of developers with a long record of suburban success, who knew, in other words, what was needed to attract the broad middle-class market. City authorities had their sights focused on the same target and a say in the design process through their representatives on the negotiating team. Both commercial and city voices—the latter representing its own notions of a middle-class paying or spending public—rejected the barrenness and the single function of urban renewal modernism. Downtown malls sought instead to create mixed uses, variety, spaces packed with activity, and the theatrical excitement needed to compensate for the persistent weakness of retail demand in central cities. Commercial projects served symbolic political functions as well.

David Harvey shows how deliberate was Baltimore's attempt to erase the memory of the riots of 1968 and overcome middle-class fears of down-town with an urban icon. Starting in 1970 with the City Fair, Baltimore had acquired by 1980 an aquarium, a convention center, a marina, hotels, and the incredibly successful Harbor Place—a shopping mall developed by James Rouse, the pioneer of large-scale renovation in a Northeastern city (Boston's Faneuil Hall and Quincy markets, open in 1976). In Harvey's words, "an architecture of spectacle, with its sense of surface glitter and transitory participatory pleasure, of display and ephemerality, of *jouissance,* became essential to the success of a project of this sort."[56] Yet, the pre-condition of downtown middle-class *jouissance* is the guarantee that crime, poverty, and decay shall be safely banned from the private public spaces where the permanent spectacle goes on. If structures must satisfy the same basic requirements of enclosure and safe access, surface is the only thing that *can* change. The pressure on cities to carry these projects out and make them work meant that the successes, real or apparent, would be rapidly imitated.

For all the efforts to differentiate the product with novel and exciting inventions, the commercial projects' programs and budgets inevitably tend toward a new conformity that does not always attain James Rouse's "com-mercialism with artistic flair" nor follow his choice of excellent designers (like Benjamin Thompson in Boston or Frank Gehry in Santa Monica). Architecture engaged in the privatization of public space is most often held to standard structures and, paradoxically, to standard amenities and stan-dard frills as well.

In addition to shopping centers, another typical downtown project was the hotel, for which the architect-developer John Portman set the trend in the 1967 Atlanta Peachtree Center. Its enormous atrium, "free-standing" glass elevators, fountains, cafés, and internal vegetation have earned for Portman's prototype the nickname "Jesus Christ Hotel" (because dazzled first-time visitors gasp "Je-sus Chee-rist!"). It was repeated and imitated by the dozen in the hotel boom of the 1960s and 1970s, notably in Portman's own Bonaventura Hotel in Los Angeles and Renaissance Center in Detroit.[57]

Just as ambitious architects had learned to work with government in the 1930s and with community activists in the early 1970s, they learned to work with the developers and the "public–private" ventures of the 1970s and 1980s. The effects of this collaboration were superimposed upon the re-evaluation of modernism in which the profession had been autonomously engaged since the 1960s. The commercial need for "product differentiation" and the competition among cities to create a sense of their own uniqueness were thus perfectly attuned with the evolution of architectural discourse.

From the mid-1960s on, design theorists had been reducing the radical innovations of modernism to just another voice in what Jameson aptly calls "the imaginary museum of a now global culture." As he says, "the random cannibalization of all the styles of the past," the clever mobilization of nostalgia, the inventiveness of pastiche, and the cinematic techniques of collage and fragmentation (which architects felt increasingly free to use) promoted the role of design in the competitive phase of "postindustrial" urban development.[58] Together or separately, city governments and developers learned to exploit the old mechanism of architectural competitions to find monumental and "original" designs for projects always touted as unique yet ultimately much alike in their uses and looks after being built.

The point I want to stress is that structural forces converged with the internal evolution of architectural discourse to revaluate the symbolic dimensions of urbanism and architecture. As the manufacturing industries abandoned the cities with the effects that we have seen, hard-pressed city managers, hard-headed businessmen, and architects in retreat from modernism discovered that the production of ever-renewed and ever-diversified images and meanings is a constitutive dimension of postindustrial economic activity. The production of images and meanings is not restricted to the obvious and crucial fields of information, education, advertising, and the media in the postindustrial economy. Commodities (among them buildings), valued more for what they mean in terms of status than for their actual use, are the lifeblood of late capitalist commerce.

As meanings and images themselves became the objects of production, architectural designers found new demand for their work, though often not for the reasons they would have preferred. With the government's welfare functions in retreat and the seedy (or just the poor) downtown quarters erased by redevelopment and gentrification, a population of marginal and evicted citizens has become the generic "homeless," haunting the new private public spaces as the very present ghost of needs not served. Their daily struggle with private guards and municipal authorities is about the classification and the use of urban spaces: As city after city strives to enforce the rule that stations (or parks, or shopping malls) are not for sleeping, they disclose the real social functions of "public" architecture and tight zoning principles.[59]

ARCHITECTURE AND THE PRIVATE SECTOR IN THE AGE OF LAISSEZ-FAIRE

For all the significance of spectacle in unique downtown projects, the boom in office building of the 1970s and early 1980s was a much more important source of large-scale work. New York's predominance in the office building market began to be challenged in the 1960s, an indication that economic restructuring was extending to the whole country: While the thirty largest metropolitan areas doubled the volume of new office space of the 1950s (and again, in the 1970s, increased the volume of the 1960s by 150 percent), New York's share declined from one-half to one-third of the total. Then, as Frieden and Sagalyn report, "a construction boom without parallel produced more downtown office space from 1980 to 1984 than during the entire decade of the 1970s. From 1960 through 1984, 1,325 office buildings were built or started in the downtowns of the thirty largest urban areas, supplying almost 550 million square feet of floor space—the equivalent of 250 new Empire State Buildings."[60]

For the noted expert Anthony Downs, what happened in real estate capital markets in the late 1970s and early 1980s amounted to a "revolution." Two interrelated outcomes of this revolution had direct effects on what was built: The first was the retreat from the social priority assigned to financing homeownership since the New Deal; the second was a tendency toward chronic (as against merely cyclical) overbuilding in nonresidential commercial real estate.[61] The partial deregulation of the thrift industry (which Downs stresses) influenced both outcomes through its effects on capital markets; but the effects of federal tax policy were more direct and at least equal in importance. From 1981 to 1986 in particular, the depreciation allowances of Reagan's Economic Recovery Act helped create the flurry of office construction in the 1980s.[62] Let us briefly outline Downs's technical argument.

Inflation had made it impossible to continue operating the thrifts on the traditional principle—long-term mortgage loans at fixed rates and short-term borrowing through saving deposits. From 1979 to 1982, successive deregulations allowed the thrifts to compete on the financial markets, diversify their rates, and enter businesses other than mortgage lending while still enjoying the advantage of federal insurance on deposits. After the savings and loans catastrophe of the late 1980s, it hardly needs repeating that when interest rates rose, many thrifts financed riskier and riskier real estate projects in an attempt to recoup their losses.

On the one hand, deregulation eliminated the sheltered position that housing had enjoyed in the credit markets. On the other hand, it induced competition, which led to higher interest rates and less affordable housing. Another crucial contingency was the combination of large fiscal deficits under President Reagan with the Federal Reserve's anti-inflationary monetary policies. Both nominal and real interest rates reached much higher levels in the 1980s than in any of the three preceding decades. However, as a consequence of capital markets' great uncertainty about inflation, interest rates, exchange rates, and security prices, financial capital still flooded real estate markets in 1983–84.

Downs links the "real estate bias of capital markets" to tax policy and to the socialization of risk offered by federal deposit insurance. To this I must add the extremely generous depreciation and interest-payment deductions allowed by the 1981 tax reform. According to Downs, the favored financial institutions that invest in real estate shift from residential to nonresidential property when they expect inflation: They insist on acquiring equity in the properties they finance, which is something that homeowners normally refuse. In the late 1970s and early 1980s, the financial community was looking for protection against inflation and a share of future capital gains. Therefore, thrifts and banks joined the new real estate syndicates in their search for nonresidential property in which to invest. A further enticement in many large cities was the rapid rise in nonresidential rents of the late 1970s, owing both to inflationary construction costs and shortages of space.

After the short recession of 1982, a second boom in nonresidential construction followed that of 1978–81, even though the thirty-one largest metropolitan areas "showed a continuous rise in vacancy rates from under 5.0 percent in early 1981 to 15.3 in early 1985. Downtown office vacancy exceeded 10 percent throughout 1983, the same year in which commercial mortgages (in 1972 dollars) increased by 48 percent more than their highest previous annual gain."[63] The excess of capital in the real estate markets continued to favor new construction, which allows much higher depreciation rates than the purchase of old buildings.

At the same time, however, the high cost of money directed smaller developers toward the less expensive renovation of older structures. Helped in some cases by tax credits for historic preservation, they attempted to capitalize on the increasingly high residential rents of some cities, spurring on the phenomenon of gentrification, to which I will return.

Overbuilding of commercial property and the need to compete for tenants in nonresidential buildings encourage a desire for "product differentiation" that has implications for architecture. While location is still the primary factor in real estate price, good design represents a differential advantage both in leasing and in resale. Indirectly, the trend had been highlighted by the corporations that in the 1970s started adopting new and striking forms or surprising historicist styles for their headquarters. For the corporations, it was a matter of acquiring not only space but a symbolic presence to use as advertisement. One of Equitable Life's vice presidents gives a true "postindustrial" reason for high prestige architectural packaging: "You don't sell financial services the way you sell soda pop. You have to feel this is a sound financial institution. I don't know if a tall, big building is a subtle way to establish the reputation of a financial institution, but you don't do it through billboards."[64]

Developers were quick to exploit the notion. Gerald Hines, the developer who went from Johnson and Burgee's Pennzoil building in Houston to a nationwide reputation as patron of architectural celebrities, explains:

> I discovered that extra quality in buildings would make our product stand out; we found if we had a product that was differentiated, we had a chance of getting a better class of client. . . . The fact that Pennzoil was two buildings didn't scare us. . . . In fact, having the two buildings represented a lower leasing risk: it enabled us to secure a second major tenant, which reduced our exposure—the name of the game in the development business.[65]

As New York's Citicorp discovered, after keeping about 100,000 square feet for itself in Hugh Stubbins's striking towers, it got premium rents for the rest. The reasons had to do not only with the systematic use of design for product differentiation but with aggressive marketing techniques.[66] While looks distinguish a building among a plethora of neighboring others, the architect's name and reputation, if appropriately publicized, can become an increasingly important asset. In the marketing of redundant office space, an *international* reputation becomes one more difference that the public relations department can put to good use. One result is to intensify the "media" element of high-level architectural careers.

Vincent Scully has bitterly observed of the astounding urban boom of the 1980s: "Office buildings are intrinsically less interesting and lively than almost any other kind of building, than houses, farms, or factories, for example, and much less complicated and dense in meaning than temples, or cathedrals or even city halls. . . . *Never before in human history have cities been dominated by forms growing out of a program so fundamentally inane.*"[67] The other side of downtown office building, as Scully crisply notes, is the suburban house.

We have seen that financial deregulation and high interest rates made housing less affordable after 1974, especially in regional markets like California, where speculation had run rampant. The price of housing relative to income became especially onerous for people who bought homes after 1979 and for first-time home buyers. However, it is not inconceivable that the events of the 1970s and early 1980s had a positive effect for the "boutique" practice of residential architecture.

Downs points out that homeowners benefited greatly throughout the 1970s from two things: First, rapid inflation diminished the burden of long-term fixed-rate mortgages on their incomes; second, they made great profits from their equity by selling at much higher prices than they had paid. Millions of households were thus able to make down payments on more expensive homes than those they sold, a favorable factor for architecture's ability to attract potential clientele.[68] Furthermore, the relative advantages of people who buy or upgrade their homes continued growing during the Reagan years. While the household incomes of American families had become more equal from 1948 to 1969, growing inequality seeped in gradually from 1969 to 1978, accelerated rapidly from there to 1982, and has stabilized since at high levels. This inequality concentrates disposable income in the hands of the rich, who are more likely to spend it on luxuries such as second homes and architects' designs.

The substantial increase in real disposable income per capita under Reagan concealed two main forms of inequality: (1) the growing distance between the higher fifth of the income distribution class and the fifth immediately below and (2) the increasing polarization between the rich and the poor. The richest fifth of households became richer (partly due to Reagan's tax abatements), the middle class shrank, and the poor became poorer while also losing much in terms of social programs. *Household* income continued to be supported by the massive entry of women into the labor market. Yet, on aggregate, the advantage of dual-income households was offset by the crushing disadvantage of single-female heads of household.[69]

In some cities (for instance, Montreal), female single parents of modest means have been able to buy homes for the first time in central working-class areas, remaining close to their jobs and to services. This has not been the norm in the United States: Here, central working-class areas are characterized by gentrification, a trend that tends to be linked to the growth of the urban professional and managerial strata. In the United States, dual-income households have been much better able than female-headed households to take advantage of the "rent gap"—the difference between actual and potential real estate prices that location and amenities produce in some older residential or industrial neighborhoods.[70]

GENTRIFICATION AS A NEW CLASS ACTIVITY

Neither the corporate services that support the large firms nor the "third sector" (made up of government and nonprofit organizations in education, health, social services, and cultural activities) can flee or have fled the cities. Even as the population of older urban areas contracted during the 1960s, service employment expanded.

"Service" denotes a large and heterogeneous sector polarized between the top and bottom tiers of income distribution. "Professional, managerial, technical, and kindred" workers, whose entry into careers and class position depends primarily on higher education credentials, cluster at the top. The bottom tier provides "dead end," low-paying, nonunion jobs to the largely nonwhite, young, female, and often part-time population that pushes the brooms, runs the errands, tends the copying machines, serves the food, and supplies personal services to the upper tier.

The increase of the professional and managerial categories and the related decrease of working-class positions have been continuous in the last decades.[71] A 1982 study, expecting stagnation in the economy and in state employment, had predicted a slowdown, perhaps a reversal, in the proportional increase of managerial, supervisory, and expert classes. Yet the 1987 follow-up showed the opposite: The growth rate of the managerial class within economic sectors, far from slowing down between 1970 and 1980, had increased from 5.9 percent of the total work force to 11.7 percent; for experts, the rate had gone from 7.8 percent to 9.2 percent; while the class of supervisors was still growing at a steady annual rate of 5 percent. In the census years 1960, 1970, and 1980, the proportion of managers was 14.8, 16.3, and 18.4 percent respectively; that of supervisors, 11.5, 12.4, and 13.2 percent; and that of experts, 5.6, 7.4, and 8.6 percent. "Managerial class positions" had expanded in all sectors except the extractive one. In the 1970s as in the 1960s, professional and state services accounted for most of the expansion in the managerial and expert categories.[72]

The acceleration in the growth of managerial and professional classes during the 1970s corresponds to the entry of the baby boom generation into the labor force. The number of persons between twenty-five and thirty-four years of age increased almost by 50 percent in that decade: Twelve million young adults, comparatively better educated and better traveled than ever before in history, presumably took many of the managerial and professional jobs that were opening at a fast rate.[73] Many of these jobs were in architecture and design. While the proportion of architects in the labor force remains very small, their numbers increased during the 1960–80 period much faster than those of other professional groups. Architecture is a professional producer service, the fastest-growing category among the services.[74]

The majority of educated and affluent baby boomers still lived in the suburbs. Yet those who chose the city created not only the "yuppie" stereotype but also new patterns of consumption and entertainment that attracted sophisticated suburbanites. In particular, they provided large contingents to the ranks of middle-class "gentrifiers."

Research shows some common characteristics of the latter: They have college degrees, professional, managerial, or technical jobs, and incomes above the city median and especially above that of the neighborhoods into which they move. They concentrate in the age groups between twenty and forty, most are white, their households are small, and they have few if any children; couples can be married or unmarried, heterosexual or, frequently, gay; the majority do *not* come from the suburbs. They add their hard work—their "sweat equity"—to a relatively modest initial investment, and they expect to be rewarded as real estate appreciates, sometimes very rapidly, in their neighborhoods.

Needless to say, gentrifying neighborhoods invite speculation. But while developers' "revitalization" is associated with wholesale evictions and the direct displacement of the previous residents, gentrification by homeowners proceeds more subtly. As property values rise, the city reassesses them and raises real property taxes, sometimes rapidly and by a large amount. In the word of one researcher, "long-term residents living on low and fixed incomes eventually become asset rich and income poor." Their inability to keep up with rising taxes makes them vulnerable to indirect displacement.[75]

Economics is not, however, the only important factor: The conflict of "life-styles" in the neighborhood is also significant. As anyone who has seen gentrification can tell, the clash between people who drink beer on their stoops and those who sip white wine in their backyards, between Irish taverns and bars overrun with ferns, between old-time merchants and the newcomers' French cheese, between aluminum siding and restored Victoriana is not a trifling matter but one overloaded with resentment and with indigenous people's justifiable feelings of dispossession.

Indeed, if gentrification was only a matter of rational economic choice, it would have direct but limited relevance for architecture. There is partial evidence that a majority of architects not only live in large cities but prefer to do so. With their urban jobs and limited incomes, with their construction know-how and their design expertise, architects themselves are gentrifiers of choice. Moreover, small practitioners and especially architects who start to work on their own get most of their commissions from referrals—the latter, in particular, from friends, relatives, and a circle of acquaintances. Judith Blau's systematic study of New York City firms established that renovation work had become a primary source of income for many small firms trying to survive the crisis of 1974–79.[76]

Yet the remodeling of old homes and the transformation of old storefronts into trendy boutiques can hardly constitute an architectural change. They represent, at best, a special niche in the segmented market for architectural services, although one in which architects face the strong competition of builders and small contractors. Gentrification is much more significant as an indicator of the complex shift of perceptions, cognitions, and tastes that constitute the inchoate base of postmodern culture.

For the postmodern sensibility, history is buried under a thick layer of images and simulacra that mimic an impossible recovery of the past. Synchrony, the simultaneous and ephemeral presence of events in space, eclipses temporality. Or, as David Harvey argues, "fiction, fragmentation, collage and eclecticism, . . . suffused with a sense of ephemerality and chaos" are perhaps the only possible cultural responses to the enormous compression of time and space effected by the global marketplace of objects, images, and ideas.[77] A multiple self, one that makes itself over with each mask it takes, cannot engender the unitary expressive style that modernism searched for.

We may wonder what this has to do with the carefully repainted facades and restored interiors of gentrified homes, with the countless hours spent exposing brick and sanding beams, with the conversion of industrial loft buildings, occupied until yesterday by small manufacturers, into "archeological finds." Michael Jager has observed that the gentrifiers in a Victorian neighborhood of Melbourne applied the Protestant ethic of hard work to the project of reclaiming nineteenth-century homes and borrowing status from their grandeur. They copied the Victorian middle-class's imitation of the higher bourgeoisie, but not cheaply: Their "sweat equity" gave them moral justification.[78] Cleanliness and orderliness are close to godliness in the bourgeois gospel: gentrification, returning things to their pristine original form through hard work, embodies all these moral virtues.

The gentrifiers' often exaggerated respect for authenticity is more than just an attempt to restore the "aura" of the original object. It is also a search, a way of building equity in a past in which much of the "new class" has no roots. Gentrification thus corresponds to a special kind of nostalgia for the past, a moralistic attempt to appropriate it through an active form of consumption. An often compulsive concern with spatial and physical reordering is a morally justifiable form of denying what has happened and what is happening to decayed old neighborhoods. The ideology of positive environmentalism, with which I started this chapter, meets the ideology of art in an ordered environment where disalienated objects (beautiful, creatively preserved or put together) are taken as signs of a conquest over an alienated social life.

The concern with order that finds powerful expression in design may also be seen as an attempt to stave off the postmodern sense of cultural chaos. The insecurity inherent in advancement through hierarchical organizations, the uncertain fit between graduate credentials and the job one is really expected to do, the ephemeral nature of symbol manipulation, the fragility of purely symbolic capital—all these characteristics of the positions of the "new class" should make its members sensitive to cultural disorder. The new class unconsciously absorbs a sense of fragility in the chaotic daily rounds of electronically mediated "postindustrial" work and jarring, disintegrated urban experiences. In the same ways that buildings offer identities to "postindustrial" conglomerates, the past can be a therapeutic illusion for their employees. Both things readily lend themselves to commercial exploitation.

A fine study by Sharon Zukin analyzes both the spontaneous and the manipulated aspects of gentrification.[79] From the late 1960s on, multiple grass roots initiatives, contingent successes, and conflicts among tenants, landlords, and developers transformed the industrial lofts of lower Manhattan into prized studios and expensive housing. In the process, New York's official center for contemporary art moved from Midtown to SoHo.

Zukin shows that a convergence of structural and cultural forces helped to cause this unexpected development. On the one hand, ongoing disinvestment and restructuring were accelerated by New York's economic and fiscal crisis in 1973–76. The crisis favored promoters of a "postindustrial" strategy in their competition for space with small manufacturers and also increased pressure on the city to find alternative tax bases. On the other hand, the explosive development of the arts and interest in art during the 1960s and 1970s was pivotal. On this convergence, Zukin builds a general hypothesis about the integral role of cultural consumption in the postindustrial mode of capital accumulation.

Artists in search of studio space were, indeed, the first outsiders to enter a SoHo that had been rapidly losing industrial tenants since the 1950s. In the first phase, city planning authorities accommodated them by rezoning industrial and commercial lofts for artists' use. In succeeding phases, eligibility for loft living was extended from art occupations to those who could give even vague proof of their "commitment to art." As middle-class residents with a taste for the "loft life-style" moved into SoHo, developers were quick to grasp that the presence of artists was an asset for real estate valorization. The unplanned success of SoHo led to deliberate speculative moves into Tribeca and, in the late 1970s and 1980s, to the totally planned construction of Battery Park City.[80] However, as Zukin ruefully notes, it is inconceivable that "living like an artist" could have appealed to the middle class before World War II.

During the 1960s, the emergence of wider public support for art and historical preservation culminated at state level with the creation of the National Endowment for the Arts in 1965 and by passage of the National Historic Preservation Act in 1966—each, and especially the latter, backed by a skilled and effective political constituency. Diana Crane reports that "support for the arts by the National Endowment for the Arts . . . increased from $1.8 million in 1966 to $131 million in 1983. Corporate spending increased from $22 million to $436 million. Support by all state governments increased from $2.7 million in 1966 to $25 million in 1983, while foundation support increased from $38 million in 1966 to $349 million in 1982."[81]

Of the corporate art collections that existed in 1980, 76 percent had been founded in the 1960s and 1970s, as had 67 percent of the New York art galleries studied by Crane. When New York grabbed Paris's position as the world's art capital after the war, it also became a center of the art auction market; contemporary American art began to be auctioned and to gain in price in the 1970s; the number of serious art collectors grew into the thousands. One million people declared their occupation as "artists" in the 1980 census, against 600,000 in 1970.

Interest and participation in the arts had been growing since the end of the war in close relation with the rapid growth of college enrollments. Both undergraduate and graduate arts programs kept pace with the development of higher education, demonstrating that "a career in the arts" was becoming at least conceivable for a vast middle-class public. For the lucky artists, teaching provided an alternative source of support at the same time that a booming art market encouraged artistic careers.

The attention of the mass media and the renewed vitality of local art centers throughout the United States were further evidence that the traditional "high bourgeois" interest in the arts was becoming much wider. The arts and crafts movement of the 1970s, which appears to have been particularly attractive to middle-class women, extended interest in design (as well as some technical know-how) deep into middle-class life-styles. In sum, the 1960s and 1970s made it both possible and almost necessary to integrate aesthetics into production intended for middle-class consumption. Professional artists and specialists in aesthetics had become an integral part of the new "service class."[82]

In implicit response to these developments, Susan Sontag observed that a new nonliterary culture was both educating and shaping a new sensibility: "The model arts of our time are actually those with much less content [than literature] and a much cooler mode of moral judgment—like music, films, dance, architecture, painting, sculpture. The practice of these arts—all of which draw profusely, naturally, and without embarrassment upon science and technology—are the locus of the new sensibility." Closer on the one hand to the style of science, modern art was on the other hand erasing the barrier between "high" and "low" culture. Indeed, the new attitude toward pleasure in art no longer associated it with edification; it would henceforth be possible to enjoy popular art forms without either moralism or condescension.[83]

If, in Weimar Germany, architects compelled by the political climate had symbolically joined the politicized art avant-gardes, the opposite was happening in the 1960s in America: Professional artists were joining architects in the ranks of a much widened professional-managerial class. Their positions as specialists in aesthetics were sustained by the democratization of interest in the arts and possibly helped by the apolitical, less elitist, and less didactic sensibility detected by Sontag. As more cities turned to the arts for help in their postindustrial conversion, a 1984 study found that the cities with the highest proportion of working artists were also those with the highest rates of downtown gentrification and condominium conversion.[84]

Gentrification provides an appropriate close for this analysis of the postindustrial matrix of architecture. As a symbol of spatial and physical reordering, gentrification expresses the ambiguities of the professional and managerial class to which architects belong. Disinvestment and restructuring made gentrification possible; the displacement of indigenous residents makes it a cause of social disorder. In the cities of late capitalism, private reordering cannot be disassociated from the dispossession and disruption caused in "other people's" lives. The causal link between gentrification and homelessness is not as direct and certainly not as massive in its effects as large-scale urban renewal and redevelopment. But at least rhetorically, homelessness appears as the dark side of all forms of urban revitalization.[85]

It would be a mistake to reduce gentrification, or, for that matter, "commitment to art" and aesthetics, to economic self-interest or to a preoccupation with social distinction. Of course, much of both propels the new sensibility forward. But the postindustrial passage also contains the latent possibility of transcending the narrow utilitarianism, the overriding concern with production, even the blindness to injustice and alienation that characterize industrial capitalism.[86]

Not much of the positive potential seems close to becoming reality. From the standpoint of the 1990s, there appears to be less political will and fewer known political ways for the actualization of dimly envisioned possibilities. Yet, in the same way that architects do not claim to be artists *only* to exploit an available opportunity, the taste for ordered and pleasurable urban environments and the appreciation for beautiful objects and good food are not necessarily callous attitudes of conspicuous consumption. Aesthetics and entertainment are basic human needs that deny the subjection of everything to the hegemony of economic logic. Capitalist businessmen understand this well, or else they would not systematically try to make these needs amenable to profit. Neither beauty nor pleasure nor fun are morally objectionable, as the reproving tone of leftist critics often implies; it is the social context in which these needs are affirmed that makes them so difficult to disentangle from other morally obscene effects.

This survey has recorded the appearance of different roles, at different historical moments, in the repertory of the architectural profession in America: service professional, businessman, technocrat, corporate servant, social activist, subaltern consultant to developers, and artist. In the moment of postmodernism, the artistic role was ascendant in at least one important revisionist sector of architectural discourse.

Other sectors of the profession were less theoretically than practically inclined, yet they still took "art" (not efficiency or technology) as predominant legitimation. Postmodern eclectics, indeed, sought to abandon the adversarial aesthetics of modernism extolled by Lionel Trilling for either an aesthetics of everyday life or one of pleasure and entertainment, which could be adapted and revised for commercial use.[87]

By the 1970s and 1980s, the pitfalls of earlier periods had discredited the technocratic alternative, while the government's retreat from housing helped to further disassemble a public role that has never received much sustained support in the United States. Still, we shall see that the memory of those alternatives persists in the lore of the profession.

I turn now to the elite architects who played a part in changing the profession's discourse. In the next chapter, the protagonists will guide us, from their local and particular viewpoints, through the ways in which structural change has impinged on the making of architecture.

CHAPTER FOUR

The Perception of Structure

Firms, Clients, and Career Settings
in the Design Elite

Rob Quigley, a much-awarded San Diego architect, remembers that one of his developer clients kept telling him: "Rob, this is not going to win an architectural award, is it? Each time a building of mine got an award, I lost money!" Most clients, indeed, do not seek architectural services for aesthetic reasons. The usual corporate and commercial client seems to think that the artistic part of architecture is dangerous for the control of construction and maintenance costs. As a producer service, architecture is expected to contain costs by rationalizing construction. Much of this service is provided by firms experienced in proven, routine solutions or "in house" by architects who work within large engineering or construction firms or for the largest residential developers. That is not where new ideas come from, however.

In the saturated field of real estate investment, the new patterns of upper middle-class consumption have made commercial clients aware of the potential of architecture for differentiating and marketing their product. The developer Gerald Hines states it candidly: "The basic intention is to establish an identity for the building which is individualistic, that makes the tenants say, 'that's my building, and I'm proud of it.' After all, our buildings are products that have to compete with other products."[1] The strategic search for "quality," "distinction," and "identity," known to major corporations since before World War II, is relatively new for commercial developers. It directs them to outside architects whose names are recognized (or, more rarely, to rising younger ones), the client's emphasis on uniqueness matching and encouraging the profession's own postmodern eclecticism.

In an interview with Hines, Peter Eisenman asked how postmodernism's nostalgia for the past fit with the self-image of corporate America; the answer delineates where the choice between style and cutting costs ultimately lies:

> The new architecture fits into the mold that corporate America imagines for itself. I think the style is very strong. For example, the Republic Bank Center project for Houston by Johnson/Burgee is a very strong statement. At first we were a little concerned, but it has received an excellent reception from clients. . . . *The clients' acceptance of a particular system really leads the trend.* If your clients are buying post-modern buildings, your builders are going to build post-modern buildings. But if your customers can buy modernist curtain wall systems at prices lower than post-modern stone buildings, then we are going to see a move back in that direction.[2]

George Kassabaum, of the very large St. Louis firm Helmut Obata Kassabaum, used to say that there are "clients who want it good" and "clients who want it Wednesday." Consumption patterns and architectural eclecticism seem to have inaugurated a new relationship between large commercial clients and smaller firms with a reputation for innovation, but the new type of client seems to want it all: fancy new ideas, reasonable price, on-time completion, and efficient delivery. The money lenders reinforce the normal tendency of corporate clients toward conservatism, and they also often encourage cost savings at the expense of quality.[3] If clients do not find it all in one architectural firm, they increasingly tend to split commissions between design architects and production architects (who sometimes work in the client's own architectural department).

Large and knowledgeable clients have fostered specialization and fragmentation in the architectural profession.[4] "Signature architects" and "idea firms" may be allowed qualified movement, for publicity's sake, across the boundaries of market niches, but this cannot reverse the profession's increasing bifurcation between "a small number of large corporate offices who are assuming control over the largest percentage of architecturally designed work, and the large number of firms small in size, doing small-scale buildings and a proportionately smaller percentage of architecturally designed projects."[5]

After the demise of modernism, the elite of designers who make architectural discourse is likely to be found in the latter group. Since the mid-1970s, the prize put on novelty has allowed a few talented designers in middle-sized or even small new firms to take large-scale work from large firms and to outshine those large firms identified with modernism.[6] This should not be surprising. As Robert Gutman observes, "the small office includes more architects and other technical personnel than it used to. . . . [It is] a bigger small office than it was in the recent past."[7] But large comprehensive offices cannot be discounted. Whether or not they hire innovative designers, they can satisfy clients, achieve recognition at the official levels of the profession, and, last but not least, obtain conspicuous billings, and they can do these things more easily than small firms can.[8]

Drawing from experience and extensive research, Weld Coxe's noted group of management consultants proposes three ideal-types of architectural firms:

> *Strong-idea firms,* which are organized to deliver singular expertise or innovation on unique projects. The[ir] project technology . . . flexibly accommodates the nature of any assignment, and often depends on one or a few outstanding experts or "stars" to provide the last word.
>
> *Strong-service firms,* which are organized to deliver experience and reliability, especially on complex assignments. Their project technology is frequently designed to provide comprehensive services to clients who want to be closely involved in the process.
>
> *Strong-delivery firms,* which are organized to provide highly efficient service on similar or more routine assignments, often to clients who seek more of a product than a service. The[ir] project technology . . . is designed to repeat previous solutions over and over again with highly reliable technical, cost and schedule compliance.[9]

Strong-idea firms associate more and more frequently—often on client demand—with firms of the second or the third group. In fact, association is obligatory for highly specialized projects, such as hospitals or laboratories, and for projects out of the designer's own state or abroad. We can safely assume, however, that elite designers will not be found in the third category.

Predictably, the large majority of the architects I interviewed over the period 1988–90 are principals or partners in strong-idea firms of variable size. However, I also interviewed architects known for their design talent and ideas in large strong-service firms.[10] While Coxe's ideal-types make sense, for the purposes of this analysis they must be complemented by the firms' (and their principals') positions on a different aspect that I call the discursive dimension of architectural practice. Ultimately, it is the recognition granted within the autonomous discourse of the profession that gives architects elite status and lifts them above the level of a small or purely local practice.

Nowadays, an architect's professional recognition is contaminated by the designer's "media celebrity," but its chief expression is still the standing it confers in the circles that follow the profession's discourse. Standing may be local, national, or international; it includes a good measure of client satisfaction, especially for strong-service firms; yet it depends primarily on publications, awards, professional societies, rankings in important design competitions, lectures, nominations to juries in awards programs or elite schools, faculty appointment in a renowned school—in sum, the marks of recognition bestowed by esteemed fellow architects, educators, and architectural critics.

The design elite to which I am referring is therefore not the same as the notorious architectural "star system," although it includes many "stars."[11] All the architects I interviewed know about the others' work, talk about one another (frequently with malice), and often know each other very well, even if they are located in different areas. Yet, despite these real or invisible networks, we cannot speak of one design elite, for it has many layers and many centers.

Undoubtedly, New York architects and influentials believe that New York is the capital of American architecture as it is that of American art.[12] With its schools, museums, exhibitions, lectures, critics, foreign visitors, and debates, New York's architectural scene is more "discursively active" than that of any other city in America and perhaps the world. But it would be much too simple to assume that New York's cosmopolitan and intellectual elite co-opts and anoints the architects of regional or local repute.

In terms of what architects build, Chicago and Los Angeles are strong and independent centers in their own right. In San Francisco, Philadelphia, Boston, San Diego, Santa Fe, Miami, and smaller cities as well, elite designers receive national awards, win national competitions, and build across the nation and abroad. The saying attributed to Antoine Predock of New Mexico—"A regional architect is one who only builds in his own state"—rings true, but it must be corrected by two observations.

First of all, elite reputations are made by and within the medium of architectural discourse. New York influentials have direct access to New York and probably to European critics as well, but in order for these critics to exercise their influence, they need new names to make. The architectural critics of the *New York Times,* because they need interesting stories, must scout for new talent and interesting work, as also do architectural museums outside New York (such as the reputed Walker Art Center in Minneapolis or the new Canadian Center for Architecture in Montreal) and museums and galleries of contemporary art all over the United States.

Vittorio Gregotti, the renowned Italian architect, long associated with CIAM and with the journal *Casabella,* observes:

> The star system is no longer tied to a group, as in the time of CIAM. There no longer is ideological solidarity as there was then. The stars all know and compete with one another. In America, the construction of charismatic personalities gives a much greater authority to the architect, but also a shorter life. What *is* this life? Finally, it is only the life of the schools. The schools perform the "cooling" operation, transforming the ideas into style and minding the changes of fashion.

Particularly in the United States, the nationwide system of universities with reputed graduate schools of architecture is directly connected to the making of architectural discourse. Through publications, lectures, and teaching in what graduate students in the best schools simply call "the circuit," architects in peripheral locations gain direct access to the discursive field of architecture.

Finally, competitions (especially the international ones) provide another important point of entry to a widely broadcast discourse, for the winners as well as the most noted finalists.[13] The case of Robert Venturi, for instance, seems more extreme than it is unique. He became world famous after publishing *Complexity and Contradiction in Architecture* in 1966 without a single major building to his credit, although he did include several competition entries among the examples of his work. Nowadays, even local architects, helped by their reputations and by direct contacts with clients who operate internationally, not only enter architectural discourse but also achieve international commissions.

The second important observation is that architecture is primarily a *local* activity. In the United States, the state and local chapters of the American Institute of Architects make sure that national design awards are geographically representative. Thus, publications, exhibitions, and visiting lectures rapidly bring local and regional reputations to the attention of the profession at large. Moreover, except when times are really bad, established design elites may not care too much about work beyond their area. Some of the architects I interviewed have as much work as they need in their state or do not need much because they have chosen to practice a local, craft-oriented kind of architecture. I will explain in conclusion how the discourse of the profession "amplifies" their achievements.

In architecture, as in other fields, the distinction between "locals" and "cosmopolitans" is more a matter of frame of reference than of geography. At present, there are several ways of finding clients, practicing architecture, and becoming part of a design elite because there are many different points of entry into architectural discourse. More important than locale is the interaction between the clients and the firm, which jointly determine what and where architects build. And professional discourse, almost by definition, transcends locale.

In this chapter, I let the designers describe the settings in which their careers unfold and the changes they deem important in their practice. I start by considering what these men and women have in common: namely, their relationship to the enterprise of building in a firm that is also their means of livelihood. Their different types of careers involve different strategic choices at the outset or at the classic "turning point." Among elite designers, the latter means either starting one's own practice or joining the firm that will allow one's career to develop. In the second section, I examine the beginnings of architectural careers and some of the indigenous concepts by which architects describe both their careers and the lives of their firms.

In this segmented market, certain types of firms tend in principle to go with certain types of clients, but the principle may be transcended by the designer's talent, the firm's reputation, or the client's will. In the third section, the architects discuss some of the factors on which they depend for negotiating and realizing (that is, building) design work: different types of clients, repetitive and unique commissions, the vanishing public client, the skyscraper as a building type. Architects' relations with developers are treated as examples of a special case in the fourth section.

My account of how careers are organized in firms, how the firms find clients, and how architects see clients and commissions centers on the tensions *architects* perceive and express, often in their own voices. I deal with the clients' side only occasionally. In the last section, I organize these findings into types of design careers, including alternatives to the traditional patterns of the architectural elite.

WHAT DO ELITE ARCHITECTS HAVE IN COMMON?

All elite designers, like all independent practitioners, are *in business*, either as small entrepreneurs or as partners in a large firm. Such is the aleatory nature of real estate financing that, even in elite practices, a good client and a good commission are, first and above all, a commission that gets built and a client with the power and the money to build it. "Getting work in" is the lifeblood of the firm. Fred Clarke, Cesar Pelli's managing partner, considers the office, which allows the firm to obtain work, "the space shuttle that gets you to the moon," organized as a buffer that absorbs pressures and liabilities.[14]

In many elite firms, the division between design and managing partners is meant to insulate the former from the tasks of running the firm and finding clients. Other partnerships are more egalitarian in the distribution of business chores. In any case, the division of tasks cannot be a division of interests: The brilliant design partner can be allowed to forget the business part of the practice but never to ignore it. In the smaller firms, unless they find a way to rationalize management, "running the business" risks becoming a devouring and therefore, at the same time, always sloughed-off part of the designers' work. Architects in precarious practices obviously worry about the effects of this on their careers and on their selves more than architects in established firms; yet, once the office exists, supporting it becomes an important concern and a potential burden for *all* architects.[15]

Architecture's dependence on clients whose decisions reflect the larger socioeconomic situation is the major element of contingency in architectural practice. The initial recognition of "real" architectural talent, as opposed to theoretical or symbolic recognition of "paper architecture," depends on clients and on the nature of the commission. Despite the autonomy claimed by its "geniuses," architecture is a structurally *heteronomous* profession. The client's choice of architects, the visibility of the commission, the project's realization by the construction industry, all involve an element of luck. John Burgee, for example, tells an interesting story about how Philip Johnson and he topped the list for the famous AT&T headquarters building:

> They sent out a fairly big questionnaire, asking a lot of very specific questions. I had been talking to a friend of mine at AT&T about the possibilities of someday working with him, and I thought this was just a form that he sent, the kind that you fill out when you've got time. . . . So about two weeks later I got a call from my friend at AT&T and he says: "We had no response." And I said: "Oh, did you want that back in a hurry? I thought it was just for your file." He said "No, it's for our headquarters building. We sent out fifteen or sixteen, whatever they were, we got all fourteen back within three days except yours. . . . Are you going to submit it or not?" So I said "Oh, my God, I'll get down there tomorrow." Not responding to their request . . . that *did* surprise them, got their attention, somehow.

Many of the architects I interviewed seem more willing to accept the role of luck than that of sponsorship, recommendations, and awards. This may be a way of justifying the irrationality of success in a heteronomous profession, but "luck" also recalls another logic—the charismatic logic of genius—amidst all the rational steps taken to market the firm and insure its success. Here I examine elements of occupational identity that are held in common by these elite designers, some of which will inevitably reappear in the next chapter, when they explain their visions of architecture and approaches to design.[16]

It bears repeating that these men and women are all in business, no matter how self-consciously elitist and restricted their practices. Some of them can afford to lose money, but not for too long. Architects lose money, we could say, by extracting their own unpaid labor time: They spend time on work that the client will not *pay* for while overhead costs keep running. As one elite architect puts it, "the negotiation of the fee is the single most important thing: it gives you the leeway to *spend the time.*"[17]

A sole proprietor like Rob Quigley of San Diego can decide to lose money on projects he cares for; large successful firms like Kohn Pedersen Fox of New York lose money in competitions, for which architects never get enough compensation, by diverting paid staff from paying projects; smaller prestigious firms keep going by paying their designers with proximity to the "masters" and interesting work rather than good wages; and most architects engaged in prestigious work need supplementary sources of income, often from academic work.

Elite architects are not exempt from clients' abuse. Gene Kohn, the founder and managing partner of Kohn Pedersen Fox, summed up the essence of "developer stories," which occurred repeatedly in my interviews. In the early stages, Kohn said, developers do not have the financing to build large projects and refuse to pay out of their own pockets; they expect architects to subsidize them with free work. Many, if not most, of the less secure firms accept this demand in hopes of getting the job and seeing the project built.

For practically all these designers, being an architect means first and foremost *building,* for obvious economic reasons and for equally important ones of self-realization. Few would be bold enough to speak like John Hejduk, a member of the "New York Five" and a very influential architect through his ideas and his role as the dean of the Cooper Union in New York: "I'm in my mid-fifties now and I feel I am just ready to build. . . . What I don't agree with is the emphasis on *building* rather than *architecture.* The very thing an architect can do is to affect your psyche and spirit—that's his job. It's simply not enough for him to answer only to the physical. Unfortunately, that's what's been done today. We have builders, not architects."[18] Talented designers seldom take their talent, or their ambition, lightly. Peter Eisenman, for instance, explains that he left his "power position" as director of the Institute of Architecture and Urban Affairs in New York because he was bored with his fifteen years as an intellectual impresario. Twice he connected the turn to practice with the personal transformation of psychoanalysis and divorce. And Charles Gwathmey, like many students who passed through Yale's graduate program when Paul Rudolph was there, sees his mentor as almost determining his personal choice. "Rudolph was like a sort of principal in an office full of talented people, himself a strong, a major architectural force who was aggressively building buildings. . . . I never could work for anybody. I always had the idea I would have to work by myself, and I was a victim of Rudolph's 'you-got-to-build-immediately' ethic."

If building is importantly connected to the architect's self, *not* building or building trifling things can be costly. Denise Scott Brown is eloquent about what this meant for Robert Venturi in the 1970s, when their firm seemed to be a permanent "runner up" in all the important projects it attempted to get: "I always said, why *would* we just do little houses when we have the talent to do more? . . . In Milton's sonnet on his blindness there is a phrase that fits Bob perfectly: 'that one talent which is death to hide / Lodged with me useless. . . .' Bob had an ability that he could not use because he didn't have the opportunity."

The respect, even the reverence, with which these designers speak of building and buildings is obviously consonant with a lifetime commitment. Building is the distinct occupational *interest* that architects pursue, defend, and invoke to justify their choices and assuage their doubts. In order to place building more exactly within the professional ideology, we need to compare the psychological costs of *not* building important things with the other side of the coin.

Craig Hodgetts, winner of several major awards in the 1970s, once seemed headed for a successful career. He is now by choice on the outskirts of architecture, teaching and doing sundry projects with his architect wife in his eight-person firm. His account of how he started doubting architecture is instructive. Back in 1980, at the first Venice Biennale with an architecture section, Craig was struck by the bitterness of "all his heroes, the most wonderful architects and luminaries." He explains that their cynicism and inner despair result from being involved in the building process:

> Here's the client, there's a contractor, there's the legal system, there's the consciousness of the urban situation, and so forth, and the only continuity between all of those is the architect. . . . Everybody is terrified. The risks are enormous. The architect assumes the mantle of all those anxieties and sacrifices whatever his own emotional needs may be in order to husband these projects through. . . . The project's lifespan is five, ten years, something like that. It has no immediacy, it is this strange phenomenon of living in a projected future which is somewhere

else. By the time it is built and open you [as the architect] are . . . numb, kind
of past life, and you look at it and think "Gee, I wonder why I did that."

Furthermore, for this reluctant and reflective architect, architecture as it
has been defined since the Renaissance is not and was probably never
worth it. It only seems so important because it is so expensive: "Why *should*
it matter what it looks? Just because it cost *x* million dollars? . . . There is
a kind of merchandising alliance right now because the architect is called
upon to magnify the importance of his client, and that of course is not a
reasonable role in society today; it is not a healthy role."

Designing buildings is the livelihood of all architects. After a design is
done, a long and difficult process results in a finished building that represents the culmination of the architects' work. But the building can also
symbolize the frustration of the architects' intentions. Artist-architects tend
to see building as something more. Thom Mayne, for one, talks about it in
a clearly romantic key, as the objectification of a search. Its aim is "producing places that are appropriate for our time. And I am not interested
in defining those. My explanation is in the work, and . . . I have said it all
when the work is done. There's really nothing left for me to say except this
is a bedroom and this is a living room—stuff I am not even interested in."

Building, then, is the central self-expressive activity; it is what distinguish-
es "real" architects from "paper" architects; it is where architecture can show
itself to be an art. And yet, of course, building is service, the embodiment
of architects' dependence on clients and their programs. The contradiction
should no longer surprise: In this occupation, building is the specific and
preeminent interest created in its members, but it also is the mystified
mainstay of its ideology.

In reality, architects do not build anything; at best, they supervise those
who do. Historically, the art of design is founded on the separation of
conception from construction and on the architect's appropriation of the
former. In conceiving a design that is to be built, the architect must con-
front (and if possible surmount) the basic heteronomy of design work.
"Building," as the sign of the true architect and the foremost expression of
creative autonomy, is a mystification. It is meant to hide that which it
inherently represents: the architect's dependence on both the patron and
the real executants.

I turn now to the different ways in which architects transact the difficulties of finding "buildings to build." I begin with basic differences among
firms, for the firm is both the organization that supports (or hinders) an
architect's career and the first materialization of his or her ambition.

GETTING STARTED AND GOING ON

For elite designers, as for other architects, a decisive choice is whether to seek employment in an already existing office and stay there or to strike out on their own (and, if so, when and with whom, since only six of the twenty-nine designers I interviewed were sole principals). From this point of view, the most basic distinction among firms is whether, having been founded by the principal or by partners, they represent entrepreneurial ventures or not. If the firm was founded by its present principals, the career of the elite designer is parallel to that of the firm and synonymous with getting it started, going, and well known. In a firm that the elite designer joins as a hired employee (no matter at what level), the identification of career and firm is in principle not as close.

Unless entry is at the partner level, the designer's career in an extant architectural firm revolves around classic organizational questions—openings "at the top," the time it takes to get to them, and the compatibility of one's professional goals with those of the firm. There are, of course, contingencies; being a talented woman when the firm needs to show openness may be one. Because of their size and security, large firms can offer better and stabler employment as well as longer career lines. Gene Kohn emphasizes, as do other large-firm principals, the policy of giving every carefully screened employee the opportunity to work in all areas, "from feasibility to design to detailing to production to supervision," but here too luck plays a part: "Some . . . happen to be in the right project at the right time; it goes ahead and they get to stay with it. Or we are very very busy and, suddenly, something comes in and one of the young people who is asked to study it does a great job and gets discovered."

At SOM-Chicago, young designers come up through the ranks as project managers and heads of studios (a concept started by Bruce Graham in 1972, the studio is a team that stays together and executes several projects, almost like a small office). What count here are the usual career assets in organizations—showing leadership, getting along, and being placed on the fast track by a senior executive. But bringing in clients of one's own (because of an impressive reputation, through well-cultivated contacts in the community, or, rarely, because of previous professional contacts) is quoted repeatedly as an obvious and almost determinant factor. In large firms that are interested in creating a reputation for design, the awards and the professional standing of talented designers can help their advancement to partnership.

Practically all architects must serve an apprenticeship in someone else's office before registration. None of the elite designers admitted to stealing clients from their apprenticeship firms (the pattern so feared by law firms); in fact, most reported more precarious beginnings. However, they frequently found their partners in their former employers' firms. Besides acquiring experience of different levels and scope in their previous workplaces, they also formed networks of acquaintances and reservoirs of good will, which turned out to be helpful in getting recommended to clients. In fact, the medium-sized entrepreneurial firms of the design elite often seem honor-bound to mentor the former professional employees who get started on their own. Indeed, turnover is expected in firms where there is little room at the top and where the charismatic designers leave few design opportunities to their associates. Yet Michael Graves points to a common experience of beginning architects when he observes that the referrals they get from their former employers, who are their seniors in the profession, tend to be for "work that is not wanted by somebody else, because the job is either insufficient in size or in some way shaky and uncertain."

Entrepreneurial beginnings are modest. Some elite designers started out "drawing in my kitchen," "in a warehouse that belonged to my partner's parents," "in a garage," or "in my apartment"; or, like Graves, they sacrificed a good part of their academic salary to rent an office while waiting for clients. It is usual for architects to moonlight while in the employ of others and not unusual to act as a small developer.

After returning from two years with the Peace Corps in Chile, Rob Quigley's seven months with a very fine San Diego firm gave him an understanding of architectural practice that hardened his resolve to go out on his own:

> The kind of attitude in the drafting room was, I think, typical of most offices in the country. "Boy, you know, we could do great work in this firm if we had a great client," or . . . "if it weren't for all those building codes," or . . . "if we just had the budget to do it." Hearing this, day in and day out, I began to believe that you could not do good work unless you had a "patron of the arts" client, and once you start believing that, *you are dead.* And I escaped, and luckily I got a commission to do a small house, got a commission to do another small house, . . . then I put together a small investment group to do a four-unit, three-story apartment building. I acted as a general contractor because I wanted to learn from the tradesmen. That gave me enough work to go out on my own.

For employed architects, moonlighting includes not only projects too small to support an independent practice but also unpaid work, especially submissions to competitions and award programs. If nothing else, this effort keeps one alive and active in the discursive field of architecture. Placing as a finalist in a significant competition or receiving an important

award (for small-scale work or projects) may act as a trigger for the decision
to start an independent practice, provided there is a supplementary source
of income. Philip Johnson quips that architects either have to be born
wealthy or marry into wealth and then apologizes for this "rich boy's statement"; the fact is that a spouse's income can help entrepreneurial ventures
in architecture as in other businesses.[19]

Three concepts recur in the architects' accounts of their careers: breakthrough, track record, and range. I analyze them in turn, but, first, I briefly
describe their interrelations.

Architectural breakthrough refers to a phenomenon that includes the
accumulation of symbolic capital—Pierre Bourdieu's concept of the legitimate authority to speak *in* and *for* the specific field where one's achievements count—although it cannot quite be measured in the same terms.[20]
Because of this profession's fundamental heteronomy, a breakthrough must
necessarily confer authority on the architect in the eyes of the potential
clients. After the breakthrough, an architect should ideally go from project
to project, accumulating a track record (an ensemble of realized work)
without suffering major interruptions. Breakthrough and track record are
the fundamental building blocks of orderly careers. Range, however, is
different: It refers to architects' efforts to shape their careers with relative
autonomy from the market and to escape their specialized niches. By striving for range, architects implicitly resist client pressure to confine them to
a limited track record.

As I hinted above, peer recognition provides confirmation of individual
or collective ability, but it is seldom enough to bring the breakthrough of
which designers speak. Breakthrough is a complex notion. First of all, it is
highly retrospective, constructed by looking back from the vantage point
of a developed career. In a sense, only an established architect can say
"*that* was my breakthrough," as if *that* building had created the career that
followed.[21] It is next to impossible to know whether architects recognize
breakthroughs when they happen; younger architects assess their achievements cautiously, for reversals of fortune are common and can happen
quite easily.

For instance, Julie Eizenberg and her husband, Hank Koning, got a First
Design Award from *Progressive Architecture* in 1987 for two complexes of
affordable apartments built in Santa Monica. Their work was reviewed by
Paul Goldberger in the *New York Times,* and the award helped Julie get a
teaching job at the University of California, Los Angeles. On the other
hand, the Santa Monica Community Corporation, Eizenberg and Koning's
client, thinks they have hired them too often and would "like to spread

their work around"; Eizenberg and Koning's next project, a community services center, while big enough to put them "in another league of work," was still only "a hole in the ground" in 1989 and not yet part of their track record. Julie refused to see these considerable achievements as a "real" breakthrough.

Second, the breakthrough is tied to symbolic capital in the field. It is work that brings attention and standing in architecture: It gives the designer "presence," the status of a potential or emergent member in the eyes of the profession's elite. Presence allows strategizing behaviors and political moves in the profession's discursive field. Thus, a man as strategically placed as Michael Graves considers the remarkable project with which he won the competition for the unbuilt Fargo-Moorhead Cultural Center in 1977 as a breakthrough because it led directly to the Portland Municipal Services Building, his first major realization. His account of what happened after winning in Fargo-Moorhead with enormous expenditure of time, energy, and money, tells of the anxiousness attending architectural work:

> I worked *so* hard to get the commission, got it, but never built a building. Now, those drawings were published everywhere. They were imaginative. It was really the first postmodern things that were published a lot . . . covers, and so on. That's *not* what I wanted; I wanted *a building!* But, from that, I was invited to give a lecture in Portland, so the net continues. . . . The AIA invited me, and Ed Wundram [the Portland competition organizer] sat next to me at dinner after the lecture, and he said: "We've got a competition going out here. . . . What do we have to do to encourage *somebody like you* to enter?" I said: "Ask!" I mean, "somebody like you!" He thought I was too grand, but, here again, he thought that Fargo would be built. I did too at the time. Even when it looked as though it was very shaky, you continue to think and to say to people "There's every hope that it *will* be built," though things are not going well, or they didn't raise the money, or they didn't pass the bond issue, or whatever it was, which is all true. Golf courses got 51 percent [of the vote] and the cultural center 40 percent. *Then* it was dead, but by that time we had Portland.

Professional standing and the attention of sound clients must go together in elite careers. Standing, however, is not the same as position in the field. Having attended an elite school, having met the right people, and having an effective "old boy network" can substitute for the traditional family ties of the "gentleman architect," but with two conditions. First, an architect's mentors in the field must have positions of influence and be willing to use them; second, the protégé's work cannot threaten the mentors' own professional standing. The beginner's work should bring credit to the mentors and reinforce their influence, but it should not take clients from them, unless they have plenty to spare. Mentoring is self-reproducing: In a competitive and male profession, it tends to exclude women and other outsiders. It also tends to work against dissent, or at least against architectural challenges that cannot be contained within a market niche other than the mentor's own.

The third and most important characteristic of "real" breakthroughs is that they should insure a relatively continuous flow of work. Because clients are the crucial factor in this, breakthroughs must be important enough to elicit not only the attention but also the trust of clients. It is ultimately by the grace of clients' choices that architects constitute their track record, the compendium of experience and recognition that is the prerequisite of important architectural work.

The trajectory of Venturi Scott Brown and Associates illustrates the discrepancy that may arise between a breakthrough in the discursive field of architecture and the track record, which is the first thing a client wants to see. Fame gave a prestigious standing in the field to the Venturi Rauch Scott Brown partnership, nourishing their high expectations. But precisely because their reputation was controversial, they needed to accumulate a substantial track record to neutralize the effects of fame. Therefore, their "real" breakthrough (Wu Hall at Princeton University) took from 1964 to 1978 to come. Denise Scott Brown gives a vivid account of the tyranny of the track record:

> They don't trust new young firms, that's the first thing. They don't trust firms who are not well connected in the society, which we weren't. They don't trust firms who . . . can't show buildings, and then they don't trust firms whose work they don't like the looks of. But if everyone else is saying they are marvelous and they have a whole lot of other commissions and they have a strong track record, then you feel reassured about the fact that you think it ugly. . . . Hiring us was a risk. Princeton was the seal of approval that removed the risk element for many clients. Obviously, we still don't get whole categories of clients who are not interested enough. But now we get enough who *are*.

Real breakthroughs and impressive track records can never eliminate the element of uncertainty from the lives of even the best entrepreneurial design firms. Their principals vividly and repeatedly refer to this uncertainty as the "roller coaster" of architectural practice. In hard times, it does not spare the large corporate firms either.[22]

Large strong-service firms must be started too, and the time at which they do so is significant. The small partnership of Skidmore Owings Merrill was founded in the late 1930s, when there was practically no architectural work. According to the late Gordon Bunshaft, SOM's success after the war was facilitated by the disappearance of many rivals (firms identified with the Beaux-Arts approach) in the depression. The building boom and the change in clients' taste completed a constellation of factors favorable to modernism:

> We never had to *sell* modern. They just accepted it. . . . At one meeting we presented partial models for the exterior of Chase [the Chase Manhattan build-ing in New York]. We had made samples of stainless steel and glass and one in aluminum; Owings thought he had to do one in granite. . . . The key man on this board was about ninety. . . . He came into the meeting before anybody, he walked up to me and he said: "What's this?" I said: "That's a granite thing." He said: "Hell, we don't want any granite today, we want a *modern* building!"

Kohn Pedersen Fox, one of the most visible firms of the 1980s, is a likely challenger to SOM's position as corporate design leader. Its beginnings involve a strategically planned anticipation of clients' desires. The firm started in 1976, in the middle of the recession. Gene Kohn met his partners while all three worked (Kohn as vice president) in John Warnecke's office, a large firm that was rapidly declining because Warnecke wanted neither to share power nor prepare his own succession. Kohn explored the field with the marketing and managerial acumen for which he is famous. He got the ideas of "six or seven key people about what a good firm should provide in terms of service, talent, energy." One of his contacts got him an open line of credit with Chemical Bank, which was exceptional for a new office in 1976; but there was no work to be had, "none, zero."

From July to September 1976, KPF made a breakthrough so remarkable that the bank credit was never used. Crucial to it were the extended con-tacts created at Warnecke's and a first commission with ABC, the media network, where Kohn and Fox knew two "key vice presidents" and to whom they offered their services for the planned renovation of an old armory. "A good interview and no competition, basically," led over fifteen years to twelve buildings, master plans, and interiors.[23]

What mattered most to their first clients, according to Kohn, was getting three senior architects present at all the meetings and involved in all the phases of the project. After three years and a dozen buildings (three for ABC), KPF had itself become a marketing tool: A Chicago developer tried to lure ABC to a relatively risky real estate area by retaining its favorite architects. Ultimately, Pedersen produced for the developer, not for ABC, one of his most publicized designs at 333 Wacker Drive: a dark green blade of glass that curves softly along the river front with razor-sharp lines and clean massing. KPF was the first outside firm to penetrate Chicago's jeal-ously guarded architectural preserve in the postwar period.

In sum, KPF owes its meteoric ascent during inauspicious times to Kohn's aggressive and effective marketing of an experienced architectural team distinguished by William Pedersen's brilliant design talent. Kohn says: "People have to like you, and they have to respect your talent; some other third party has to say something nice about you, and, finally, the press has to give its blessing. When those come together, they form a pyramid that points the job." But the editor of *Progressive Architecture* gives them more credit than that: KPF supports the now customary "contextual" approach to the urban environment by a carefully prepared architectural, social, and economic history of the place. According to John Dixon, this approach is "tremendously persuasive" for a client.

KPF is a large-scale practice with eight partners, two hundred employees, and a hundred more in Conway Associates, its separate interiors branch; at any time in the 1980s, it was working on thirty to forty projects in different stages of development; it has many "repeat" clients; it has projects overseas; it participates at a loss in competitions for different building types. But it has not yet had the breakthrough it so desires in prestigious institutional building. All the public relations, all the talent, all the care in detailing and construction, and all the concern with mobility within the firm seem insufficient to release KPF from the constraints of success within one major building type.

Strong-service firms, therefore, need their breakthroughs as much as the entrepreneurial strong-idea firms. However, there seems to be a sort of trade-off between security and variety in the constitution of the track record: Repeat clients risk locking the firm into a relatively narrow (though immensely profitable) market niche. For the corporate and the entrepreneurial firms, growth has different implications.

Since its take-off at the end of World War II, SOM has built a worldwide reputation of technical competence and excellence in the design of very large buildings for business, government, and large institutions. In the 1980s, it has tried to diversify an approach too closely identified with the modernism of the 1960s, enraging its retired partner Gordon Bunshaft, a fierce gatekeeper of modernism against the postmodern challenge.[24] Bruce Graham, the powerful senior partner at SOM-Chicago, has recently started to collaborate with elite designers such as Charles Moore, Frank Gehry, Venturi Rauch Scott Brown, and Stanley Tigerman. These designers see this as a welcome attempt by SOM to spruce up its design reputation, an action that might spread large-scale work around. Graham implicitly contrasts the entrepreneurs' "roller coaster" with the stability due to his own firm's size and internal organization, which he sees as requirements for securing work: "It's harder for them. Frank [Gehry] does not like to have more than twenty-four people, so he can't keep a backlog of things. He can't move those people into the next phase while *he* gets involved into the *next* phase. If he had three studios, he would be able to do that better." Gehry might respond with what he told me: "Thirty people is the absolute limit here. We won't hire the thirty-first, so that means we have to choose the jobs, and it *is* hard." Yet his complaint that corporate clients who are courting him want him "to be SOM" lends indirect support to Graham's diagnosis:

> If they come in with a senior vice president in charge of real estate and . . . a junior real estate division manager, they would like the office to have their kind of parts, so *that* one can meet with *that* one. . . . It's almost like putting a key in a lock! When they come *here*, they don't know *how* they're going to fit. I think the president, the boss, usually can relate to me if I just spend time with them, but the lower levels have trouble with this. . . . They want that fit!

Although size is a sign of success and organizational health, it appears to be a recurrent concern in the growing entrepreneurial elite firm. A corporate architect like Graham implicitly takes size as the counterpart of good organization, but entrepreneurial design principals mention size almost apologetically. They are well aware of the old architecture school notion that one architect cannot supervise more than five others. Their prominence in the field matches in many cases the studio set-up of their offices, run by the master as an old-fashioned atelier. Obviously, the larger the size, the more difficult it is to preserve this atmosphere.

Most strong-idea firms cultivate an informal appearance: renovated lofts; art books and models lying around; the occasional piece of very fine art or the master's own creations (in Gehry's office, his fish-shaped lamp and paper furniture); open drafting rooms never too far from the principal's office. As an example of this last item, Robert Stern's office is one of elegant simplicity carved out of the huge drafting rooms (an oval room with no doors, separated by large arches from a corridor with the loft's glass wall on one side and the entrance hall on the other). The atelier atmosphere, reminiscent of art schools, is one of the nonmaterial rewards for always underpaid professional workers.

Elite entrepreneurial architects often engage in the ideological masking typical of the sellers of symbolic goods. As Pierre Bourdieu observes, "the vendor deceives the customer only insofar as he deceives *himself* and is sincerely sold on the value of what he sells."[25] These architects see in large size both a cause and a symptom of the transformation of architecture from "a way of life" into "a means of livelihood." Yet, when the "roller coaster" is down, it is clear what comes first: Employees are reluctantly but no less relentlessly let go.

Some elite firms admit to having a stable core of partners (not all of whom design), experienced project captains, and technical people, around which revolves a larger professional staff expected to move on after a few years—the justification being that the best people have the ambition to leave in order "to do their own architecture." Yet managing partners of entrepreneurial design firms recognize that they do not provide good technical training to their professional employees. Instead, they depend on preexisting technical competence, acquired by their staff in "firms that do not get published" or in those that do. SOM, in particular, has the reputation of a graduate school in practical construction skills.[26]

Robert Stern Associates, with one hundred people in its employ, has acceded to the status of large firm, although the looks of Stern's office reveal a reluctance to identify with a straight "corporate" practice. Stern says he is the first to be surprised, since he thought for so long that his teacher Paul Rudolph's "ideal office size"—twenty people—was a lot. He justifies the course he has taken by invoking a modified but "natural" model of career development:

> I imagined I would have the kind of career that Rudolph before me had had . . . if you use Rudolph as a model, small houses in Sarasota, and then he got Leslie College and suddenly New Haven parking garages and architecture buildings and then big office complexes for IBM. . . . But setting up practice in 1969 with all hell breaking loose and then a declining economy! . . . When you have a five-hundred-men office and it gets cut back to two hundred, it's one thing, but when you have a three-men office and it gets cut back, it's pretty terrible. . . . I suppose I am getting the kinds of projects I imagined I would have had fifteen years ago, but also large projects for developers. Let's face it, being trained in my generation at a place like Yale, developers were not even *imagined* as possible clients for a good architect.[27]

Stanley Tigerman, Stern's friend and former classmate at Yale, has a thirty-person firm in partnership with Margaret McCurry, his wife. Tigerman is convinced that supporting a larger firm than that is "like feeding a big animal": You need to get more and more work to "feed it and feed it and then, what's next? You!"

In sum, size is determined by the uncertainty of architectural practice, and it becomes an important element in the designer's ideology. Tigerman, like Gehry and many architects of the entrepreneurial elite, believes that big firms change the nature of architecture from a profession that believes in good craftsmanship and the free play of fantasy into something that is "like going to work for IBM. IBM, SOM, it's the same."

Bruce Graham would dispute that his firm is "like IBM." It has much less regimentation than the New York office had under Gordon Bunshaft, Graham says. His own goal in organizing SOM-Chicago "was to design firms *that could build cities* [emphasis added], and big pyramidal organizations won't be able to do that because the heirs become assistants and they soon die, the firm dies. . . . You don't build cities in your lifetime, you build them in milleniums." "Building cities" (standing for large-scale planning and even infrastructural design) is, in fact, a practical part of SOM's diversification strategy. But it is also an ideological notion by which Graham implicitly counters the new superiority of the smaller strong-idea firms in designing "beautiful buildings." Other designers of corporate towers mention large-scale architecture *as if* it were the same as urban design, as if the sheer amount of urban land and sky their buildings cover produced "cities" by accretion. Graham, however, is clear about what *he* means. He chairs the Chicago Central Area Committee, "the most powerful business group," a position he owes to being *both* an important executive and an architect. Yet he only mentions the latter, contrasting the real power of Chicago architects with New Yorkers' mere influence. For him, "building cities" is a function of power.

SOM is the very model of a firm closely integrated with the capitalist firms it serves. Its clients, its projects, and its practice are definitely more secure than those of most entrepreneurial architects. It has offices in Chicago, New York, Washington, San Francisco, and London. It is a large partnership with internal career lines and a definite policy of *not* hiring partners from outside. Senior partners can deal as equals with their powerful clients, for the partners are backed by organizations and influence comparable to those of their clients. The organization's internal labor pool takes care of succession, and the continuity of the firm is not a problem; competitiveness is, however. This involves being concerned with "new blood," or new design ideas.[28]

The next chapter will show that design work at the partner level is not essentially different from that in smaller firms, only better supported by organization and technology. Yet design reputation in large comprehensive firms is a *collective* attribute. As Gerald Horn of Holabird and Root notes, "in a large firm, it's really *the firm* that they are hiring; only occasionally they'll name a person."

In architecture, as in the law, sophisticated corporate clients tend to push the firms that provide them with professional services toward the organizational form that they, as clients, find most reliable. The market of services thus comes to consist of distinct niches. Robert Gutman observes:

Each niche or segment is made up of clients with particular needs and architectural offices that attempt to serve these needs. . . . Fragmentation within the profession is a condition that clients help to generate and are probably interested in preserving. Architectural firms also find it to their advantage to preserve the pattern, at least once they have succeeded in understanding it and mastering its implications.[29]

Yet, as we have seen, architects with design ambitions emphasize peer recognition, breakthrough, and track record, regardless of the type of firm in which they work. Therefore, the organizational distinction between entrepreneurial ventures and large corporate firms (like the overlapping division between strong-idea and strong-service firms) must be corrected. In terms of design, the kind of symbolic capital that each type of firm (and each firm) accumulates makes a difference.

The examples of SOM and KPF suggest that a firm's age connects its symbolic capital to the evolution of architectural design. A firm like SOM is old enough to have built a diversified track record at a time when the relative uniformity of the modernist language helped both the firm and its individual designers pass from one building type to another. After all, museums, libraries, Air Force academies, and office buildings did not *have* to look all that different. Today, SOM looks to renew itself by opening its design gradient to new, albeit not too audacious, experiments.

The pluralism of styles of the postmodern period seems to tie new service firms with design ambitions more tightly to their track record (namely, the large commercial projects to which every large firm must give primacy for economic reasons). Savvy clients in search of product differentiation "demonstrate time and time again a high degree of openness to new approaches and new faces," as the repeated use of competitions demonstrates.[30] Regardless of the size or the nature of the project, such clients can push design architects (or strong-idea firms) to work in association with strong-delivery firms, turning for novel ideas to entrepreneurial designers, whose names rest on uniqueness, variety, and innovation.

THE NEGOTIATION OF DESIGN

Clients are crucial for the economic survival of architectural firms. Furthermore, clients are the ones who ultimately choose architects and architectural styles. Changes in the nature of major architectural clients appear to have coincided with the eclecticism of the postmodern period and reinforced it. Experienced observers such as Weld Coxe and Robert Gutman insist on clients' resourcefulness and on their power to dictate what services each kind of architect shall be allowed to provide. Yet, as Craig Hodgetts noted earlier in this chapter, the risks of such an expensive enterprise are immense. Organizational clients try to minimize risks by seeking different architectural services in different kinds of market niches. However indirectly, this demonstrates the clients' uncertainty in a period of stylistic disunity and escalating construction costs.

Turning to the elite designers, I let them explain, first, the basic distinction between clients who are able to act as one and clients who act collectively. Second, I examine how the designers see the related, but not equivalent, distinction between "one-of-a-kind" and repeated commissions. Third, their account of the decline in public commissions forms the backdrop for their ambivalent relationship with developers, which I examine last.

INSTITUTIONAL VERSUS INDIVIDUAL CLIENTS

Thinking aloud about "a marketing argument for KPF," Gene Kohn latches onto the logical inconsistencies of market niches: Architects known for their museums *must* have done one for the first time, and it must have been good, or it would not have led to the second and the third, so why can't he find clients willing to believe that KPF could bring "a fresher approach" to the museum than firms that have done many? Part of the answer lies in the way institutional clients are constituted.

Like other patrons of large-scale architecture, institutional clients tend to be represented by committee, which often projects the organization's own internal conflicts upon its hired experts. Universities, for instance, put together committees of administrators and hierarchically determined "representatives of the users" (professors may be included, and sometimes students, but seldom, if ever, support personnel).

Joan Goody relates how university administrations, particularly the physical plant divisions, tend to "assume [that] the academics don't know anything and [that] they are already fighting with each other." Infighting and the presence of "in house" professional advisers in large organizations produce, as she says, contracts that are "a sort of compendium of all the problems they ever had with every architect they have ever had."

Even in the best of cases, the architect must spend an inordinate amount of time in meetings and presentations to accommodate all the different "heads" of the corporate client.[31] To smooth the conflicts over, she must be lucky. Joan Goody ruefully suggests that, regardless of her track record, she would do better being a man:

The Frank Lloyd Wrights in their capes and broad-rimmed hats . . . came across as being the Magus. And these strong men (and the clients *were* men) would allow themselves to be beguiled by men, although this was somehow a female role which represented the artistic "other world." . . . When *I* come to the 10 percent leap of faith and I say "Trust me, this is the way it will look better, I have done many buildings of this size" . . . they can't quite do it.

Male or female, architects who face committees often cannot tell who is really in charge. Their traditional function of "arbiter of taste" for the ruling class becomes difficult, if not impossible, to perform. This may well prompt the men to rely on charismatic male bonding, as some of them report. Yet the dominant trend points in another direction: Large corporate clients (like universities, businesses, or government) do not deal with their hired architects directly, especially if construction looms large among their activities. The norm is for an expert in architecture and construction (the corporation's own architect or architectural department or a "third party" architectural consultant) to mediate between the client and the designers, much in the way that internal legal departments intercede between corporations and outside law firms. Several elite designers report difficulties in relating to a sometimes timid, sometimes arrogant intermediary who must be treated as an expert but cannot be treated as a colleague.

To many innovative architects, this type of institutional client seems to be structurally averse to risk. Yet it appears that the profession's own postmodern diversity compounds the insecurity and the irreducible variety of the corporate client's taste. Uncertainty, playing upon the costs and the permanence of building, pushes the collective client toward safety or compromise, which means conformity with styles that already exist. But if what is desired is a new image, minimizing risk compels the client to "style" the building superficially—the massing, the facade, the lobbies, the skin—while keeping the invisible routine and the costs down.

The designers I interviewed have too much savvy to believe in a harmonious conception of the "patron."[32] Yet the niche structure of the market objectively takes the place of an older ideological notion that I call "the match made in heaven." Thus, a sense of preestablished cultural harmony between architects and those who choose them ("They know what *we* do; they would not come *to us* otherwise") can still slip unawares into architects' talk. Whatever the scale at which architects work, they have good *practical* reasons for preferring clients with enough power to make a decision that "sticks." Among the desirable characteristics of the client, taste and artistic discernment thus seem secondary to a ready capacity for decision making, which is more often lodged in individuals than in groups.

Gordon Bunshaft of SOM-New York links the "golden era of American architecture" (the 1950s and 1960s) with the fact that he "never dealt with anybody but the boss of the company." The architect enjoyed an authority parallel to that of the CEO. Bunshaft's nostalgia shows in his account of how SOM dealt with clients in the past (the change of tense from past to present is significant here):

> We never show them a design of a building; we show them *plans.* And perhaps it took us a year to get the plans accepted and all worked out. . . . And when we are all done, *we* have been studying the outside and the masses, but we never showed it to them. . . . They knew the plan and the building was just the natural outcome of the *plan* [note the axiom of the Beaux-Arts *and* the modernist approach that the plan comes first and generates the building]. *This is how architecture is done.*

Peter Eisenman would probably agree about little with Bunshaft, but he too sees a direct link between the internal stratification of the multiheaded client and the historicist brand of postmodernism, which he, like Bunshaft, detests:

> CEOs are the ones who are excited about what I have to say. Middle managers are entirely threatened, because their job is to get things done on time, for cost. They don't give a shit for aesthetics or *any* ideology. Postmodernism has been really useful for middle management because they don't have to think about anything. They get a comfortable, nonthreatening . . . nonideological, perfect commercial architecture.

Philip Johnson says about the pediment-coiffed AT&T landmark in New York that John deButts, AT&T's chairman, wanted a building to supersede Mies van der Rohe's Seagram:

> With the Seagram, Sam Bronfman got too many kudos for doing that different building; deButts wanted to be on the act for *his* generation. . . . Some people on the board disliked it just on concept, but deButts said "That's not a glass building. I like it." Then so many people hated the top that he got worried and we did lots of other tops. Then he said "I like this top. Any questions?" In other words, it was not a committee decision.

In sum, it is always easier to sell to one person, especially one who has the power to decide. Denise Scott Brown thinks her firm clinched the commission of Wu Hall at Princeton by showing beautiful beach houses, after showing all the campus buildings in their track record. It is a strategy of corporate jet salespeople, she says, to "sell" middle management on efficiency and the president on "raw beauty."

The profession's eclecticism, however, has lodged beauty more than ever in the eye of the beholder. Today, the residual ideology of "the match

made in heaven" is a feeble echo of Gordon Bunshaft's account of a past
in which architects, together with the brilliant and powerful men "who
became personal friends . . . established the character of a building."

Thus, while a first set of difficulties in getting commissions big or significant enough to be public comes from the corporate constitution of the
client, a second set seems to lie in the profession's eclecticism. For elite
designers, the competitiveness inherent in the increase in the number of
firms has been compounded by the pluralism of taste that the profession
itself has promoted. The lists of candidates in closed or invited architectural
competitions illustrate this situation.

Competitions are used with increasing frequency to adjudicate important commissions, reflecting in part the client's uncertainty about what to
choose. Despite their complaints about uncompensated costs, architects
dearly aspire to being included, and even more so in the lists of potential
architects kept by major corporations. The reigning diversity leads many
expert advisers to think it their duty to present clients with "one of each
kind." As a result an architect may be invited on the basis of personal style
then candidly be told that he lost "because of aesthetics." Since the aesthetics were well known beforehand, all that is conveyed is an offensive
neglect of the architect's scheme and its adequacy for the program and the
site. Postmodern eclecticism, in sum, has complicated the task of a design
profession that has never quite left the age of patronage but must work
without Maecenas.

REPEATED VERSUS ONE-OF-A-KIND COMMISSIONS

Given the difficulties and costs involved in finding clients, the most rational
policies for an architectural firm should be to concentrate on clients who
continue to bring in work and to specialize in commissions that represent
a repeated building type. This is what strong-delivery firms strive for, but
it is equally important in the success of a new corporate firm such as KPF.
Michael Graves explains:

> If Kohn Pedersen Fox is doing, say, a dozen towers . . . they're doing many and
> they are *big* buildings with decent budgets. We have some too, and now I know
> the economics of that, and if you are doing many at the same time they are
> repetitive buildings. You are paid by the budget and the size of the building;
> and if floor twenty-three is like floor thirty-three, it is not so hard to punch it
> out on the computer. Yes, you must compose it originally, and, yes, you must
> spend more time to get the materials in the hands of the contractor, etc., to get
> it built. All that is true, and it takes longer than let's say my little building in San

Juan Capistrano, but the financial rewards are *much, much, much* greater, and so that is what makes profit for an architect, that kind of practice.

There is a tension, however, between economics and architectural ambition, which wants relief from routine work. Diane Legge, who in 1988 was a young partner at SOM-Chicago, phrases it clearly:

> Hopefully, you build up a clientele who keeps coming back to you. Hopefully, you work on projects that have brothers and sisters after that . . . [Musingly] Many of the projects *I* work on are one of a kind. . . . The client I work with will probably *never* do another race track; and the Boston Globe is probably *never* going to do another printing plant, because these buildings will last for fifty years. . . . They'll go beyond me.

The concept of "range" (the array of different types and sizes of projects) expresses the conflict between architectural ambition and economic rationality. It is a concept repeatedly invoked by elite designers, who see range as an insurance against the routinization of talent. They unanimously believe that architects mature, refine, and renew their abilities by careful consideration of new and diverse problems. As Graves and Legge suggest, the economics of the firm are the first major obstacle in achieving range. The second obstacle, of course, is the tyranny of the track record.

Charles Gwathmey also emphasizes "the tension between the business of architecture and the need to face new discoveries."[33] He describes his first speculative high rise proudly, yet he doubts that it will be enough to open up a new niche for Gwathmey Siegel:

> Listen, *it took us twenty years of practice to have someone trust us enough to let us do a building we had never done before.* . . . The real estate people evaluate it as having the best floor plan of the buildings available in New York . . . [but] no one else has come knocking at our door. We are perceived as difficult, committed, expensive. . . . We are no more expensive than other well-known architects in this town. *We don't take more time.*

In a fundamentally heteronomous profession, the high value placed on range indicates something more than the expert's desire to create new knowledge in the confrontation with new problems. Striving for range is an ideological strategy by which architects assert and pursue autonomy. Range defies the market's compulsion to force architects to specialize. It is not a coincidence that architects invoke it to justify getting involved in a process as economically irrational as the competition: They argue that competitions are strategic because of the odd chance of extending their range with otherwise "inaccessible" types of buildings.

Second, striving for range is a way to say "I can do it." It places one's confidence in one's own firm and one's own talent above the judgment of clients who do not know or care enough about architecture. Finally, range embodies a subtler rationality than that of sheer specialization: In fields that produce symbolic goods, the symbolic capital attached to the name of an architect or a firm increases when it is transferred from project to project. Metaphorically speaking, such moveable assets can go in search of the best returns, insuring continued and expanded accumulation to the owner. David Denton, Frank Gehry's managing partner, puts it succinctly: "There has been a big shift from the large firms of the modernist phase who did all the work. . . . *But to establish yourself as a name designer, you have to do a lot of types, and that costs a lot.*"[34]

THE WANING OF THE PUBLIC CLIENT

Government is by definition a multiheaded and bureaucratic client. Despite all the problems involved in working for the government, it still is the institutional client of choice. The federal government's share of the total budget for new construction went from 22 percent in 1981 to 15 percent in 1984, while the percentage of total receipts that architectural firms drew for public and institutional facilities went from 36 percent in 1972 to 26.6 percent in 1982. Yet the federal government is still the largest single client for new and renovated buildings of all kinds in the United States. Since the passage of the Architect-Engineer Selection Act in 1972, the General Services Administration's selection process has become open to "hundreds of firms that once thought they would never have a chance to design a major government building."[35]

Yet the elite designers whom I interviewed perceive a rapid retreat of the public, and especially the federal, client: some because they focus for political and ideological reasons on subsidized housing, which was drastically reduced under President Reagan; others, perhaps, because of the increase in competition for fewer commissions. Thus, depending on the architect's orientation, the contrast with France's "royal" program of public monuments under Mitterrand or with the commitment of northern European social democracies to affordable housing and environmental planning seems painful to consider. In my interviews with architects, the government often figures merely as the source of regulations and reviews that slow down the approval process and diminish the architects' autonomy in many projects.

The drastic curtailment of the federal government's social role under Republican administrations has directly and indirectly brought to an end the involvement, characteristic of the 1970s, of a postmodern generation in community projects and public housing. Don Matzkin of Friday Architects is clear about what this meant for him and his partners, who were known before even being published for their community design work in Philadelphia. In 1972, their breakthrough had been their fifth community center, funded by Model Cities, which led to eight more community and religious projects. Don says he would not mind designing community centers all his life, but, "with Nixon and Reagan, community money dried out and we had to figure out what was marketable of that experience. . . . Reagan forced us to work for the private sector!"

Postmodernism thus seems to have coincided with a greater emphasis on private commissions. Besides the shrinking of federally subsidized housing and community funds, some building types—like the small train station, for instance—have practically disappeared from the public landscape of the United States.[36] Others, like the post office, regional prototypes of which used to be commissioned from outside architects, are now modified or produced by government design offices to cut costs. All civic monuments are adversely affected by the chronic fiscal crisis of local governments.

Architects denounce the shrinking of the public client at the level of single buildings. This is not because there is no will to build city halls, public libraries, post offices, public schools, or even fire stations *as civic monuments* (as some architects seem to believe) but because funds for renovation or new buildings are scarce. Often, elite designers win competitions for projects which there are no funds to build (Michael Graves with the Fargo-Moorhead Cultural Center, for instance, or Barton Myers with the Phoenix Civic Center). Others must accept commissions from municipal governments who desire for their buildings the extravagant interior spaces made fashionable by hotels and shopping malls, but these lavish interiors consume the budget to the detriment of detailing and materials.

The retreat of government is also felt at the level of environmental planning. Barton Myers, a noted architect and urban planner,[37] emphasizes three factors in U.S. architects' retreat from physical planning: the devastating heritage of modernist planning, the fiscal and political incapacity of cities, and the fact that postmodernism arrived when architects in the public sector were already struggling with "burn-out." He says:

> Those architects who were interested in working in cities or being involved with reform in the early 1970s all left [he mentions Richard Weinstein, Jacquelin Robertson, and Robert Stern in Mayor John Lindsay's Urban Design Group in

New York]. They have all gone to the development industry. At the same time
. . . postmodernism was attacking what had been built. . . . Most architects said:
"Well, all this concern with social issues in America is not getting us anywhere.
Let's go back to being better architects." So they went back to being architects
who basically focus on making objects.

Myers's insistence that "postmodernism has almost no instinct for planning" on the one hand exaggerates the effectiveness of architects (or, for
that matter, planners) in the physical solution of urban problems. On the
other hand, it seems to slight postmodernism's sensitivity to context and
its preoccupation with usable public spaces. Yet Myers's criticism captures
the retreat of designers toward concern with the single building while also
suggesting that contextualism, symbolism, and preservation do not make a
match for the total urban vision of modernism. From a European perspective, Vittorio Gregotti concurs: "In the 1950s, architecture had an infe-
riority complex with regard to urban design. In the 1980s, it was reversed;
it became then opposition to planning in general. *That is when postmodernism became antimodern.*"

Recognizing circulation as the lifeblood of the modern city, modernist
planning delivered it to the automobile. But the physical problems created
by the automobile require regional solutions, in which public-transporta-
tion policy has a decisive part to play. For the developer Gerald Hines, "If
there is tax increment financing the development patterns will change, but
you have to bring in the transit system first. . . . Only when cities start to
strangle, like Houston, do people really start to study mass transit; only
when people need seventy lanes to get downtown does mass transit become
the only alternative."[38] The response to modernist planning, therefore, not
only exceeds the competence of architects and urban designers but also
seems far beyond the reach of the political capacity that can be presently
mobilized in the United States. It is indicative that the most widely praised
achievement of "postmodern" American planning—Andrés Duany and
Elizabeth Plater-Zyberk's (or DPZ) 1983 plan for the new resort of Seaside
in Florida—is, first, based on the exclusion of the automobile; second, is a
small private project for the upper middle class; and, third, is a frankly
nostalgic mixture of American small town and English village that has nothing to say to the large cities. The success of Seaside has led DPZ to perfect
its "neotraditional" approach to small-scale urbanism in over thirty planning projects, the bulk of which predictably consists of private suburban
plans. Duany's campaign against the typical American suburb is still waiting
for the broad public policy that could take it beyond merely local
developments.[39]

In sum, architects design mostly single objects. They tend to find their range in unique commissions, for these demand more creativity than repeated types. While the bulk of one-of-a-kind commissions comes from residential clients, residential work can only support independent practices that remain deliberately small and have a renewable pool of rich clients from which to draw.[40] Therefore, institutional clients are the most likely to provide work at a scale large enough to be profitable, interesting, and prestigious; there are, however, relatively few of such clients, and their financial stringencies often relegate architectural considerations to the background. A very small elite of no more than two dozen architects can aspire to be considered for prestigious international commissions. If we add to this the perceived retreat of the governmental client, elite designers seem to be left with business corporations and developers for major sponsors.

Today, the most visible (and yet the most repetitive) commission that developers entrust to elite designers is the schematic design of skyscrapers. Both to close this section and to introduce the relationship of architects with speculative clients, let us hear what some eminent designers say about the most conspicuous of modern building types.

DESIGNING THE SKYSCRAPER

The "tall office building" has been called a stunning architectural phenomenon, and its urban impact and cost certainly are stunning. Its designers admit that the skyscraper is mostly a massive sculptural form or, as Vincent Scully says, "an architectural one-liner, intended to knock our eyes out for a fleeting instant as we glimpse it from behind the wheel."[41] Yet they also talk about the discipline and responsibility its design entails. Here is Frank Gehry, a relative newcomer to this building type:

> The problems are incredibly more complicated and yet simpler. Complicated to solve architecturally because the repetitive nature of windows . . . is pervasive. You can't escape it; it's like peg-board; you *have to hand it over to the rental program.* . . . The freedom of the smaller buildings is you don't have to put those goddamn windows every five feet. You can move them around, so you have opportunities to make different forms. [emphasis added]

Philip Johnson declares that the problem of form in gigantic size is intractable, yet he accepts this risk as an almost inescapable consequence of the type:

> The problem is the middle. . . . It isn't hard to [design] an interesting bottom. You can't go wrong with a big enough pier, and you can't go wrong with an amusing top of whatever flamboyance you want, but the rest of it! It is a piece

of dullness that is just unbelievable! . . . You have the problem of the taper, of
the top, the middle, and the bottom as always, but the form, the outline is the
basic thing that you are always faced with. . . . Gae Aulenti [the Italian woman
architect of international renown] says "the skyscraper is not the subject of architectural thought." . . . Wait until she does one!

A ferocious rejoinder in the name of service comes from the late Gordon
Bunshaft, who *did* design many skyscrapers: "Architecture is the simple
thing of enclosing space for various human functions. I don't hear anybody
talk about whether the building *works*, whether the client or the employees
are happy. . . . Mr. Goldberger [the *New York Times* critic] thinks all those
buildings are built for silhouette from a distance, so they all put pyramids
on the top or little domes or crap." Finally, Joseph Esherick, the West
Coast architect who won the AIA Gold Medal in 1989, speaks of skyscrapers almost as an immorality of design:

> The skyscrapers and a lot of these buildings are just basically big teapots or big
> pieces of jewelry. There is nothing easy about designing a good teapot: It
> shouldn't leak, you should be able to pour out of it, it shouldn't burn your hands,
> and it is something you focus on. There are technical sides to it, but the mate-
> rialistic demand is that the thing be focused on [in the sense of attracting atten-
> tion]. It's very hard, I think, to do something like that and give it any kind of
> spiritual quality.

ARCHITECTS AND DEVELOPERS

How elite architects see speculative clients depends, first of all, on whether
they work for them or not. Practically all the large firms do.[42] Yet elite
designers are somewhat ambivalent in talking about their relationships with
developers. For the layperson confronted with the results of the 1970s and
1980s building boom, the most obvious reasons for ambivalence are expressed in questions that few architects can afford to ask: Is still another
speculative office building necessary? What is the impact of another tower
on a dense urban environment and an overloaded infrastructure? What
people and what social needs does it displace? Architects are no worse in
this than other hired experts: They leave ultimate "value judgments" to the
political sphere.

Most of the elite architects I interviewed are liberals who were in their
thirties during "the sixties." So in principle they welcome, as does Robert
Stern, the emergence of "an informed, articulate, *and armed* public, who
must be included in the process in a way that was not imagined before the
mid-sixties." But our society's fragmented spheres of action appear to justify forgetting *one's own* active citizenship in the performance of a spe-

cialized technical function. There are, after all, special arenas for "the armed public" to represent itself and special agencies set up to represent the public interest (even though elite architects are often quick to denounce their "invasions" into the design process).

Contemporary architects in the United States cannot be held directly responsible for their own disengagement from social architecture. Depending on the kind of business they run, the crux of architects' relationships with speculative builders is not a lack of social responsibility but a lack of alternatives. Bruce Graham implies that architects, if they were to accept responsibility for what is *not* built, would let the real decision makers off the hook: "The problem of housing is *not* an architectural problem. It is simply a financial and political responsibility. If the society decides to build [housing], then the architects can do it, but making it cheap is not the answer."

Graham is wrong; building cheap often *is* the answer. It certainly was in Europe and in the United States in the 1930s. It certainly is an important answer in the Third World today. And finding new design solutions for unimagined levels of poverty taxes the architect's skill far more than a skyscraper (an architect working for Habitat for Humanity mentions Indian reservations, where families have an income of $250 a month, and Mississippi—in both places Habitat must build for $10 a square foot).[43] If, however, architects cannot be held responsible for wrong social priorities, they *should* be held responsible for taking the notion of architecture-as-art as a special ideological shelter.

In our century the educated bourgeois has learned to suspend moral and political judgment in front of works of art, making it convenient to leave hard questions aside. In practice, aesthetics ("guaranteed" by the famous architect's name) are traded off by developers to review boards for a few more stories or an infraction of density regulations. In ideology, heated debates on the aesthetics of a building hide questions about priority and consequences from view. Aesthetic talk further mystifies the architectural object, making it a thing that has value only in discourse. Too often, elite designers speak as if the most important issue about a building was whether it is beautifully and sensitively designed or not. This might be taken as just another example of the congenital moral idiocy of experts were it not that the lingering ideological notion of an art avant-garde still associates art with progress and with a critical "antibourgeois" position.

The postmodern erosion of barriers between "high" and "mass" culture has allowed architects to present purely commercial buildings as potential works of art. Yesterday's "gentlemen architects," steeped in tight distinctions between "culture" and "commerce," would neither have argued nor conceded the point. As Philip Johnson puts it, "When I was a kid, developers were called speculators and they were all evil and that was that. . . . You don't do work with people in the alleys!" The ideology of art gives a further twist to experts' *generic* abdication of individual responsibility. Architects (like other experts) seem to argue tacitly that one individual cannot go against the whole structure of the division of labor—therefore, one individual's moral choices cannot count all that much. Yet artists' faith in their own genius requires them to believe that it would, indeed, make a difference if someone less talented was hired in their place. The two contradictory positions can be held together, except that the latter ("it would be worse without me") demands a minimal preservation of one's personal integrity as a designer. The working relationship with developers seems problematic even for the consciously limited responsibility of the expert in aesthetics.

The first distinction elite architects tend to make is that between mere speculators and a "better kind" of developer. Frank Gehry's is by far the most colorful: "The very basic essence of the developers is to make money. That's obvious. Then, if they are responsible developers, their second priority is to make some kind of good building, whatever that is, in the end. They don't want to take the world. They don't want at the end of the project to have people say 'Oh, you bastards, you created this thing!' " But the other developers, especially around Los Angeles:

> They are led by their greed and street smarts. Their lives are spent in the jungle. . . . If they were sure that [good design] was going to make them money, they would use it! There is no clear evidence of it, because they can build a junky apartment house quicker. I would take twice as long. Julie Eizenberg would *work* to make something better. And we *have* to charge more! I can get an architect to do a building for a third of what I do, and they do it faster . . . and *it builds* cheaper. The technicians (it's an overstatement to call them craftsmen) can slam bam, wham bam, thanks Sam, get it up, finished! It's sloppy bullshit but the users don't make any judgment on that. . . . They buy their fancy chairs and their glitzy fixtures and for very little money they create a look they feel comfortable with.

Perceptions are obviously shaped by particular experiences, but the distinction between the category as a whole and the exceptional developer (the architect's own) is recurrent in this rhetoric of implicit self-justification.

In Chicago, distinction and rhetoric take a regional turn. Gerald Horn contends that even Chicago bankers have a different, Midwestern, attitude toward building: "Just to last one winter in the Chicago climate means it's going to last twenty or fifty or a hundred years in California. . . . The bankers in the Midwest . . . want things that will stay there for all the winters. They say 'I don't want this glitzy thing on it that looks good and makes it fashionable.' "[44] Other Chicago architects agree that their city is different, but they also believe that the same kind of "slap-dash" developers who have built Chicago's suburbs may be taking over downtown building. Bruce Graham thinks it makes a difference that banks and insurance companies were involved directly in Chicago's urban development, but what matters most is that architects have deliberately sought to collaborate with developers: "Our office in New York built the monuments . . . but the developers were building the city. We deliberately went out to do work with developers so that . . . bad architects wouldn't take over Chicago. And it wasn't just us! Harry Weese did the same thing, and Holabird and Root and [Bertrand] Goldberg."

The prevalence of the large firm in Chicago tends to support Graham's argument in several ways. Large architectural firms have power, and they also need large-scale work to support themselves. Chicago being poorer in corporation headquarters than New York, it stands to reason that government work (for which connections with city government count a lot) and speculative projects were the main alternatives. The large firms could never have afforded to behave like "gentlemen architects" for reasons that have nothing to do with their principals' upbringing.

Firms such as SOM bring to the client the organizational and technical insurance that things will be done on time and on budget. Therefore, they are not likely to work in association (and much less likely to accept association) with strong-delivery firms, a working arrangement that developers often demand of the smaller elite firms. Association is said to spread the work, to raise the construction firms' standards of professionalism, to be the only way of working nationwide and internationally, and, above all, to limit growth and overhead expenditures for the principal firm. But the problem of how much and whether one can trust the associate firm looms large. David Denton points out, for instance, that "if a project comes in above budget, construction architects tend to go back to the [materials] specifications and simply change the quality without changing the design." The best solution seems to be the costly one of delegating full-time a highly trusted and technically competent employee to "linking" with (in fact, supervising) the associate firm.

Most of the elite architects I interviewed, even if they go into lengthy justifications of these "forced marriages," end up admitting that the abdication of control over the working drawings is a risky contingency of doing developer's work.[45] In fact, the trend toward association seems to represent for American architects a potential loss of occupational power and control. Logically, for those who are in favor of it, association presages not a loss but a transformation.

While the working drawings for a large project can keep a good-sized firm busy for three to four years at a time, "design only" lasts about six months. Therefore, firms such as Robert Stern's and Cesar Pelli's, which work in association for all large-scale projects, must compensate for the loss of construction work by keeping a lot of work coming in. The track record, however, can belong to the construction firm instead of the design architects, who are thereby free to transfer their signatures and charismatic personas from project to project. Association, indeed, allows elite designers to expand their range beyond what is possible in "all-around" work. Elite architects who work for big developers insist that their clients have become better educated and more socially ambitious. (Charles Gwathmey, who does not work for the big ones, says their motives are "ego and money: They like driving around and saying 'that's *my* building; Philip Johnson built it *for me;* he is *my* architect.' ") Robert Stern admits that developers' first objective is always profit but thinks that "good" developers have their own reputations to maintain. Above all, many architects want to believe that developers have discovered the economic value of their work: It helps with zoning boards to have a famous signature, and good design helps the approval, the rental, and the resale of buildings.

John Zuccotti, who represents major developers in New York, partially confirms their hopes: "Good design solutions helped me, as the attorney for the client, in securing the decision. Good architecture helps in a political sense . . . and it also helps in the basic truth that good design does solve problems that arise in the approval process." Ron Siskolne, vice president for planning and development of Olympia and York, Zuccotti's most important client, sees architecture simply in terms of marketing:

> We are building a product, like laundry detergent. We need to know what kind of design is going to appeal to the consumers, who have become much more design-conscious, across the board. Design is a secondary, added feature, but it is gaining more importance. . . . We try and include [in invited competitions] some less-experienced architects that we think might stretch to work in a new scale, if the marketing objective is that we don't want buildings to be all that similar. We are *not* dealing with the public at large: *The media* generate the interest in the designs that we develop.

There is nothing radically new in using architecture as *sign*. Mansart's Versailles was meant as a sign of Louis XIV's power. Yet, there is a semiotic difference between a building erected in an unbuilt place and a building conspicuously inserted in the dense fabric of a city to create an urban event. The former kind—like Versailles itself, or Frank Lloyd Wright's 1936 masterpiece Johnson Wax Administration building in Racine, Wisconsin, or, today, Frank Gehry's Design Museum for the Vitra chair company in the small German town of Weil-am-Rhein—makes *a place;* the latter kind creates a new "sign system" around itself, and *that* is its semiotic significance. Gordon Bunshaft was proud to point out that design was already worth a lot in free publicity in 1952, when he designed Lever House for a soap company; two years later, Mies van der Rohe's building for the Seagram Corporation introduced the name of a liquor manufacturer (a twentieth-century Medici) into the annals of "high art." Unsurprisingly, after the demise of the "glass box" in the mid-1970s, American corporations have rivaled each other in putting up towers aptly defined as "giant architectural logos."[46]

Robert Venturi's postmodern manifesto of 1966 emphasized the communicative power of architectural ornament. In once again freeing appearance from structure, Venturi unwittingly prodded architects to the deliberate production of architectural images. The postmodern theory of architecture thus foreshadowed its own absorption not in *industrial* production, as modernism had done, but in the prolific production of signs of the postindustrial age.[47]

IDEAL-TYPES AND ALTERNATIVE CAREER SETTINGS

We have viewed elite careers in connection with the firm, the organizational support by means of which and in which they evolve. From this point of view, there are two ideal-types of elite career settings in the profession of architecture in the United States.

One ideal-type of elite career depends on the reputation of a large firm for service *and* design excellence. Individual architects contribute to this reputation, though not in the visible and original manner that ideology associates with artistic talent. The other is the individualistic type, associated with the entrepreneurial firm. The table on page 134 summarizes some basic features of these two ideal types.[48]

Both types of firms can promote their protagonists to high levels of national and international visibility. Reputation includes them in both ideal and real rosters of architectural talent, considered by critics and potential clients for important commissions, invited competitions, international exhi-

Organizational form	Individual's position	Orientation to practice	Typical product
Entrepreneurial; loose structure	Principal "guru"	Strong-idea, innovative	Unique solutions
Corporate partnership; structured project teams	Design partner or director	Strong-service, diversified, high competence	High repeat; projects "personalized" for each client

bitions, and juries—the events that go into the making of "architectural history."

A large organization and a corporate practice are almost prerequisites of longevity among American architectural firms. In the first ideal-type, architects come up through the ranks of a preexisting firm that values design talent. The loosening of the modernist canon and clients' desires for product differentiation have facilitated competition. This appears to have spurred elite strong-service firms to diversify their approach to design. Speculative clients may take an active part in this process by "arranging marriages" (in Ron Siskolne's words) between the more established firms and "genius designers."

The operation of the large firm has an essential element of impersonality. The late Gordon Bunshaft scoffingly suggested that SOM had been prompted to single out individuals (something not done in his time) by the press's compulsive search for "charismatic designers." Corporate firms with a design reputation may build up some partners' names, but it is extremely rare for an elite design career to emerge within ordinary service firms.[49]

The second ideal-type, based on an entrepreneurial practice, is built around the personal talent and reputation of one designer (or no more than a few), known for innovative design and sought out by clients for prestigious or unique commissions. The life cycle of the firm tends to coincide with the architectural career of the design principal. Breakthroughs come between one's late thirties and mid-forties, and track records that spell success are seldom accumulated before one's late fifties. But even the longest and most productive careers come to an end, and firms too closely identified with individuals find it difficult to survive their succession.

In the falsely democratic atmosphere of firms that employ between fifteen and ninety professional employees, there is not much room at the top to prepare seriously for succession. Nor are there many opportunities for creative and conceptual talent to emerge when a charismatic (and egotistic) leader must put his mark on every project. The "star system," to the extent that it touches an architect's career, further aggravates the problem of firm survival.

Today's star system functions symbiotically: The general press (helped by architectural journals) creates "design leaders" and feeds their names to potential new clients after it has been fed the names of new "stars" by savvy marketeers.[50] The genius architects of our century (Frank Lloyd Wright, Le Corbusier, Mies van der Rohe, Alvar Aalto) did not have successors; but today's stars (unless they have extraordinary personas, like Philip Johnson) must go on succeeding themselves within a system that creates fashions without much architectural reason and consumes them in increasingly rapid cycles.

In the United States, the charismatic star system appears to complement the separation of design from production. Together, these two trends may support a hybrid empirical type of elite firm, which uses the "guru's" symbolic capital in its attempt to live two lives: One is the traditional life of the all-around (strong-idea *and* strong-service) firm, for smaller and more prestigious projects; the other life, for large and repetitive projects, tends to be that of a consultantship in silhouette building, siting, and embellishments, as opposed to the constructional role of structural, mechanical, and air-conditioning engineers. The service part of the practice may weather the crisis of succession but lose the international visibility "owned" by the charismatic designer.[51]

Below this level we find "architects' architects" and more traditional elite careers. At this second level, elite careers tend to coincide empirically with local firms and regional reputations, although it is neither the firm's size nor the geographical or stylistic range of its work that matters. In the United States, "traditional" architects are those that make a committment to following a project carefully and therefore to being directly engaged in *construction*; it is obviously easier to carry this out when one is not working many airplane hours away from home.

The traditional firm's partners are rooted in a region that they know very well, in which their work is highly respected, and in whose schools they often teach. Their rootedness may count against them when it comes to being included in much-publicized local competitions that hunger for "name architects." Yet these are firms whose public projects tend to be loved by users and worthy of high respect in the profession's discourse.[52]

Architectural discourse therefore complicates the simple typology of elite careers based on firms. The bulk of architectural services, however technically competent and useful, does not even enter a discursive field that privileges aesthetics. *All* architectural elites exist by and within the profession's autonomous discourse. In addition, the level of highest visibility is *a media event,* architectural discourse seized upon and amplified by the general press.

Architectural aesthetics are the subject of much abstract theorizing, but the canon of architecture, which consists essentially of built exemplars, matters more. Symbolic challenges are waged against the canon to determine what exemplars will be counted as "Architecture." Thus, disputes that may seem purely ideological can rearrange positions and redistribute "cultural power" in the delimited architectural field. In according different relative weights of form, meaning, technique, and social function to architectural products, these challenges redefine not only the product but also the ideal image of the architect's role.

Publication, awards, exhibitions, and competitions are still the major mechanisms through which the profession selects work, built or unbuilt, for peer recognition. Already in the 1930s, as all the older architects report, the library was the place where one discovered Le Corbusier and the Modern Movement. But the expansion of architecture's academic base has amplified recognition beyond anything imaginable in the prewar period. The broad audiences created by schools support alternative teaching settings (like Peter Eisenman's Institute of Architecture and Urban Affairs) and make teaching essential for *academic* elite careers. These begin in relative autonomy from clients and unfold in large part or even purely through discourse.

Whatever elite designers may claim, not one of them is indifferent to peer recognition or, more broadly, to the profession's discourse.[53] Practically all recent American architects included in the encyclopedia *Contemporary Architects* have participated in teaching as visitors, critics, and jurors. Most of them teach or have taught regularly; many have occupied positions of great responsibility as deans of architecture schools or vie to obtain them. Influential designers who build very little, like New York's John Hejduk or Raymond Abraham, are primarily theoreticians who teach. Teaching, then, provides a basic alternative that goes beyond merely economic support.

In 1975, when Cal Poly's Ray Kappe founded the Southern California School of Architecture, Thom Mayne was among the first teachers. He and his partner, Mike Rotondi, the school's first graduate, teach and participate in its direction. The school was for a long time their primary involvement and, as Thom says, it allowed Morphosis, their firm, to "select work that would continue our own explorations, our own investigations, without the burden of actually running a business."

Peter Eisenman, once the tireless and most ambitious intellectual impresario of architecture in the United States, started the Conference of Architects for the Study of the Environment in 1964 and in 1969 the Institute of Architecture and Urban Affairs—a unique center of research, instruction, debate, and publication (publishing not only the ambitious theoretical journal *Oppositions* but the lively magazine *Skyline* and a series of significant monographs). In my interview with him he described his student days at Cornell, his stint with the army in Korea, and his work for other architects. Then, a failed commission for his old fraternity house and time spent studying for a Ph.D. in England seemed to put him on another course: "There was nothing else I could do. . . . And then I became very ideological; I was no longer fit for the real world. And [while teaching at Princeton] I began to do this set of didactic houses. I was no longer going to have an ordinary practice. And then I started the Institute and it was not clear to me that I would ever go into *real* practice." In giving a wider resonance to "paper architecture" and to very small projects, schools, especially *elite* schools, provide a platform from which it is actually easier to launch oneself toward a real (that is practical) career in architecture. In the case of Cesar Pelli, an elite academic position has helped to move his career from one type to another: From a position in a strong-service/strong-delivery firm, he has moved to an extremely successful, large-scale strong-idea entrepreneurial practice.

Academic positions are in themselves direct channels into the discursive field: They can amplify the significance of small-scale experiments and transform an artisanal practice into an alternative to the established types of elite careers. Stuart Cohen, who teaches at the University of Illinois in Chicago, on the one hand describes work "done for practically no money," small projects that are "complicated and spatially rich and getting more and more bold." On the other hand, he takes care to mention that he owes to his writing a personal reputation larger than that derived from his projects.

The discursive challenges of the early postmodern period have been waged in the arenas of teaching, writing, and debating. In Chicago, setting up alternative arenas or taking over the existing ones was the preliminary phase in the attack against the dominance of the large firms and the "descendance of Mies." Cohen describes a movement that started when Tigerman, Tom Beeby, and himself organized the "Chicago Seven" exhibit in 1976:

> After our show we formed the Chicago Architectural Club in 1981. I would say *literally* in that period, because of the visibility that we created collectively for

ourselves and for other small firms doing high quality work, *that* became an option. We were educating a clientele. . . . We were creating a market for the work we were doing and convincing people that they could make a go at it rather than having to sit at SOM and draft all day long. And the number of little firms has grown astronomically! . . . We were all conspirators in a sense. I was teaching at Illinois. Tom Beeby at IIT [the Illinois Institute of Technology]. We used to talk about how *dismal* both schools were, and Tom and I and Stanley said "What are the possibilities of making a first-rate school of architecture?" It was like our agenda for the city of Chicago. . . . Our dean resigned, and I nominated Tom. Then Stanley came and the year after Tom Beeby came, and it was like hitting a critical mass there in terms of change.

The amplification and the alternatives provided by symbolic challenges are significant. Their objective, as we have seen, is to renegotiate and redefine the architect's place within the delimited field. And yet, beyond it, as Rob Quigley says, architectural elites "are mute; the laypeople couldn't care less what architects think."

Quigley belongs to a genus of architects who attempt to redefine the architect's role in broader social terms. They struggle with what little remains of the weakest architectural option in the contemporary United States: designing decent housing for people of modest means and dignified buildings for community life. Architects hope that the revision of the modern precludes a repetition of the urban renewal disasters of the 1950s and 1960s. But there is no broad government sponsorship for the programs of jobs and housing that could bring a new life and a new domestic architecture to the urban ghettoes (or the poor rural areas) of the United States; there are mostly local efforts. The Massachussetts Housing Finance Agency has subsidized Boston's Tent City, on the site of the 1968 squatting protest by displaced residents, and Goody Clancy has designed on the site a remarkable "mixed incomes" complex. Also in Boston, the Bricklayers and Laborers Union has acted as developer for William Rawn's simple but eloquent housing projects. In San Diego, Rob Quigley has paired with an adventurous developer whose beginning "niche" in the jungle of southern California real estate was profitable SROs (single room occupancy hotels):

> He was smart enough to see that there is no place for people to go when the redevelopment agency clears an area. He realized that if he created a flop house or a slum or something undesirable, that was not in his best interest. So he thought of going to a visible architect who in San Diego at least is considered the avant-garde. He didn't think I would be interested and he was only willing to pay what he would pay a draftsman. . . . It covered about half our cost. When he proposed it, I was just *overwhelmed.* This is where whatever our talents are should be focused. And so we agreed to do it, and *there were no models.* It hadn't been done in seventy years.[54]

In Quigley's political analysis, "there are no bad developers. . . . Their values mirror our society's values." He is aware that a compromised role is the normal fate of experts striving to do the best they can with their work.

In large firms, in entrepreneurial ventures, in hybrid types, in traditional local practices, through discourse and in building, *all* the architects on whose accounts I have drawn attempt to reconcile the business of architecture with their own conceptions of art and service. Peers, or clients, or both concede that these men and women have more than ordinary talent. The architects too believe themselves capable of doing work that is worth more than just its material significance. We should read their mystifications of architecture (building, art, building cities, crusade) as different signs of an ideological struggle to affirm the value of their work.

The social conditions in which architects practice have changed. The analysis based on their perceptions does not contradict the general argument outlined in chapter 3: The demise of modernism has increased the fame that some architects can expect to gain through their work. The clients—corporations, developers, even city governments—try to use for profit, publicity, or both the designer's name in symbiosis with their designs. Yet, while there seems to be more appreciation for architects' ability to conjure up *images,* both their control of the process of building and their centrality in it have diminished. In particular, the architects committed to a socially responsible architecture find it more difficult to pass from paper projects to building. Taking refuge in the pure aesthetics of architecture appears as a consoling and ever-ready temptation.

Looking at practice through practitioners' eyes, aesthetics and the profession's discourse are obviously important, so important, in fact, that architectural elites in the United States may constitute themselves exclusively within discourse. Discursive battles are therefore always endowed with practical significance. In the next section, I consider the main discursive battle of the period 1966–85—the revision of the modernist canon—from two angles: I examine in chapter 5 how elite designers view the creative substance of their work and, in chapter 6, how postmodern revisionism has shaped their views. This in-depth analysis establishes the ideological and personal parameters of architectural discourse. In chapters 7 and 8, I take a larger sample of the profession's elites: the juries who assigned design awards for the journal *Progressive Architecture* during the period 1966–85. I use their debates to reconstruct the recent transformation of the discourse and the canon of architecture.

PART THREE

The Revision of the Modern

CHAPTER FIVE

Architects and Creative Work

"You could not help getting [from Louis Kahn] this sense of hope that architecture was ultimately poetry and art, transcending accommodation, shelter, and program." This statement has the generality of a cliché. Yet Charles Gwathmey pronounced it with absolute conviction, and one can see it emanating from a man's serious involvement in his work. Less celebrated architects than Gwathmey also take it for granted that art and meaning make architecture more than mere building. Here is, for instance, the principal of a commercial firm with a three-generation history and a more recent one of making production drawings for many famous designers: "I think art has a lot to do with architecture. . . . What you want is a businessman who is willing to spend a little bit of money so the buildings you are designing have an ability to say something. We have a number of jobs that we think have a lot of art in them." The creation of meaning— "saying something"—still appears to be the distinctive quality of architecture, but it is implicitly quantified and made into a commodity. If "a lot of art" can go into a building, it is also possible to put in "a little" or none. One can only tell when it is "enough" by the money it costs.

The skeptic might see these two preceding statements as candor on the one hand and pretension on the other. Yet architects are wont to repeat (with variations) Gwathmey's notion that architecture must transcend the requirements of practice and therefore go beyond its conditions of existence. Joan Goody, for instance, treats architecture as the architect's secret intention in a constrained process. She does not try to say what it *is*, except the undefined beauty that could not be quantified and is not paid for: "Architecture is the most valuable, the hardest to make of the things that we do. . . . They pay us to be sure they make it through the building inspectors and the zoning, that the clients will be happy, that they are rented . . . but the extra layer of beauty we have to sneak in." Because of general properties inherent in building, it is difficult to articulate what architecture *is*. Architects' occupational ideology forms around this difficulty.

As physical artifacts, buildings do more than articulate spaces within their shells: They also make the space around and between them perceptible and organized. As significant artifacts, buildings give spatial expression to the social relations and basic social hierarchies that inform a culture, nourishing its language and cosmology with spatial metaphors.[1] In this sense building is like music or poetry: It is impossible to fully describe in words what has been created, for our ability to describe depends on experiencing with our senses an artifact that has "feeling and form."

Each culture has its specific building arts, and in ours architecture is that which *our* architects do. In Western culture, architects profess to be specialists in transforming the complexity of buildings into beauty. Art critics and architectural historians specialize in telling us what that beauty consists of, but architects lay claim to its creation. Their claim implicitly rests on a syllogism characteristic of this profession: Architecture is an art. Only architects produce architecture. Architects are necessary to produce art.

The profession of architecture depends on clients, on executants, and on rival professions to whom it is often subordinate in the field of construction. This means that the profession of architecture is not autonomous but rather is fundamentally heteronomous. Yet architects "own" both the name and the discourse of architecture; the basic syllogism affirms and preserves the profession's identification with beautiful buildings. When noted designers grant interviews, the syllogism is tacitly taken for granted: The lay interviewer *must* identify architecture with what respondents do; otherwise no interviewer would be asking *them* about their work and their views.

While the syllogism of architecture establishes the profession's collective authorship of buildings, authorship for elite architects (the "gurus," as the press says) merges with charisma derived from the ideology of art. The syllogism and the authorship it claims are basic prerequisites of architectural ideology.

This ideology assumes that the art of architecture transcends the utilitarian and technical tasks of building. Beauty is what justifies a building's permanence in time and its significance in history. Architects with an exalted conception of their work aspire to do something beyond the practical services that clients require. Directly, in their work, and indirectly, in what they say about it, they make rhetorical choices intended to prove architectural quality to their peers, their clients, themselves, and something undefined they call "the public"—in this order.

In this chapter I consider, first, how architects articulate the object of architecture (the thing to which they are committed) and the subject of architecture (their role as author). We should not expect them to penetrate what the critic Reyner Banham, borrowing an image from science, calls architecture's "classic 'black box,' recognised by its output though unknown in its contents."[2] Rather than the specific substance of architecture, their rhetorical constructions reveal different parameters and expressions of the occupational ideology.

The contours of this ideology become clearer in the second section, where I examine the orientations that architects have toward three ways of seeking transcendence in their work: by creating meaning for their buildings, by emphasizing the craft of architecture, and by highlighting the enhancement of life that architecture provides. Each represents for elite designers an attempt to transcend the narrow mandate of their work.

ARCHITECTURE'S SUBJECT AND OBJECT

Architects talk about the art of architecture in four main ways: in general terms that do not tell us how it is different from other forms of building; in personal terms that focus on the frustrations of a misunderstood and threatened enterprise; in very specific terms that explain what they want to achieve in particular projects and how they go about it; and in prescriptive terms that offer specific critiques or variations on the theme "this is not architecture."

There is no theory of architecture or, as one historian writes, "none that has not been used to justify totally different styles of architecture over the past two centuries."[3] Peter Eisenman, the architect and cultural entrepreneur, thinks that architecture lacks "cultural power" because it lacks theoretical foundations. This implicitly explains why architects have difficulty imposing their syllogism, or, which is the same, their own distinction between architecture and building, on the public and potential clients. Comparing architecture to law and economics, Eisenman argues that architecture has always vacillated between extracting theory after the fact from realized projects and engaging in "ideological practice," which proceeds from developed theory. The opposite of theory is, for him, the business of architecture; only theory can provide autonomous criteria for judging the results of practice: "In architecture, the theory is under-valued because it does not matter. . . . Everything is concerned with selling, with the media. We seem to have no corrective, no notion of what the discipline *is* against which to measure results."[4] Eisenman's argument implies that "the capacity to shape society as law and economics do" depends on the recognition of professional criteria by the state and by relevant others: "When the government wants a legal opinion it goes to the Harvard Law School or the Stanford Law School for advice. When there is a question of development or environmental concern, nobody goes to the architecture schools for advice."[5] Now, in the United States as in Europe, practicing architects (rather than academics) invariably sit on fine arts commissions, design review boards, and city planning committees, even if their advice is often ignored. Eisenman's point is that they are not taken seriously because their expertise does not rest on autonomous theory.

Eisenman's argument was part of an exchange with Henry Cobb, whose reply (as the senior partner in I. M. Pei's firm rather than the chair of the Department of Architecture at Harvard's Graduate School of Design, which he was at the time) is significant. Architecture, Cobb implies, must choose between *doing* anything and advancing as a purely theoretical form of knowledge. But the choice is already made: In order to exist, architecture needs realizations. Invoking the theoretical authority of an outsider, Cobb cites Michel Foucault: Architecture belongs among the composite practices (like the practice of government) that the Greeks called *techne;* it is "a practical rationality governed by a conscious goal."[6] Cobb then implicitly returns to the basic syllogism of architecture, suggesting that it is bound to fail: "Architecture by definition gives three-dimensional form to the society from which it springs, portraying it in a form so vivid and influential that it has the status of a cultural artifact; on the other hand, this cultural power does not invest architects or architecture with the kind of direct manipulative power that . . . lawyers and the law or economics and economists have in the shaping of society."[7]

The culturally significant, socially valued, and long-lasting products of architecture are *both* the insignia of clients' power *and* the expression of architects' autonomous artistic aspirations. Historically, the problem of authorship was that the architect had to distinguish his contribution from the power of the patron. In addition to this, modern architects must also fight for place in ever-more-complex rosters of building specialists.

As a form of cultural production, modern architecture must simultaneously convince and deceive the client. For Vittorio Gregotti, this cunning is the architect's critical duty:

> Modern culture involves a radical discontinuity: it is a *critical* culture, it *cannot* be organic vis-à-vis the society that exists. Because [Albert] Speer and [Marcello] Piacentini wanted to be organic, they interpreted our relation with nazism and with fascism. The typical duplicity of the architect is precisely that of having in mind two different goals simultaneously—architecture as autonomous culture *and* the client.

Yet, because the autonomous culture of architecture matters only to other architects, they must resolve ideologically the problems of authorship and of "double coding" the object—for the client and for the cognoscenti.

In the public, nonspecialist discourse of architects, the ideological construction of architecture moves on a continuum between two poles: On the one hand, discourse must establish the architect as the *creative subject* of architecture, proclaiming the superiority of the idea over its realization. On the other hand, it must construct the significance of the *created object* in a mostly "nonarchitected" environment, emancipating the building from either utilitarian or hedonistic vocations. The rhetorical strategies by which practitioners sustain the collective claims of their profession move imperceptibly from one focus to the other. My argument is that both remain central, even though contemporary professional ideology has abandoned the "strong programs" with which they were once associated.

Let us begin with the architect as subject in Le Corbusier's manifesto of 1923:

> The Architect, by his arrangement of forms, realizes an order which is a pure creation of his spirit; by forms and shapes he affects our senses to an acute degree and provokes plastic emotions; by the relationships which he creates . . . he gives us the measure of an order which we feel to be in accordance with that of our world, he determines the various movements of our heart and our understanding; it is then that we experience the sense of beauty.[8]

While few architects would dare to talk in these terms today, the glorified role that architects seek among other design professionals silently evokes them. Architects' willingness to assume practical and legal responsibility for all aspects of good construction (functional and environmental performance, beauty of form and adeptness of space, respect for materials and structural economy) implicitly asserts authorship.[9]

Similarly, the fact that architects' discourse almost inevitably veers toward description or graphic exhibition of their intentions, moves, and procedures in specific designs indicates another way in which architects claim creative responsibility. Indeed, it is not only the case that architects feel more comfortable with specifics than with generalities but also that the active "I" of their descriptions assigns them a protagonist's role, rivaled only by the buildings they claim as their creations.

The fusion of creation and creator comes through in the prose of Louis Kahn, the great American architect, who reinvigorated the principles of Beaux-Arts planning learned from his teachers in Philadelphia:

> Architecture is a thoughtful making of spaces . . . spaces which form themselves into a harmony good for the use to which the building is to be put.
>
> I believe the architect's first act is to take the program that comes to him and change it. Not to satisfy it, but to put it into the realm of architecture, which is to put it into the realm of spaces. An architectural space must reveal the evidence of its making by the space itself.[10]

Architects often say that architecture animates inert matter. This ability of architecture is captured in common language that employs anthropomorphic terms (walls rise and turn corners, roofs drop, windows look down, moldings run, buildings have character) and in more vivid metaphors in architects' discourse (spaces form themselves and slide into one another, fifty-story buildings cannot stop rotating, and an urban square leaks space). Beaux-Arts teaching was centered on the generative properties of the plan—a principle as important for Le Corbusier ("the plan is the generator" that "holds in itself the essence of sensation," he wrote) as it was later for Kahn.[11] The phrase "the powers of the plan" is a specialist's way of metaphorically attributing powers of agency to built space. This metaphor links the architectural principles of modernism to the social-engineering orientation of its professionals.

Incorporating, among other things, the idea of the generative plan, the Modern Movement developed a more absolute principle: The exterior of a building *must* be an expression of its structure and its interior. But the principle could be knowingly contradicted (as it often was by modernist masters), and the facade could be built up as the boundary between the inside and the outside. Yet the principle that form must follow plan and structure (a more exact phrasing than "form follows function") rephrases the general conception that architecture is the *active* organizer of space. This is the architectural counterpart of the "strong program" of architectural determinism, which extends (on an ideological level) the agent powers of architecture from space to its occupants.

For an architectural determinist, "architectural design has a direct and determinate effect on the way people behave." Writing in the 1960s, the sociologist Alan Lipman observed: "In this psychologically and sociologically conscious period, the profession's traditional belief that it satisfies aesthetic 'needs' can be extended to psychic and social 'needs.' It is difficult to imagine a more gratifying belief, one which could better recompense the architect for the vicissitudes of his professional activities."[12] No contemporary architect would credit architecture with reordering social powers; yet traces of the basic metaphor of architectural agency survive. Paradoxically, they inform the formalist emphasis on architecture's aesthetic meaning.

Obviously, architecture must have some purpose and meaning for people who devote their lives to it. The point is that even Richard Meier, an architect known for his uncompromising aestheticism, attributes to architecture the power to create and convey meaning for society *in general:* "I am not sure [that architecture] shapes or reorders society, but I think it gives some focus, some sense of purpose or meaning that otherwise might not be there in the chaos of our time."[13]

"Meaning" has become an essential ideological justification of postmodern revisionism. Having retreated by will or by force from exalting architecture as an agent of social reform to exalting its single products as works of art, their authors must still insist on making them "speak."[14] Signification, as Meier suggests, extends beyond the signifier.

The idea of communicating through architecture is old. One historian sees in the eighteenth century the emergence of "a tradition in architectural writing . . . of ignoring the origins and importance of 'style' and of explaining architecture away as a consequence or a manifestation of something else."[15] In the nineteenth century, Victor Hugo noted that Notre Dame, "the gospel of stone," had lost its powers of denotation to the printed word; connotation, however, is never lost. It was therefore logical that a profession rendered doubly insecure, by the disintegration of its neoclassicist language and by the revolutionary change in the relations of patronage, would look for justification outside its own canon.

In the second half of the twentieth century, the advance of academicization has changed the substance of architectural criticism and extended its public. Criticism uncovers methods of composition and spatial results that are not only difficult to interpret but even to see by untrained eyes. Yet academicization also promotes the continuing search for external theoretical legitimacy: It goes on, looking to science and technology or, on the aesthetic side, to philosophy and literary theory.[16]

Despite all the talk, architecture cannot be read like a written language: The basic vocabulary of doors, windows, walls, ceilings, floors, and columns does not compose a text to be read but a building to be lived in. Functional elements and ornamental figures are more readily accessible than "spatial grammars," yet they are inseparable from practical and historical connotations. Therefore, the conventions of building type, the multiple practical functions, and the social origins of buildings always persist as "impure" associations in the viewer's memory.

In sum, theory or, more simply, the esoteric analysis of architectural objects cannot displace whatever it is that the large numbers of viewers or users "read" in them. An obvious contention is that people mainly see size, place, and use in a context that is always already social—a meaning as far from the "purely architectural" as its users' behavior is from being caused by the built environment.

TRANSCENDENCE AND IDEOLOGY

In the discourse of contemporary American architects, three ways of seeking transcendence in one's work stand out: First, architects seek to create meaning for their buildings, an effort that can be called signification; second, they emphasize the process, the quality, or the craftsmanship that goes into thinking architecture; and, third, they highlight the enhancement of life that architecture provides as it looks beyond clients and users to a general notion of human fulfillment. These orientations are not incompatible, although they can become contradictory.

In the aesthetic inheritance of modernism, art should not represent something outside itself but should reveal the very process of its making and the conflicts overcome in its creation. For this aesthetics of specialists and cognoscenti, serious architecture is one that shows the tensions the architect has attempted to resolve. As one critic puts it, writing of Le Corbusier's 1930 house in Chile: "[It] displays an intention not only of accommodating the occupants' basic needs but of creating a basic confrontation between architecture as an abstract idea and architecture as craft and tradition."[17] Despite ideal or actual confrontations, meaning, craft, and service all concentrate on the single architectural object. All three orientations to some extent reflect an ideological distance from the obligatory team work of more comprehensive projects; they reflect a turn toward individuality.

SIGNIFICATION

Robert Venturi called on architects to enrich the experience of architecture by making *deliberate* use of the multiple connotations of the architectural sign. "A valid architecture," he proclaimed in 1966, "evokes many levels of meaning and combinations of focus: its space and its elements become readable and workable in several ways at once."[18] Contemporary critics tend to see a clear bifurcation in the search for meaning in architecture: on the one hand are the heirs of modernism, who concentrate on signification accessible to still very small circles of specialists and cognoscenti; on the other, traditional postmodernists (who should more properly be called premodernists) deliberately look to the past of architecture for symbolic associations, accepting the "impure" pomp, power, and grace that the past evokes.

I mentioned in chapter 2 Robert Stern's distinction between "traditional" and "schismatic" postmodernism, as well as Charles Jencks's proliferating categories.[19] Whatever the validity of the classifications, all the revisionist tendencies remain within the basic parameters of the architectural ideology. None rejects the identification of architecture as an art, and all equate this art with what architects do. Furthermore, in the revision of the modern, all the tendencies are interested in signification. Even the self-proclaimedly radical "deconstructive" tendency appropriates for architecture the task of communicating the "impossibility of meaning." Here, for instance, is Peter Eisenman's text for a hotel competition in Barcelona:

> The resulting form and space no longer can mean in the conventional sense of architectural meaning. . . . In this sense it means nothing. But because of this meaning nothing, another level of potential significance previously repressed by conventional meaning is now liberated. . . . Thus this project not only symbolises the spirit of new Spain in the world of 1992, but also the new world of an architecture possible for the 21st century.[20]

If embodying the *Zeitgeist* seems a bit much for a hotel, we should remember that formalism elides considerations of program and function and thereby hints at the waning of distinctions between commercial and "high" art.

Signification crosses the boundaries of approach and style, adding its quest for transcendence to the syllogism of architecture. While architects seldom challenge the Western idea of art as personal expression, they professionalize it: Signification (like beauty) becomes a manifestation of their expertise. *They* and no others will determine what there is to be said and how to say it best. But, of course, to whom they say it (the client, the users, or the ideal audience) determines in large part the formal strategies of architectural signification. Proposing signs that will be legible only to certain publics creates at the same time special market positions for their makers.

For a theoretically sophisticated formalist like Eisenman, being misunderstood and accused of arrogant hermeticism is, on the one hand, the inevitable consequence of being at the avant-garde:

> Essentially the profession sees itself as providing comfort. It is a consumer profession, and the elite is *not* producing comfort. . . . Deconstruction deals with the questions of text and absence and displacement . . . certainly too much for the public to deal with, but it's not too much for a *literate* public. There *is* a class of literati, but what is interesting about them is that they have no sensitivity to architecture *at all!* The intellectual public, which is appealed to by philosophers, scientists, theologians, literary critics, *are only interested in comfort when it comes to architecture.*

On the other hand, Eisenman is accumulating an impressive international track record from his special market niche: "I get clients, basically, that no one else will get, because there is no one else occupying my territory. I beat Michael Graves in Cincinnati *because* I took the, quote, 'radical risky position,' the unsettling, unstable position, and I've always done that from the first of my clients. . . . The thing is how do I remain unestablished?"

Communicating with the "happy few" and shocking the rest is the classic position of the avant-garde. Traditional postmodernists reject in principle the elitism of this position. With different architectural elements, different measures of eclecticism, and different degrees of reflexive irony or seriousness, architects like Robert Venturi, Charles Moore, Michael Graves, Robert Stern, Stanley Tigerman, Thomas Beeby, Stuart Cohen, William Pedersen, and even Philip Johnson (to mention only some we have encountered) rely on traditional or vernacular forms to make their architecture more accessible. In other words, they aspire to a different and possibly a much broader market than Eisenman.[21]

The different stages of Michael Graves's work illustrate different levels of tension between broadening "meaning" (and thereby reaching a larger public) and veering too far from the narrow professional foundation of fame, toward an architecture that strives to delight on "the other's" terms. Of all the American postmoderns, Graves has probably the most consistently sought to use the simple elements of architectural composition—doors, windows, walls, ceilings, floors, and columns—in a personal language. In the early 1970s, he moved away from an abstract formal repertoire derived mainly from Le Corbusier toward a vocabulary that he thought richer and more intelligible: color and figures and meanings taken from the "high" traditions of the Renaissance and mannerism. He explained his gradual shift from schismatic to traditional postmodernism this way:

We can't have any purposeful ambiguity in our language unless there are abstractions. But at the same time we run the risk, if we are not figurative enough, of losing our audience. There has to be some balance between what is figurative, what is associational, what is understood as symbolic in terms of its figural association, and what is multifaceted in the sense that the abstraction allows the several readers . . . to read what they want into the composition.[22]

For the historian Alan Colquhoun, Graves's formal choices reflected a "nostalgia for 'culture' which is characteristically American, and . . . depends on the existence of a type of client who has similar—though less well defined—aspirations." Graves's work of the late 1970s was becoming "a meditation on architecture," in which "the substance of the building does not form part of the ideal world imagined by the architect. . . . The objective conditions of building and its subjective effect are now finally separated." Graves's architecture was becoming image.[23]

In the 1980s, Graves's work for an emblematic client, the Disney Corporation, completed the passage toward an architecture that is pure sign. Disney epitomizes the culture industry's tremendous capacity to create mythical figures and the most effective simulacra of real "places." The audiences for these images never share in direct social relationships—the lifeblood of traditional communities and autochthonous myths.[24]

Doing architecture for Disney sends multiple messages beyond the buildings themselves. In the new world of indirect and mediated social relationships, Graves's implicit message to architects is that architecture as it *used* to be can no longer compete with the connotative powers of the culture industry. In the Swan and the Dolphin hotels at Disney World, Graves designs "cosmic cartoons in toto, their shapes abnormally few, obvious and vast."[25] Yet "entertainment architecture," as the company defines it, and expensive hotels designed for "vast conventions of sober-suited executives" are not cartoons. In a tightly controlled private town with not a shadow of democratic government, the architecture points beyond itself and beyond Mickey Mouse: The Magic Kingdom represents a phantom public life—one, however, that must be *paid for*. The architecture, like all the other forms of delightful simulation, is a piece in the vast marketing strategies of the archetypal postindustrial corporation.[26]

Precisely because they represent extreme cases of image-making, Michael Graves's brilliant designs for Disney illustrate inescapable problems of architectural signification. Walter Benjamin, the Frankfurt school critic, saw architecture as "the prototype of a work of art the reception of which is consummated by a collectivity in a state of distraction." He saw that architecture, like the cinema to which he compared it, pointed a way out of the "rapt attention" and the reactionary aestheticism that surround art in Western culture. Architecture, embedded in social relationships, was appropriated habitually "by use and by perception or, rather, by touch and by sight."[27]

Benjamin was wrong about the culture industry. Disney's world of paid entertainment proves that most people pay attention not to architecture but yes to the fantastic images and associations it connotes. The viewers do not relate either to each other or to the architecture by habit or use but rather by the imaginary bonds of spectacle.

For the critic Mark Girouard, modern architecture had failed "to produce images of enjoyment or entertainment or images of domesticity with which any large number of people could identify."[28] The case of Disney architecture, like the architecture of films to which it is so close, reiterates the dilemma of contemporary art: caught between the esoteric advancement of a specific art and signifying something for a broader public— essentially by giving it what (artists think) people want. Only world-famous architects, whose names have market value, actually ever face a choice that stark. Even so, the client always has the last word.

With clients less experienced than Disney in the creation of images, the choice is already made: Architects who aspire to make a mark on architecture—the subject of professional discourse—seek the client's license, in order to communicate with those who pay attention. Thus, despite Venturi's original pleas for a nonelitist "pop" architecture, the traditional revision of modernism has been identified chiefly with the revival of the neoclassical language and with the search for a vernacular style.

Contextualism, the hallmark of postmodernism, inflects the architecture of single buildings toward the discovery or invention of vernacular forms. For the public, contextualism tends to mean only conformity with what is already there. For the designer, it means that signification emerges from the insertion of one object within a preexisting system of built objects and from their spatial and temporal relations. The predominance of neoclassicism (among other high styles of architectural history) has a reason: it has a long history in the urban environment. In the visual and vital chaos of many modern cities, there is no vernacular and no discernible "context" capable of ordering the design of single buildings. In this account by William Pedersen, we detect an almost inevitable return to the tried language of the "high" architectural tradition:

> Since most of the contexts we were building in gave off confusing and contradictory signals, wasn't it possible for the building itself to be composed of different pieces, each drawn in reference to different conditions within the context?

. . . Certainly, a large building could be more sensitively scaled to the city if it was made up of distinct pieces. . . . [But] the individual building could only go so far in representing the complexity of the city. Consequently, our buildings became less complex. . . . The issue of the tall building, addressing the public realm, presenting a facade to the street which would join other buildings to make a continuous and cohesive unity out of the street, became a dominant preoccupation in our work. *We started to introduce classical compositional techniques, primarily those that were aimed at encouraging the textural environment and unification of surface.*[29]

In suggesting the difficulty of contextual design, Pedersen shows that accommodating the single building to its environment can be a supreme expression of architectural craft. A new object can be fitted into its surroundings if the architect pays enough attention to detail and creatively interprets the past and present context. But it can also be made to fit in mass and facade if the architect uses rapid gestures and a silhouette, vocabulary, and ornament that satisfy zoning boards and commercial clients. The emphasis on craftsmanship does not reject signification but the quick creation of illusion.

CRAFTSMANSHIP

Architectural craftsmanship requires care, technical competence, proverbial attention to details, subtle handling of spaces, efficient and elegant interpretation of the program, and ingenious and sensuous use of materials; above all, perhaps, it requires considering the consequences that each move implies. Craftsmanship *takes time*—and time in architecture is, of course, money. An inventive designer can achieve scenographic solutions and brilliant effects in less time than it takes the craftsman architect to design a small building. This is one reason developers are not the latter's typical or choice clients.

Craftsmanship entails a reverence for embodied perfection. The perfect objects produced deserve permanence and respect. Indeed, craft-oriented architects emphasize that their designs will last—or *would* last, if construction was as good as the care that went into the designs. Well-crafted architecture seems "naturally" contextual, like the architecture the great Bay Area architect and educator William Wurster called anonymous—so married to the site, so simple and so lasting, that it looks like a Tuscan farmhouse or a wood barn in California, something that has always been there. For Joseph Esherick, an architect in Wurster's tradition, "the ideal piece of architecture is one that you don't see." The disappearance of the architect as creative subject is, of course, a rhetorical strategy, for viewers and users *know* that these perfect syntheses cannot just happen, that an invisible human subject was responsible for devising what was made to be forgotten.

Although independent of size, well-crafted architecture connotes both an emphasis on control and a close relationship with the client, both of which seem easier to obtain in the design of smaller projects—notably private houses, unique commissions in which the client-user has a personal stake.

Houses occupy a large place in Stanley Tigerman's practice. Predictably, he sees small projects as a much more fertile ground than large-scale buildings for the development of new architectural ideas. This is, in part, because small buildings admit his playful vision of architecture "as commentary," even as joke (as in Bruno Taut's motto of 1920, "Down with seriousism!"), while all the enormously expensive "humorless buildings . . . *are* the joke." The owner of several south Florida burlesque houses, dying of intestinal cancer, came to Tigerman to ask him to design a beach house. Tigerman decided he could only try to make him laugh. Accordingly, he developed (and explained to everybody) the plan of the very successful "Daisy House" as a phallic emblem. Ten years later, its main occupant was still alive!

Tigerman's account of his practice typifies the emphasis on craftsmanship, including the ideological notion that the match with the client is "made in heaven":

> It's like when I was a teenager, you would see an attractive girl . . . you'd never let her know that you wanted to go out with her! You wanted her, *somehow*, mysteriously, to *find* you. So I have been waiting for them mysteriously to find me. I don't want to *find* anybody. . . . I just want to sit and do work. Of course, I don't want too much. . . . If you have too much work, you can't do it well. You can't. You start doling it out to the people in your office to do. I only want the work *that I can do well*. . . . Whatever it is. If it's a back porch, a little store, a house, a skyscraper, a business, *it's a building!* I want to do what somebody comes to me and wants me to do. . . . I don't do marketing. I resent architects who do it. What I think an architect should do is sit in his or her office *and work*.

Tigerman is such a public figure in Chicago, so active talking, writing, teaching, drawing, exhibiting his work, and organizing events, that it might indeed be true he does not need to do more than that to find clients. As we know, discursive activity is a necessary amplifier for the craftsman-architect's work. Yet discursive activity is not quite enough for Tigerman; he may *prefer* his small practice, but he has been actively involved with

Stern at Euro-Disney and with Bruce Graham of SOM in the now defunct possibility of a Chicago Fair.

In theory, craftsmanship should not be a primary orientation toward architectural work but an ancillary one, an orientation to supplement others. It can be pressed, of course, into the making of architecture as art with meaning of its own. Yet, as Holmes Perkins perceptively notes, originality and craftsmanship are two different dimensions, and architectural judges perceive them as distinct and reward them differently. When Perkins was at Harvard in the 1930s, "the people who were real leaders in our eyes were breaking new ground. . . . One of the dilemmas in breaking new ground is that the new is almost always crude, and it takes maybe another generation or so to polish it up. I think the difference between the polished up version and the original is very very visible!" Because craftsmanship ultimately chooses integrity of process over other aspects of architectural work, it may orient itself toward "perfection," away from the possibility of failure (which lurks in expressing "meaning" or, simply, original ideas). Yet because craft work recognizes the primacy of the client's needs, it has affinities with the form of transcendence that I have called the enhancement of life.

ENHANCING LIFE

The close relationships that architects like Tigerman establish with their clients show their concern for their clients' purposes. In addition, architects show a concern for clients' lives that is typical of the *architectural* craft.

Architectural craftsmanship tends to see architecture as providing a setting for social life. Speaking for many architects, Joan Goody declares, "It's a bad setting if it obstructs that life and makes itself the star." She describes her idea of a *good* setting a little less modestly:

> Architecture . . . can be intellectual in the way it is conceived, but it's got to appeal to the senses once it is built. . . . It feels good when light enters in such a way that it opens up a space rather than making it oppressive or cramped; when the proportions of a facade feel comfortable, in harmony; when the materials, colors, textures are appealing to the eye. This is a sensuous reaction, as opposed to an intellectual one, where you need a scorecard to understand that one piece of a structure alludes to something that's three blocks away and another is an ironic comment on something else three centuries away. I think one should be able to respond to a building with one's eyes and one's body.[30]

"Feels good . . . comfortable, in harmony"—these are dimensions of architecture that a theoretician like Peter Eisenman despises. While all

professional architects (and all professionals!) try in different ways to enno-
ble the service they render for money, this form of transcending mere
service tends to steer architects toward certain types of clients and especially users. The aspiration to enhance life by means of architecture rises
above the commonplace by exalting the concrete needs that are served.
Therefore, its choice settings are those that represent the needs of everyday
life: houses, workplaces, roads, airports, schools, community centers.

   Insofar as the first motive is not profit but augmenting the quality of
life, the creation of new needs (or rather, the direction of unrecognized
needs toward new forms of fulfillment) is the contribution of all professions
to the civilizing process.[31] Architects who spend unpaid labor time on projects they hold important seem close to that in intention.

   Joan Goody, once again, illustrates how to serve unrecognized needs.
In my interview with her she discussed the renovation of worse than half-
abandoned public housing at Boston's Harbor Point. Cross-ventilation had
been the overriding concern of all public housing from 1945 to 1960, resulting in the cross-shaped concrete towers "tossed around" in such a way that
they "line up next to one another and become a single wall." Her "selective
demolition" has re-created the traditional grid system of streets and opened
each one to a vista of the harbor. Besides making it safe for people to get
home, "the point was to get people to walk on the street."

   Rob Quigley explained that the single-room project for the homeless
"was neither an apartment building nor a hotel, and the building codes
penalized the design of such an animal," and then described almost apologetically how he worked on the developer's idea: "A working wall that
incorporates the toilet in the room, a sink with garbage disposal, a spot for
a microwave oven for rooms that are 10 by 10 feet. These are simple little
trivial things, but it is a precedent setting idea, that you can have a bathroom not legally called a bathroom. . . . What it means in comfort, dignity,
sense of privacy to not have to walk to a common toilet at night is unmea-
surable." Not surprisingly, Quigley echoes the vision of the Frankfurt architects in the 1920s, the vision that Paul Tillich called "a religion of everyday
life."[32] The issue here is not transcending service but, much more ambi-
tiously, transcending life itself by enhancing its "everyday-ness": making
efficiency gracious and grace efficient.

   The aims of architecture, as Sir Henry Wotton defined them in 1624,
were tripartite:

> . . . the end must direct the Operation.
> The end is to build well.
> Well building hath three conditions:
> *Commodite, Firmenes and Delight.*[33]

Few elite architects are inclined to care about comfort only, and few define signification independently of delight, except, at their most theoretical, the "deconstructive" architects with their philosophy of "violating" and rupturing form. Most architects seem to believe that "delight" is still possible and acceptable in a world like ours. Too often, they slide into believing that beautiful architecture is *good* in itself.

The central objective of ambitious design is to achieve this good and the "firmness" that will make it last. To their peers and to interested circles, architects of recognized talent seem able to achieve it more often than others. In the following chapter, I examine, first, how they explain the process, basic to their work, which they call design. Second, I consider the revision of modernism through the eyes of its protagonists, exploring how it has affected their way of conceiving their work.

CHAPTER SIX

Design and Discourse in a Period of Change

The Protagonist's View

To Reyner Banham, the persistence and centrality of drawing, the Renaissance *disegno,* make for the distinctiveness of our building art. It follows in his logic that computer-aided design may well have destroyed the mystique of drawing, and hence of architecture, "not by mechanising the act of drawing itself, but by rendering it unnecessary."[1] Obviously, the process of design *includes* an ability to draw, as well as the much more basic competence to read two-dimensional representations of three-dimensional space. But my analysis will show that Banham greatly underestimates the complexity of what architects call design.

I begin with two eloquent accounts by Adrian Smith and Diane Legge, both of them partners at SOM-Chicago. Their firm makes available to them the most sophisticated computer technologies that exist and the technical support required to use them efficiently. It is therefore instructive to consider how they describe the formal origins of a design. In studios, architects draw as they speak about what they draw. But the accounts presented here do not rely on the combination of "drawing and speaking," which Donald Schön identified with "the language of designing" in direct observations of teaching studios. Yet, Smith and Legge think in terms of the "normative design domains" that Schön recognized.[2]

Both Smith and Legge are *explaining* to a lay interviewer (with faint echoes, perhaps, of how they talk to clients) the emergence of a composition. In Smith's account, siting and form predominate; precedent and the "felt path," the user's experience of moving through the created spaces, are most salient in Legge's. Both make brief technical references, either directly to structure and technology in the case of Smith, or indirectly, by representing problems in the language of measurement or by common technical notations such as "scale" and "section." Both give much importance to the constraints of program; Legge alludes vaguely to those of cost.

In the language of the French Beaux-Arts, architects often call their first approach to a specific design problem the *parti:* in Stanley Tigerman's words, "the plan-wise organization of something, typologically, categorically, so that you can understand it formally, not by function, but *by formal type."* Adrian Smith explained the genesis of a *parti* for the Rowes Wharf complex on Boston Harbor, an invited developer-architect competition that SOM won out of a field of eight. The Redevelopment Authority's guidelines required that the Broad Street axis remain open down to the water, and Smith's solution ultimately included a spectacular arch spanning the space between two corps of building:

As you look at the city from the air . . . as it hits the water's edge, it fans out: You see all these finger piers sticking out into the water. It was just *very apparent* that this building had to have a continuation of those fingers sticking *out* of the water and that there should be an urban edge which relates to the strong street that rims it. In between the finger piers and the city is this highway that makes a very strong kind of figural piece through the city. . . . The client and his people and we, we all felt that we wanted to have some strong kind of figural piece that could be identified and identifiable as the project's memory of things.

Smith is not talking about composition but relating the genesis of a governing conception. The idea, at this level, is still vague; if it involved drawing, it would be one of the rapid sketches (sometimes clay massings) with which lay people identify, so wrongly, the architect of genius. The configuration of the site plays a determining role, which is immediately modulated by the guideline's constraints and the client's wishes; as Smith continued, he moved quickly in technical and *political* directions: "The arch came about from the fact that we had to span about 80 feet. If we built over it at all, we had to span it. . . . The arch became an important kind of entry way into the city. Our initial designs did not have it, because I did not think we would win the competition if we spanned over [laughs], but after we won, we were allowed to change it!"

Diane Legge reiterated the primacy of a governing idea:

All of the work I had done in architectural school, plus the work I had done for firms, was very small-scale. It seemed to me that a large project probably *was,* in a sense, a collection of smaller projects put together. *In the end* that's how you tackle it. . . . [Yet] in order to work at a large scale you have to think of it as *a single* problem. . . . We try to reduce it basically to *one* overriding idea that *directs* this very large project. Once that idea is established, and you have tested it and made sure that it *will* work, *then* that idea translates itself into different subsets that influence the components of the project.

Her commentary summons up the idea of the architect's governing role in a complex design process. This role is in almost perfect correspondence with the role that primary producers assume in the flexible, "postindustrial" organization of production.[3] Her concrete example is a vivid illustration of the architect's imagination at work:

So, for example, I am working on a race track for Arlington Park. . . . We believed that the overriding idea of the grandstand in the new complex should be a *long, low* building in the tradition of the older great race tracks. . . . (But we have a much more energetic and large program than you normally see in European race tracks; you can see in section it is a tallish building, because you have to get up to 30,000 people in it.) . . . *The magic of racing is being outside and seeing the horses. So that was the basic idea.* Now, how do you carry that out? You've got to keep the grandstand open; it has to have a roof, but it is not enclosed. The building is as *long* as we could make it: 800 feet long. (We really can't make it longer than that because of price constraints.) The paddock . . . needs to be a place where the pageantry of horse racing in the greatest tradition of the sport is played out, and so we've brought in earth: It's an amphitheater with a great walking ring at the center, and people move from the building out to the track and back into the garden space. So the *long, low* relationship . . . to the ground, to the scale of the horse, of a person, is played out through the whole building. . . . And yet, 30,000 people can be there at the same time, all experiencing this flow of "look at the horses, go out and watch the race, come back and look at the horses," so there is *a flow* back and forth. . . . You think of the massing of the building being long and low in the traditional sense.

In Legge's account, the building's particular *looks* come well after the directive form and the program:

Then, as you begin to think of the exterior, you still keep *that* in mind. . . . So we looked for the larger buildings that you see in the Midwest, and actually barns and stables were very close. . . . The building is all in white, it has clapboard siding on it and long verandas and porches on the back, so it always has a sense of the barnlike roofs that you see in the Midwest. It's all white, like all our barns here, and stables. And you just keep layering and layering the architectural ideas and solutions onto the original concept.

Smith and Legge can use computers both to generate drawings or materials specifications and to simulate how a building would look in its urban context (SOM's software can take a specific site in a specific city and peel it away, like an onion, from different viewing points). Yet there is no way that a computer could have provided the creative effort that seems guided by experience, by the intuition of directive form, and by constraints. In these accounts, the process of design apparently begins, in Diane Legge's words, by synthesizing "literally thousands of ideas and bits of information in our heads."

Both accounts are highly contextual. In Smith's, the urban context seems to immediately suggest the form; the arch is identified later as a physical and symbolic organizer of space—a gateway to the city. In Legge's explanation, the context consists of *precedents*, which she first takes from traditional interpretations of the building type (she accepts both the *character* and formal conventions of the race track grandstand) and, second, *creates* from a Midwestern vernacular, regionalizing a design characterized by its type. Her eloquent references to the imagined movements and evolving feelings of clients inside the building suggest how good she must be at talking to clients.

Neither Smith nor Legge refer to "high" architectural precedents. They are both talking to a lay interviewer, and it may be that only architects with an academic bent commonly use historical antecedents as a sort of shorthand in conversations among themselves. Contrast their accounts with this excerpt from an interview that a Chicago architect conducted with Thomas Beeby (just appointed dean at Yale) about the firm's work:

> Right, there is a progression. First, National Bank of Ripon and the Fultz House were both sort of Miesian/Palladian schemes, with nine-square-bay *partis*. Then, with the Champaign Library and Hewitt Associates, . . . there are free-form figural elements, vaguely Corbusian, as filtered through John Hejduk, juxtaposed with the more Miesian, orthogonal pieces. . . . The bank in Northbrook . . . comes from Kahn, but is also based on a little tomb by [Friedrich] Gilly. It's German, super austere classicism. . . . There used to be this magic little book floating around here, the German neo-Classicists. . . . It had Gilly, von Klenze, Laves, as well as Schinkel.[4]

To the layperson, the account seems unbearably pedantic. It suggests, however, that elite designers may well take their formal cues *directly* from the evolution of types or from architectural history, while nonelite followers take it from what is current. If this hypothesis were true, then while Beeby looked at Schinkel, the ordinary architect would look at what Beeby published or at SOM. In any case, the architect's creativity does not consist of inventing original forms but in discovering how to use form as a directive concept.

For Donald Schön, designing is a reflexive "conversation with the materials of a situation."[5] The designer evaluates the implicit potentials of some initial decisions and considers them in the light of criteria drawn from the normative design domains (see note 2). But constraints were weak and cost did not play any part in the teaching situation Schön studied. Contrast how Charles Gwathmey describes a work process in which thinking-as-drawing plays a large part:

> Bob [his partner, Robert Siegel] and I talk the problem through at length, all the aspects of it. We evaluate all the information and all the constraints and prioritize the components of all the parts of the problem: *site, overlaid with program, overlaid with budget.* . . . We get a *deep* picture of what the problem is. Then we respond *as architects,* not as philosophers or theoreticians. *We take notes that are drawing notes about form and plan and section simultaneously.* Quickly, right after that, there is a notion of image, but it is not preconceived. And we try to make a building . . . whose idea has longevity . . . strong enough in its own right and tolerant enough to adapt, to readapt, to be renovated, and still to withstand as a recognizable valid idea. (emphasis added)

All architects repeat that there is no good architecture without a program, which means that there can be no real design work without constraints. Constraints also mean that the emphasis on *one* directive concept in Smith's, Legge's, and even Gwathmey's account is either provisional or a rhetorical strategy. Once the real process of design gets going, *devising alternatives* becomes an integral part of it. William Pedersen gives another reason that alternatives are fundamental to designing:

> It is one thing to design a building, and another *to convince a client of that design.* . . . I presented [to the City University of New York] what I thought was an excellent solution, but because it was the only solution I presented, I gave them no means of comparison. . . . An architect has the obligation, I learned, to present many possibilities. *Then the logic of the right choice will be more evident.* I went back and worked out six or seven alternate schemes and presented them in clay massing models. The next presentation went much better. I had given them the tools by which they could get involved in the problem.[6]

The overriding importance of program and constraints in real design situations suggests, in fact, that the *active* part of designing involves politics more than drawing or even imagining. Politics means, among other things, trying to commit the client to an idea and deciding what and when to compromise. Joseph Esherick speaks for many architects in affirming: "When I spend time talking to clients, *I call that design.* Same if I am arguing with our central engineer."

For elite architects, design is emphatically *not* only drawing, nor even essentially drawing. It is both creative synthesis and an eminently political activity: the negotiated assumption of full responsibility for construction.

The directive ideas of form (and, just as important, the details of the plan and the construction) must be expressed in the technical language of architectural thinking-drawing. Yet two collaborative and potentially conflicting processes are essential in the formation of ideas and details: what Steven Izenour of Venturi Scott Brown and Associates calls "the tussle" with the client and, just as important, the ongoing critique of a collaborative team. When architects emphasize program, they evoke the client's active or silent presence. But the profession's traditional ideology of charismatic authorship and the related emphasis on directive, and therefore singular, form tend to ignore the vital collaboration of the team. In the offices of great designers, ideology insures (at least for a while) the professional staff's complicity with this neglect.

Returning to the acknowledged "tussle" with the client, Denise Scott Brown's story about the firm's and Venturi's approach to design suggests that excellent designers *listen* perhaps better than others; however, they also know how to stand firm for their directive ideas, once they are formed.

> A lot of times people say things like "You sound as if you really listened to us. You didn't look as if you were going to ram something down our throats." That's very important. Bob *listens*. But there comes a time, and it may be a year into the process, when he says "Look, *it's been decided now*. Don't try to change pieces because it won't work that way." . . . The president of Princeton [University] tells a beautiful story about it. One of the trustees had questions whether that flattened column with the tiger on top in front of Wu Hall should be there at all, and whether it should have a tiger on top. Bill Bowen pushed Bob. He imitates Bob crossing his arms and saying: "I am perfectly *happy* with my tiger." And Bill Bowen said "OK." . . . You try to be as negotiable as you possibly can, but there comes a time when you can say, *even in the tussle*, "Look, for the way this building is happening, you really do need the stairs going in this direction. If you go in the other, then we will need a whole *new* point of departure, a whole new philosophy." Saying "take that element off the building because I don't like it" will lose you your architects. The architects will feel their baby has broken a leg.

So, good design is clearly more than satisfying the client. It is, in Cesar Pelli's words, "*choosing* what you can control, because you cannot do everything." It is quitting a client who wants to mix and match parts of different alternatives, as Joan Goody did, because architecture is not "a Chinese restaurant, where you order one from column A, one from column B." It is Frank Gehry talking about the program for the Los Angeles Disney Concert Hall to the members of the orchestra, one by one, to help *them* find the "Ten Commandments" essential to the project: "One is the fidelity of the musical delivery, and with that the *experience of listening* to the music which connects with the way the lighting works and the room is designed. That means you cannot select an acoustician who comes in and says 'Either you do it this way or like that' because then . . . you are saying that the acoustics is more important than the *experience* of listening to the music."

In sum, not all design is a political activity: Good design *becomes* political because its authors have a competence, and often a reputation, on which to stand, and that gives them authority and something to defend. This competence is complex. It consists not only of aesthetic talent, which must bow to the belief that "everyone has his own taste." It does not consist only of thinking-drawing formal ideas that organize space. Good design is *imagining building*. Among other things that mere building technicians do not normally pursue, this implies the sensitivity to materials for which Frank Lloyd Wright and Louis Kahn are rightly famous.

The architects I interviewed still speak eloquently about materials. Materials do not matter to the architectural imagination because they are precious. Although elite architects like the luxury of expensive materials, they insist that architecture does not depend on it; somehow, they are more articulate when they talk about *cheap* materials, perhaps because there is not much that needs to be said about travertine, except that it does not age well in certain climates.

For instance, Cesar Pelli's long-standing interest in the architectural possibilities of glass dates from his work in the commercial practices of DMJM and Gruen, to which clients came "looking for building, not for architecture." As a designer, he was free to concentrate mainly on the building's enclosure or "skin," for the designs were for the most part standard spaces. Pelli explains that his commitment to glass as a material that is both cheap and architecturally "active" dates from that period:

> Several architectural decisions were necessary to create the appropriate conditions for the delightful surprises of interpenetration and overlap. First is the dominance of the glass wall; the glass is not contained in a frame or hanging from a fascia. Second is the presence of a thin grid of mullions that define the surface of the glass and the form of the building. Third, the thinness of the mullions and their minimum projection . . . do not obscure the reflections; they help maintain the plane of the glass and the tightness of the surface. Fourth, the choice of tinted glass. . . . Fifth, the balance of outdoor and indoor light, which allows both reflections and transparent perception to take place at the same time. Sixth (although minor), the glass wall brought to eye level, where most of the points of reference, inside and out, occur. Seventh, the position of the building in relation to its immediate environment; the environment becomes absorbed in the architecture; through transparency the figure becomes ground and in the reflections the ground becomes figure.[7]

A cheap material like glass became a worthy substitute for stone and a hallmark of classic modernism; Pelli suggests that the fragility and transparency of glass make it now a symbolic medium for a new phase of our modernity.

Frank Gehry also became famous while using the humble, mass-produced materials of the industrial age. The choice was initially dictated by economics: Gehry worked for a long time with tight budgets, very unlike today's $100 million budget for the Disney Concert Hall. His imagination, primarily similar to that of a plastic artist, found enormous possibilities in omnipresent materials like corrugated metal and chain-link fencing.

> What fascinated me about the chain-link from the beginning (I never *liked* it either!) was that the amount of it that's been installed into the world culture is *staggering!* And there was so much denial about it! And when you used it intentionally, everybody hated you for it, and *that* really excited me! . . . I said in one lecture "I do not know what's ugly and what's beautiful," and it got quoted. I said it in the spirit of a lawyer who asks "What *is* the law?" It's a good question to ask. . . . "How do you put a box around this thing they call Law?" How do you put a box around beautiful and ugly? I've been confused about it because things I find beautiful sometimes are the things people find ugly, and vice versa. And they have immediately tagged ugly something that's made with cheap materials.

His friend, the painter Michael Heizer, thought that with expensive, lasting materials there could be a chance that someone, some day, would eventually like Gehry's work. But Frank was more interested "in the momentary and what was going on and how I saw it" than in architectural permanence. The irony is that his stucco and chain-link are holding up better than the precious, fancy buildings: "No, it won't last the two thousand years! but I did a little house in stucco that looks as good as anything, and that was 1964. . . . There is a little travertine building down the street that Dan Dworsky did. The travertine is not as nice as it was; it has lost its feeling, it has lost its spark, where my funny little stucco building has retained the energy I put in it. . . . *It's the idea that counts more than the object.*" Whatever the size, the scale, the function, the environment, and the cost of a project, architecture for these architects *should be* about ideas that transcend mere service to a program. While drawing is only a specialist's "language," *design* is the creative process (technical and political, hence collaborative) that gives content and substance to the ideas. The process is so complex and so difficult that ideas have to be controlled: Ethically, they should not interfere with the client's needs (in practice the client often has the power to forbid this interference). Joseph Esherick says about Frank

Gehry and powerful architectural ideas: They "can actually *help* solve the very particular problem that he has in front of him. But not if he lets his search for a particular *Weltanschauung* get in the way. . . . I think *he* will always remain responsible to the task at hand. Nobody ever said that you cannot give to a project more than what's in your contract." Ultimately, Esherick believes there is so much to think about in designing architecture that it is pure romanticism to think one can even remember the *Zeitgeist:*

> That's the problem with historicism: You've got so much to do that you cannot assume a historicist position without excluding the whole process of design. Nobody I know can integrate it into the complexity of the issues—the methods are sloppy, vague, heuristic. . . . What really happens is that they solve the problem by very ordinary methods *and then* they lay all this historicist junk on it. It is a sort of add-on thing. The same if you have some particular world view: You *have* one, and it exists, but *I* wouldn't be able to *consciously* go through designing with the idea that somehow I am going to express my world view or that of my social group! It is conceivable that I may have two different ideas (and I consider it a failure if I only have two!), and *then* I might say which one is the more likely expression of my particular world view. . . . You can never tell, I might take the *least* likely! The process is very messy and, you know, you just do it!

Good designers trust their own competence. Professional and artistic self-confidence are necessary for the apparently arrogant task that involves *imposing* a form upon a site and *taming* a program, if necessary by means of an arbitrary discipline. In the legend of the genius architect with a manic ego, the formal discipline is an act of the creative will, but, as the designers tell us, architectural form is never invented. It is taken from a historical and typological repertoire and from a canon that, it is true, has been broken open by architecture's most recent evolution. It is to the architects' personal visions of this process of change that I now turn.

MODERNISM, POSTMODERNISM, AND BEYOND

This is not the place to review the flood of literature on modernism and postmodernism; while architectural discourse may have started the flood, it is now a small stream compared to the rivers of literary criticism and philosophical debate. The American architects on whose views I draw belong to different generations, represent different types of practice, and are at different stages of their careers; nonetheless, a majority of them have played an important role in the revision of the modern. Postmodern revisionism is in part a generational challenge. It is intertwined with the intellectual construction of "modernism" as its target. How architects view modernism and its revision obviously depends on their age and professional status; less obviously, the kind of professional transcendence to which they aspire influences their construction of the postmodern passage. They are able to say more about the passage itself than to draw a conclusion from an evolution still in the making. Tolerance of eclecticism, which has replaced the International Style, appears to have left them with a sense of malaise, as if something very important had been lost and could only be recaptured now as a historical memory.

THE DEFENSE OF CORPORATE MODERNISM

Since challengers and defenders need to construct their enemy, it is helpful to start with an interpretation of modernism that brooks no doubts about how it was practiced in the United States. For the late Gordon Bunshaft, "the period after the war, until about 1970, is probably the greatest and most unique building period in the history of architecture. . . . We were building a kind of architecture that was not derivative from anything— maybe that will be bad or good, I don't think anybody can judge now, but it was *unbelievable* and it became worldwide and there was a tremendous amount." Bunshaft does not distinguish the derivative modernism appropriated by American business from the modernism of Le Corbusier (as much his idol as most revisionists') and Mies van der Rohe. Formally, it is the same architecture, and his generation "owned" it. He does not see any difference either between his kind of modernism and the schismatic revisions of architects who try to redefine modernist aesthetics at the source: "The best work that is done today is all modern." There has been *no* revision. Bunshaft limits the postmodern challenge to the eclectic historicism of the "gray" variety ("ugly on purpose," like Venturi's buildings, or "freaks," like Graves's, or "copies," like Stern's), *and it has failed.* He complains about the proliferation of Venturi's lunette windows all over Long Island houses (yet he does not consider houses "important architecture") but never mentions the modernist glass boxes that spread all over the world mainly because they were relatively *cheap* to imitate. He caps his defense by resurrecting the aesthetic enemy of the 1920s and 1930s modernists: "Victorian is now back. If somebody can tell me there is any aesthetic quality in Victorian, I'll eat my shirt. It's all heavy, clumsy, and overstuffed."

Bunshaft's polemic traces an unbroken formal line from the beginning of our century to the 1970s. Other defenses of modernism admit its formal complexity, as does Bruce Graham, who belongs to the cohort of SOM-Chicago partners following Bunshaft.

Graham takes care to distinguish the American modernism of the 1890s from that of Europe in the 1920s, which was "a highly revolutionary movement, inspired by painting and poetry, against the history of Europe, against imperialism, and mainly against the First World War." The first American modern architecture, as Sullivan and Wright have themselves claimed, "was actually a result of building cities in a hurry . . . rather than a negative idea. And it was a search for a democratic expression in architecture, one that expressed the people. . . . The European movements were completely devoid of decoration, while Sullivan and Wright were decorative, and [their] symbols, like the onion, were symbols of Chicago and the Midwest." But when Graham drafts a sanitized version of post-World War II modernism, he does not maintain his previous distinction between ideological and commercial orientations. Graham's Hancock and Sears towers were going up in Chicago when architecture, like other professions in the late 1960s, began to stir. In the late 1980s, Graham was about to retire but was still at the apex of professional power. In my interview with him he took the 1988 special issue of *Progressive Architecture* on private houses and dismissed all but one from the field of architecture with a common theme: "What does this mean to building cities? It's fashion, it's nice, but so what?" This rhetorical move is an integral part of a defensive reaction to the attack on the modernist aesthetic.

Graham (like Bunshaft) appropriates postmodern contextualism for his side, citing the convincing example of his Banco de Occidente in Guatemala City ("The building is not air-conditioned, it is all naturally ventilated, naturally lit, with colors that deal with Guatemala, which is not the same as Mexico, quite different"). By avoiding the accusation of ignoring (or destroying) the context, an accusation frequently waged against the International Style, he thus opens the way to a protective account of the architecture of the 1950s and 1960s: It was only the result of what clients wanted and of what a public insensitive to cities allowed. On the one hand, government ("with a lot of influence from Europe and a lot of Easterners who looked at it as social scientists") dumped people into buildings that were "abstractions."[8] On the other hand, clients prevented architects from putting shops on the ground floor "to bring people in and make the building part of the street."

The 1960s changed the public's perception of buildings and their role: "At first, it was probably in universities, *not* so much Vietnam, as simply a consciousness of looking around and seeing how ugly things were. *And that became a power for architects to use, so we used it*" (emphasis added).

Graham credits Jane Jacobs for much of this change. But for younger architects, it was Vietnam.

THE POPULIST CHALLENGE

Stanley Tigerman makes a forceful connection between events of the 1960s and the discourse of his profession: "Bob Venturi was to architecture what Vietnam was to America: . . . They both made the subject fall from grace. . . . The Vietnam War was one of the most stunning examples of a country coming to grips with its own imperfection. Similarly, architecture was thought to be high art . . . until Venturi came along and pointed out that Las Vegas was part of our heritage and that this was OK."[9] Instead of focusing on the confusion of the 1960s and the complexities of architectural discourse, I will take the postmodern challenge strand by strand.

In the excerpt above, Tigerman, like many of his contemporaries, combines two distinct processes that converged for a time in the delimited field of American architecture: One was the broad social and political ferment of the 1960s; the other a critique of what the aesthetics of modernism had become. The political movement fueled a professional critique that had started independently before the late 1960s. In this composite movement, the definition of the object of criticism determined to a large extent where the challenge would be headed.

Briefly, the different phases of the postmodern challenge were as follows. In the 1960s and early 1970s, the concern of younger architects with their role in society transpired in architectural discourse about form and meaning. In the late 1970s and the 1980s, as the political movement ebbed, discourse veered toward transforming architectural objects; it seemed crucial then to obtain architectural legitimacy for diverse kinds of professional realizations. In other words, the challengers by and large kept themselves within an established professional identity, limiting their defiance to challenging the boundaries of legitimate professional discourse. As defiance ebbed and business more or less as usual returned in the late 1980s, the social and formal dimensions of architecture tended once more to diverge. Because of the legitimacy that had been gained for projects of all sorts, small-scale architectural craftsmanship emerged as a credible alternative to subordinating one's talents to power. Let us consider how these elite designers see different moments of this passage.

Tom Wolfe has flippantly dismissed the barren functionalist vocabulary of the once hegemonic International Style as "workers' housing."[10] Yet its most visible embodiments were quite the opposite: the towers that changed streets and urban skylines in the United States and the world during the long boom that ended in the mid-1970s. A younger generation of architects, having as yet no vested interest in the design of downtown office buildings, could afford to attack simultaneously the architectural language *and* its foremost type of building. Corporate architects could not.

We understand, then, why Bunshaft's formalist defense completely avoids the issue of building types and also why Graham concedes the negative urban effects of freestanding monoliths without questioning their presence or functions; why, in fact, he dissolves objections to the skyscraper's program into a technocratic ideology about the physical "building of cities." We can imagine younger architects responding to Graham that suburban houses for the rich are distinctly less harmful than crowding the world with office buildings, even though they may be just as inane for society and the collective welfare.

Tigerman's combined reference to Vietnam and Las Vegas is more perplexing. First, the barrenness and brutal antiurbanism of International Style skyscrapers had capitalist sponsors. A government fully identified with capitalist interests was waging a savage war against Vietnam, and losing it. It was easy to defy the whole by challenging its parts. Metonymy was a major rhetorical recourse, not of architecture only but of most disciplinary challenges in the 1960s.

An exhausted International Style continued clothing the same tall boxes of capitalist architecture with eclectic detail. For some revisionists (such as the New York Five), opposition meant a search for general architectural principles and a return to a truthful form of modernism. For most architects, it was imperative to find a new kind of urbanism. Many elite designers of the postmodern phase—including Graves, Eisenman, Stern, Tigerman, Venturi, and Scott Brown—started their careers with research into new types of urban housing and planning.

As we have seen, urban renewal was a more proximate factor of architects' dissent than the looks of corporate architecture. Black insurrections responded to segregation and displacement, not primarily to the housing provided, which was always too scarce. Yet the different appearance of public projects accentuated the stigmatizing power of segregated housing, rendered unlivable by lack of maintenance, vandalism, and tenants' problems.

While few architects mistook the public "high rise" for the ghetto, several younger ones discovered architecture's *social* dimension through their work with lower-class communities threatened by urban renewal.[11] This moved them further away from social engineering ideas and closer to conceptions of housing and planning despised by the International Style.[12] For Tigerman, the 1960s were the turning point:

> [It was] the first time I saw a visceral, poignant human connection that would have an architectural implication. . . . The social view was obviously intrinsic to the modernism of Europe in the Teens and the Twenties, but never in America. Because I was teaching and working for the group that Saul Alinsky had put together, a black group on the South Side that was fighting the University of Chicago and the city, and because I was working in Bangladesh, and East Pakistan was on its way to a revolution . . . all these things conspired to subvert the way I had been trained as an architect. . . . At Yale there was nothing that collapsed the distance between an architect and his or her work. What we learned was "Architecture" with a capital A.

This is where Venturi and Las Vegas come in.

The "populist" challengers were not naive about consumer culture. But in order to reject the urban uses of "high" architectural language, they had to find something to put in its place. Venturi, Scott Brown, and Izenour's *Learning from Las Vegas* was therefore serious research in architectural form. It was followed by the exhibit "Signs of Life: Symbols in the American City" and the unpublished *Learning from Levittown*. Scott Brown has explained many times that the research was, first, about trying to extend architectural services to "taste cultures" that have nothing to do with architects' work or upon which it is imposed. Second, it was about analyzing the ugly and ubiquitous cityscapes of America, not to glorify the "ruthless shlock of casino culture," as has been written, but to learn what was architecturally worth preserving—for instance in South Street, Philadelphia, where a low-income black community, assisted by Scott Brown, was fighting a freeway. Third, the objective was to erase the barriers between "high" and populist vocabularies and symbols to make a *modern* architecture, which the Venturis conceive unremittingly as an art of its time. They and many "populist" followers understood both the research and the challenge as exercises in cultural humility; Scott Brown asked rhetorically in a reply to Kenneth Frampton: "Why must architects continue to believe that when 'the masses' are 'educated' they'll want what architects want? I distrust the presumption behind the social critique that a society which gives freer rein to its architects and planners will find its life improved."[13]

Critics from *both* the left and the right criticized postmodern "populism" from the vantage point that sees architecture as uncompromised art. But while a conservative such as Hilton Kramer defended the established "high" art of modernism, a leftist such as Frampton inveighed against

"populist" notions in the name of "critical" architecture, the idea that architecture must sever its ties to (capitalist) modernization.

Frampton had summoned architects to reject the bulldozing, "*tabula
rasa* tendency" of modernism and to divorce architecture from modernization. "The capacity of the body to read the environment in terms other
than those of sight alone" is the public's ability that architecture needs in
order to develop its full potential. Critical architects must heed the tactile
and tectonic principles of architecture and hold them above the scenographic dimension. An architecture of "critical regionalism" thus opposes
"the rhetorical techniques and images of advertising," from which the
"populists" were borrowing architectural purpose. "The *communicative* or
instrumental sign," Frampton warned, "seeks to evoke . . . the sublimation
of a desire for direct experience through the provision of information."[14]
In fact, Frampton's idea of critical architecture returns to an ideological
concentration on the aesthetic and semiotic properties immanent in single
architectural objects, as if they were by themselves capable of reversing
the effects of modernization. The effect is to render the real social implications of building even more opaque.

Ironically, a most representative illustration of the divergent under-
standings of architecture's functions comes from two traditional postmodernists: One is Robert Stern; the other, the influential European "theoretician" Leon Krier, bases his critique of modernism on the counterutopian
vision of a classic preindustrial city that never existed.[15] The object of their
disagreement is the urban-renewal plan for a public-housing complex commissioned from Charles Moore's firm. To Krier, Whitman Village is just
"a kind of nostalgic suburban collage": "It was the ideal of CIAM to build
buildings in the park . . . whereas if you want to make an urban composition
that has some complexity, you need . . . the relationship between public
and private, you need big collective buildings in relation to private buildings, and so on." Stern's counterattack looks beyond buildings and
composition:

> You deny not only the American suburb, but also all those parts of cities you
> admire that don't conform to your view. . . . *This is public housing made to look
> like rich man's housing; it is not made to look like "existence minimum" even
> though it is.* . . . Moore has picked up the thread of making cheap housing in
> the image of luxury housing—a thread, like so many others, which was thrown
> out in the revolution of the '20s.[16]

Stern falls for the illusion that class can be spirited away, but he understands that people sandwiched between a railroad and a highway do not
need any more stigmatizing physical signs than those. Krier completely

ignores both class and race, not least the need for cheap housing in Huntington, New York. In his abhorrence of modernism, he refuses to acknowledge that, in the early 1970s, the likely alternatives to Whitman Village were either bleak modernist towers or nothing.

The final word, however, belongs to Cesar Pelli. In the same debate, he accurately observes that architects are affected by "how good the architecture is, regardless of how good it is for people, regardless of how good it is in terms of signification." At the end of the 1970s, the protagonists of postmodern revisionism were retreating toward the traditional ideology of architecture: What *one* object is (or looks like) reaches universal significance by its excellence—or by its connection to the ideas of beautiful form and truthful expression. In 1977, for the second edition of his pathbreaking *Complexity and Contradiction,* Robert Venturi wrote the usual modest rejection of architectural totalities: "The architect's ever diminishing power and his growing ineffectualness in shaping the whole environment can perhaps be reversed, ironically, by narrowing his concerns and concentrating on his own job." But, astonishingly, he concludes: "Perhaps then relationships and power will take care of themselves."[17]

Should architects accept a limiting program in a project with social merit or refuse to compromise their *architectural* principles? And, having chosen practice over theory, whom should they try to please—the users or themselves—when programs are always determined by clients? Robert Stern argues forcefully for pleasing the client and (hopefully speaking) the user, an attitude that avant-garde architects in the European mode consider the worst sin of uncritical postmodernism: "We are not in the business of educating or transforming human nature. We are in the business of responding to the human condition. We are not reformers or revolutionaries. I don't think that is cynical at all. I think it is much more cynical to say, screw it; they'll understand eventually what it is."[18]

In the careers of ambitious architects, the idea of trying to serve differentiated publics of modest means tends to last for a limited time. As the example of Moore's Whitman Village illustrated, the programs offered to socially responsible architects are limiting, their possibilities and their qualities often insulting to those they are meant to serve. They are easy commissions to discard once greener pastures have opened up. Then, when the main choice is among commissions that are for the exclusive use of the rich (like private houses), or that tend to be used much more frequently by the upper-middle strata than by others (like museums, theaters, or the much-desired commissions in prestigious universities), or that are intended to make their owners rich (like most commercial and developers' buildings), architectural discourse logically turns once again exclusively upon itself and upon the intrinsic virtue of its creations.

The postmodern challenge in architecture started with nonacademic and nonspecialist aspirations. For all architects, the new revisionist concern with the plastic and formal aspects of architecture defied attempts to "scientificize" it and reduce it to construction systems. The political activism of the 1960s merged with the architectural criticism of corporate modernism, going against *both* its style and its favored building types. The early phase of postmodernism harbored hopes of developing a different type of urbanism and significant public commissions. The hopes floundered in the recession of the 1970s and disappeared in the political reaction of the 1980s. The issues of "scenographic" versus "architectonic" value, "historicism" versus "modernism," "signification" versus "craftsmanship" may still be infused with rhetorical fervor, but, to repeat Rob Quigley's diagnosis, "the laypeople couldn't care less what architects think."

By the late 1970s the modern/postmodern debate in American architecture returned to the aesthetic and business components of the professional ideology and ended there. Retrospectively, many elite designers think it was "all only about style." A curious continuity is thereby implied between what modernism became in the United States and its recent revision, since style is architecture's only hallmark in the absence of new programs. For Joseph Esherick, protected against the International Style's excesses by both Bay Area regionalism and his own sense of craftsmanship, "modernism in architecture is a lot of different things, but the attack was on it as a style. . . . That wasn't the issue to begin with, but it was inevitable that postmodernism become a style because it was in those terms that the battle got joined in the first place." Let us consider how some of the protagonists now see the battle and the battlefield.

THE RETURN TO ARCHITECTURAL DISCOURSE

What elite architects say about the transition to (or through) postmodernism focuses on three interrelated matters. First is the place of modernism in the evolution of architecture, on which place notions of continuity or discontinuity depend. Second is the focus on formal freedom and the question of appropriate sources for a contemporary architecture, from which derives the consistency, or the diversity, of architectural vocabularies. Third is the problem of controlling diversity, which entails the question of "scenographic" versus "tectonic" principles or its proxy—applied signs (or decoration) versus structural and technological aspects of architecture.

Much of the academic debate still centers on how the European Modern Movement became the American International Style and incorporates questions that architects asked in Europe soon after World War II. To a revisionist movement that tends to concern itself increasingly with form, the movement's contrast with Europe before *and* after the war seems stark. It appears, in particular, that no other version of the Modern Movement than one reduced to architectural—hence professional—discourse may ever have crossed the Atlantic.

In the evolution of architectural taste, no other architect practicing in the United States has played as important a part and for as long as Philip Johnson has. No one doubts that the set of modernist rules that he and Henry Russell Hitchcock brought to New York in 1932 was already divorced from the collective aspirations of Europe in the 1920s. Johnson doubts it least of all. Divorcing aesthetics from politics was a conscious and deliberate attempt on his part to reconstruct the traditional ideology of architecture. Johnson says it was imperative for him to return "the conception of [architecture] *as an art* and whether [it] looks good or not" to the forefront; he claims to have modeled his attitude on Mies: "There were all those who didn't like Mies because he wasn't an architect who did housing, and he said, 'Well, you give the workers some more money and we can build them some wonderful housing.' Marvelous answer. It undercut all the bleeding hearts."[19] The faith and excitement Johnson says he felt in 1932 were definitely about architecture, not social democracy. Yet the period impressed upon him, the aesthete and arbiter of taste, a specific kind of architectural morality: "I cannot free myself from starting designs with the program as outlined by me or my clients. I know that other periods have begun with shapes and only later shoehorned the uses into the shapes. *I am too 'modern,' too puritan for pure form.* I am, in spite of speeches to the contrary, a functionalist; but perhaps, in contradiction, also an eclectic."[20]

With the perspective of age and historical erudition, Johnson considers that defining clear phases of architectural change, as he once tried to do, is problematic. The traditional emphasis on the history of forms has the merit of simplifying the problem. If one takes the customary characterization of European modernism as an ideological and political movement, Johnson says, then the International Style was ending in 1932, but he could not have known it. He knew, however, that only the epigones took as prescriptions stylistic principles that the masters felt free to apply as they pleased. Now, he sees the aesthetics of the decade 1922–32 as just one polemical episode of antihistoricism that turned dogmatic: "postmodernism is really . . . legitimizing eclecticism, which is paradoxically essentially pre-Modern Movement."[21]

Johnson the postmodernist thus reconstructs a formal continuity longer than Bunshaft's. For if architectural reformism begins in romantic responses to the industrial revolution, the modernist *style* belongs to the *longue durée* of Western architectural history. This is also the stance of traditional postmodernists like Stern, Beeby, or Stuart Cohen or eclectics like Cesar Pelli. Modern architecture is for them the Western architecture that emerged after the Gothic; it is the whole architectural corpus produced by specialized designers of buildings.[22] From the "long" perspective, postmodernism, as Cohen says, was "reentering architecture."

Johnson the modernist indirectly introduces the focus on formal freedom and diversity. Unwilling to dismiss so easily a stylistic revolution that he promoted, he issued in 1977 a verdict about the work of Venturi and Stern applied many times since then to his own skyscrapers: nothing new in plan or section, "essentially coating modern architectural space with a new dress." In fact, Johnson understood early on that postmodernism justified not only "a style for each job" but also the license to experiment, at least in surface, with form and applied ornament. This was his reading of Venturi's plea for "decorated sheds," though Johnson was not about to coat them with "symbols of the ordinary."[23]

Among the elite practitioners who are now in their early or mid-fifties, all except Peter Eisenman recognize that the postmodern challenge, *even* stripped of its social aspirations, gave them three things: a new concern with context, a concern for creating single architectural objects as identifiable "places," and, above all, the freedom to choose formal sources from the entire repertory of architecture. Within the latter, the radical, heroic phase of European modernism can be given the ordinary place of one more historical source. Architects who still consider themselves modernists simply choose *that* source; they too welcomed postmodernism as a movement of ideas in Venturi's theoretical work.

Charles Gwathmey (whom Vincent Scully describes as "unreconstructedly International Style") is a good example:[24] "Learning the lessons of history, for a student from the late fifties and sixties who was in the throes of dogmatic modernism, . . . forced us to a critical reevaluation of why we did things. The postmodern debate was confrontational, motivational. For us, it confirmed our commitment to cubism, to abstraction, to principles that are insistently pure." Logically, since Gwathmey confirmed his stylistic convictions in the debate, he is severe with the work of eclectic historicists. Like Esherick, however, he attacks them mainly on the grounds of craftsmanship and "tectonics," accusing them of having a "sloppy" attitude toward detail and materials. In fact, many architects who, like Gerald Horn or Rob Quigley, bear no grudge against historicist or "pop" allusions (and may even contemplate using them at times) complain about the indirect effects of postmodernism: Architects tend to neglect real technical improvements, and manufacturers tend to concentrate on untested cosmetic innovations, such as the ubiquitous sheets of glass-thin granite.

The fear and resentment here are not based on style but on its implications. The victory of developers' "scenographies" accompanies the reduction in the expected life of an office building from a hundred to perhaps thirty years. The architectural historian Leland Roth comments that "the ethic in building today seems to be 'Don't build anything that lasts beyond the depreciation period allowed by the IRS.' " And another historian echoes the structural concerns of the architects I interviewed: "Unless you use the same materials and methods, if you try to mimic the style of McKim Meade and White [the great Beaux-Arts turn-of-the-century firm], you might be giving your client a headache in twenty years."[25]

For Craig Hodgetts, the issue of architectural vocabulary is profound. He believes that architectural expression is, first of all, *technological:* using the technologies that are available in novel ways and exploring their aesthetic and symbolic capability, in the tradition of the Modern Movement. In the 1970s, Hodgetts was exploring social architecture (industrial park modules, community centers, youth centers, mobile theaters) in a "high-tech" vocabulary. He implies that the emergence and commercial success of traditional postmodernism may have cost him his career: It *"ruined* something that was an important way of working to me. There were *no* clients, simply no one in the United States. That's why Richard Rogers [the architect of the Beaubourg in Paris and Lloyd's in London] is still not built here, because we have a society that is extremely insecure about its lineage."

Traditional postmodernists like Stern, Beeby, Graves, Cohen, and (most ideological of all) the "theoretician" Leon Krier, or the planners Andrés Duany and Elizabeth Plater-Zyberk, curiously echo some of the modernists' architectural determinism. Implying once again that cultural *objects* may have the power to reshape lived culture, they hope to prepare "a cultural resynthesis," or even a regeneration of cities and suburbs, by giving the past a physical presence.

The elite architects who have come out of the International Style opting

for an abstract or a "technological" idiom see postmodern traditionalism
as pure nostalgia for a past that never existed. In what is now a cliché, they
say it is "the architecture of Reaganism." Aware that their own modernism
is just another style in a chaotic plurality, they see in this plurality the true
expression of the *Zeitgeist*. Frank Gehry puts it this way:

> I would say, "Gee, I'm of our time, I'm using chain-link and corrugated because
> it's a time of belt-tightening and unpretentiousness." Well, it isn't. It is a time
> of Reagan and Michael Graves, so I don't know what's of our time. That is my
> interpretation of the present, and Michael is making his, . . . and they both can
> coexist at this time. *That's the present,* that they can both coexist and that's the
> interesting thing, finally.

Less predictable than Gwathmey's, Hodgetts's, or Gehry's is Venturi's condemnation of traditional postmodernism. In the 1982 Walter Gropius Lecture at Harvard, he began observing that traditional, or historicist, postmodernism, as "the major manifestation of the new symbolism," had not
achieved authentic diversity. Not only had it seldom drawn from both "high
art *and* Pop—Scarlatti *and* the Beatles": too often, it had *copied* the past
instead of engaging it in reflexive dialogue. Thus, by lack of irony, postmodernism had failed to illuminate the provisional present. Worse yet,
these unnamed postmodernists "have substituted for the largely irrelevant
universal vocabulary of heroic industrialism another largely irrelevant universal vocabulary—that of parvenu Classicism with, in its American manifestation, a dash of Deco and a whiff of Ledoux. . . . [This] transition . . .
manifests architects' continuing formalist predilection for simplification."
In an indictment reminiscent of Frampton's warning *to him* against the
rhetorical strategies of advertising, Venturi diagnoses the co-optation of the
postmodern challenge: "Formal simplicity and symbolic consistency make
architecture easy to identify, name, copy, learn, teach, promote, publicize,
publish, draw, and exhibit."[26]

Today, architects are bitter about what Venturi's emphasis on repro-
ducible architectural *discourse* was only hinting at: It is easier for the press
to make "stars" when their style is identifiable by the broad public, easier
still when it shows consistency and can be readily appreciated. Architectural
work that lends itself easily to reproduction and diffusion contrives to make
an oeuvre out of single buildings scattered all over the world. This coherent
existence "on paper" is an ultimate blow to the notion of architecture as
organizer of the human environment.

Cesar Pelli, erasing the great majority of architects from view, explains
that the fame of the architect and the constitution of "signed" oeuvres
require eclecticism: "No architect worth his salt is going to say 'O.K., I am

going to design background buildings that nobody will notice.' We don't
have anonymous architecture anymore; there are no anonymous architects.
They all have names and they want their names known. Also, that's just
about the only way today to get new work."[27] The statement could not be
clearer: Architecture and individual architects that clamor for attention are
both easier *to sell*.

If architects' views of the postmodern shift is to be characterized by one
statement, it should be that they look with reluctance at the formal and
stylistic freedom they have acquired. Autonomy within the discursive field
is undoubtedly much greater than in the early 1960s. Yet the elite architects
who have lived the generational challenge of the 1960s are aware that the
fame and glamor of a few do not compensate for the profession's weakness
or its strategic withdrawal into discourse. The glamor, the seductive exemplars, and the heated discourse attract a growing number of recruits to a
perennially weak profession that has trouble guaranteeing them a future.
The freedom to imagine and conceive appears to have been paid with
irrelevance and exacerbated professional segmentation.

Even the most famous of architects cannot be quite sure that their work
is *followed* by anyone. Their manufactured charisma, vested in objects that
may not last, sounds hollow. The temptation is therefore great to reactivate
the old ideology: Perhaps as critiques, perhaps as sources of cultural
change, objects of art can transcend the social relations in which they are
born.

In the next two chapters, I turn to a broader roster of architects and to
a more general reconstruction of the postmodern transition. To close this
analysis of personal accounts, let us hear a voice very far from the "star
system," definitely *of* the professional elite, yet outside the main currents
of architectural discourse. Justifying the Gold Medal of the American Institute of Architects that he had just received in 1989, Joseph Esherick suggests why, beyond modernism and postmodernism, architecture may matter still:

> [This] is an award that goes to a bunch of ideas and attitudes rather than to any
> individual. It recognizes ideas that exist all over this country and a lot of unrec-
> ognized people who are, for one thing, *serious*. I think they have a traditional
> view of architecture: It is just automatically required that it should meet all of
> the technical demands; but beyond that, *beauty is appropriate,* and I think archi-
> tecture ought to make you feel better. It ought to leave people the opportunity
> of being, doing whatever it is *they* want to do rather than fit people into a system
> or a style. . . . I don't think it should necessarily control social requirements or
> make people feel better *for what it does;* it should *never get in the way.* . . . The
> ideal piece of architecture to my mind is one that you don't see.

CHAPTER SEVEN

Mapping a Paradigm's Demise

The View from a Symbolic Reward System

Established professions, academic disciplines, and other organized forms of cultural production periodically bestow honors and distinctions upon some of their members. These annual events represent more than just rituals that call the attention of specialist audiences and the interested public to the names of distinguished individuals. They are exercises of autonomous authority, by which the symbolic gatekeepers of each specialized field try to preempt the judgment of outsiders with their own.

Even in the most insulated fields, producers of culture seldom hold the ultimate "purse strings." Symbolic rewards are therefore easier for them to control than material ones. If, as is often assumed, lack of control over material resources compromises creative freedom, symbolic rewards administered by creators themselves should, in contrast, encourage innovation. However, symbolic gatekeepers have their own personal standing and ideological positions to defend.

How the elites of a field deal with innovation may test their objectivity, but the autonomy of symbolic rewards systems resides elsewhere. Organized producers of culture affirm the superiority of their judgments by striving to establish a "feedback link" between that which they do control and that which they do not. The symbolic rewards that elites grant to their colleagues are intended to impress the elites' judgments on relevant outsiders and to make the acquisition of material rewards more likely. In turn, achievements that bring fortune and public fame are reinterpreted in terms of a field's specialized discourse so as to bring more symbolic recognition.

Both strands in this feedback link reinforce the elite position of the symbolic gatekeepers.

If the qualities that experts choose to reward appear indifferent or undesirable to the outsiders who hold the purse strings, the feedback link obviously fails, and failure is endemic in architecture because the profession's attachment to aesthetic values is often at odds with what clients want most—service and commodity. The symbolic rewards that the profession autonomously grants to itself matter only to special kinds of clients. Thom Mayne of Morphosis, a much-awarded Los Angeles firm, thinks that the clients who plan to use the building themselves are the only ones who care. "With the somewhat shaky clients who are not all that secure . . . they have already spent much too much time and too much money, all this investment on a young architect that nobody knows. . . . You bring them the AIA award, the chapter, the national, *PA*, all the awards, and they feel they have made the right choice and they might make it again." From the point of view of business, awards and recognition by user groups (such as hospitals or school boards) or specialized user-oriented publications (for instance, *Health Facilities Management*) are just as important. In fact, they are more likely to bring new commissions.

Yet, for the design elite constituted by official recognition, the profession's own symbolic rewards are obviously important, and they are also important to any architect who aspires to participate in the making of architectural discourse.[1] Both elites and followers share the feeling that no one understands architecture, or no one cares. The symbolic rewards administered by the profession thereby acquire the aspect of consolation prizes: Like other specialists engaged in esoteric pursuits, architects distribute them to one another to reaffirm the importance of what they do.

Regardless of how outsiders view them, symbolic rewards express the internal dynamics of specialized fields. In a process in which specialists address other specialists, honors and awards embody the models and standards that the field's elites (legitimizing their judgment by their position) want to encourage or uphold. But as standards change, so do the honors and awards that are administered. The evolution of symbolic rewards reflects what constitutes good work, legitimate innovation, and acceptable challenges to cultural authority in the eyes of the symbolic gatekeepers.

Thus, professional awards are both an official badge of approval and a significant indicator of change in a profession's discourse. But we must not forget that awards—like the slick architectural magazines that publish them and other noted buildings—mystify both the collaborative aspects of architectural work and its harshly competitive reality.[2] Design awards help to perpetuate not only the profession's attachment to its artistic identity but also the charismatic ideology of single authorship.

This chapter and the next examine a system of adjudication for symbolic rewards in American architecture over the years 1966–85. In a period that saw the rise and the normalization of postmodern revisionism, the judges' responses to the work of their peers represented deliberate attempts to influence the evolution of architectural discourse. These responses are the data on which I base my interpretation of the shift in architecture.

THE ANNUAL DESIGN AWARDS OF *PROGRESSIVE ARCHITECTURE*

The source of my data is the annual awards program for architectural design of a professional magazine, *Progressive Architecture* (*PA*, in the profession's lingo). It is a fertile source for a number of reasons.

First, the program's declared intention is to identify the major trends in design for the year ahead. The January awards issue is an obvious boost for the journal's wide readership.[3] According to the editor, it is "eagerly awaited by the American architectural community. Even the cynics . . . pounce upon a copy to see who among their colleagues was premiated, to comment upon and to criticize the choices, to examine them (or scoff at them) for indication of current trends."[4] Predictably, the editors believe in the program's efficacy, but so do many others in the profession. In 1967, for instance, at the beginning of postmodernism's ascendance, one judge worried in this way about the three design awards (out of nineteen) given to Venturi and Rauch: "This magazine is going to be coming out in January and every kid is going to be turning the pages and saying, 'Wow! this is it this year!' You'll see half-moons swinging all over the place!"[5]

Second, the program has become a professional institution in its own right. In the thirty-five years since it started, 224 renowned judges "have reviewed some 26,000 submissions and chosen 849 for recognition."[6] In 1980, the medal of the American Institute of Architects recognized *PA*'s design awards as "the catalyzer of the best talent and work in this country for years, producing a lively contest between—and a valid platform for— both young and older professionals to test their ideas."[7]

Being a judge is an honor that the most famous architects are eager to list on their résumés. Cesar Pelli, former dean of the Yale School of Architecture and twice a juror in the period under study, sees the design awards as "the only continuing program of architectural criticism . . . done by top level architects of the selected work of their peers."[8]

Every year brings numerous submissions that are easily recognized as those from the most prestigious names in architecture. Rob Quigley, who was a judge in 1987, describes the screening process:

> There are 700 projects in front of you [in fact, 790 for that year in Architectural Design alone], and the quality level is incredibly high. In the first ten minutes projects by famous architects go on the floor . . . literally on the floor because you have them all on a big table and you start discarding and you know you are throwing Philip Johnson's and Michael Graves's work on the floor. . . . Of course they all submit; they see a *PA* award as enormously prestigious; they all want that sanction from the community of architects. Michael Graves submitted seven projects for one award.

Third, the *PA* awards program illustrates one profession's effort to establish a feedback link between symbolic and material rewards; its goal is "to recognize the most promising architecture before construction, thus supporting forward-looking schemes when they are most vulnerable to compromise."[9] The juries give awards to "paper architecture" (schemes, renderings, plans, and sometimes models with accompanying text). Yet the submissions must be for real clients, even if still in the project stage. The candidates are supposedly close enough to a real commission to have developed fairly complete schemes for their probable client. The program transforms this probability into a symbolic reward, by which it seeks to insure both the commission and the integrity of the design.

Finally, and most important from my point of view, *PA* is the only journal that accompanies iconographic presentations with excerpts of the judges' debates. Caring not to offend anyone, the sanitized transcripts do not reproduce either the most heated exchanges or the actual dynamics of the jury. Still, they tell us a great deal. The excerpts convey the editorial staff's opinion of what was important in the discussions, which judges dominated the proceedings, and what trends are represented in the awarded projects. *PA*'s Annual Design Awards Program can therefore be seen as a complex set of messages that professional elites send to their peers and followers with the important mediation of the magazine's editorial staff.

The awards may be pooh-poohed as irrelevant by the designers who do not get them and even by those who get many, like Steven Holl, who says "an award may give you a little push, but it doesn't make a client find the money if he doesn't have it." But Thom Mayne, whose firm first received national attention through *PA*'s awards, is emphatic in his support:

> The first four years . . . we were working out of my own home. Mike [Rotondi, his partner] was working for someone else, I was teaching . . . and the *PA* awards can be seen as a competition. It is a way of motivating yourself, you know. . . .

Publication is the termination of a project. . . . *PA* is an incredibly useful program, an opportunity for people who are not gentlemen architects, like we certainly are not, to be there, to establish some sort of presence. . . . *For our firm [the awards] did that: they established our presence, period.* It's the only way that you get some kind of recognition, that you become known *within the profession.* (emphasis added)

PA's editor, John Morris Dixon, who has been making a second career in architect selection committees, invokes the insider's knowledge he has gained to argue that awards influence from *within* the development of professional careers:

The word of an award seeps through a network. The influence is not direct . . . it wouldn't get you this or that commission; it makes you more likely to appear on a list of possible . . . anything: possible jurors in a competition, possible participants in an invited competition, possible architects for a job. In a committee for architect selection, everyone is asked to write a list of who should be contacted, and then the list is brushed over and boiled down and everyone is asked for qualifications. When [architects] submit qualifications for a job, all those awards are in there. They never leave them out. If they've been on our jury that's never left out either.[10]

PROGRESSIVE ARCHITECTURE'S JURIES

American architectural magazines do not have the authority of some of their European counterparts or the institutional aura of the American Institute of Architects. The juries and the selection process must give legitimacy to the sponsor rather than the other way around. *PA*, therefore, chooses its judges for their eminence and their representative positions in the field.

In addition, the editorial staff must hold on to the magazine's readership. Balancing the juries is therefore an important concern: If one year's decisions have been controversial, the editors tend to load the next year's jury in the opposite (or in a different) direction. The authority of the jurors is to some extent on the line, and they tend to respond self-consciously to what they perceive as bias in the previous year's awards. This double balancing may impart a pendular movement in style and type to both the awards and the entries. The contestants, knowing the judges' names through the program's announcement in June, often tailor their submissions to what they assume to be the jury's preferences.

Thus, in a time of growing eclecticism, the choices of both *PA* jurors and editors may tacitly induce a yearly pattern of action and reaction. Yet, as we shall see, the turning points in the *PA* awards juries correspond faithfully to turning points in the profession's discourse.

The editors' concerns with readership and with professional legitimacy command the basic composition of the juries, while the magazine's "trendiness" means that the editors will try hard to represent the leading edge of architectural discourse. John Morris Dixon says that the only selection rules are serious reputation and regional balance. Yet a former member of the editorial staff insists that the magazine adopted parameters that are not merely geographic, but stylistic and technical as well: no more than two "avant-garde" designers, as long as they were well known, and always one juror to represent concern with social issues, user needs, or technical solutions. Geographic spread used "to mean a West Coast architect, until the Californians became too 'avant-garde.'" Then balance had to be sought elsewhere, and such questions as "Does anyone know somebody in Arizona?" started popping up at editorial board meetings.[11]

The expert in technology is often an engineer, as if in recognition that few architects are competent to judge complex technological issues on their own. Similarly, it was acknowledged after 1971 that architecture and planning have taken separate paths; a team of two specialists was invited thereafter to judge the entries in urban design and planning. Since 1974, the eight-member jury has consisted of three teams: four judges in the most numerous category of architectural design, two each in urban design and in the new category of "research." After a first day of screening, the jury comes together in the last day to discuss each team's nominees. Architectural design invariably elicits the most disagreement.

The juries' debates provide a direct insight into the making of architectural discourse. The choice of jurors, the jurors' choice of winners, and the editorial staff's choice of comments worth recording give us, over the years, a microcosmic view of the recent history of American architecture, built or unbuilt. Although the entries give substance to the symbolic gatekeepers' reflections and delimit their range of choices, the rejected entries (which would be the architectural historian's choice object of study) are unfortunately not available for analysis. For the sociologist, the juries themselves, in their capacity as symbolic gatekeepers, are the real protagonists of the awards rituals.

Analysis of their debates confirms, first of all, one theoretical assumption: Judgments of architectural quality are inseparable from normative conceptions of the architect's social role and from realistic concerns with practice. From 1966 to 1985, one revisionist tendency emphasized architectural aesthetics abstracted from program and function. Yet even that exclusive emphasis on the autonomous evolution of form may be construed as a strategic response to the practical circumstances of the profession (see Appendix).

The years 1966–85 may be considered a period when one paradigm was destroyed but no other rose to take its place. My analysis starts in 1966, the year that Robert Venturi published *Complexity and Contradiction in Architecture*, his call to reject a frozen and reductive modernism. I look at this beginning in the first section. In the second, I explain the importance of the private house in the juries' debates. I use it, in the third, as a tool for mapping the emergence of different revisionist trends.

THE ONSET OF REVISIONISM

When the awards program started in 1954, the hegemony of the International Style seemed assured. In the early years, the juries "talked a lot about 'good design' and 'work that could be truly called progressive,' but they rarely spelled out exactly what they meant; it was assumed that anyone would know what was meant and that any explanation or justification of the jury's choices would be superfluous."[12] The first *PA* First Award went to the Back Bay Center in Boston, a multiuse development by an "all star" team that included Walter Gropius's Architects Collaborative, Pietro Belluschi, Carl Koch, and Hugh Stubbins; the project itself was a megalithic expression of urban-renewal modernism. Yet, even then, jurors of impeccable modernist credentials found the ensemble of submissions poor in "gaiety, excitement, fancy."

Three years later, Thomas Creighton, then the editor of *PA*, noted "an obvious, restless search on the part of many talented people in many parts of the country, for plasticity and an expression which has an emotional, rather than a withdrawn intellectual impact."[13] Among other "new but backward-thinking movements," he detected a trend (which was to dominate the *PA* contest during the years 1958–63) toward neoclassical forms and symmetrical compositions.

Even through the lens of a symbolic reward system, even "on paper," modernist hegemony seemed fragile. No sooner was it recognized by the incipient program than it began to be challenged by judges who partook in the "restless search" of the late 1950s. The dissatisfaction of the elites betrayed the profession's seeping discontent with its own interpretation of an imported style.

Ten years later, aesthetics were subsumed under a larger challenge. For John Morris Dixon, *PA*'s editor since 1972, intellectual and political questioning, which aimed at the core of the profession's identity, rushed an always partial stylistic consensus to its demise. "Good or progressive design is *no longer the sole criterion for premiation;* in fact, in recent years some juries have seriously questioned whether design, as it is traditionally understood, should even be a criterion for judgment.... Now the jury questions even the program, and asks whether a building should happen at all."[14]

The 1960s and 1970s were years of ferment for much more than just American architecture. Politics energized American culture; multiform attacks spread outward from many centers against all that was taken for granted. The men and women who came of professional age in those years, especially if their own youth or their ties to the university kept them in contact with the student movement, were not likely to remain untouched. On *PA*'s juries, the men and, since 1974, the women placed among them in response to the feminist movement, also could not ignore what was happening.

Frank Lloyd Wright had died in 1959 and Le Corbusier in 1965; Mies van der Rohe and Walter Gropius were to die in 1969; despite the important presence of Louis Kahn, there was no successor in sight. In 1966, architecture as a cultural force was without leaders and seemingly without direction. In his editorial for the 1966 *PA* awards issue, Jan Rowan commented: "Dissatisfaction with much of the work currently being done is increasing each year.... Different jurors, with different backgrounds, experiences, attitudes and aims make remarks that are becoming repetitively similar; the only change is the increasing intensity of dissatisfaction." For Rowan, the problem was the frustration of architects subjected to "lack of vision and direction on the part of those whom they serve—individual clients, corporate clients, institutional clients, and society at large."[15] But the 1966 judges diagnosed a different, endogenous disease: "overdesign," the exaggerated display of architectural skill.

Only Charles Bassett, partner in the San Francisco office of Skidmore Owings and Merrill, represented unalloyed International Style aesthetics on the jury. Kevin Roche was the collaborator and successor of Eero Saarinen, known among architects as an early advocate of "a style for each project." Vincent Scully, Yale's charismatic architectural historian, was an early critic of corporate modernism and a supporter of both Louis Kahn's and Venturi's departures from the canon. William Conklin, the designer of the new town of Reston in Virginia, had a strong reputation for sensitivity to context and an early commitment to preservation. Even the jury's engineer, August Komendant, had been for years Louis Kahn's consultant and collaborator.

The reaction against buildings that tried "to knock your eye out" became this jury's consensual criterion, as singled out by Scully: "These winners probably represent on the part of the jury *a tendency toward selecting the most modest project,* toward urban renewal, toward the working out of a few simple problems. . . . What we're really having here is a movement out of the '50s when monumentality developed."[16] Kevin Roche, an architect not noted for inconspicuous design, complained that every project was "based on an exercise considerably beyond the needs of the problem," and Bassett joined him in deploring the immaturity of the submissions ("You give a guy a box of sand, and by noon he's got a mountain!"). August Komendant, on his side, implied that "art" is to blame for design without principles: "Architects . . . think architecture is art, but it isn't. There must be guiding principles behind it. So many of these designs are too rich, too soft, without principles. . . . How much Lou Kahn there is, but done so badly!"[17]

The judges' condemnation of overdesign conveyed their sense of being at the end of an architectural era. Lamenting the exhaustion of inventiveness that marred the submissions, Scully implied that there had been better sorts of monumentality: "When you look at this group . . . the general effect is not sculptural at all, but is a kind of weakening out . . . of gentling out of a lot of the forms that were around a few years ago. . . . We are representing a kind of disgust with [monumentality's] last and sick phases."[18]

Their preference for modesty, however, did not extend to the designer's role. The charismatic conception of the architect as artist lurks in this unattributed exchange about the Second Award, an alternate urban-renewal scheme designed by Troy West for a Pittsburgh citizen group:

—It has the passion of one man's image.
—A very strong scheme, and therefore gratifying in the abstract sense to the architect. I'm reacting to it as a great building and huge, empty spaces.
—The steps go up, but the building they're going toward goes down, which is really a sensational thing. It's such a great *ruin.*
—The resultant form has nothing to do with what's going on. It's preconceived form.
—All art is form, and form is the meaning of any work of art. In architecture, all conceptions, all attitudes, all studies in the end are form. . . . You have the embodiment here of a tremendous force, of a terrific and . . . tragic vision of the character of life. It's not a good solution or a bad one. It's a tremendous and moving and stupendous sense of what it is like to be here in the vast city.[19]

The jury's call to abandon heroic aesthetics appears to proceed from a tightening of formal standards, not from a revision of professional identity. To the five different judges on the jury, architecture seemed to have veered so far toward sculptural grandiloquence and surface innovation that they rejected all formal experiments as trite. Still, they bestowed their First and Second awards to grand and ambitious projects: In Cesar Pelli's and Anthony Lumsden's First Award for a new urban nucleus in the Santa Monica mountains ("the first time I have seen a city which is a building, where the whole community is a building," as one judge put it), the governing ideal is still the total control of the built environment, the creation of whole public spaces through the design of single buildings.

To Scully, a veteran of the battles against the destruction of New Haven by urban renewal, the rejection of modernist planning was political. It was practical for Conklin, who had realized an alternative in Reston. The logical response to isolated monuments was the concern for the urban context apparent in Scully's vague exhortations to "design . . . for the way the street ought to be."[20] Five years after Jane Jacobs's epoch-making *Death and Life of Great American Cities,* this group of designers did not have an alternative sense of urban public space to propose against the comprehensive planning derived from the Modern Movement, other than to respect streets that were still there.

The call for restraint in the design of single buildings appears as a moral as much as an architectural plea. Yet caution and restraint did not count for much in the jury's conception of the architect's authority. From 1966 to 1985, the tension between a utopian (or perhaps even a critical) vision of architects' social role and a realistic assessment of their modest capacity for social intervention underlies the debates of *PA* juries.

The design entries considered by *PA*'s judges feature different building types. In discussing them, the juries implicitly assign different values to different kinds of architectural practices. This is nowhere clearer than in their responses to the single-family house, which, throughout this period, is a focus of implicit confrontation between the ideology and the practice of architecture.

THE HOUSE AS DOUBLE METAPHOR

"There are only four cases where an individual house is not embarrassing," Vincent Scully declared in 1966: "(1) if it is a specially useful prototype of a mass urbanistic development; (2) if it does something really important on a street or a square, to teach us something about urban design; (3) if it represents a breakthrough in plastic imagination, even if it might not be justifiable in terms of a house; or (4) if it is ironic, and thus expresses the human condition."[21] Scully does not say anything specific about how the single-family house could meet common needs and be beautiful or about technological and economic efficiency. Underlying his criterion of architectural legitimacy, we find, in the following order, references to (1) the classic Deutsche Werkbund concern with *Typisierung*, the elaboration of standardized prototypes appropriate for mass production;[22] (2) the emergent emphasis on adjusting single interventions to the urban context; and (3) the architect as creative artist, for whom the private house is a field of experimentation or the medium for an existential statement.

Scully's prescriptions for the architecturally valid house avoid the tension between professional service and art characteristic of the architect's idealized identity. He makes no reference to the profession's obligation to serve a client and a site well but gives equal weight to the potential for affecting the environment on a large scale and the creation of formal or symbolic values. He thus transforms the difficult tension between "commodity" and "delight" into the difference between large-scale problem solving and artistic expression, which may come in any scale.

In deeds and words, Scully had expressed his conviction that the foremost duty of architects is to struggle for the humanization of redevelopment plans, if necessary by working directly for the government.[23] The implications are different when architects with corporate clients (architects such as Bassett and Roche) deny the architectural legitimacy of the private house. By dismissing small-scale practice from the domain of "important architecture," they restrict the latter to projects that are no less privately owned yet become "public" by their sheer size.

We shall see next how the recognized and the ignored architectural functions of the house fared in the juries' debates. In brief, Scully's emphasis on *Typisierung* did not seem utopian in the mid-1960s, despite the intensification of the Vietnam War and the domestic consequences it portended; the Housing Act of 1970, for instance, was still ahead. The waning of government support for public housing and the eclipse of large-scale work during the recession of the 1970s would change the juries' notions of what was possible. But it was not economic realism alone that compelled them to readmit the single-family house, on its own merits, as part of "Architecture." Inside the profession, revisionism mounted a multipronged attack against what the elites identified with modernism considered exemplary.

Architectural critics responded, on the one hand, to urban protest, for which stopping urban redevelopment often was an immediate objective. On the other hand, a major revisionist strain asserted the primacy of design and of meaning, for which any building type could be the vehicle. This was a strain identified with theorists (notably, Peter Eisenman at the Institute for Architecture and Urban Affairs) and young architects with strong ideas and small practices.

To illustrate how the house becomes a sign for all the divisions of architecture, let us skip forward to an exchange among the divided judges of 1977:[24]

DINKELOO:	We have too many houses. If this is architecture, let's forget it.
HODGETTS:	The houses have content; at least they have ideas.
DINKELOO:	The individual house has no place in American culture any more.
HODGETTS:	Rather than 'no place,' it has a *rare* place.
GWATHMEY:	The house has always been a critical reference point in design. It is a complex building. Architects learn by doing them.
HODGETTS:	An expensive house can afford to be an important benchmark. They should be as idiosyncratic as possible.
GWATHMEY:	*We are tending to make value judgments about houses that we don't make about other building types.*[25]

So why does this particular building type serve as lightning rod for the different values held by divided professional elites?

A preliminary consideration is that the majority of *PA*'s architectural entries almost always consists of private houses. Because residential commissions represent a good part of the practice of small and beginning firms, the private house is a good symbol of the artisan side of architectural work.[26] In the juries' debates the single-family house becomes a metaphor for each side in the antinomies of professional practice. In this sense, the house is an ideological proxy for the opposition between the rationalization of professional work in large firms and large projects, on the one hand, and the practice of architecture as a craft and perhaps an art, on the other hand. As a symbol for the organization of architectural work, the house metaphorically sums up a chain of implicit oppositions. These extend from the substantive opposition between "corporate" and "artisan" forms of practice to much larger ideological antinomies: art and business, traditional and modern organization of production, fantasy and discipline, frivolity and seriousness. This is not all, however.

Expensive private houses are an obvious symbol of the architect's dependence on wealthy individuals. Taken as metaphor for a subordinate and trivial professional role, the house governs a different set of ideological oppositions, best summed up by the contrast between house and housing. This set counterposes the socially inconsequential design of single objects to the comprehensive shaping of built environments; individualistic self-expression to collective responsibilities; the private to the public dimension of architecture; architecture as art to architecture as service to society; and luxury to need.

As a metaphor for both actual practice and ideal social role, the house generates two different sets of semantic oppositions. The judges must evaluate *program*, which embodies the clients' mandate, and *design*, in which architects manifest their competence and imagination. Their evaluations entangle the two semantic sets. Displacing terms and meanings from one large metaphor to the other, the judges' emphasis moves back and forth from program to design, according, no doubt, to the relative quality of different types of submissions but also to the ideological position the judges defend.

By keeping the building type constant, my focus on the single-family house allows a clearer view of the contending positions in a self-transforming professional discourse. The juries start with a technocratic notion of social responsibility, expressed in a modernist bias toward large-scale work. While they do not critique urban-renewal projects directly (in part because exemplars seldom reach *PA*'s contest), their critique appears indirectly in the revaluation of the private house. It proceeds from two main sources: One is the priority accorded to design over program, thus overriding the service aspects and the social function of architecture; the other is a concern with preservation, opposed by definition to the wholesale demolition of the existing stock of buildings. In both cases, as one critic notes, architectural discourse tends to confuse "disalienated" objects (buildings that have been saved from the ordinary fate of for-profit construction—ugliness or sterile functionality—by either inventive design or preservation and reuse) with the utopian disalienation of the social relations housed in these buildings.[27]

THE PRIVATE HOUSE AS A BAROMETER OF CHANGE

In the first years of the period 1966–85, few juries were interested in private houses. Then, in the 1967 *PA* awards, postmodernism made a strong appearance in Robert Venturi's "architecture of allusion" and in the presence of Charles Moore, another leader of the movement, among the judges. Musing over Venturi and Rauch's four submissions, the planner

David Crane summed up (with unwarranted optimism) this jury's ecumenicism: "I am interested in the fact that in the next twenty years we are
going to build as many cities as we have already built. Someone like Venturi
is not interested in that; he is interested in individual, particular, special
things. But I agree . . . that *architecture really is bigger than either my
architecture or Venturi's; it's a more inclusive thing.*"[28] The inclusive line
thus reconciled the design of single architectural objects with that of whole
environments. In 1968, the judges' twelve awards (among which were one
house, a church, a chapel, and a high school addition) appeared to continue
the same line. And yet, though much had happened between the lines in
1968, the judges contradicted the professional diversity recognized by the
awards by their unanimous endorsement of large-scale projects as architecturally superior.

Lawrence Anderson, dean of Architecture and Planning at M.I.T., identified large projects with progress. Since the future of materials development resided in industrialized construction, the individual house was not
important to him, "not on the technical end, anyway." For the planner
Richard Dober, "a multi-client aspect" explained the higher quality of
large-scale work, and SOM's engineer Fazlur Kahn, the brilliant designer
of the type of structure that supported the tallest buildings in the world,
concurred: "The large projects seem almost always to be *more rational*. . . .
One of the reasons . . . is because large projects involve more people and
bring in other disciplines as a total team." The architect Gunnar Birkerts,
known for his industrial, corporate, and institutional practice, underlined
that the new and challenging problems posed by large-scale projects were
"really purifying for our profession." Finally, Romualdo Giurgola, the noted
architect and educator who had come from Rome to study with Louis
Kahn, began by observing that the issue was not size but meeting "the real
needs of today," yet he immediately corrected himself. Because architects
could not take large design projects as "a personal exercise," the greater
discipline required by these projects made them *architecturally* superior:
"A more genuine architectural language has always been set by projects of
a comprehensive nature that have influenced the character of smaller
ones."[29]

The 1968 jury had many large institutional projects and two remarkably
innovative experiments in low-cost housing from which to choose. Their
bias, which can easily be stretched to include corporate modernism,
appears not in the nature of the awards but in the slippage in the emphasis
of architectural meaning: from socially responsible large projects to the
virtues of large scale per se. This slippage associates design discipline with

"multiclient" and "multispecialist" teams, emphasizing both technical innovations that require economies of scale and aesthetics that can be gen-
eralized across building sizes. Conversely, the small-scale projects are
denounced—in Birkerts' words, for extreme "form-consciousness" that
leads to the fashionable monotony of sloped roofs and diagonal lines. "The
older guys [meaning more established architects] did not go for it, because
they have a chance to play around with the real stuff, and big things too."[30]

The attribution of intrinsic superiority to large-scale work reproduces
the notions of architectural significance reflected in the established professional hierarchy and in accepted career patterns. The 1968 judges did
insist that the individual house should be a "laboratory for experimentation," but this seems no more than a cliché, belied by the notion that large-
scale work (and, indirectly, the program) is the primary generator of innovation. In successive years, as the *PA* editors begin to include the revisionist
representatives of small "idea firms," the inclusion of what might be called
"boutique architecture" becomes less of a token gesture.

In 1970, two architects of equivalent though antithetical fame—Robert
Venturi and Bruce Graham of SOM-Chicago, the architect of the Hancock
and Sears skyscrapers—pick up the issue of the single-family house. Venturi places it neatly on the artisan side of architectural practice:

> On one level, this kind of house is insignificant and is not responding to the
> social crisis. But in a funny kind of way you solve problems by indirect routes,
> and who can say that the little house for the rich man is not one of them.
> Architects don't get many research grants as yet and especially for a young man
> who is lucky enough to have a rich uncle, it's a fine opportunity for experi-
> menting. . . . *I think the architect is essentially a craftsman who can do what the
> society allows him to do.* . . . Thank goodness there's an opportunity for the
> young architect who does not want to go immediately into an organization to do
> his individualistic thing!

Graham's response mixes and displaces meanings from the two metaphorical sets:

> You could use [a house] as an experiment with the technical tools. For instance,
> if someone has designed an expensive prefabricated house, it would be very
> relevant. It also gives you the opportunity to create new spaces, a kind of poetry,
> an experiment with a new way of life. A lot of people resent this since it implies
> that their present way of living isn't so good. . . . I am not really interested in
> anyone's love affairs, therefore I'm not interested in a house that becomes too
> personal—then it's not really for others to discuss. I think *it has always been
> true that great houses have had social impact.* . . . Breuer's early houses . . . were
> all related to one another so that they became a sequential group of *art forms,*
> and for this reason . . . they were very important.[31]

Starting with technology (as a good modernist should), Graham moves quickly to embrace its "opposite," architecture as art. Endowing art with the capacity to change life, as did the European modernists, he nods in passing to the criticism of architects who impose their own preferences on the users. Then, in a sarcastic tone, he opposes the personal dimension of a small-scale design and the collective responsibility of architecture. But he refers to the architect's social role only to confuse it, as he equates "social impact" with great art in a specific reference to the Bauhaus architect Marcel Breuer.

This is still an ambiguous and reluctant endorsement of the designer's ability to transcend even inconsequential programs. Art transcends service *if* it acquires a direct social function. The ambiguity disappears in later juries with the affirmation of the tendency that Richard Pommer has aptly called "architectural supremacism."[32]

"Supremacism" appears in Peter Eisenman's 1975 pronouncement that the architectural potential of the house lies precisely in the fact that its program is well known, conventional, and insignificant: "Most other types of buildings differ from houses precisely because the functions are so explicit; consequently they have no room for any kind of statement about iconography, meaning or intention; the ideas are subsumed in the program."[33] Eisenman's tribute to the house relies on the building's potential as a metaphor for the architect's ideal role but *reverses* the positive values, from social responsibility and service to self-expression and art. Yet the preeminence of design over program is an ideological position that corresponds to specific conditions of practice. Supremacism is therefore still addressing, even if silently, the antinomies of practice evoked by the first house metaphor.

This was 1975, two years into the worst recession since the end of World War II. The New York Five had just been created by the Museum of Modern Art and the press. Peter Eisenman had been at the helm of New York's Institute for Architecture and Urban Affairs since 1967. His architectural record consisted of unbuilt projects and a few houses, as did that of Michael Graves, Eisenman's former colleague at Princeton and fellow member of the New York Five. Seven years later, during the shorter recession of 1981–83, Graves had won the Portland and Humana competitions and left small-scale work behind. Nevertheless, in the *PA* jury of 1982 he still traced a mixed connection, romantic and realistic, between design talent, the private house, and the architect's practice.

In that jury, the planner and feminist historian Dolores Hayden complained about the award conferred to Ralph Lerner, a young man on the

Princeton faculty: "This mountain-top palace for a Brazilian tycoon seems to come out of the far distant past, when one thinks about architecture as a service for the very rich and the very remote." Graves rushed to his colleague's defense: "I would be quite delighted to have this architect design a city hall or a children's home or almost any other kind of project involving the public at large because of the incredible sensitivity to . . . [our] size and proportion . . . as we occupy the rooms . . . [and] as we identify collectively."[34] While Graves sees talent as an inalienable asset that the individual transfers from project to project, the hidden reference to the constraints of practice is unmistakable: Young architects demonstrate their talent in whatever way they can. Viewing residential commissions with favor and asserting the primacy of design thus merge in defense of the potential of architects who do small-scale work.

In fact, the ideological "art" element present in both semantic sets is what joins the individualistic, artistic side of the house as metaphor for the architect's social role to the "artisan" side of the house as metaphor for architectural practice. This joining, however, is not only ideological: it involves a realistic assessment of the work available to architects—young and not so young—in hard times. Recessions, we could fairly say, make realism compulsory.

In 1976, one year after Eisenman's proclamation of design, the entries were reduced to an all-time low of 462; nothing seemed to deserve a First Award for architectural design, but four out of ten citations went to private houses. The architect Arthur Cotton Moore voiced the jury's regret that good multifamily housing projects and planned developments had been as absent as good commercial buildings: "The major thing that's going to happen in cities is commercial and speculative investment development [a prescient statement, as we know]. . . . The few submissions we had were inept, obviously indicating that *the architects had no actual power or causal role in these things*. They were absolutely just fluff. . . . In the end we have to fight like demons to keep from picking all single-family houses."[35] Raquel Ramati, juror for planning and urban design, noted that even in the very competent plans she had seen, the architect's influence was missing. Nor were architects involved "in the design of suburbia or of mobile homes, where most people really are affected." Stating the obvious, she confirmed Moore's interpretation: Architects' concentration on the house was a strategic but forced retreat "into an ever smaller realm where [they] can operate."[36]

To conclude this point: The revisionists' reappraisal of the single-family house proceeds from an ideological view of "pure" design that reflects the practice of architects with nothing better (or bigger) than single-family houses to do.

Concurrently with the rise of "architectural supremacism," a complex revaluation of the house was emerging from the critique of large urban complexes and from the preservation movement. The preservation movement's historical beginning may be traced in the accounts of the East Coast architects I interviewed. John Morris Dixon remembers "about 1960 marching to save Penn Station," the grandiose 1910 building by McKim Mead and White, replaced by the drab anonymity of Madison Square Garden Center at the end of the 1960s. The preservation movement, Dixon believes, reversed more than a decade of academically induced, doctrinaire contempt for historic architecture:

> I think our generation [he graduated from M.I.T. in 1955] had a kind of aversion to recognizing the value of historical structures. . . . But as soon as these things began to happen, you had to think of what it was about these buildings that made them worth preserving. I had had very little exposure . . . only *one* course, in my senior year, at M.I.T. Seeing them as I did, working on the AIA Guide for New York, I began to learn to identify and distinguish historic styles.

Preservation and contextualism compose what I call a principle of "environmental nondisturbance." In a blanket reaction to modernist urban renewal, it induces a revaluation of the house as a potential art object, not *despite* its program but *for* its nonobtrusive program. Let us examine the steps involved in this reassessment.

Disdain for the single-family house is a logical complement of the "large-scale bias" that transforms the undeniable public impact of large projects into a significant public good. This bias is aligned on the public, collective side of the house metaphor, bespeaking the architects' ambition to play a significant social role. But significance is a contested notion, as is the role of architects in large urban complexes that rarely satisfy the users' conception of what is good. The ambition to have a positive effect on collective welfare reflects long-standing utopian aspirations. But the exclusion of the users from the planning and design of public projects almost inevitably gives a technocratic slant to professional ambitions. In contrast, the single-family house can be revalued as an antidote to the invasive and technocratic implications of large buildings. Both the preservation movement and the emphasis on craftmanship are pivotal in this new set of attitudes toward the urban house.

Preservation appeared in the 1960s as a middle and upper-middle class response to the destructive invasion of cities by urban renewal. The juries' taste for different architectural vocabularies shifted various ways during the period under study. Yet preservation and reuse became the focus of a movement that outlasted, for instance, the concern with energy-saving design following the 1973 oil crisis. The *PA* awards began to reflect this crucial change of attitudes in 1969. The award given to James Polshek for the headquarters of the New York State Bar Association—three old townhouses renovated and connected by a multilevel terrace to a new building in back—was hailed by Roger Montgomery "as possibly the most portentous of all the projects that we finally selected," a sign of modern architects' "coming of age . . . in terms of their leadership of responsible preservation efforts."[37]

Preservation obviously influenced the architecture of historicist and vernacular allusion that architects call "postmodernism," although architects express regard for the past in different ways. One way is *image*, which emphasizes fitting single buildings into their environments by choosing appropriate proportions, vocabulary, and ornament for their facades. Urban contextualism preserves the preexistent architectural order by "writing in" new components, as it were, in a compatible design language.[38]

Contextual and sympathetic design applies to all building types, but the house comes in through the preservation movement's essential concern with program—more exactly, with making preservation and reuse a premise of all new programs. Thus, with its simple, conventional, and flexible program, the relatively nonintrusive town house becomes a favorite object of the urban "nondisturbance principle." At the same time, its constructional complexity redirects the designer's attention from formal innovation to craftsmanship, another facet of the house as metaphor for antitechnocratic architecture.

The potential for successful collaboration between architects and users is more likely to be realized in a small and manageable project, especially one as dear to its occupants as the private home, than in any other kind. Thus, as the metaphor for *practice*, the house may come to represent a "publicness" more subtle than what either large size or collective ownership imply: In the process of applying expert knowledge, diminishing the distance between the professional and the layperson is a way of opening the process and increasing the client's access to knowledge. However, gentrification and other types of residential reuse in cities most often limit the reduction of distance to relatively affluent clients. The antitechnocratic potential thus remains circumscribed within the relations of good craftsmanship.

The craftsman does not look to change the canon of his or her métier but to produce a lasting object, adequate to its functions, its circumstances, and its users. In architecture, attention to the program predisposes the craftsman to respect the environmental considerations imposed by the site. Although the concentration on doing a task well for its own sake can apply to all projects, it is compromised by the complex division of labor (and by industrialized construction) in the largest ones. Small scale makes it possible for the professional to practice architecture as service, design, and construction.

A craftsman tends to respect traditional type-forms—conventional cultural notions of what an office building, a factory, a school, a church are supposed to look like. Despite its merits, this respect for type-forms appears conventional by contrast with loftier architectural aspirations. Craftsmanship and propriety tend to be prime criteria of evaluation when the juries, having withdrawn from technocratic ambitions, also become critical of an abstracted notion of "Art." In a period of paradigmatic demise, these criteria are insufficient to reconstruct a consensus.

The conflict of standards was strikingly illustrated in 1978, when the presence of Natalie de Blois on the jury subtly infused gender into the debate. She resisted giving a First Award to a large suburban residence and was outvoted by Charles Moore, Richard Meier (the most prominent of the New York Five, known for uncompromising aesthetic purism and allegiance to Le Corbusier), and Edward Bain, partner in a first-rank Seattle firm. The implicit ideal of a well-crafted, adequate solution runs through her objections to equating overdesign with art:

> Richard likes it because of the form, I dislike it because of the form. The forms and the spaces inside are so confused, the whole thing is so arbitrary that the resulting spaces are small and cramped. . . . It is tedious to approach the building on the long walkway. There is no service entrance for the kitchen, for bringing in groceries, removing garbage. . . . An enormous amount of space is used for circulation . . . [and given] to closets, to toilets. There has been an awful lot of effort to create a jungle gym on the outside.

Charles Moore's rebuttal is remarkable: "Given the incredible and altogether gratuitous task that he has taken on, . . . [he] does manage to bring it off with power, verve and a sense of danger." He responds to a casual question by de Blois that such a house could not have been designed by a woman: "It has a kind of aggression that one has associated with males. With all my strong reservations about it and my sense that it is just on the verge of collapse and chaos, I'm strongly attracted to it and I want to give it some really fancy prize."[39] While the three men took the large family house as "the appropriate setting for an experimentation process," it is difficult to imagine a woman endorsing power, a sense of danger, and male aggression *in a house*. Craftsmanship informs de Blois's sense that a house should serve the client's purpose with propriety and within conventions, the opposite of an "incredible and gratuitous" task. It also restrains her from encouraging originality.

The house, as building type and metaphor, has held program constant, letting the emphasis on design per se fluctuate according to the jury's position. The contending positions are now in place, but they are not permanent: modernist dogmatism is definitely on the wane. Yet there is not one clear successor. For this reason, eclecticism must be tolerated. The architectural supremacists' emphasis on design admits historicism for single buildings and contextual "blending in" as much as daring, idiosyncratic, theoretical new departures from modernist abstract geometries. While the concern with preservation and "nondisturbance" nourish both historicism and a return to the craft of building, the connection with art and theoretical developments remains more closely wedded to audacious formal invention. On both counts, the notion of the architect's social and public role appears to be either suspended or drastically revised.

We may proceed now to analyze the chronological transformation of architectural discourse during the period 1966–85. This period encompasses two declines of construction during the 1960s, the severe recession of 1973–76, and Reagan's recession in 1981–83. At its center, there is a professional crisis. The juries' debates increasingly reveal the double toll taken by the economic recessions and the internal crisis of meaning. Architectural supremacism, which makes a clear entry into the jury's debates in 1975, is a turning point. I take the priority accorded to design as an attempt to find a symbolic resolution for the internal crisis. This ideological reordering cannot resolve (even symbolically) the real crisis of the profession, but it still becomes a principal axis of the postmodern transformation.

1.   (Above) Le Corbusier. Plan Voisin for the rebuilding of Paris. Model. 1925. Courtesy of the Museum of Modern Art, New York.

2.   (Below) Maya Lin. The Vietnam Veterans Memorial, Washington, D.C. 1982. Photo: Charles Larson.

TWO STARKLY DIFFERENT VISIONS

3. (Above) Walter Gropius. Apartments at Siemenstadt, Berlin. 1929–31. Photo: Roland Schevsky.

4. (Below) Bruno Taut. Hufheiser Siedlung, Britz,
Berlin. 1925–31. Photo: Roland Schevsky.

GERMAN SOCIAL ARCHITECTURE IN THE 1920s

5. Ludwig Mies van der Rohe with Philip Johnson.
Seagram building, New York. 1956–58. Photo: Ezra Stoller.
Courtesy of Joseph E. Seagram and Sons, Inc.

THE ARCHETYPAL TOWER OF MODERNISM

6.   Philip Johnson John Burgee. AT&T World Headquarters, New York. 1984. Photo: Richard Payne.

AN ARCHETYPAL TOWER OF POSTMODERNISM

7.   (Above) Venturi and Rauch. Vanna Venturi's house, Philadelphia. 1962. Photo: Rollin la France. Courtesy of Venturi Scott Brown and Associates.

8.   (Below) Joseph Esherick and Associates. Sea Ranch, Calif. 1965. Photo: Peter Dodge. Courtesy of Esherick Homsey Dodge Davis.

REVISIONS AND DIFFERENT VOICES

9. (Above) Stanley Tigerman. Daisy House, Porter, Ind. 1976–78. Photo: Howard N. Kaplan. Courtesy of Tigerman McCurry.

10. (Below) Robert A. M. Stern. Residence at Chilmark, Martha's Vineyard, Mass. 1983. Photo: Wayne Fuji. Courtesy of Robert A. M. Stern, Architects.

11.   Esherick Homsey Dodge Davis. An early example
of urban reuse: shops at the Cannery, San Francisco. 1966.
Courtesy of Esherick Homsey Dodge Davis.

12.   (Above) Cesar Pelli. Pacific Design Center, Los Angeles. 1971–75. Photo: author.

13.   (Below) Michael Graves. Municipal Services Building, Portland, Oreg. 1980. Photo: Paschall/Taylor. Courtesy of Michael Graves, Architects.

14.   (Above, right) Kohn Pedersen Fox with Perkins Will. Procter and Gamble Headquarters, Cincinnati. 1985. Photo: Jack Pottle/ESTO. Courtesy of Kohn Pedersen Fox.

15.   (Below, right) Cesar Pelli and Associates. World Financial Center, New York. 1981–87. Photo: Cesar Pelli. Courtesy of Cesar Pelli and Associates.

THE INCORPORATION OF POSTMODERNISM

16.   (Above) Venturi Rauch Scott Brown. Gordon Wu Hall, Princeton University. 1980. Courtesy of Venturi Scott Brown and Associates.

17.   (Below) Kohn Pedersen Fox. 333 Wacker Drive, Chicago. 1979–83. Photo: Barbara Karant. Courtesy of Kohn Pedersen Fox.

ARCHITECTS' BREAKTHROUGHS

18.   (Above) Adrian Smith/SOM. Rowes Wharf, Boston. 1987–88. Photo © 1987 Nick Wheeler/Wheeler Photograhics. Courtesy of SOM.

19.   (Below) Diane Legge/SOM. Race track. Arlington, Ill. 1989. Photo: Hedrich-Blessing. Courtesy of SOM.

20. (Above) Gwathmey Siegel. Taft residence, Cincinnati. 1977. Photo: Richard Payne. Courtesy of Gwathmey Siegel and Associates and Richard Payne.

21. (Below) Michael Graves with Alan Lapidus. Disney World Dolphin Hotel, Lake Buena Vista, Fla. 1990. Photo: Steven Brooke. Courtesy of Michael Graves, Architects.

THE CONTRASTS OF PLURALISM

22. (Above) Frank Gehry. Edgemar Center, Santa
Monica, Calif. 1984–88. Photo: Tom Bonner.

23. (Below) Peter Eisenman with Richard Trott. Wexner Center for the Arts, Ohio State University, Columbus.
1989. Photo © Jeff Goldberg/Esto.

HOUSING IN THE 1980s

24. (Above, left) Joan Goody. Renovation of Harbor
Point, Boston. 1989. Photo: Anton Grassl. Courtesy of
Goody Clancy and Associates.

25. (Below, left) Koning, Eizenberg. Affordable housing, 5th Street, Santa Monica, Calif. 1988. Photo: Grant
Mudford. Courtesy of Koning Eizenberg.

26. (Above) Rob Quigley. Baltic Inn, San Diego, Calif.
1987. Courtesy of Rob W. Quigley.

CHAPTER EIGHT

The Autonomous Transformation

Paper Architecture, 1966–85

In 1966, the *PA* judges recorded extreme dissatisfaction with the architecture they were seeing. Though normative in tone, their response to the submissions was mixed in content. They recommended aesthetic modesty while desiring for the architect an implicitly powerful role.

A deliberately nonmonumental and simple architecture is not incompatible with important interventions in the built environment. In our century, antiheroic architectural standards and high social impact have marked the alliance of modernism with social democracy. However, in the mid-1960s, the architectural profession was on the verge of discarding a modernism that had become frozen and unprincipled at the same time.

As the last unifying hold of the modernist paradigm dissolved, confusion increased. In the juries' debates, the internal crisis of the discipline became apparent in the disconnection between program and design—the constitutive elements of architecture that symbolize, respectively, social function (through the mandate architects receive) and aesthetic competence.[1]

The professional elites who serve as gatekeepers in the *PA* awards program have no client, no sponsor, and no user to please, only themselves and their peers. Their debates represent, therefore, highly autonomous instances of professional discourse. In this chapter, I consider those debates chronologically and analyze, first, the rise of architectural supremacism in a profession marked by the political impact of the 1960s. I show this rise not as a paradox but as a strategy for restoring professional identity. Second, I examine how the contest about the place of image and sign in architecture intensified as an ambiguous outcome of the formalist strategy.

The lionization of celebrity architects by the "star system" and the use of their signatures to valorize both real estate and luxury objects parallel, ironically, architecture's loss of power as a specialty of construction. Architectural formalism insists on the "art value" of architecture. Calling attention to the transformation of art and artists into commodities highlights only one of the contradictions that plague architectural work. At the end of this period, contradictions and structural weaknesses return, unresolved, to the center of the juries' preoccupations. After the phase of struggle and polemics, the irreducible pluralism of postmodern architectural discourse may be interpreted quite simply. It mirrors the conditions of practice in the contemporary United States, meeting their structural divisions with a conciliatory eclecticism.

1966–75: THE RECLAIMING OF DESIGN

When architects respond to specific programs, they work with type-forms. As David Crane put it to the 1967 jury: "We start with names for certain problems—house, shopping center, apartment building, etc. These names have already designed it before we start."[2]

The variety of building types expresses a complex and changing hierarchy of social needs. The type, importance, and visibility of the buildings are already present in their programs, which connote the unequal professional status of the architects from whom they are commissioned. In contrast, the concentration of architects on design stresses the distinctive competence shared in principle by all legitimate practitioners. It thus reaffirms professional unity. The problem, however, is whether the diversity of type-forms admits any common quality of architectural design beyond basic technical competence.

The modernists' answer to nineteenth-century eclecticism was a unified interpretative framework or style. The abstract geometries and industrial forms of the new style sought to express the idealized rationality and the universality of modern construction. As a by-product of its postwar triumph, the modernist style was stretched and weakened beyond recognition. Postmodern revisionists then moved to disconnect aesthetics and symbolism from construction, opening the door to a plurality of design codes. We have seen some judges meeting the disorder of resurgent eclecticism with principles that were moral as much as architectural—such as the recurrent generic appeals to simplicity and modesty. Others welcomed the new ecumenicism of taste.

On the one hand, the inclusive architecture proclaimed by Charles Moore in 1967 admitted the ineradicable diversity of architectural types. Inclusiveness subsumed professional inequalities within the embrace of one profession, in which all can produce "architecture." On the other hand, the disconnection of aesthetics from construction dissolved common standards of judgment, forcing the juries to judge a work as being "good, of its kind." To many architects, this meant that the professional elites were incapable of issuing any coherent message about what architects are *supposed to do*.

Yet, as long as all other things were equal, the expanded conception of architectural legitimacy replaced an exhausted aesthetics with a sense of liberation and discovery. So it was for the 1969 jury. Meeting after a 6 percent rise in the volume of new construction, judging more entries and picking more winners than in 1968, the jury exuded a tone of exalted optimism. "The pluralism of aesthetic intentions today is something we have to recognize. . . . Everything is alive simultaneously," declared Roger Montgomery. His sanguine advocacy of Lester Walker and Craig Hodgetts's expandable, demountable, and economic rental building for an industrial park—"Come on, be bold, do something, make a gesture. Brave New World is around the corner!"—echoed Cesar Pelli's forecast: "In five years . . . there's going to be a radically different architecture. . . . *We are not concerned with objects anymore, but with process. We are not concerned with detail, but with emotional responses. We are not concerned with order and clarity, but with excitement.*"[3]

Process is activity, not product; emotional response and excitement are effects, not criteria of good design. The jury's First Award was conferred in part on an effective *image*. Witness this exchange between Cesar Pelli and Lewis Davis, principal of a respected strong-service firm in New York:

DAVIS: We're not in control of what we build or how we build. The politicians
           are making the decisions; the bureaucrats are doing all the planning;
           and whatever drifts down to us we do the best we can. . . . And the
           technological, industrial breakthrough is not going to be made by the
           architects. It's going to be made by Boeing, or GE, or Westinghouse.
           They have hundreds and hundreds of architects working on this right
           now.

PELLI: The First Award is dealing with technological images—not technology,
           but a technological image. *Images are what architects deal with.*

R. M. Gensert, the engineer on the jury, had to remind the architects that the image of architecture as progressive technology was no longer persuasive:

GENSERT: Architecture should express occupancy of the building and not the
             Machine Age. This so-called new image is a loss of identity. It says
             that what goes on inside a building, where it sits on the site, and
             how it relates to other buildings is meaningless. You could put this
             on a mountain or . . . in a valley and you'd get the same thing.
PELLI: Like a car.
GENSERT: I don't live in my car.
PELLI: You sure do. More people have cars than have houses and the same
             car is used in Texas or in Alaska, New York City or Dubuque . . .
DAVIS: I don't feel we're giving it a "design" award but a "message" award.[4]

Architects learned to exalt their own social role through the symbolism of
futuristic technological icons in the progressive modernist battles of the
1920s. As Robert Gutman ruefully remarks, "Expressing technological
ideas through symbols and images makes architecture *appear* relevant,"
even when architects have lost technological control to other specialists in
the construction process.[5]

In 1969, designers whose vision was still governed by the geometric
forms and technological allusions of modernism could develop a common
symbolic strategy. In following years, the proliferation of aesthetic codes
made it increasingly difficult for the judges to agree. Short of explicating
their reasons, most of them appeared content to have their own preferences recognized, if necessary by trading off one award for another.

As the juries retreated toward case-by-case adjudication, the basic
dimensions of service and craftmanship took precedence over the divisive
issue of design but left the disciplinary crisis unaddressed. Service, indeed,
ignores the architects' artistic and theoretical aspirations, while craftmanship, in its characteristic concentration on the perfect object, rises only
occasionally above the isolated building. Neither one resolves the problems
of conceptual and symbolic content brought forth by postmodern revisionism. The architect Earl Flansburgh noted in 1972 that technological competence is not what makes architecture: "The fact that an extremely difficult problem has been overcome . . . to me only brings [the architecture]
up to ground zero. I think we should not give an award if the problem was
difficult, if the architect simply solved it but did not advance the art."[6] Yet
the crisis of modernism meant, precisely, that architects no longer agreed
on what was art. And if there is no agreed-upon stylistic code within which
to work, it becomes impossible to appraise "advances." Furthermore, the
plurality of design codes only compounded that of professional roles.

In different ways, each possible way of being an architect was called into question in the 1960s. Take, for instance, the design of mass housing. Critics within the profession anathematized technocratic "big projects," yet independent architects had practically no part in the mass production of suburban houses or mobile homes. Or take urban planning and redevelopment: The influence of architects was challenged by the rival profession of planning, yet architects shared the blame for the displacement of former residents and the awfulness of buildings. The modernism of the large architectural firms continued to thrive, yet a new generation of architects attacked it from below for its sterility and subservience to business interests. The expanding alternative careers in the academic world brought regular income to teachers of architecture yet could not help them put their new ideas into practice. The growing academicization of architecture nourished the intellectual debate but contributed also to what critics have called graphism, "a fascination with the evocative power of drawings and models."[7]

In this situation of disarray, architects looked outside their field for some compelling way of reconstructing the parameters of their discipline. Two European scholars identify "populism" and "scientism" as the two main ways. The former took user participation as the sole determinant of good design, putting it in place of obsolete stylistic norms; the latter sought to make architecture "rational" by means of imported scientific methodologies.[8]

Scientism officially entered the process of symbolic rewards in 1974: The *PA* awards program recognized architectural research as a separate category. A good part of what came under this rubric incorporated changes in construction technology that minimized aesthetics.[9] Populism, under the tutelage of Community Development Grants, inspired the search for alternatives in community architecture and advocacy planning. Attuned to this development of the 1960s, the 1975 jury made user needs (or the methodology to represent them) into a normative standard of *PA*'s urban design awards.

In the architectural juries, populism emerged in the democratization of both building types and symbolic sources. Charles Moore was the first to argue in 1967 that architects must become the interpreters of popular culture. He praised Venturi's submissions as an effort "that seems to me of enormous importance, to include a set of allusions to our cultural heritage à la T. S. Eliot and allusions to the pop life that would hopefully bring a set of architectural forms into a much deeper meaning for the people who are using them."[10]

Architects like Moore and Venturi were pursuing an iconography and a

set of associative symbols to which large strata of users could relate immediately and with delight. To some critics, this pop-art inspiration either led
to an objectionable revaluation of kitsch or was a mockery of low-brow
taste, performed ironically for the pleasure of the cultured public. In the
1970 jury, Timothy Vreeland objected to Venturi himself that a symbolic
architecture was impossible; architects, he said, did not share symbolic
codes with the vast public. Venturi rebutted:

> We live in a communication era teeming with symbols. Don't forget that words
> and letters, which inundate almost all of our environment, are symbols. *We like
> to say we haven't an accepted set of symbols the way the Middle Ages had, but
> we do, via all the advertising media, in great variety and complexity.* The valid
> base of often superficial supergraphics is that it is architecture connecting with
> the idea of communication in space.[11]

We must note for future discussion that Venturi accepts without qualms
the metaphorical passage of architecture into the dematerialized realm of
signs. Turning then in reciprocal praise to Charles Moore's First Award,
he added his well-known plea for the "ordinary." Moore's Pembroke College Dormitory at Brown University

> in one sense is symbolic because it is ordinary architecture and is symbolic in
> being ordinary. But in another sense, it is anonymous and fits in very beautifully
> with the programmatic way of living of college students who really want to do
> their own thing in this building and *there's no reason why the architect should
> be doing his personal thing.* . . . In its anonymity, [this architecture] marks the
> stage before the symbolic appliqué comes back. Architecture is now in
> between—the architecture itself is the decoration; this is doing all it can to be
> commonplace . . . and can thus *take* the decoration.[12]

The architect acknowledges that it is not *his* meaning that matters. Yet at
no time does Venturi suggest that an architect ought to yield either his
authority or his strategic interests to choices determined by "the people."
The architect designs the structure and will also design the applied decoration that Venturi wants to bring back.

Here, the designer's task is to provide the anonymous (though decorated) shed where the users live as they want and create their own meanings. Venturi phrases the architect's mandate exclusively in terms of design,
keeping it securely within his professional purview and forestalling moves
to wrest control away. But he offers no solution to the problem of standards.

Timothy Vreeland had intimated that "ordinary" architecture runs a
double risk: failing to convey its popular symbolism to "the people" while
losing in aesthetic persuasion and turning off the "happy few." Vreeland's

alternative was to emphasize the technical mastery of structural and mechanical construction. But technology does not go beyond "ground zero," and it is the monopoly of engineers. Design thus remains the crucial thing.

When symbolic gatekeepers cannot strike a balance between constructional and aesthetic competence; when they reject formal experimentation but no longer have a formal tradition on which to rely; when they distrust innovators yet are bored with the commonplace, the notion of good architecture seems to dissolve. Professional service and technical competence often appear as recourses against trendiness, as in these representative positions:

> The results of the jury's work seem to say to me that we are voting against fashion fascism. . . . Perhaps this jury is saying that *there are no establishment rules, but only tasks to be tackled.*[13]

> Just take a guy who has an office and he has a problem. . . . What is the body of information . . . that he can lean upon to help him solve it? *It's a tradition.* He can make a competent response. I object to using the word *architecture* as "the art of it," because it's so subjective.[14]

> Some very old fashioned basic questions . . . like the clarity of circulation and the clarity of the process of building and how that comes through in the space itself . . . get sacrificed or ignored for the sake of a certain literal kind of architecture, an architecture that has its roots in words and in abstract geometry rather than in space and the light that goes on in space.[15]

But old-fashioned common sense is dull. The following position is equally significant: "The only things that catch my eye are those things which indicate a new direction or a fresh approach.[16] The problem, as we know, is that there are no clear standards and no tradition by which to judge the merits of novelty. Judging each case on its own merits, the juries of the early 1970s concentrated instead on the architects' response to the programs. In the heated political climate, they gradually shifted their doubts from the service itself to that which architects were asked to serve. Questioning the programs became for these professional elites a corrosive exploration of the legitimacy, and ultimately the powerlessness, of their profession.

In 1971, the latent tensions between program and design took an antiarchitectural and antiprofessional tone. The jury rewarded the following: a fifty-five acre retreat in Texas, in which the designers provided only three anchoring points for a VW camper and one masonry fireplace, for being "non architecture—nature" or, at least, "a different kind of imagery"; the "straightforward anonymity" of an office building in Oregon; and the idea, not the concept, of modular housing by Fred Koetter and Jerry Wells— three programmatic options which, were they to become prevalent, would eliminate most of the profession's work.[17]

Other juries exaggerated the architect's responsibility not *to* but *for* the program, as did Moshe Safdie and Earl Flansburgh in discussing the 1972 awards:

SAFDIE: We attach a responsibility to the architect in having gone along with any program. . . . That is where our value judgment comes in about how land should be used.

FLANSBURGH: Let's say that an architect questions whether or not a school should be under a railway and, having questioned it, finds it is physically possible, and he has successfully done it, even though it may not have been anything we thought ought to have been done.

SAFDIE: It is crazy for us to give recognition to a scheme that has solved something which we think in the context of schools is wrong.[18]

Unlike the antiarchitectural choices of 1971, this kind of questioning leaves the professional assumption of competence and authority intact. However, challenging the program to the point of turning the commission down places the architects' function in jeopardy, forcing them to admit that socially responsible architecture is impossible.

In the context of the symbolic adjudication of the early 1970s, some gatekeeping elites were urging others to question the program while presumably continuing with "business as usual" in their own practices. Their dialogue during these years is marked by rhetorical sensitivity to social concerns. The mounting doubts are compensated by a sense of professional solidarity.

Thus, in 1973, one juror reminds the others that the submissions "were sent to P/A by architects to be judged by architects . . . because existing procedures, processes and institutions have not satisfied real, given problems that have to do with what architecture is." In other words, "what architecture is" matters mostly, if not exclusively, to other specialists, and the autonomous award process gives it the recognition that practice cannot. And Hugh Hardy, of the New York firm Hardy Holzmann Pfeiffer, a rising architectural star, adds, "At least it isn't gloomy. . . . People haven't given up. *It may be silly and naive, but they're still out there trying*—which is remarkable, really, considering where the society stands."[19]

Shifting the blame to society is a realistic justification for going on with business, but business would not continue "as usual" for long. The recession hit building and architecture in 1973. At the end of that year, Paul Kennon, the director of design of Caudill Rowlett Scott (one of the largest firms in the United States, based in Texas) prefaced the jury's expression of interest in preservation with the warning that "we are running out of money as a nation."[20]

The economic downturn amplified the crisis of standards and the turmoil within the profession. In the face of grave external difficulties and of internal uncertainties about architecture, the settled normalcy of professional life seemed an impossible pretense.

Meeting in the middle of the recession, the architectural jury of 1974 conferred nine citations and only one award, for the recycling of an old factory building in Massachussets. The architect and planner Barton Myers proposed an award for "the concept of urban homesteading, although it was not submitted, to call attention to that and other movements in housing." Although his colleagues on the jury refused to change the terms of the award program, they adopted Myers's message. Devising titles that stressed the moral implications of different kinds of projects, they put "Recycle" and "Environmental Response" on the positive side; on the negative side, their strict design categories ("The Machines" and "Le's Maisons," from *Mad* magazine's parody of the New York Five's cult of Le Corbusier) ridiculed the two most fashionable idioms of the moment.[21]

The judges did not see their quest for responsible performance as moralizing but as good policy, a way to rebuild credibility in the midst of a serious economic crisis. Jacquelin Robertson, urban design juror with Denise Scott Brown, gave a more direct and practical response. To Scott Brown's criteria ("quality of life, way of life, and kinds of living in these environments"), Robertson saw the need to add a nontraditional roster of client groups. As he affirmed, unexceptionally: "If the client groups effectively don't include developers, then architects will have only a tiny effect on what is built."[22]

In the middle of the most severe recession since World War II, the majority of architects must have been well aware of the fragility of their professional status. A collectivity in crisis is more likely to seek reassurance in the restoration of traditional identity than to plunge forward into uncharted lands. Neither the critique of programs nor the extraarchitectural concerns of the early 1970s were likely to reduce professional anxieties.

In this context, affirming the importance of design and formal search restores the traditional occupational identity of the architect. On the *PA* juries, the move was announced by Peter Eisenman as early as 1975. Uncommonly articulate and cultivated, Eisenman was committed by force of circumstances to developing architecture *theoretically*. He started by making his position clear: "For the record, I would like to say that in contradistinction to last year's jury, this year's reasserts the necessary aspect of architectonic quality and development toward a solution, as opposed to process only or good intention. *I think this restatement of the architect's role, the spatial answer to a programmatic statement, is reassuring.*"[23]

Eisenman did more than just reassure. Having stressed the intrinsic virtues of design as the specific competence of the architect, he moved then to propose a full-fledged ideological interpretation of the architect's role as avant-garde artist. Here is how he praised an expensive house in a dense Miami suburb by Rem Koolhaas and Laurinda Spear:

> This house is above all a critical gesture at architecture today and at society.... It breaks from the Corbu tradition; there's no Venturi, no Giurgola, none of that; it's a-stylistic and that's what I like about it. It's one of the few submissions that makes a comment about the suburb, the private house, the way it occupies space, about the metaphorical nature of our personal lives. *It's a kind of utopistic gesture in the midst of this awful middle-class suburbia; it thumbs its nose at the middle-class,* and in the end it's a poetic gesture of the sort you can perhaps only do in a private house.[24]

This rapid turn away from the wider social role that architects had sought during the 1960s may surprise. But Eisenman appeals, on the one hand, to the ideological assimilation of aesthetic with social and political avant-gardism.[25] On the other hand, the profession's disarray called for a restorative strategy.

For the critics Tzonis and Lefaivre, the emphasis on design is a recurrent "narcissistic" reaction of architecture to market downturns. Narcissistic formalist emphasis makes the architectural object "precious, alluring, desirable"—in a word, saleable.[26] The plurality of design codes legitimized what it was economically imperative to explore: the search for a more seductive and widely pleasing architecture. Within the profession's new discourse, one could invoke Venturi's intellectual authority in justification of symbolic forays across the barrier between "high" and "popular" culture.

Nothing, however, was further from pleasantness than the architectural intentions of Peter Eisenman. His contempt for traditional postmodernism was declared; his experiments with linear or planar elements generated abstract forms; what he described as "a logical and linear sequence of moves" presupposed and revealed, as in chess, the existence of rules. In a written dialogue with himself, Eisenman justified the hermeticism of this work: "When one denies the importance of function, program, meaning, technology, and client—constraints traditionally used to justify and in a way support form-making—the rationality of process and the logic inherent in form become almost the last 'security' or legitimation available."[27] In *Oppositions,* the heavily theoretical journal edited by Eisenman, the critique of modernist architecture, which had started as the critique of a socially embedded activity, had rapidly become disembodied. In his analysis of the journal's eleven years, Vincent Pecora notes that "opposition" becomes purely internal dissent within the discursive field of architecture. In that shift "can be read much of the development of postmodernism as a self-proclaimed 'deconstruction' of an earlier and monolithic humanist tradition. . . . Architectural thinking once again reveals where the primary critical values are always already to be found: in the defamiliarization of built form by built form, in the autonomous dialogue of architecture with itself."[28] In this internal dialogue, Eisenman's ideological assertion of the primacy of design had unintended consequences. Design is only the *general* ability to provide spatial answers to a program. In severing appearance from structure, the demise of modernism had multiplied the conventional idioms of architecture; the *looks* of the architect's spatial answers had become indeterminate. Architectural supremacism could heretofore be invoked to legitimize *any* kind of stylistic experiment.

To recapitulate: aggravated by the economic recession, the disciplinary confusion of architecture had endangered traditional notions of professional identity. Reestablishing design and the development of form as central criteria of excellence was a restorative strategy. It strengthened the shared and distinctive competence of architects but was unable to reunify the aesthetic codes.

Moreover, since form can be explored graphically, the primacy of design helped reduce the generational "achievement gap," for it allowed young architects to produce and be taken seriously "on paper." In other words, it allowed them to start their careers without waiting for rare commissions. "Graphism," however, could not provide constructional experience, and it left untried architects open to counterattack by their more experienced elders. In the following ten years, underneath the stylistic differences, we find the PA juries rephrasing the profession's historical cleavage between art and service as a conflict between formalism and construction. This opposition captured, without resolving, the structural divisions of the profession.

1975–85: CONJUGATING CONTRADICTIONS

By 1975, pluralism was on its way to official acceptance. Yet the formal and stylistic diversity of the submissions could not please all the PA judges at the same time.[29] The debates of this period show various strategies by which the juries implicitly sought either to contain or to deny professional disunity.

The rarest strategy by far was the deliberate choice of one stylistic tendency over the others, as happened with "traditional" postmodernism in 1980. The typical strategy was agreeing to disagree, either procedurally, by accepting divided votes, or substantively, by finding projects that offered something for everybody. This strategy compromised the rearticulation of common standards, but any effort to rearticulate them would have been divisive in the crisis atmosphere of the 1970s. Later, with construction on its way to recovery and "style" or "image" as common scapegoats for what was wrong with architecture, that effort became less divisive. Redefining standards became almost a ritual of the 1980s juries.

The main line of conflict in 1975–85 was drawn between the predominance of images and a more traditional holistic conception of architecture. Predictably, what the PA judges thought of a project on paper often contrasted with their opinion of it as built form. But in all cases the juries were judging only drawings. Therefore, the contrast is only symbolic; it connotes a cleavage, with generational overtones, in their way of *imagining* architecture. If, as Henry Cobb suggests, the training of an architect "should be about learning how to construct a concept of space through graphic means without actually having to build a space,"[30] then the more seasoned and pragmatic architects should be better able to imagine buildings from drawings and also less willing to suspend this act of imagination.

Large-scale commercial projects objectively contribute to the practical separation of structural and formal responsibilities. On the one hand, the predominance of industrialized construction tends to limit the architects' intervention to exteriors, public rooms, and circulation schemes.[31] On the other hand, the recent appearance of trained construction managers further tends to take away from architects the function (traditional in the United States) of coordinating multiple building specialists. In contrast, custom-made, small-scale projects allow architects to retain craftsmanlike control over the building process.

It is logical, therefore, that the cleavage between "paper" and "built" form should have appeared many times in the discussion of single-family houses. We have tracked it in Natalie de Blois's objections to the three

men on the 1978 jury, while its generational connotations were clear but
unexpected in the systematic alignment of the modernists Harkness and
Dinkeloo against Gwathmey and Hodgetts. Here is an example:

HODGETTS: OK, there is a need for "commodity" building, architecture with-
               out a capital A, but it is not award material. *Society needs a cer-
               tain stable and comfortable framework, but it is not the architect
               who needs to do that.* Architects can stimulate, they can focus on
               certain very important things. To me the role of a jury involves
               that too.

HARKNESS: Do you have to have an "idea," or can you do something that
               might have been done ten years ago and you are doing it well?

GWATHMEY: What makes architecture a great place is where ideas are work-
               ing, where there is *speculation.*

HODGETTS: Is [the architect] a technician who moves forward with a lot of
               craft and aesthetic sensibility, a curator, or a space explorer?[32]

One would expect the younger architects to defend what is truer of smaller
projects than of big commercial ones: the crafting of design, the careful
control of building by ideas. They are, however, in open polemic with their
elders' experience. Their vague notion of architectural "ideas" descends
from an ideological rejection of the axiom that form emerges from structure.

   In turn, the older architects choose to read the advocacy of "ideas" as
a cavalier attitude toward the client and as professional irresponsibility.
Thus, while Hodgetts justifies the complex abstraction of Peter Eisenman's
House X because it has "two lobes," one for the support of the family, the
other for the intellectual nourishment of the architectural community, Dinkeloo blurts out: "You're saying 'If you can find a sucker, let him have it!' "[33]
More gently, Natalie de Blois had answered Richard Meier in the same
vein:

DE BLOIS: It's a nice looking building. It's a lot better than most.

MEIER: I don't see any idea in the building that has any redeeming value.

DE BLOIS: *Does a house have to have an idea?*

MEIER: I think *every* building has to have an idea.

DE BLOIS: *You* may not think it's an idea. . . . It addresses itself to solar prob-
               lems, heating problems; they are properly ventilated, shaded,
               there's cross-ventilation. The idea is kind of basic, but they've cer-
               tainly forgotten it in many places.[34]

De Blois's position was a dissenting one in 1978. Yet many judges were
to react with increasing dissatisfaction against "meaning" and "ideas,"
which seemed to presage a dangerous slide into mere "image." Then, as
we know, concerns with construction and service return to the fore. But

bringing design back from image-making is difficult without the modernist symbiosis of structure and form.

The analysis of symbolic adjudication in these years suggests that a tactical solution was to identify historicist and eclectic postmodernism as the culprit. However, not even the partial consensus about a whipping boy could alleviate the dissolution of common standards. Let us follow this process step by step to its ambiguous outcome.

We have heard Cesar Pelli calling in 1969 for emotional responses and excitement. Ten years later, an established and sedate jury similarly celebrated architecture as "the making of objects and spaces *which are events.*"[35] Neither exciting events nor stylistic eclecticism have to be superficial or facile. In fact, most juries took pains to denounce, case by case, what they saw as trendiness—either contrived originality or imitation without any architectonic or programmatic reason. However, the divorce of appearance and construction having authorized eclecticism, evaluators could not invoke a shared language of design against the seduction of "effects." Without a positive countervalue, the denunciations of facile effects converged in the early 1980s upon a negative: the "antimodern" imagery of eclectic postmodernism. Predictably, the reasons for this negative agreement were different and often incompatible.

Unreformed modernists, while they admitted variations and faintly historicist or neoclassical forms, had never accepted that structure and site do not by themselves generate form. On the other hand, "schismatic" modernists (such as the New York Five or Craig Hodgetts and Frank Gehry) detested in "traditional" postmodernism the nostalgia for an irrecoverable past, the symbolic association of neoclassical ornament with imperial power, the repudiation of the present and its doubts.[36] The schismatic revisionists accepted the separation of building and appearance, without abandoning the notion that architecture must somehow embody the *Zeitgeist.* Yet, in truth, some of them recognized that eclecticism *was* the precise postmodern expression of the times.

For instance, in the awards program of 1983, the two younger jurors (George Baird, a Toronto architect and educator, and the young Bay Area architect Mark Mack) disagreed with the famous British architect James Stirling and with Alan Chimacoff, professor at Princeton and winner of many awards for his sober and elegant work. The older men argued for the architectonic quality of a small neo-Gothic chapel added to a Gothic Revival cathedral in Ontario. Baird and Mack objected to the figurative symbolism of the chapel, invoking the obligation to "reinterpret architectural form" and "reflect our times a little better."[37]

Like James Stirling, Peter Eisenman did not object to historicism in itself but objected to its adoption without serious architectural and archi-tectonic reasons. For Eisenman, "the burying of modern architecture by the 'postmodern' savants (who one suspects have always known it is easier to sell a pitched roof than a flat one)" was a deliberate attempt to excise the critical potential of architecture.[38] The "pristine, ideal forms" of mod-ern architecture

> not only have been in decline stylistically . . . but have also lost the capacity to sustain the once-symbolic iconography of their often literal machine forms. In their place has arisen something called "postmodernism," a catchall term . . . for every form of non-mechanistic and eclectic imagery. The ruin and the fragment have become the staple iconography of the new "follies" of this new "-ism" . . . the collaged fragments of Robert Stern's or Michael Graves' historic icons—pediments, gables, cornices and moldings grafted together and disassociated from their formal and functional contexts.[39]

Returning to the *PA* awards program, the rejection of "historicist post-modernism" had there a more proximate cause: its apparent enthronement by the 1980 jury. What strikes one most in the debates of this jury is not the intention to grant hegemonic status to a style but the acceptance of image as a central and legitimate concern of architecture.

The 1980 design jury consisted of an established local professional from Boston and three men—Frank Gehry of Los Angeles, Helmut Jahn, part-ner for design in the Chicago firm of C. F. Murphy Associates, and Robert Stern—who were each to claim a place among the best-known architects of the decade. Helmut Jahn had been chosen for balance because of his Miesian allegiances, but his opposition to most of the chosen projects did not make a dent.[40] The jury recognized thirteen small-scale projects, mostly residential, out of nineteen.[41]

Perhaps because of the entries' relative quality, Stern's taste for histor-ical eclecticism appears to have carried the day. One staff member later observed in jest, "We ended up giving an award to anything that had a pediment." The resultant triumph for "traditional" postmodernism was to provoke an uproar among the readers of *PA*.[42] In their discussion of the most controversial awards (Michael Graves's three house projects), the judges staked out a significant terrain:

JAHN: These houses . . . only address themselves to a particular element of architecture which is the aesthetic, cultural side, and not to the side that deals with the more real problems . . . of getting buildings built.

STERN: The aesthetic is the only important thing about building. When archi-tects get together to talk about the state of their art, *aesthetics is the only interesting thing, although there may be many ways to talk about it and many ways to define it.*

GEHRY: The forms are simple, and there's clarity in them, and no complication
             about building them that I can see. The complication is in transferring
             the aesthetic quality implied by drawings.

Jahn voices constructional and professional objections clearly. Gehry's contention is that building may not capture the beauty that Michael Graves
renders on paper. A different concern with paper architecture surfaces in
the comment of Blanche van Ginkel, urban design juror, about a house in
Delaware by Venturi Rauch and Scott Brown. "A paper facade," she
thought, marred the house's beautiful organization of volume. This exchange followed:

STERN: Well, the taste for paper—thin planes—seems to pervade our times.

GEHRY: And this example is well done, it's really American.

JAHN: Are you saying that anything goes in America?

STERN: Yes, that's the nature of the American experience . . . a very pluralistic
             society with diverse cultural heritages and regional styles . . .

GEHRY: Forgetting the imagery, what a beautiful composition!

JAHN: But why?

STERN: Because it's built in America and it uses American techniques and
             because composition is composition.[43]

Stern, invoking national culture and defending paper thinness, appropriates
for architecture the immaterial power of *images*, even if he seems to believe
in some universal criterion ("composition is composition"). What he understands by image is clarified later on:

VAN GINKEL: I see most of the submissions as representing the very rich des-
             serts of a very rich people, and you're not going to find how to
             make good, wholesome, whole-wheat bread out of them.

STERN: . . . Wholesome whole-wheat bread . . . has been translated as
             safe and sanitary housing—the most depressing environment to
             live in imaginable.

VAN GINKEL: No, they're not wholesome . . . they're the packaged white bread,
             without soul.

STERN: *The need to embellish architecture* . . . can be applied to all build-
             ings in all sectors of our society. The impoverishment, the quest
             for minimalism, has too often been translated into "make it sim-
             ple and cheap and get on with it."

PREISER: If you publish this kind of work, some public-housing decision
             maker will say "Hey, yeah, let's make some porticoes and col-
             umns and adorn our public housing."

STERN: I would hope so. If the portico stands for a front door to a build-
           ing, whether it's a single-family house or a 30-story high-rise . . .
           that would contribute enormously to the dignity of the people
           who go in and out of the buildings.[44]

With generous intentions, Stern is drawing architecture, through ornament
and embellishment, into the domain of illusion.

In the colonization of aesthetics by marketing, the designed commodity
(a piece of a building, a pair of blue jeans) and the designer's signature are
intended to confer instant status and instant identity upon the consumer/
owners of the image. Status is traditionally connected to the stylization of
life in real (albeit amorphous) communities.[45] With the mass media and
the mass market, stylized signs of status become comprehensible and accessible to enormous audiences that share nothing except diffuse meanings in
a universe of proliferating signs. In a disconnected society, the most readily
available form of identity is as a consumer of significant commodities.
Indeed, the consumption of signs is one of the crucial processes on which
analysts predicate postmodern culture, and the United States has been far
ahead of any other society in both the mass production and the mass consumption of goods that are images and of signs that are values.[46]

What we see here is a new stage in the long and uncertain march of
Western architecture from the service of plutocratic status ambitions into
the domain of popular consumption. The postmodern medley of historical
styles allows the designer to offer not only whole architectural compositions
but also *fragments* as status-conferring signs.[47] Eclectic postmodernism
reclaims the aristocratic lineage of architecture by allusion, not so much in
the service of ideological nostalgia as in that of differentiated mass consumption. In the process, the architect's name becomes itself a sign to be
consumed.

In the *PA* juries, a majority of the elite adjudicators overtly resisted the
assimilation of architecture into postindustrial consumption. The "pastiche
architecture" that James Stirling derided was easy to recognize and easy to
target. The choice of it as target perpetuated the impression of a lingering
stylistic battle against modernism; but it is important to recall that the
demise of the modernist canon had *institutionalized* "stylistic debate"
within the profession. Style no longer meant a hegemonic compositional
approach nor the convergent characteristics of spatial organization and
vocabulary that distinguish the architecture of a historical period. To the
established architects whom the editors favored for the juries after 1980,
"style" meant rhetorical design gestures and closeness to fashion.

Rapidly co-opted by developers and corporate builders, the cheapness of applied ornament and the pleasing, accessible looks of "traditional" post-modernism typified the inclusion of architecture in the aesthetics of product differentiation. Beyond this, the jurors seemed to fear a progressive and irremediable leaning of architecture toward the fashion-determined cycles of nondurable goods. As Alan Chimacoff put it, the alternative was either "to impose limits of style . . . in a permissive age in which there are no accepted canons of judgment" or to "look beyond style . . . to a basic quality of architectural organization or space-making."[48]

In the architectural discourse of the 1980s, style seems the opposite of permanence. In part, this reflects the increasing importance of graphic diffusion. Publications and exhibitions accelerate the conversion of superficially identifiable novelties into stylistic trends. The most telling effect is on aspiring and apprentice architects, seduced by an architecture that accents superficial and rapidly recognizable traits.

Conversely, resistance to style as image and effect emphasizes the constructional use-values that "real" architecture traditionally provides. Constructional principles reveal purely rhetorical departures from architectonic sobriety, but they cannot unify design unless form is once again ideologically predicated upon structure.

In the 1980s, modernism was gone, as ideology and as style. The professional elites could not ignore that novelty is in itself much of the excitement that clients (and architects) look for. Besides, they had no way of ruling out diversity and no desire to do so. The 1980s' recurrent calls for unity were unable to generate a uniform language of design, and they reflect the typical professional drive toward unified discourse rather than actual reintegration.

The architectural jury of 1981 (by deliberate editorial decision, we may surmise) included neither "avant-garde" nor "traditional" postmodern representatives.[49] Its chairman—Romualdo Giurgola, whom we met in 1968—opened the debate with a message of exemplary vagueness:

The manifestoes have been issued, the polemics written and now the time has come for the painstaking working through of all that has been proclaimed. This return in the cycle of the Modern Movement is the period of reintegration . . . and it is *this quiet yet intense search for unity* which we found manifested again and again in this year's presentations.[50]

Giurgola was offering reconciliation, redefining the discursive battles of the recent past as cycles of a single, long movement. The jury, on the other hand, condemned the building type that embodied facile innovation best, rejecting all the large office buildings submitted (there were many, thanks to the private building boom). Robert Frasca explained: "When we struggled with the big office buildings, we found that, though *they all tried to say something different, they obviously had nothing to say.*"[51]

It was no longer size or building type that makes architecture "dumb" but the commercial demand for distinctiveness, passed on by architects as some sort of meaning. An architecture "speaking" in too many tongues (for too many ideal audiences but too few kinds of users) encouraged this subterfuge. In Giurgola's opening statement, reintegration ultimately depended on subjective qualities for, indeed, "quiet and intensity" suggest *personal* efforts that yield "unity" only by the action of some unnamed invisible hand.

Subsequent juries became more explicit in stating few prescriptive criteria: Architecture must establish physical connections to its context (as William Pedersen asserted in 1985); "ideas" must go beyond the surface, involving, in James Polshek's words, context, technology, appropriateness to human habitation; ambiguity makes for experiential richness. . . . The prescriptions are general, easy to endorse even from contradictory positions.[52]

For instance, in 1984, the eminent German architect O. M. Ungers, former dean of architecture at Berlin's Technical University and chairman at Cornell, specified in this abstract way the permanent and universal qualities of architecture:

> First, clearly expressed concepts which in turn lead logically to the form and style of the building. . . . *The elements are ordered under a higher ruling principle.* Second, . . . *an urban quality* . . . even in the rural context, because I find it rather naive, these days, to design houses . . . that pretend to be part of the nice, unspoiled world. . . . The third quality [is] *the dialectical aspect of architecture.* . . . The initial idea should be exposed to its dialectical opposite, thereby leading to higher complexity.

Julia Thomas, a Los Angeles architect, chair of the board of a development company, declared herself in total agreement with Ungers, yet went on to invoke the opposite principle, consumer appeal:

> We can find more excitement in American cooking and restaurants now than in architecture. . . . [The entries] are still addressing issues that were addressed in the magazines a year or two ago, and they are still searching for a unifying theme. . . . I do not park in parking structures as they are now organized and would not live in most of the houses presented here.[53]

The profound differences of conception among the jurors were unresolved. In consequence, the only explicit push toward unity was their determination to accept plurality in the canon and in their own persuasions, for it was better to select strong designs of different tendency than to water down the awards in a futile search for agreement. Basic forms and plans could be legitimately historical (to the point of imitative reconstruction, as in the neo-Gothic chapel I mentioned), but fragmentary historicism was ostracized. In fact, the symbolic gatekeepers made the repudiation of "incoherent" historicist allusions a substantive indicator of their own seriousness. Defining a common antagonist, however, did not reconstruct a common identity.

Toward the end of the period, the critic Kenneth Frampton recognized the "refreshing . . . absence of any dominant trend" yet deplored the fact that "the continuity of the Modern Movement as a critical culture is still inadequately represented."[54] To Frampton, "critical" means the (necessarily autonomous) architectural discourse that transcends serving the client or pleasing the public. As he had explained in another context, "Architecture can only be sustained today as a critical practice if it assumes an *arrière-garde* position, that is to say one which distances itself equally from the Enlightenment myth of progress and from a reactionary, unrealistic impulse to return to the architectonic forms of the preindustrial past." The strategy that Frampton calls critical regionalism "mediate[s] the impact of universal civilization with elements derived *indirectly* from the peculiarities of a particular place."[55] Despite Frampton's allegiance to social architecture, his analysis concentrates on discourse regardless of the social function it serves. Here, Frampton understands the critical much as Peter Eisenman does the ideological: as the noblest potential of architecture, yet one which expends its critique solely within the bounds of the disciplinary canon.[56]

Frampton found that Eisenman's project for the Ohio State Wexner Center for the Visual Arts and Bernard Tschumi's red kiosks for the park of La Villette in Paris were the only rigorous modern works among the awards of 1985. Not much is "regional" in Tschumi's fragmented diagonals, except perhaps the effort to express the conflict and discontinuity of a great city. Eisenman's design, on the other hand, has resulted in one of the decade's most interesting "contextual" buildings.

As the university's leaflet points out, the diagonal line that organizes the building on its site represents "the convergence of the campus and city grids" (the former skewed by 12.25 degrees from the latter in Frederick Olmsted's 1880s design). The intersection of the two grids organizes the complex internal spaces; outside, it commands a "scaffold-like structure, a delicate layering of rhythmic grids rising toward infinite space." Seen through the variously patterned curtain wall and the skylights of the long sloped corridor, the white lattice frame accompanies the visitor's ascension toward the exhibition rooms.

For Vincent Scully, the abstract contextualism of the diagonal is in part responsible for "a spatter of small forms blocking the major ceremonial entrance" to the campus's central oval.[57] Indeed, the diagonal roof of the underground theater interferes with the broken brick towers and partially hides the arch that Eisenman uses to invoke the Armory, "a treasured landmark" that was located on the site until it burned down in 1958. The "contextual" towers are not powerful or large enough, says Scully, to keep the eye on the building and its grid. But they are Eisenman's parody of historicism, representing not the past itself but the impossibility of resurrecting it. The building's complex allegory takes on not the constructional principle of modernism but its abstract geometries. It is a deeply revisionist creation.

The dilemma of disunity subsists, however. The atmosphere of pluralism may be refreshing, but Tschumi, Eisenman, or new architects like Steven Holl each adds only one more voice to those the cognoscenti recognize. Separated from critical analysis of a building's *social* function and meaning, even the return to the forms of early modernism appears as just another stylistic gesture, or as a merely personal search.

Architectural formalism goes hand in hand with artistic individualism. Eric Moss, a young Los Angeles architect, made the point in response to Frampton's comments:

> People like Venturi, [Norman] Foster, Stirling and Graves really did move architecture toward a new stance. The architectural kit is now filled with another set of parts—symmetry, historical references, contextualism. Ten thousand people are now dipping into four lexicons. For this reason, I certainly wanted to find works that attempt to end run the conventions, old and new, *by delving deeply into personal issues.*[58]

Contrast Moss's "personalism" with the last part of James Polshek's statement the year before:

> We are moving away from producing architecture as pastiche, architecture as marketing, architecture as packaging, architecture as a kind of self-generating animus wherein the next project flows from the previous one by virtue of its . . . *conscious loading with "meaning" . . . defined primarily by the architect with no relevance for those using the building.*[59]

Return then to Eisenman's distinctions among types of practice: Excising the commercial is not enough to resolve the divergence of service and meaning. Professional motivations (in which the "concern with society at large" is obviously open to contestation and conflict) still clash with *both* aesthetic and ideological ambitions.

Thomas Beeby—perhaps out of his own experience at the helm of a smaller firm in Chicago, the city where the large architectural firm was invented and still predominates—voiced still another kind of insurmountable division. Anchoring the antinomies of postcrisis and postmodern architecture in the sociological reality of professional practice, he observed:

> Another paradox of today seems to be the incredible schism that exists between the large commercial work done by big firms and the more self-conscious artistic work being done by small practitioners. If these two disparate professional groups could only learn from each other, it is possible that architecture of the quality of Richardson or Sullivan would be possible once more. The apparent disdain existing between these two groups tends to vitiate the impact that architects have on the built world of today.[60]

Eisenman presented differences of orientation in architectural practice as voluntary choices. Frampton's exhortations to critical regionalism also emphasized voluntarism. Beeby's statement recognizes that, beyond the architect's individual choice, contemporary architecture is determined by segmented market niches and unbridgeable structural divisions. Its identity, reproduced by schools and in discourse, and its nominal unity, maintained with much effort by the organized profession, are both grafted onto the divided basis of practice.

FORM FOLLOWS PRACTICE

The *PA* system of symbolic rewards has given us a microscopic view (particular but detailed) of architectural discourse during the instatement of postmodern pluralism. To follow the juries negotiating the boundaries of legitimate architecture, I have had to ignore the important issues discussed in urban design (energy conservation, transportation, preservation, interpretation of the American urban vernacular). I have ignored also the attempts to systematize architecture and the varied investigations considered under the rubric of research. The design focus mirrors in its very narrowness a basic problem of architecture's traditional identity.

Design is an essential part of the profession's specialized discourse and the core of the *PA* awards program. Because it is open, this program reflects the interaction between professional elites who hold the key to semiofficial discourse and practitioners who aspire to participate in its making.

In the twenty years under study, the architectural language associated with the hegemony of large firms ceased to be dominant in the discourse of the profession. The initial impulse came from dissatisfaction with a paradigm stretched beyond recognition. The design elites did most of the stretching, although dissatisfaction reached far beyond their narrow circles, as indicated by the reception of Venturi's book in 1966.

In academic enclaves, opening architecture to other disciplines appeared as a path to reconstruction. But soon, the sixties proferred one with much broader appeal: It involved small firms, community advocates, academics practicing on the side, students, and users in the task of redefinition. As the 1960s turned into the crisis of the 1970s, untried intellectual architects moved to rescue "pure" design from what they saw as external diversions and meretricious seductions.

At the specific level of the "pure" geometric idioms adopted, the "architectural supremacism" proposed most notably by the New York Five could only fail. Various vocabularies (allusive and figurative or abstract) and various ways of doing architecture competed on the unsettled architectural scene. The "supremacists" were too young, too intellectual, and too idiosyncratic to be able to provide a unifying code for a profession in the throes of both intellectual uncertainty and economic crisis.

Yet, at a deeper level, supremacism as ideology aimed at restoring the professional identity of architecture and the confidence of younger professionals in their own basic competence. Tacitly accepting a retreat from larger social ambitions, the advocates of pure design were extremely successful in reconstructing the architect's traditional artistic role.[61] They did not have (or not yet) either enough professional power or sufficiently compelling solutions to rule out competing views. This came later on.

Established professionals and even the principals of large firms had to accept both eclecticism and professional diversity into the profession's discourse. Only thus and only then could there be enough support for ostracizing the most superficial and spectacular gratifications of postmodernism. The chosen target was eclectic historicism. Earnest historical reconstructions, attuned to the enthusiasm for preservation, seemed acceptable and are now considered serious.[62] More than admitted, the ideas of traditional postmodernism about context (working with the context and respecting its fabric) have passed into architectural common sense, as has tolerance of plurality.

The passing of the polemical phase means also a return (at times with a vengeance) to professional common sense. My analysis may have overstated the disjunction between program and design because I was considering the uncertainty about standards at the level of pure discourse. In practice, as we know, architects always design for the program and with the program in mind. Therefore, the juries' insistence on constructional quality and their condemnation of architecture-as-image reveal something more than concern for the program.

Surface imagery, rhetorical persuasions, and status appeal are what clients, in particular "professional" commercial clients, hire architects to provide. An autonomous conception of the architect's mandate, including a firm hold on architectonics, is what elites need to defend as their expertise. Their contrasting purpose may be interpreted as ideological resistance, not only to the severe but circumstantial threat posed by the recession of the 1970s but also to the long-term reduction of the architect's role in industrialized construction.

The lionization of celebrity architects is part of the client's marketing strategy and a sign of architecture's proximity to the culture industry. In this guise, it helps to valorize both real estate and luxury objects. But insofar as "signature architects" become mere consultants in styling, the negative side of their celebrity is the loss of power of architecture as an occupation.

We should not, however, take postmodern revisionism as the discursive expression of a surrender. The profession has not simply accepted a more superficial version of its ancient role as the dresser of power and the provider of its emblems, now far less durable than in centuries past. Paradoxically, it is the ineradicable segmentation of the profession that helps preserve a repertory of possible roles.

Among these varied roles, the modernist attempt to negotiate a responsible public function for the architect has left an indelible mark and a self-critical legacy. By 1985, in the messages issued from the *PA* juries, architecture had returned to all the concrete and divisive variety of its practical existence. As if to complete the cycle, the 1987 jury, celebrating thirty-three years of *PA* awards, gave two First Awards to affordable housing.

One went to apartments in simple modern language by Hank Koning and Julie Eizenberg for the Community Corporation of Santa Monica; the other to three little houses for needy families in Madison County, Mississippi, inspired by traditional vernacular forms—the work of Samuel Mockbee, Thomas Howorth, and Coleman Coker for Madison Countians Allied Against Poverty. The jury, noting that "nothing seemed to have happened" in low-income housing in the last decade, praised the Santa Monica design for its artistic interest, its internal courtyard, and a presentation that could almost be used to build. The Mississippi houses, praised by one juror for their architectural and climatic competence, showed that "elegance has nothing to do with cost." Their design, said the historian Thomas Hines, "is timeless; it speaks to both the condition and the aspirations of the people for whom it is designed." Perhaps, another juror added, the human qualities of the little houses could become "possibilities for much more elaborate, substantial housing schemes."[63]

The "restless search" that the editor had noted in the third year of the *PA* awards program seemed to have come home thirty years later to varied, local, and specific conceptions of architecture. There, if art happens, it is precisely as a conquest over the social, ecological, constructional, and economic requirements from which architecture cannot be abstracted.

CHAPTER NINE

Conclusion

In the late 1960s and early 1970s the revision of architectural discourse coincided with challenges waged from inside the profession against the architect's subservience to power. The coincidence came from different groups of architect-activists taking dogmatic modernism (which had made architecture part and parcel of the relentless modernization of cities) as a common enemy.[1]

In the United States, modernism-as-modernization primarily referred to the large-scale urban renewal that started in the 1950s. In the late 1970s, an extraordinary wave of real estate speculation succeeded the momentous economic crisis and spurred on architectural revisionism (at least of one kind). Clients with more credit than capital wanted their buildings to look rich, playful, and different. Developers' much-vaunted discovery of design contributed to the fame of a few "signature architects," but their main criterion in selecting design was and continues to be product differentiation. Postmodernism was bound to become tainted by its alliance with invidious status distinction, "image-making," and mere visual variety.

Architects' commissions and the glamor associated with the profession in the 1980s registered the effects of financial deregulation and the redistribution of income from poor and middle strata to the wealthiest. When architects and critics scoff at traditional postmodernism as an architecture "for the age of Reagan," they refer mainly to *style*. Few architects identify an age by the types of commissions that became prevalent or extinct. Yet the architectural sign of the period was less a style than the overabundance of office and retail space, luxury hotels, rich men's homes, and cultural institutions for the elite.

During the revision of the modern, divergent ideals clustered around the conflict between "image" and the "reality" of architecture. These terms can be read as transpositions of the basic disjunction between conception and execution in architects' work, for architects always design images (plans and working drawings are technical images of the building to be) while others do the building. That image and reality occupied a central place in the postmodern contest suggests that something was perceived to be changing (by will or by chance) in the architect's basic social identity.

The problematic relations of architectural image and reality call into question the place of aesthetic conception in the economy of building. If, indeed, architects are increasingly and primarily hired to embellish buildings and attract customers with images and symbols, their social function has changed. In Scott Lash's words, symbols have "a purchase on meaning but not on reality"; unlike signs, symbols have no referents. Buildings (or cities) do not refer to anything, they are. They can function as symbols, but their reality is overwhelmingly material and utilitarian. They are not circulating goods (cultural or material) but the primary stage of life and commerce on which goods are exchanged and consumed.[2]

If the best architectural work becomes the projection of symbolic and cultural significance, then architects are resigned to abandon to others the material design of the environment. It may, of course, be argued that they have never designed but a very small part of it. At issue, however, is their collective intention to provide the keynote.

Architectural supremacism, a professional ideology that extolled design for design's sake, rose in the mid-1970s on a contested and insecure professional scene. In the beginning, it had attempted a return to the imperious and autonomous self-definition of modernism, but it was too late. Not only did supremacism abandon earlier efforts to rethink cities gutted by modernism-as-modernization; its proponents did not have the professional power to restore modernism by a "working through" of partially developed aesthetic possibilities. Yet tacitly admitting all building types to the legitimacy of architecture in reality functioned as a reconstructive strategy.

At the same time, an ideal of environmental "nondisturbance" was inspiring a powerful middle-class movement, risen to preserve what was left of the ravaged urban fabric. This movement was also in part too late.

The precedent of massive urban displacement and the explosive protest of poor residents cast a different retrospective light on the preservation movement.

Its goals transposed the urgency of urban protest into an aesthetic and nostalgic ideological key, dear to cultivated and politically empowered professionals. In turn, the historicist or populist styles of architectural revisionism transposed the concerns of preservation—care for the old, the meaningful, the picturesque, the layered diversity of the urban fabric—into eclectic allusions to the remote or recent past of architecture. The resulting pastiches often collate fragments that never had a historical existence together, with disturbing effect. Perhaps more disturbing is the dim sense that pastiche harbors a double reversal of collective concerns: First, pastiche reverses the concern with security and a decent life into concern for the old neighborhoods in which these people live; second, it reverses the concern for preservation into a preoccupation with cute historical allusions.

Rejecting traditional postmodernism became *de rigueur* among professionals in the second part of the 1980s, but this should not conceal other facts. First, any style can be impressed in the service of speculative profit. Second, the urban working class and the poor suffered more from renewal than from remodeling and restoration. Third, the emphasis on context, the respect for the labyrinthine streets and motley construction of living cities is one of traditional postmodernism's most positive and significant contributions. Fourth, the proponents of contextualism can help invest even preservation with oppositional force. Last, at the level of the architectural objects themselves, the essence of postmodernism is not one style but the tolerance of multiple languages.

If "a thousand flowers bloomed," it is because the growing numbers of architects found (with difficulty) increasingly diverse clients for a great variety of projects. Either these diverse clients wanted stylistic novelty and excitement, or they could be convinced to accept new and momentarily different architectural idioms. A recession that aggravated the perennial structural problems of the profession pressed all but the most recalcitrant dogmatists to accept, even to encourage, the blooming. When postmodern pluralism is expressed in these terms, the situation after 1980 becomes clearer.

Architecture emerged from its double crisis with a restorative professional ideology—the formalist emphasis on pure design—and a pluralism that applied both to styles and building types. Having reconstructed the traditional identity of the architect-as-artist, formalism helped designers to effect a strategic retreat toward the individualism of one-of-a-kind commissions.

In the United States of the 1980s, social commissions and democratically oriented public architecture had all but vanished. The ideological comfort that formalism tendered to architects was excellence for excellence's sake, in either the playful or the rigorous delights of an eclectic discourse. The profession of architecture thus entered the speculative boom of the 1980s with new gatekeepers and a varied design elite but neither a common style nor a common vision. No group had enough power or enough influence to propose a direction, much less enforce common standards for the disparate professional enterprise. Yet the adoption of traditional postmodernism as favored style of the real estate boom made it easy to take it for a dominant style and blame it for what was happening to architecture.

Denying legitimacy to the use of architects as scenographers or stylists and of architecture as "packaging" matches the revaluation of craftmanship and service, which architects emphasized when aesthetic standards became uncertain. But despite their importance, constructional and pragmatic standards cannot define what architecture will look like (except multiple in form).

In sum, in our century architectural modernism went from technocratic social engineering to the service of corporate power. With the loss of social impetus, the aesthetic vision became routine. Strains and revisions multiplied at the level of discourse, quickening aesthetic disintegration. When an activist generation ignited political dissent and criticism inside the profession, the primacy of practice forced the symbolic gatekeepers to admit the ineradicable de facto diversity of architects' work.

Viewed from this angle, postmodern pluralism is a legacy of the antiauthoritarian politics of the 1960s, but the transformative impulses were contained within the specialized limits of a still weak and basically untransformed profession. The most substantial change was therefore in architecture's official discourse. The oppositional content of postmodernism (its emphasis on urban community, its advocacy of accessible design and authentic symbolism) struggles on within practices perforce devoted to the places of work, life, and leisure of the new urban middle class.

ARCHITECTURE AND CULTURAL TRANSITIONS

I have shown throughout this study that architecture is special, both as an intellectual discipline and as a professional practice. Despite this overdetermined specificity, its recent evolution suggests that transitions in the production of culture may have some common traits. I submit them as tentative hypotheses.

First of all, the study of architecture indicates that change in specific cultural discourses has local origins. This goes further than the well-established notion that modern cultural practices are "self-legislating."[3] Identifiable impulses toward change start within the specialized practices of identifiable agents and within specific circles of producers. Thus, what I was able to show about postmodern revisionism concerns the specialized discourse of architecture in the United States in a specific period.[4] The postmodern accent on relativism and particularism agrees with the localism of architecture, the practice of which begins in a concrete locality, even if it can go international after that.[5]

Second, discontinuities within specialist discourses do not *necessarily* respond to much more vast external discontinuities. World War II's awesome sequence of stasis, destruction, and reconstruction brought the Modern Movement from a minority position (already past its prime in the mid-1930s) to a universal and totalizing style. In turn, the global triumph of a banal and impoverished modernism compelled architects to react. The monotony and dreary sameness they call "exhaustion of forms" set in early, crying for aesthetic innovation and theoretical rearticulation. Not the catastrophic discontinuity of war but a later movement of young and educated people meant that a younger generation did both tasks.

Third, youth and education would not have been as significant without large numbers. The pressure of numbers within a delimited field deserves special attention for it is likely to engender competition for finite rewards. Competition, in turn, has been related to cultural innovation in settings as diverse as Islamic religion, nineteenth-century French painting, and twentieth-century American science.[6]

The booming economy probably absorbed most of the fast-growing numbers of architects produced by American schools in the 1950s and 1960s. Nevertheless, pressure for elite standing was bound to increase in the narrow and self-contained circles that make up the "scene" in major art centers, the "circuit" of elite graduate schools, the boards of major journals, and the juries of major contests. Moreover, the strongest push for aesthetic innovation and typological diversity coincided with the mounting pressure of "overproduced" architects on a field beset by the economic crisis of the 1970s. Without prejudging in any way the form or the content of cultural innovation, I expect that a larger number of players makes it more likely to emerge. Architectural postmodernism thus reinforces the rough correlations between numbers, competition, and innovation in the narrow ranks of specialized producers of culture.

Fourth, the partial overlap of personnel creates concrete connections between specialized cultural fields and larger political and social movements. The latter inspire and sustain within the former homologous actions of dissent, the objective of which is to redefine dominant intellectual paradigms and prescriptions about the specialists' roles.

Postmodernism could not have replicated the deliberate and fiery merger of artistic and political avant-gardism of the 1920s, for the revolutionary conditions of 1918 were not present in the 1960s in countries rich enough to afford an architecture. Yet what oppositional content there is in architectural postmodernism derives from the phase when, on both sides of the Atlantic, the New Left was raising its antitechnocratic banner.[7]

Implicit in the above points is a fifth one, the most important corollary of cultural specialization: The interaction between producers of culture and their potential audiences (and even, if one so wishes, the expression of the *Zeitgeist*) is always mediated by conditions of the producers' practices and by the historical circumstances that surround them. From this sociological position, it follows that bypassing the specific and localized analysis of cultural practice is unsound. Rushing to determine what cultural objects "say," one risks ignoring the experience of those by whom culture is "spoken" and of those to whom it "speaks."

Two things stand out in the practice of the American design elite during the postmodern transition. One is the sheer complexity of the architectural task, a good part of which is the economic and organizational difficulty of keeping the business of architecture going. To paraphrase Joseph Esherick, there is no time at all to think of the *Zeitgeist*.

Besides, even if an architect conveys a personal vision of the times, polysemic objects are always open to multiple and conflicting interpretations. Yet in architecture one interpretation clearly prevails upon any designer's message. Although building type is understood through and by means of stylistic conventions, the social function that type denotes is more broadly and immediately accessible than style or aesthetics. The idea that significance can be exhaustively explained by the author's intention is thus conspicuously doubtful in architecture.

The second thing that stands out is the convergence of parts of architectural work with parts of the culture industries. The material base of this convergence is clearer than its moral and social implications, and I will limit myself to sketching the former.[8]

Postmodernism has marked the ascendancy of small- and medium-sized idea firms within the discourse, not the business, of American architecture.[9] Their relations with organizational clients recall those of the creative technical producers with the organizational and managerial core of the culture industries. Like musicians for record companies or independent producers for television, architectural firms have no tenure beyond their project contracts. Because the smaller firms organize production in an almost artisanal way, overhead costs tend to be relatively low. If costs are reliably controlled, the firms enjoy full autonomy: The high level of professional competence (for which architects are presumably hired) makes it too costly for the sponsor to deny them responsibility.

Product selection occurs in architecture, as in the culture industries, at the "input boundary." Architects propose a range of alternatives (much expanded by postmodernism) to clients; like managers in the culture industries, large clients sponsor a selected sample for realization. In the large developers' offices, there is increasing professionalization of both "talent scouts" and marketing personnel, charged with co-opting the "mass media gatekeepers" (although in a minor way, compared to the culture industries). In the culture industries, book, music, film, or TV critics can strategically block or facilitate the "diffusion of particular fads and fashions."[10] In architecture, media critics have probably less power.

Elite designers do their own marketing to find clients, but big commercial clients market the architects, their names, and their personas as part of the commercial packaging of a new project. However, star architects' access to reputedly autonomous critics (and, for some exceptional designers like Robert Stern, access to their own television programs) does not sell more products. It can "sell" a project to users and the architect's ideas to the vast ranks of followers in schools and offices across the land. Therefore, in architecture, the "diffusion of fads and fashions" does not depend as much on the general media as on the organized profession, the specialist press, and especially the system of training institutions. The design process is still too complex and too highly professionalized, and, above all, building is still too expensive for clients and banks to permit momentary fads.

These caveats suggest that elite architects see image-making as a qualitative jump, more than just a further loss of control over the construction process. The decrease in the fiscal life of buildings, the multiplication of images from which clients can choose, and the increase in the media's emphasis on the architect as "culture hero," all conspire to subject stylistic conventions (the most noticeable sign of a building's architectural aspiration) to rapidly exhausted trends. Architects have not only moved closer to providing images instead of buildings; the life cycles of the images themselves have moved closer to those of the fashion and culture industries. The providers of these images can run after newness or imitation, for the decisive factor is what each can add to rental or resale values.

As an activity, postmodern architecture epitomizes material forces that tend to erase the differences between "high" and "mass" cultural production. Hired for their creativity and granted freedom to innovate, specialized cultural producers constrict their creative autonomy in anticipation of the client's choice. A subtler and more pervasive heteronomy channels cultural practices in the general direction of what sponsors can accept. This is in marked contrast with the autonomy of discourse.

Indeed, in most cultural fields, academic expansion and the continued growth of educated audiences allow increasing theoretical sophistication to develop in discourse. Architecture reveals a dialectic that appears with variations in many cultural fields: The autonomy of discourse encourages technical producers to take risks in cultural practice, while the costs of realization (a good indicator of producers' dependence on markets and funding) hold them back. This general condition helps us understand why theorists and philosophers take architecture as a pivotal allegory of postmodernism.

ARCHITECTURE AND THE POSTMODERN ALLEGORY

Postmodernism has been presented as a period, a new aesthetics, a theory, a philosophy, a new epistemology (by Lyotard), a "structure of feeling" (borrowing Raymond Williams's expression), a "regime of signification" (by Lash), a dominant in the cultural logic of late capitalism (by Jameson), or its fragmented consciousness (by Harvey).[11] In all these versions, the shift is of concern mainly for the intellectuals who theorize it. Yet the "over-theorized" phenomenon of postmodernism is in fact not theorized at all. A phenomenon for which each theorist provides a disparate objective basis, if not a different theory, is incomprehensible as a whole.[12] If postmodernism indeed represents an ongoing transformation of culture, it should be approached modestly, part by empirical part.

In this discordant chorus, however, a minimal consensus seems to form around architecture. Philosophers like Habermas and Lyotard take opposite stands on the universality of rational claims yet concur in making architecture a parable of the postmodern moment. They give modernism, not postmodernism, as the reason for architecture's conspicuous place in their theories.

Lyotard understands the modernist project as "a last rebuilding of the whole space occupied by humanity." Its abandonment is the first step in Lyotard's definition of the postmodern.[13] His second, more-developed point is that postmodern means "incredulity toward metanarratives." The great philosophical justifications from which Western knowledge drew sustenance and legitimation have become unnecessary. In particular, the metanarrative of universal emancipation through science has become untenable; there need be no more proof than a list of names—Auschwitz, Hiroshima, Vietnam.[14] Architecture, intimately linking modernism to modernization understood as social progress, points to this terrible discontinuity.

Habermas, more precise than Lyotard, disentangles modernism from its consequences. Everyone deplores "the soulless 'container' architecture, . . . the solitary arrogance of the unarticulated office block, of the monstrous department stores, universities and congress centers, . . . the lack of urbanity and the misanthropy of the satellite towns," but the Modern Movement is "still the first and only unifying style since the days of classicism," a style born from the avant-garde spirit, powerful enough to create its own models and itself become classic, from the outset international, from the outset aiming to penetrate everyday life.[15]

The valence is different but the diagnosis is the same. The program of architectural modernism in the 1920s was so strong and (Habermas fails to add) its co-optation by capitalist democracies after the war so complete that the challenge against it acquires emblematic clarity.

Yet how can architecture so readily become an emblem of change? No other art (except film) is as expensive, which means that new ideas take longest to materialize. And no other recognized art is as useful and as intimately linked to economic investment and the fate of cities. The two attributes are at odds yet concur in lending architecture allegorical power.

First, change in architecture takes much longer to become visible than in other arts; as a corollary, architects become famous (and, to clients, trustworthy) late in life. The mid-fifties is an advanced age for a "young Turk." Ideas are therefore expressed on paper, in words and drawings, with a kind of extremism that would be unthinkable (if not undoable) in cement and steel. The debates and battles are not only more vehement on paper: They last longer than in other visual arts, insofar as it takes much longer to get to the "real thing."

Habermas, Lyotard, Jameson, Derrida, and others are theoreticians: they follow discourse more closely than any other medium. "Paper" architecture captivates them both by the starkness of the modernist project and the fervor of the challenge. Architectural discourse, moreover, is free to dress itself up with all the important words that populate *their* philosophical and literary debates: postmodern, poststructuralism, deconstruction, marginalization, estrangement, "the unconscious of pure form."[16] Is it any wonder that they should ignore how little the structure of dominant building types has changed or how the architect's intervention is circumscribed to "facade and lobbies?"[17] Architectural change, for the philosophers, happens in words as much as in built exemplars.

The exemplars, long as it takes to build them and hard as it is to build them as designed, give architecture the opposite kind of force: the presence of ineluctable materiality. Indeed, these are not words, not paper, not merely texts, but buildings. They must (even by law) be sound. Formidable or modest, they occupy a place, they transform a landscape, they loom in front of our eyes, they can be inhabited. They are the stage of power, commerce, worship, toil, love, life. The art of architecture has never abandoned the "sphere of our sorrow," has never moved into the rarefied domain that art occupies in bourgeois ideology. It is among us.

Against the overintellectual discourse of postmodernism (by which I mean a debate addressed to intellectuals alone), we experience architecture sensuously, holistically, and, as Benjamin pointed out, habitually and in a state of distraction.[18] In an intellectual culture governed by the abstraction of the linguistic metaphor, the materiality of architecture is inescapable. This is the art that does not represent and does not signify but *is*.

It is, in part, the environment, a formidable capital investment, the archetypal durable good, not a commodity but the container of commodities. What happens in architecture will be received, in due time and distractedly, by people who will not have access to other arts. As the stage of social life, architecture (good or bad) becomes the embodiment of a historical period.

A PERSONAL CLOSURE

The sociologist's job is in large part analysis and demystification, but this should not rule out deeper meanings and experiences. So, in the end, I will state my own perplexity about our architecture. Throughout the book I have avoided passing any judgment on its products; yet, I could not hide my sympathy for those architects who try hard to find opportunities for a social practice. Equally, I find in the modernist architecture of Germany and Holland in the 1920s the promise, for lack of a better word, of democratic and egalitarian aesthetics: The decent, dignified housing exudes repose and sometimes attains beauty. Moreover, it makes the great monuments legitimate.

Architecture is praised as a knowledge combining aesthetics and technique, theory and practice. It is often praised today for its distinctive, critical, and holistic pedagogy. From the modernist phase onward, it has also presented a model for the enlightened exercise of expertise. The high-rise buildings and the postwar new towns have tarnished that model, although there too the case is neither one-dimensional nor closed.

In the commons and winding rows of cottages in a lower-income Swedish suburb, for example, the signs of careful planning are almost moving: playgrounds, sand boxes ready for the icy winter, bike paths, common laundry facilities, meeting rooms, sheds where people keep the tools for painting, cleaning, gardening together. Only on such a background, I thought, can architectural monuments cease to be at the same time "documents of civilization and barbarism."[19] But I am fully aware that works of beauty often seem to require quite a different soil to rise. Architecture's ritual and aesthetic power can exceed the social circumstances of its production.

Vincent Scully notes that the most beloved and visited architectural work of the profligate 1980s was not a hotel nor a museum but the Vietnam Veterans Memorial in Washington. Its designer was not a famous architect but a young woman, Maya Lin, still an undergraduate, who rose from a vast field to win the 1981 competition with a black marble wall inscribed with the names of the dead. Today, crowds walk silently along the wall, reading names, looking for the one they know, touching it. The arrow-shaped wall points at one end to the obelisk and at the other to the Lincoln Memorial. The pomp of the monuments to great men dissolves into fifty thousand or so names; the wall shimmers with the dark light of grief, sloping imperceptibly toward the open sky. Memory has found a lasting form.

The *Progressive Architecture* Awards, 1954–87

During the period 1954–87 in the life of the *Progressive Architecture* awards, the strictness of the judges shows the trace of mounting doubts. The differences in the ratio of winners to entries for each year provide a very rough indication of the jurors' satisfaction with what they were seeing; these differences also reflect the difficulty in reaching a consensus about architectural excellence. Factors such as the identities of the judges and, as they would undoubtedly argue, the variable quality of the submissions are obviously involved, but the overall pattern is suggestive. Table 2 gives the numbers and percentages for each year.

In the first three years, the judges, whether uncertain, indulgent, or satisfied, named the highest proportions of winners (9.50 percent in 1954, 7.20 percent in 1955, and 7.00 percent in 1956), never to be equaled after the program became established and the juries more rigorous. In the years after 1956, the average proportion of winners was 2.89 percent, with the highest percentage of awards (5.2 percent) in 1978, at the end of the recession, and the lowest (1.15 percent) in 1966, the year in which the detailed study presented in chapters 7 and 8 begins. The 1966 jury, as we have seen, recorded its dismay with what the submissions said about American architecture.

The proportion of awards given is rarely correlated to the number of entries.[1] Leaving aside the years of the economic crisis (1972–78) and the indulgent first three years, we see that the number of awards varies inversely with the number of entries in fifteen out of the twenty-four remaining years. After 1957, the percentages show a year-by-year reversal of direction (decreasing after an increase and increasing after a decline) in fifteen out of thirty-one competitions, as if the jury were reacting to the dearth or abundance of winners in the previous year. Since the editorial staff is under some obligation to show equanimity in a divided profession, it is likely to seek some balance, year after year, in the composition of juries. A

TABLE 2.   *PROGRESSIVE ARCHITECTURE* AWARDS,
1954–87

Year	Number of entries	Number of awards	Percentage (awards/entries)
1954	600	57	9.50
1955	500	36	7.20
1956	700	49	7.00
1957	800	26	3.25
1958	700	26	3.70
1959	600	29	4.80
1960	600	22	3.60
1961	507	18	3.50
1962	522	12	2.29
1963	600	21	3.50
1964	692	14	2.03
1965	643	16	2.48
1966	778	9	1.15
1967	652	19	2.91
1968	671	12	1.78
1969	739	16	2.16
1970	670	19	2.83
1971	739	17	2.30
1972	655	18	2.74
1973	768	24	3.10
1974	863	28	3.24
1975	737	21	2.84
1976	462	20	4.30
1977	619	27	4.36
1978	654	34	5.19
1979	923	28	3.00
1980	928	28	3.00
1981	1049	31	2.95
1982	1066	22	2.06
1983	1040	26	2.50
1984	934	28	2.99
1985	933	31	3.32
1986	832	17	2.04
1987	805	23	2.85

different jury may thus deliberately react to the enthronement or dethronement of particular architectural tendencies. The figures suggest, however, that the juries might have been taking the profession's economic situation into account.

Because the submissions represent possible or probable commissions, their number may reflect, with some delay, the economic health of the profession. The not-fully comparable series of the Construction Census gives the annual amounts in constant dollars that are invested in different categories of construction.[2] Among the types of new construction that are most likely to involve architects (and thus have an effect on the profession's collective fate), investment exhibited a very sharp decline only in the recession years 1973–75 (32 percent), with annual rates of recovery of 2.5 and 4.3 percent from 1975 through 1977 and unsteady growth (below 10 percent annually) from 1978 to 1982.[3] Fueled by the boom in office building, these categories of investment underwent spectacular annual growth after 1983 (22.2 percent from 1983 to 1984 and 15 percent the next year); they declined slightly after that, remaining 25 percent higher than in 1982.

On a parallel course, the number of entries to the *PA* contest showed a precipitous decline from 1974 through 1976 and took three more years to return to the 1974 level. The number of awards varied exactly in the same direction as the entries from 1974 to 1978, as if the judges were reluctant to castigate competitors who, having enough material worries of their own, had been brave enough to submit their uncertain projects for evaluation. It is even more suggestive that the ratios of winners to entries should be *above* the "normalized" 2.89 percent average in practically every year from 1973 to 1978 (only 1975, the year in which Peter Eisenman "reclaimed design" and introduced tighter formal standards, is very slightly below average, with awards going to 2.84 percent of all entries). During this period, the profession was suffering the effects of the most severe recession in construction since World War II. Other observations confirm that the ratio of winners to entries either was high or tended to increase in years in which investment in the selected special categories of nonresidential construction visibly declined.[4]

Although these relationships are too rough to permit anything more than speculation, the symbolic gatekeepers (the jurors charged with distributing symbolic rewards) appear to have been taking economic decline into account. Sometimes they were explicit about it, as was Hugh Hardy in 1973. Most of the time, the concern can be read only indirectly, as for instance in 1975 and 1976. Of course, the inverse variations in volume of selected categories of construction and ratio of awards to entries may have been due to chance in the selection of jurors or in the self-selection of competitors. The submissions may also have improved because only the best architects could find work in a recession. Or perhaps all architects had less work, spending much more time and care on improving what work they had; or lack of work may have given them a special urge to seek confirmation from their peers and more time to improve their contest entries. *All* these processes may have been at work. Finally, juries may have wanted to use the symbolic rewards at their disposal to bolster the morale of a badly battered profession and confirm the importance of its calling.

Notes

CHAPTER 1

1. See John Goldthwaite, *The Building of Renaissance Florence* (Baltimore: Johns Hopkins University Press, 1980), 361–65, and Lewis Mumford, *The City in History* (New York: Harcourt, Brace, and World, 1961), 356–71.

2. Military engineering, for instance, became a specialized occupation by the seventeenth century; in eighteenth-century France, civil engineering provided the model of a state-sponsored profession that architects strove to emulate. I have analyzed the importance of this model in "Emblem and Exception: The Historical Definition of the Architect's Professional Role," in Judith R. Blau, Mark E. La Gory, and John S. Pipkin, eds., *Professionals and Urban Form* (Albany: State University of New York Press, 1983).

3. Reyner Banham, "A Black Box: The Secret Profession of Architecture," *The New Statesman,* Oct. 12, 1990, 25.

4. See David Brain, "Discipline and Style: The École des Beaux-Arts and the Social Production of an American Architecture," *Theory and Society* 18 (1989): 815ff.

5. I adopt Michel Foucault's concept of the discipline as a "system of control in the production of discourse" ("The Discourse on Language," trans. Rupert Swyer, appendix to *The Archaeology of Knowledge* [New York: Pantheon, 1972]). "For a discipline to exist," Foucault writes, "there must be the possibility of formulating—and of doing so ad infinitum—fresh propositions." Disciplines are "defined by groups of objects, methods, their corpus of propositions considered to be true, the interplay of rules and definitions, of techniques and tools: all these constitute a sort of anonymous system, freely available to . . . whoever is able to make use of them, without there being any question of their meaning or their

validity being derived from whoever happened to invent them" (222–23). I combine this concept of discipline with my understanding of the social appropriation of discourse. I believe, as does Foucault, that educational systems are "political means of maintaining or modifying the appropriation of discourse, with the knowledge and powers it carries with it" (227).

6. In architectural discourse, the term *postmodernism* tends to be reserved for the return to classicist and vernacular sources of formal inspiration in vocabulary and composition. I shall use the term more broadly, including all the revisions of European canonic modernism—not only the "traditional" return to premodern sources but also the "schismatic" treatment of modernism itself as a formal historical source. The distinction between varieties of "traditional" and "schismatic" post-modernism is elaborated by Robert Stern in "The Doubles of Postmodern," *Harvard Architecture Review* 1 (1980): 75–87.

7. Architects never attained the liberation from patronage that painters reached with the spread of easel painting and the organization of art markets. While the paintings that Van Gogh or Chaim Soutine had been tragically unable to sell could be "discovered" after their death, there is no such thing as "discovering" an architect who has never built anything, except within the specialized discourse of which only historians, critics, and architects are cognizant. The most notable example is that of Antonio Sant'Elia (1888–1916), the one architect among the Italian futurists. His extraordinarily beautiful visionary drawings with Mario Chiattone (exhibited in 1914 in Milan) are among the "sacred texts" of modern architecture. Sant'Elia's foreword to the catalog, interpreted by Filippo Marinetti, became the group's "Manifesto of Futurist Architecture." See Ulrich Conrads, *Programs and Manifestoes on Twentieth-Century Architecture* (Cambridge, Mass.: M.I.T. Press, 1970), 34–38.

8. On the emergence of the large architectural firm in the United States, see Diana Balmori, "George B. Post: The Process of Design and the New American Architectural Office (1868–1913)" *Journal of the Society of Architectural Historians* 46 (1987): 342–355, and Bernard M. Boyle, "Architectural Practice in America, 1865–1965: Ideal and Reality," in Spiro Kostof, ed., *The Architect* (New York, Oxford University Press, 1987). For an excellent overview, see Robert Gutman, *Architectural Practice: A Critical View* (New York: Princeton Architectural Press, 1988), especially 23–60.

9. On the interaction between organization and recognition of merit, see the excellent study by Judith Blau, *Architects and Firms* (Cambridge, Mass.: M.I.T. Press, 1984), Chap. 5.

10. In American universities, these different orientations can result in affiliation with either technical or fine arts faculties.

11. Niels L. Prak, *Architects: The Noted and the Ignored* (New York: Wiley, 1984), 1–2, 14–16.

12. In the United States, where architects are legally in charge of producing contract drawings (the detailed and specified drawings that go to contractors for bidding and on which the production of the building is based), professional reputations, official recognition, and informal networks help to forge cooperative ties between "design" and "service-oriented" architects. In some cases, these ties are prompted by speculative clients who want both fancy design and economic efficiency. In others, design architects seek these associations themselves for a variety of reasons, which I discuss in chapter 4.

13. The mechanisms of licensing, of course, recognize this primacy. In the United States, years of schooling are equivalent to years of practice but not sufficient to be eligible for examination by architectural boards or for professional registration. Two to three years of practice under the supervision of a licensed architect are required for the latter. It is still possible today to take the boards without any formal schooling, but only in a few states.

14. This was a finding of my research in "high volume" architectural offices. See Magali Sarfatti Larson, "Report to the National Science Foundation and the Research Corporation of the American Institute of Architects," Department of Sociology, Temple University, Philadelphia (1979).

15. Besides its specialized professional journals, architecture, like science, is also explained and presented to the lay public in the general press and the electronic media. Moreover, architectural design is featured by more or less specialized picture magazines such as *Architectural Digest* or *House Beautiful*, which have a keen sense of their readers' status aspirations. The dean of American architects, Philip Johnson, with his characteristic candor, calls them "pornography for architects."

16. See Foucault, "Discourse on Language." When I say "discursive field" I follow Foucault's more inclusive definition of discourse, which is close to Thomas Kuhn's composite notion of "paradigm" (though Foucault is obviously much broader in his usage than Kuhn). For Kuhn, a paradigm constructs, first of all, the area of nature or of the social world that scientists take as the object of their research. The paradigm rests on metaphysical assumptions that tacitly determine what kinds of questions it is legitimate to ask. The Kuhnian paradigm is not embodied in texts only—not even *primarily* in texts, axiomatic postulates, theories, problems, empirical findings, ideas, jargon, and the like—but in exemplars of scientific practice: In replicating practical models of how to do science, apprentices appropriate the paradigm, insuring its hold upon the field and the field's self-reproduction. See Kuhn, *The Structure of Scientific Revolutions*, 2d ed. (Chicago: University of Chicago Press, 1970), and Mary Masterman's incisive discussion, "The Nature of the Paradigm," in I. Lakatos and A. Musgrave, eds., *Criticism and the Growth of Knowledge* (Cambridge: Cambridge University Press, 1970).

17. Michael Graves, interview with the author, Dec. 1988.

18. Symbolic capital is, for Pierre Bourdieu, the authority to speak within and for a field, authority that accrues according to criteria determined (and often understood) only by the qualified participants themselves. See Pierre Bourdieu, "Le Champ scientifique," *Actes de la recherche en sciences sociales* 2–3 (June 1976): 88–104, and "La Production de la croyance: contribution à une économie des biens symboliques," *Actes de la recherche en sciences sociales* 13 (Feb. 1977): 3–43.

19. One century later, Michelangelo went on: "A noble house in the city brings considerable honor, being more visible than all one's possessions" (both quotations in Goldthwaite, *Renaissance Florence*, 83, 89).

20. Goldthwaite, *Renaissance Florence*, 77–83.

21. Marshall Berman, *All That Is Solid Melts into Air* (New York: Pantheon, 1988), 295.

22. Suzanne Langer, *Feeling and Form* (New York: Charles Scribner's Sons, 1953), 73, 95ff.

23. Langer, *Feeling and Form*, 97.

24. I am borrowing from the concept of a "period's eye," developed by Michael Baxandall. See his *Painting and Experience in Fifteenth-Century Italy* (New York: Oxford University Press, 1974), 29ff.

25. The concept of "art world" and the complex networks that permit production, circulation, and social appreciation of art works is elaborated by Howard Becker in *Art Worlds* (Berkeley: University of California Press, 1982), Chap. 1. On the concept of "field," see Bourdieu, "Le Champ scientifique."

26. Peter Bürger, for instance, sees the hallmark of the "authentic" avant-garde in the Dadaists and the Russian constructivists' efforts to abolish the separate institutional existence of art in bourgeois society. See his *Theory of the Avant-Garde* (Minneapolis: University of Minnesota Press, 1984) and the introduction by Jochem Schulte-Sasse.

27. Jürgen Habermas, for instance, develops the architectural metaphor in his 1981 speech in Munich on "Modern and Postmodern Architecture" (reprinted in John Forester, ed., *Critical Theory and Public Life* [Cambridge, Mass.: M.I.T. Press, 1985]). Jean-Francois Lyotard grounds the three constitutive tendencies of postmodernism in architecture's abandonment of the Modern Movement. See his "Defining the Postmodern," in *ICA Documents 4: Postmodernism* (London: Institute of Contemporary Art, 1986), 6–7. Architecture is important in literary theory, particularly in Fredric Jameson's much-discussed "Postmodernism, or the Cultural Logic of Late Capitalism," *New Left Review* 146 (July–Aug. 1984): 53–92. See also Jameson, "Architecture and the Critique of Ideology," in Joan Ockman, ed., *Architecture Criticism Ideology* (New York: Princeton Architectural Press, 1985). Other discussions of architecture include David Harvey, *The Condition of Postmodernity* (Oxford: Basil Blackwell, 1989), 66–98, and Scott Lash, *Sociology of Postmodernism* (New York: Routledge, Chapman and Hall, 1990), 201–36.

28. The design of Brasilia is perhaps the best known of the exceptions. Thanks to James Holston, it certainly is the best studied by a social scientist. See his *The Modernist City: An Anthropological Critique of Brasilia* (Chicago: University of Chicago Press, 1989).

29. The sample is not statistically representative but formed qualitatively on the advice of experts. I interviewed thirty American architects and one international celebrity whose practice is based in Italy. The American group includes twenty-one of the most noted architects of the recent period and, in two cases, their managing partners (fifteen of them are an elite officially recognized in the international encyclopedia *Contemporary Architects*, ed. Ann Morgan, 2d ed. (Chicago, St. James' Press, 1987); five of them worked in large "corporate" firms; nine are "rising" (two were once rising) architects identified by the awards and official accolades they have received. I also interviewed the principal of a firm that specializes in doing production drawings for elite designers and consulted with eleven diverse experts in the field of architecture, including the editors of architectural journals, scholars, consultants, the former manager of the Institute for Architecture and Urban Studies, and John Zuccotti, the attorney for the Canadian developer Olympia and York. The interviews with four representatives of important developers—including two with senior vice presidents of Olympia and York—are only indicative of what a few of them think of architects. This study is not about clients but about how architects understand them and work with them.

CHAPTER 2

1. Such is the influential thesis of Emil Kaufmann. See *Architecture in the Age of Reason* (Cambridge, Mass.: Harvard University Press, 1955), 181ff. in particular.

2. Giorgio Ciucci, "The Invention of the Modern Movement," *Oppositions* 24 (1981): 69.

3. Barbara Miller Lane, *Architecture and Politics in Germany, 1918–1945*, 2d ed. (Cambridge, Mass.: Harvard University Press, 1985).

4. See Leonardo Benevolo, *History of Modern Architecture*, vol. 2, The Modern Movement (Cambridge, Mass.: M.I.T. Press, 1971), 585ff., and John Willett, *Art and Politics in the Weimar Period* (New York: Pantheon, 1978), 168ff.

5. An idea of the international effort at publicizing the new architecture can be gained from the bibliographic sources listed by the historian of modern architecture Leonardo Benevolo (in *History of Modern Architecture*, 2:843). He includes: Walter Gropius, *Internationale Architektur* (1925); Ludwig Hilbersheimer, *Internationale neue Baukunst* (1926); G. A. Platz, *Die Baukunst der neuesten Zeit* (1927); P. Meyer, *Moderne Architektur und Tradition* (1928); Henry Russell Hitchcock, *Modern Architecture: Romanticism and Reintegration* (1929); Bruno Taut, *Die neue Baukunst in Europa und Amerika* (1929), translated into English the next year; M. Malkiel-Jirmounsky, *Les Tendances de l'architecture contemporaine* (1930); S. Cheney, *The New World Architecture* (1930); and A. Sartoris, *Gli elementi dell'architettura razionale* (1932). Le Corbusier's *Vers une architecture* (1923) was translated into English as *Towards a New Architecture* in 1928. In America, the most influential texts were Le Corbusier; Henry Russell Hitchcock and Philip Johnson's catalog for the 1932 exhibition, *The International Style;* Laszlo Moholy-Nagy's *The New Vision* (1928); Gropius's *The New Architecture and the Bauhaus* (1935); followed by Nikolaus Pevsner's *Pioneers of the Modern Movement from William Morris to Walter Gropius* (1936) and by Walter Behrendt's survey *Modern Building* (1937). Throughout the period, the Museum of Modern Art in New York, with a Department of Architecture and Design founded and directed by Philip Johnson, was the undisputed center for the ideas of aesthetic modernism in the United States.

6. See Nikolaus Pevsner, *Pioneers of Modern Design: From William Morris to Walter Gropius*, 3d ed. (New York: Penguin, 1960), and Siegfried Giedion, *Space, Time, and Architecture: Growth of a New Tradition*, 5th ed. (Cambridge, Mass.: Harvard University Press, 1973). Pevsner's revised edition for Penguin has a slightly different title from that for the first edition. The first meeting of CIAM was held in 1928 in the La Sarraz castle in Switzerland, property of a patron of modern artists, Hélène de Mandrot. The Germans were not heavily represented, a fact that reveals the difference of ideological approach at the outset of the Modern Movement. Le Corbusier, who was forty-one at the time, had included the older generation: the Dutchman Hendrik Berlage (seventy-two), the Swiss Karl Moser (sixty-eight), and the Frenchmen Tony Garnier (fifty-nine) and Auguste Perret (fifty-four). The CIAM's meetings became more difficult as the war approached: The fourth congress (that of Athens, in 1933) was followed by the fifth in Paris four years later. The work continued during the war in New York, in England, and underground in the Netherlands. In 1947, the British chapter called the sixth congress. CIAM ceased meeting at the end of the 1950s after acrimonious debates that started with

the ninth congress, in 1953 (see Ciucci, "Invention," and Giedion, *Space, Time,* 696–706).

7. In the foreword to the first edition, Giedion clearly announced that he saw in modernism the potential and the depth of a new classicism and that he attributed to architecture a central position in modern culture. He wrote: "I have attempted to establish, both by argument and by objective evidence, that in spite of the seeming confusion there is nevertheless a true, if hidden, unity, a secret synthesis, in our present civilization. To point out *why* this synthesis has *not* become *a conscious and active reality* has been one of my chief aims. My interest has been particularly concentrated on the growth of the new tradition in architecture, for the purpose of showing its interrelations with other human activities and the similarity of methods that are in use today in architecture, construction, painting, city planning and science" (Giedion, *Space, Time,* vi).

8. See Kenneth Frampton, *Modern Architecture: A Critical History* (New York: Oxford University Press, 1980), 29–40.

9. On illumination, heating, ventilation, and humidity control, see Reyner Banham, *The Architecture of the Well-Tempered Environment* (Chicago: University of Chicago Press, 1969). On materials and on architecture's relations with technology, see Giedion, *Space, Time,* 163–290.

10. The units consisted of "wooden ridges and furrow frames for the glass, . . . iron lattice girders on which the [glass] panes rested, and . . . cast-iron supporting pillars, bolted together floor by floor" (Giedion, *Space, Time,* 252). The construction also borrowed from the technology of railroad sheds; it was supervised by Charles Fox, a railroad engineer, and finished in four months. Heat was a major problem under the glass canopy, solved temporarily by English weather. Kenneth Frampton observes that the Crystal Palace "was not so much a particular form, as it was a building process made manifest as a total system, from its initial conception, fabrication and trans-shipment, to its final erection and dismantling" (*Modern Architecture,* 34).

11. Le Corbusier, *The Decorative Art of Today,* transl. James Dunnett (Cambridge, Mass.: M.I.T. Press, 1987), 139. On Delaunay and the tower, see Stephen Kern, *The Culture of Time and Space, 1880–1918* (Cambridge, Mass.: Harvard University Press, 1983), 143, 185, 207.

12. Walter Gropius, quoted by Reyner Banham in *A Concrete Atlantis: U.S. Industrial Building and European Modernist Architecture 1900–1925* (Cambridge, Mass.: M.I.T. Press, 1986), 203, and Chap. 3. See also Le Corbusier, *Towards A New Architecture,* transl. Frederick Etchells (1927; reprint, New York: Praeger, 1970), 17–24. The exaltation of the machine and its products indirectly celebrates the engineer's role; see Le Corbusier, *Towards a New Architecture,* 105ff., and *Decorative Art,* Chap. 8.

13. Clement Greenberg, quoted by Matei Calinescu, *Five Faces of Modernity* (Durham, N.C.: Duke University Press, 1987), 222.

14. Thomas Crow, "Modernism and Mass Culture in the Visual Arts," in Benjamin Buchloh, ed., *Modernism and Modernity: The Vancouver Conference Papers* (Halifax: Press of Nova Scotia College of Art and Design, 1983), 221 (emphasis added). Crow is commenting upon Clement Greenberg's pathbreaking essay of 1939, "Avant-Garde and Kitsch." Crow notes that Greenberg's steadfast distinction

between kitsch and modern popular culture prevented him from seeing that the art avant-gardes were not *only* repulsed by mass culture and pressured by it to defend creative freedom; they were also fascinated by vernacular materials and even by kitsch.

15. Because its producers seek *effect*, mainly through sentimental associations, "any recourse [of kitsch] to sentiment and irrationality is bound to be transformed into a rational recipe-book of imitations" (Hermann Broch, "Notes on the Problem of Kitsch," in Gillo Dorfles, ed., *Kitsch, the World of Bad Taste* [New York: Universe Books, 1969]). See also Umberto Eco's enlightening work, "La Struttura del Cattivo Gusto," in *Apocalittici e Integrati*, 3d ed. (Milano: Bompiani, 1964), 65–129.

16. See Martin Pawley, *Architecture versus Housing* (New York: Praeger, 1971), Chaps. 1–2. On Howard, see Robert Fishman, *Urban Utopias in the Twentieth Century* (New York: Basic Books, 1977).

17. Karl Marx and Friedrich Engels, "The Communist Manifesto," in Robert Tucker, ed., *The Marx-Engels Reader* (New York: Norton, 1978), 476.

18. Le Corbusier, *Decorative Art*, 133ff.

19. The canonically approved "precursors" of the late nineteenth century are found a little everywhere. Retrospectively, historians tend to include most of the innovative designers working from the late 1870s to the 1890s on, without weighing their respective influence. In rough chronological order, they are as follows. (1) The architects of Art Nouveau, which was most successful as a movement in the decorative arts. It started in Brussels in the 1880s and included the innovative architecture of Victor Horta and, later, Henry Van de Velde; the movement spread throughout Europe under the names of Liberty or Jugendstil. In Barcelona, the solitary and obsessed architecture of Antoni Gaudí is usually classified with Art Nouveau. (2) The British architects still attached to the Arts and Crafts Movement—Norman Shaw, Charles Voysey, Arthur Mackmurdo, Charles Rennie Mackintosh, and the Glasgow school (neither Pevsner nor Giedion name Sir Edwin Lutyens, the imperial architect "rediscovered" by Robert Venturi and adopted as a source by postmodernism). (3) The Austrian school of Otto Wagner, identified with the artists of the Sezession, includes Josef Hoffman, Josef Olbrich, and, importantly, Adolf Loos, author of the famous 1908 pamphlet "Ornament and Crime." (4) The Americans: Henry Richardson and, above all, Louis Sullivan and the "architect-engineers" of the Chicago school; the designer of the first steel frame building, William Le Baron Jenney; Dankmar Adler, Sullivan's brilliant engineering partner; the firms of Holabird and Roche and of Burnham and Root. The American twentieth-century master, Frank Lloyd Wright, had been an apprentice of Sullivan. Through the publication of his work, Wright's influence spread to Holland and Germany. (5) Finally, in Amsterdam, the relatively isolated work of Hendrik Berlage, who after 1911 introduced the architecture of Wright and other Americans to Europe. In the Amsterdam Stock Exchange of 1898, Berlage produced a building recognized in its own time as the first realization of a purified architecture (Giedion, *Space, Time,* 308–16). (6) The French designers who experimented brilliantly with reinforced concrete and glass fall out of the chronology: Henri Labrouste built his magnificent Bibliotheque Nationale in the period 1858–68, while Auguste Perret and Tony Garnier began to work in the first years of the twentieth century.

Before the war, innovations were particularly notable in the design of furniture and appliances. The inspiration came from England's Arts and Crafts Movement (see Pevsner, *Pioneers,* Chap. 6, and Gillian Naylor, *The Arts and Crafts Movement* [London: Studio Vista, 1971]). Interesting observations on progressive furniture design in Germany can be found in Janos Frecot and Sonja Günther, "City, Architecture, and Habitat," in Eberhard Roters, ed., *Berlin 1910–1933* (Secaucus, N.J.: Welfleet Press, 1982), 25–28. On the work of the German and the Austrian Werkbunds, see Joan Campbell, *The German Werkbund: The Politics of Reform in the Applied Arts* (Princeton: Princeton University Press, 1978), Chaps. 1–2 and the Bibliography.

20. Giedion sees the cultural crisis of the nineteenth century as the divergence between "the paths of science and the arts. . . . The connection between methods of thinking and methods of feeling was broken" (Giedion, *Space, Time,* 182).

21. Bruno Zevi, *Storia dell'Architettura Moderna* (Torino: Einaudi, 1961), 26 (my translation). See also Paul C. Vitz and Arnold B. Glimcher, *Modern Art and Modern Science: The Parallel Analysis of Vision* (New York: Praeger, 1984).

22. As early as 1836, the great German architect Karl Gutzkow, comparing England's industrial buildings to its neo-Gothic Parliament, commented: "Desperate to invent a modern style of architecture, we have turned in our newer epoch back to antiquity or the Middle Ages, and thereby admit either our extraordinary lack of spirit and imagination, or the sobering facts and utility factors behind some buildings being made preferably modern, such as granaries, housing for invalids and the like" (quoted by Heinrich Klotz, *The History of Postmodern Architecture* [Cambridge, Mass.: M.I.T. Press, 1988], 12).

23. Adolf Loos in Ulrich Conrads, *Programs and Manifestoes on Twentieth-Century Architecture* (Cambridge, Mass.: M.I.T. Press, 1970), 19, 20, 22.

24. Marcel Franciscono, *Walter Gropius and the Creation of the Bauhaus in Weimar* (Urbana: University of Illinois Press, 1971), 29–30.

25. Ian Boyd White in Tilmann Buddensieg, ed., *Industriekultur: Peter Behrens and the AEG* (Cambridge, Mass.: M.I.T. Press, 1984), ix. See in particular the articles by Tilmann Buddensieg ("Industriekultur") and Fritz Neumeyer ("The Workers' Housing of Peter Behrens"). Behrens's office attracted as assistants men who were to become the masters of the Modern Movement: Walter Gropius met his partner Adolf Meyer in Behrens's office and, in 1910, presented to Walter Rathenau a prescient proposal for prefabricated housing; Ludwig Mies van der Rohe collaborated with Behrens for several years and was directly influenced by his neoclassical side; and, for a few months before the war, Le Corbusier, who admired what he saw but harbored doubts about the office's functionalist side.

26. See Wright's 1901 lecture, "The Art and Craft of the Machine," in *Frank Lloyd Wright: Writings and Buildings,* selected by Edgar Kaufmann and Ben Raeburn (Cleveland: Meridian, 1967), 55–73, and also "The Nature of Materials," 222–29.

27. Ludwig Hilberseimer, *Architettura a Berlino negli Anni Venti* (Milano: Franco Angeli, 1981), 41–42 (my translation).

28. Futurism was primarily a literary movement, inspired and led by the poet Filippo Marinetti. The manifesto for architecture, the work of Antonio Sant'Elia, appeared in 1914, backed by a series of audacious drawings, which nevertheless remained within "the traditional canons of perspective." Sant'Elia died in World War I, and his unfulfilled experiment, says the historian Leonardo Benevolo,

remains "ambiguous and uncertain." It has been interpreted "as an anticipation of Gropius and Le Corbusier, or as an argument against international architecture and in favour of a hypothetical autonomous Italian tradition" (Benevolo, *History of Modern Architecture*, 2:396–97). Expressionism was particularly important in German painting, both before and after World War I. In architecture, its most noted representatives were Hans Poelzig (born in 1869), Erich Mendelsohn, and, despite their association with the Modern Movement, Bruno Taut, Hugo Häring, and Hans Scharoun, among others. Taut recognized Paul Scheerbart, the utopian poet of glass architecture who died in 1915, as an inspiration. The important Belgian architect Henry Van de Velde (born in 1863) was closely associated with Germany, where he directed the Weimar School of Applied Arts. Van de Velde had been one of the masters of art nouveau, from which the veering toward expressionism is logical, after the decoration is restrained. The most characteristic feature of expressionism is the emphasis on unique, original forms that tend toward the organic fluidity of nature (which, by definition, produces unique forms). Concrete, which permits the articulation of many different forms in one single material, is a favorite medium. After World War II concrete was easier to use in clearly expressionist manner, for instance, by Paul Rudolph and Eero Saarinen of the United States or by Jörn Utzon of Denmark in the Sydney Opera House. There is no doubt that Le Corbusier's later work is expressionist in part or whole, as in the noted examples of the church of Notre Dame du Haut at Ronchamps, the chapel within the Dominican convent of La Tourette, and the General Assembly Building and High Court of Chandigarh, the capital he designed at Nehru's request for East Punjab.

29. "Arbeitsrat für Kunst," in Conrads, *Programs*, 44–45.

30. Le Corbusier, *Towards a New Architecture*, 14; 210, 261–69.

31. In 1929, for instance, Le Corbusier was awarded the contract for a partially built Centrosoyuz in Moscow; one year later, Ernst May and a team of twenty-two architects, including Mart Stam and Hans Schmidt, left Germany to work in the Soviet Union; Hannes Meyer and a group of former Bauhaus students were also involved in planning; Bruno Taut moved his practice in 1931 to Moscow (Willett, *Art and Politics*, 217–18).

32. See Pawley, *Architecture*, Chap. 2, and Ronald Wiedenhoeft, "Workers' Housing as Social Politics," in *VIA IV: Culture and the Social Vision* (Cambridge, Mass.: M.I.T. Press, 1980), 112–25.

33. Charles Maier, "Between Taylorism and Technocracy: European Ideologies and the Vision of Industrial Productivity in the 1920s," *Journal of Contemporary History* 5, no. 2 (April 1970): 29.

34. Mary Nolan, "Housework Made Easy: The Taylorized Housewife in Weimar Germany's Rationalized Economy," *Feminist Studies* 16 (1990): 549–78.

35. Maier, "Between Taylorism and Technocracy." See the thesis by Jost Hermand, "Unity within Diversity? The History of the Concept 'Neue Sachlichkeit,' " in Keith Bullivant, ed., *Culture and Society in the Weimar Republic* (Manchester: Manchester University Press, 1977). Hermand argues that the Nazis attacked and condemned expressionism and the left-wing art of the 1920s. They allowed *Neue Sachlichkeit* to flourish in all but its openly left and critical forms.

36. Maier, "Between Taylorism and Technocracy," 59.

37. The most noted are André Lurçat, Pierre Chareau, the designer of a canonical glass house, Robert Mallet-Stevens, Eugène Beaudoin, and Marcel Lods, who,

in the 1930s, used economically and technically farsighted methods (metal skeleton and prefabricated infill elements of reinforced concrete as well as, stairs, balustrades, etc.) in public housing and schools. See Benevolo, *History of Modern Architecture,* 2:595ff.

38. These prototypes, famous in architectural history, were named the Domino House (1914) and the Monol and Citrohan houses (1920–22). They were partly realized in the project Le Corbusier built for the industrialist Henri Frugès at Pessac in 1925 and in the Paris International Exhibition of Decorative Arts of that year, in which, to the distaste of the exhibition's committee, Le Corbusier built, out of real materials, his "pavillon de l'Esprit Nouveau" and also exhibited the Plan Voisin for the center of Paris. See Charles Jencks, *Le Corbusier* (Cambridge, Mass.: Harvard University Press, 1973).

39. Le Corbusier's work of the 1920s and early 1930s includes the "ideal villas" built for rich and enlightened clients in the suburbs of Paris: the Cook House in Boulogne (1926), the villa for Leon Stein, Gertrude's brother (1927), the Villa Savoye at Poissy (1929–31), and the different Errazuriz Villa in Chile (1930). He had also realized two apartment buildings for the Weissenhof exhibit of 1927, the Salvation Army City of Refuge shelter in Paris (1929–33), the Swiss Pavilion in Paris's University City (1930–32), the botched Centrosoyuz in Moscow (1929), an apartment building in Geneva, and little else. His most influential projects were the unrealized competition designs for the League of Nations in Geneva (1927) and the Palace of the Soviets in 1931. The former, in particular, was an outrage to the Modern Movement; it led to the foundation of CIAM to henceforth support modern architects in competition. Le Corbusier had been selected among the nine winners, but the jury was tied. The politicians assigned the task of redesign to four traditionalist architects among the winners; their final submission, in neoclassic style, pirated Le Corbusier's plan. See Peter Blake, *Le Corbusier* (Baltimore: Penguin, 1964), Chap. 11.

40. Le Corbusier, quoted by Jencks, *Le Corbusier,* 121.

41. Pawley estimates that three million dwellings were completed between 1918 and 1933. Of these, the programs identified with the new architecture represented a small part: May's Frankfurt program realized only 15,000; in Berlin, the building society of the federation of industrial trade unions, the Gehag, produced 10,000 units in the period 1924–33, while three of the more traditional societies (for civil servants and white-collar unions) produced 71,000 units "in the form of tenements, semi-detached and detached houses between 1924 and 1929" (*Architecture,* 33). Wiedenhoeft's figure for Berlin is 161,000 new dwellings (both publicly and privately funded) from 1925 to 1931 ("Workers' Housing," 120).

42. Catherine Bauer, "The Social Front of Modern Architecture in the 1930s," *Journal of the Society of Architectural Historians* 24, no. 1 (March 1965): 48. This article is a cogent retrospective analysis of the Modern Movement's social thrust.

43. In 1925, the extremely influential book by Adolf Behne, *Der moderne Zweckbau* (Modern Functional Construction), articulated the new ideas about building.

44. Lane, *Architecture and Politics,* 39.

45. See Wiedenhoeft, "Workers' Housing," 113ff.

46. W. Gaunt, "A Modern Utopia?" *Studio* 98 (1929): 859.

47. Wiedenhoeft, "Workers' Housing," 118.

48. Pawley, *Architecture*, 28–29. I have also consulted Italian translations of German literature, in particular Carlo Aymonino, ed., *L'Abitazione Razionale: Atti dei Congressi CIAM 1929–30* (Padova: Marsilio, 1971); Ernst May, *Das neue Frankfurt* (Bari: Laterza, 1975); Martin Steinmann, "Il Secondo CIAM e il Problema del Minimum," *Psicon* (Florence), 2–3 (1975): 61–70. In English, see Catherine Bauer's classic, *Modern Housing* (Boston: Houghton-Mifflin, 1934), Part 4; Lane, *Architecture and Politics;* and Wiedenhoeft, "Workers' Housing."

49. Both quotations are in Klotz, *The History of Postmodern Architecture*, 24.

50. Of course, the fascists knew the symbolic importance of form and exploited it politically with extraordinary talent. On the spectacles designed and planned by the architect Albert Speer for the Nazis, see Lane, *Architecture and Politics*, and especially Robert Taylor, *The Word in Stone* (Berkeley: University of California Press, 1974).

51. Bruno Taut, quoted by Lane, *Architecture and Politics*, 45.

52. Conrads, *Manifestoes*, 57–58.

53. Wiedenhoeft, "Workers' Housing," 120.

54. Its avowed purpose was, in part, to defend modern architects from the injurious treatment Le Corbusier had just suffered in the competition for the League of Nations. See Ciucci, "Invention," 70ff.

55. Richard Pommer and Christian F. Otto, *Weissenhof 1927 and the Modern Movement in Architecture* (Chicago: University of Chicago Press, 1991), 166.

56. Henry Russell Hitchcock and Philip Johnson, *The International Style* (New York: Norton, 1966), 20.

57. Hitchcock and Johnson, *International Style*, 41.

58. Bauer, "The Social Front," 49. She continues: "With this dogmatic approach, the Ernst May team soon set off for Russia, where it doubtless contributed to their failure, along with their inability to cope with a backward building industry."

59. Sybil Moholy-Nagy, who lived the Modern Movement, ironically points out that Hitchcock and Johnson "slew the anti-aesthetic, expedient, economic and socially conscious tendencies of the day with arguments that would have expelled them instantly from Le Corbusier's CIAM, Gropius' Bauhaus, Mies' Werkbund and Oud's De Stijl . . . no one caught [their] schizophrenic sleight of hand, least of all the diaspora architects who only wanted to be accepted" ("The Diaspora," *Journal of the Society of Architectural Historians* 24, no. 1 [March 1965]: 25).

60. An interesting note is that Mies van der Rohe, who was to develop in America the "curtain wall" and the exposed frame, believed so profoundly in the merits of brick that learning design and construction in brick was a fundamental part of his program at the Illinois Institute of Technology (William Jordy, "The Aftermath of the Bauhaus in America," in H. Fleming and B. Baylin, eds., *The Atlantic Migration* [Cambridge, Mass.: Harvard University Press, 1964], 512–13).

61. Le Corbusier, quoted in Benevolo, *History of Modern Architecture*, 2:444–45. The contrast between "landed" and "grounded" buildings was developed for me by the architect Charles Gwathmey during an interview in which he contrasted the approach of his teacher Louis Kahn to that of Le Corbusier, recognizing both as main sources of inspiration.

62. See Giedion, *Space, Time,* 837ff., and Jencks, *Le Corbusier,* 123.

63. It is interesting to observe the increasing ideological dogmatism in an inventive architect like the Swiss Hannes Meyer, Gropius's first and most controversial successor at the Bauhaus. For an Italian collection of his writings, see Hannes Meyer, *Architettura o Rivoluzione* (Padova: Marsilio, 1969).

64. Le Corbusier, *La Charte d'Athènes* (Paris: Minuit, 1957), 87–91 (my translation).

65. Rudolf Arnheim, *The Dynamics of Architectural Form* (Berkeley: University of California Press, 1977), 10.

66. Steven Peterson, "Space and Anti-Space," *Harvard Architecture Review* 1 (1980): 91.

67. On Brasilia, see James Holston's important study, *The Modernist City* (Chicago: University of Chicago Press, 1989).

68. Alan Colquhoun, "On Modern and Postmodern Space," in Joan Ockman, ed., *Architecture Criticism Ideology* (New York: Princeton Architectural Press, 1985), 105.

69. In Barbaralee Diamonstein, *American Architecture Now II* (New York: Rizzoli, 1985), 93.

70. Karl Scheffler, quoted by Frecot and Günther, "City Architecture," 25.

71. William Conklin, "Forum: The Beaux-Arts Exhibition," *Oppositions* 8 (1977): 161–62.

72. Gropius, invited to chair the Department of Architecture at Harvard, was joined by his Bauhaus collaborator, Marcel Breuer; Mies van der Rohe, at the Illinois Institute of Technology, called to Chicago two teachers of his brief period as Bauhaus director, Ludwig Hilberseimer and Walter Peterhans; the graphic designers Herbert Bayer and Josef Albers ended up at Yale, and Laszlo Moholy-Nagy, with the sponsorship of the enlightened Walter Paepcke of the Container Corporation of America, reopened the Bauhaus as a graphic arts center in Chicago (after Moholy-Nagy's death in 1946 it was reabsorbed into the IIT; on this episode, see James Sloan Allen, *The Romance of Commerce and Culture* [Chicago: University of Chicago Press, 1983], Chap. 2).

73. Jordy, "Aftermath," 522.

74. The dollar volume of new construction rose from $25.6 billion in 1946 to $29.5 billion in 1947 (constant dollars of 1957–59); in constant dollars of 1967, the volume of new construction, which becomes $31 billion for 1947, rose to $51.6 billion in 1954, then almost $57 billion in 1955. After a brief and small decline in 1956 and 1957, it returned to 1955 levels and jumped to $63 billion in 1959, $62.5 billion in 1960, $64.6 billion in 1961, $68 billion in 1962, $72.7 billion in 1963, and $75.2 billion in 1964 (*Construction Review,* Dec. 1979, 6).

75. William Jordy, *American Buildings and Their Architects,* vol. 4, *The Impact of European Modernism in the Mid-Twentieth Century* (Garden City, N.Y.: Doubleday/Anchor Books, 1976), 222.

76. Moholy-Nagy, "Diaspora," 25. The true technological vision, indeed, was American. Since the late 1920s Buckminster Fuller had been denouncing the Bauhaus for the nullity of its technological program. See Reyner Banham's important treatise on (and partial rebuttal of) European modernism, *Theory and Design in the First Machine Age* (New York: Praeger, 1960), 326ff., for an endorsement of Fuller's technological genius demonstrated as early as 1927 in the Dymaxion House.

77. See Jordy, *American Buildings*, 4:233, 237.

78. Robert Hughes, "Doing Their Own Thing," *Time*, Jan. 8, 1979, 52.

79. Michael Sorkin, "American Architecture since 1960: Quo Vadis," *A & U* (Tokyo) Extra ed. (March 1981): 24. Arguably, American business had discovered the advantages of design much earlier than in the 1950s (though later than the German AEG!): Norman Bel Geddes, noted for the "streamlined" design of automobiles and trains, invented the profession of industrial designer in the late 1920s. See Robert Stern's interesting comments about the 1920s in the United States: "Relevance of the Decade," *Journal of the Society of Architectural Historians*, 24, no. 1 (March 1965): 6–10. See also Allen, *Romance*.

80. Suzanne Stephens, "Precursors of Postmodernism," in *A & U* (Tokyo) Extra ed. (March 1981): 334. The architects are Eero Saarinen, Edward Durrell Stone, Minoru Yamasaki, Philip Johnson, and Louis Kahn.

81. Klaus Herdeg, *The Decorated Diagram* (Cambridge, Mass.: M.I.T. Press, 1983), 79 (emphasis added). The group studied by Herdeg includes: I. M. Pei (with Philip Johnson, the most internationally established of American architects, both as a designer and a commercial success); his present partner Henry Cobb; Edward Larrabee Barnes; John Johansen; Philip Johnson; Paul Rudolph; Ulrich Franzen; Victor Lundy; and two of Gropius's partners in his firm The Architects Collaborative (TAC), John Harkness and Louis McMillen.

82. Quotations from a Gropius Master's Class Problem, in Herdeg, *Diagram*, 79.

83. Jane Jacobs, *The Death and Life of Great American Cities* (New York: Vintage, 1961).

84. Robert Venturi, *Complexity and Contradiction in Architecture* (New York: Museum of Modern Art, 1966). Jacobs influenced Venturi's thought directly and indirectly. The most influential writing by an urban sociologist in this period was Herbert Gans's study of Boston's West End, parts of which appeared in the *Journal of the American Institute of Planners* (Feb. 1959) and are quoted by Jacobs (*Death and Life*, 272). The whole study was published as *The Urban Villagers* (Glencoe, Ill.: Free Press, 1962). Gans was teaching in the 1950s and early 1960s at the University of Pennsylvania, in close association with Venturi and, especially, with Denise Scott Brown, who would later become Venturi's collaborator, wife, and partner. Scott Brown and Venturi acknowledge Gans's influence on their joint work.

85. Published in 1966, Venturi's book coincided with Aldo Rossi's *Architecture of the City*, which became highly influential in American schools after it was translated into English. Rossi's different departure from modernism speaks, in a sense, to cities ravaged not yet by "progress" but by war. Rejecting all surface work, Rossi and his followers in the new "rationalism" engage in a search for deep historical differences, which have sedimented into a morphology of types, of "urban artifacts." Apparently more confident than Venturi in both architecture and collective public life, Rossi meditates on "the historical use of geometric forms" and demands monuments whose beauty "resides both in the laws of architecture which they embody and in the collective's reason for desiring them" (Aldo Rossi, *Architettura della Città* [Padova: Marsilio, 1966]; English edition, revised by Rossi and Peter Eisenman, *The Architecture of the City* [Cambridge, Mass.: M.I.T. Press, 1982], 126).

86. *History of Postmodern Architecture*, Klotz, 5.

87. In Diamonstein, *American Architecture Now II*, 155.

88. Venturi, *Complexity and Contradiction*, 22–23 (emphasis added).

89. For instance, Mies's archetypal Seagram building illustrates the modernist's search for aesthetic, not functional, purity: Its back should look like the blank wall it actually is because of the wind's lateral forces. But Mies did not think twice about covering it with the same beautifully detailed I-beams that frame the glass panels at the front and sides. By "dressing" the back wall Mies gave to the building its intended and perfect unity of appearance. Such hard-achieved unity had to be shown off: *the perfect modern building is designed to stand alone*. Philip Johnson described to me in these words the plaza that cost Sam Bronfman (Mr. Seagram) a million dollars a year in rent: "Mies decided to put [the building] back. I didn't think of it. It didn't cross my dim brain, but it did Mies. He said 'just put it on the back of the site. There is no way you can get back to look at a building in New York, so we'll create our own foreground and you'll see our building.'"

90. Robert Venturi, Denise Scott Brown, and Steven Izenour, *Learning from Las Vegas* (Cambridge, Mass.: M.I.T. Press, 1972), 89.

91. Venturi, *Complexity and Contradiction*, 51, 52.

92. Venturi, *Complexity and Contradiction*, 102.

93. James Freed has commented that Mies "did not perceive that in the US these architectural issues would be worked out in a different way. . . . [He] unwittingly made it possible in the long run to build in a shoddier way. When Mies's followers took over with their determinist aesthetic, developers realized that they didn't have to use stone or expensive details. They saw the new aesthetic as giving them free rein to put up simple, unadorned cheap glass boxes. Mies's theories led to buildings that were too abstracted" (quoted in Diamonstein, *American Architecture Now II*, 93).

94. Charles Jencks, *The Language of Post-Modern Architecture* (New York: Rizzoli, 1977), 6.

95. Vincent P. Pecora, "Towers of Babel," in Diane Ghirardo, ed., *Out of Site* (Seattle: Bay Press, 1991), 49.

96. Hugh Hardy, quoted in Diamonstein, *American Architecture Now II*, 84.

97. The Architectural League's 1965 exhibition, "Forty under Forty" (a practice initiated in 1941), was curated by Robert Stern under the supervision of Philip Johnson; it included many of the names that were to become noted in the revision of the modern in following years. Stern noted in the catalog that the number one problem of the younger architects was always finding "the elusive client who will have confidence in a younger man" (or woman!). In 1967, the Museum of Modern Art presented "The New City: Architecture and Urban Renewal," bringing attention to a number of architects working in urban design—some, like Jaquelin Robertson and Alexander Cooper, in the administration of Mayor John Lindsay. In 1979, the influential Arthur Drexler of the MOMA curated "Transformations in Modern Architecture," a massive exhibit that covered architectural trends worldwide; its main characteristic was a raging eclecticism, which still made a large part for International Style monumentality.

98. Andreas Huyssen, "Mapping the Postmodern," in *After the Great Divide* (Bloomington: University of Indiana Press, 1986), 187–88.

99. The Institute was in a certain sense an extension of CASE (Conference of Architects for the Study of the Environment), a group of young East Coast architects and some of their teachers who had been meeting regularly since the early 1960s. CASE had self-consciously tried to emulate CIAM. Peter Eisenman says that "at various times the group included Bob Venturi [this is disputed by others], Richard Meier, Michael Graves, Tim Vreeland, Charles Moore, Mike McKinnell, Vincent Scully and Colin Rowe" (Diamonstein, *American Architecture Now II,* 72). On *Oppositions,* see Pecora, "Towers of Babel," and Joan Ockman, "Resurrecting the Avant-Garde," in Beatriz Colomina, ed., *Architecture Production* (New York: Princeton Architectural Press, 1988).

100. See Jencks, *Language of Post-Modern Architecture,* 80, and *Abstract Representation* (London: 1983).

101. Robert Stern, "The Doubles of Postmodern," *Harvard Architecture Review* 1 (1980): 76, 82.

102. "It consisted of elegant slab blocks fourteen stories high with rational 'streets in the air' (which were safe from cars but, as it turned out, not safe from crime); 'sun, space and greenery.' . . . It had a separation of pedestrian and vehicular traffic, the provision of play space, and local amenities such as laundries, creches and gossip centres" (Jencks, *Language,* 9). Note here the classical conceit of the architect: presuming that the people who had so vandalized, defaced, and mutilated Pruitt-Igoe hated *the building* and that the building had, itself, in some way caused their behavior rather than their forced displacements and their confinement with scarce jobs in the no-man's-land surrounding downtown St. Louis. Moreover, Jencks is wrong about the date of Pruitt-Igoe's demolition: only a piece was dynamited to make a dramatic point about the lack of federal funds for the long-slated demolition of a vacant project (personal communication from Roger Montgomery).

103. Dolores Hayden, *Redesigning the American Dream* (New York: Norton, 1984), 123.

104. Klotz, *History of Postmodern Architecture,* 75.

105. Vincent Scully, *American Architecture and Urbanism,* rev. ed. (New York: Henry Holt, 1988), 277 (emphasis added).

106. Johnson appeared holding a model of the AT&T building on the cover of *Time* (Jan. 8, 1979); when the design was selected, the *New York Times* gave it front-page coverage. See Todd A. Marder, ed., *The Critical Edge: Controversy in Recent American Architecture* (Cambridge, Mass.: M.I.T. Press, 1985).

107. William Pedersen, KPF's most noted designer, follows classical and symmetric principles of composition and uses classicist detail even where (as in the 1979–83 building at 333 Wacker Drive in Chicago) the overall form and the glass skin are clearly not "historicist." Among KPF's most notable designs, are the "mixed materials" and mixed vocabularies of the Hercules, Inc., headquarters in Wilmington (1979–83, design by Arthur May); the limestone and marble towers and generous site plan of the Procter and Gamble general offices complex in Cincinnati (1982–85), and a number of towers which try hard to be contextual and to respect the street (perhaps the most distinctive towers by William Pedersen are the 1982 building at 75 Federal Street in Boston and 125 East 57th Street in New York, finished in 1986).

108. Scully, *American Architecture*, 278.

109. Klotz, *History of Postmodern Architecture*, 83.

CHAPTER 3

1. A foremost example of this kind of analysis is Fredric Jameson's much-discussed article "Postmodernism, or the Cultural Logic of Late Capitalism," *New Left Review* 146 (July–Aug. 1987): 53–92.

2. It must be noted that private investment chiefly moves toward the financial, insurance, business, research, and professional services, which, like communication and transportation, are increasingly important for the production, circulation, and distribution of goods in the "postindustrial" phase.

3. The situation of American cities is closer to one long known in the Third World: Economic capitals become more dependent on world trends, while regional centers increasingly depend on decision-making nuclei seated elsewhere. I draw extensively in this chapter from several works: Scott Lash and John Urry, *The End of Organized Capitalism* (Madison: University of Wisconsin Press, 1987); Robert B. Cohen, "The New International Division of Labor: Multinational Corporations and Urban Hierarchy," in Michael Dear and Allen Scott, eds., *Urbanization and Urban Planning in Capitalist Society* (New York: Methuen, 1981); John R. Logan and Harvey L. Molotch, *Urban Fortunes: The Political Economy of Place* (Berkeley: University of California Press, 1987); and John H. Mollenkopf, *The Contested City* (Princeton: Princeton University Press, 1983).

4. See Magali Sarfatti Larson et al., "The Professional Supply of Design," in Judith R. Blau, Mark E. La Gory, and John S. Pipkin, eds., *Professionals and Urban Form* (Albany: State University of New York Press, 1983).

5. Francis T. Ventre, "Myth and Paradox in the Building Enterprise," in Paul L. Knox, ed., *The Design Professions and the Built Environment* (New York: Nichols, 1988), 165. Robert Gutman reports that managers, especially "for buildings in which professionals and other upper-white collar personnel are employed," often solicit the views of staff and workers about their space needs and preferences. "One of the reasons . . . is the belief that designs that are more responsive to worker needs will improve productivity and morale" (*Architectural Practice: A Critical View* [New York: Princeton Architectural Press, 1988], 89).

6. I borrow the term *symbolic analysts* from Robert Reich, who points out that most of the jobs of the most successful fifth of the labor force "consist of analyzing or manipulating symbols—words, numbers or visual images." Of course, Reich's thesis is that most of the new elite either refuses to live in cities or "lives, shops and works in areas of cities that, if not beautiful, are at least esthetically tolerable and reasonably safe" ("Secession of the Successful," *New York Times Magazine*, Jan. 20, 1991, 42, 44).

7. Philip Siller, interview with the author.

8. For a pioneering approach to the issue of savings and investments, see Fred Block, "Bad Data Drive out Good: The Decline of Personal Savings Reexamined," *Journal of Post-Keynesian Economics* 13 (1990): 3–19.

9. Manuel Castells, *The City and the Grassroots: A Cross-Cultural Theory of Urban Social Movements* (Berkeley: University of California Press, 1983), 302.

10. Fred Block, *Postindustrial Possibilities* (Berkeley: University of California Press, 1990), 19.

11. Carolyn Teich Adams, *The Politics of Capital Investment: The Case of Philadelphia* (Albany: State University of New York Press, 1988), 24. For the distinction between economic and social overhead capital, see pp. 6–7. Mollenkopf, *The Contested City,* and Logan and Molotch, *Urban Fortunes,* represent the "progrowth" coalition approach. Paul Peterson, *City Limits* (Chicago: University of Chicago Press, 1981), is one of the best-known examples of "economic structuralism." Adams's lucid study of Philadelphia's investment politics supports the last view better than the first. But she also discovers that a strong redistributive tendency toward poorer neighborhoods was sustained through the 1970s, even as the city's total budget for capital outlays shrank.

12. Logan and Molotch, *Urban Fortunes,* 57. Morton White and Lucia White discuss the American distrust of cities in *The Intellectual versus the City* (Cambridge, Mass.: Harvard University Press, 1962). On Progressivism and the preaching of an antiurban ideal to the urban working class, see in particular Gwendolyn Wright, *Moralism and the Model Home* (Chicago: University of Chicago Press, 1980); Roy Lubove, *The Progressives and the Slums* (Pittsburgh: University of Pittsburgh Press, 1962); and, in general, Paul Boyer, *Urban Masses and Moral Order in America, 1820–1920* (Cambridge, Mass.: Harvard University Press, 1978).

13. Adams, *Politics of Capital Investment,* 33ff.

14. John Mollenkopf reports that "in 1919, some 5,838 central offices controlled . . . 7.8% of all plants and one-third of all industrial employment. By 1929, roughly the same number of central offices accounted for 12% of the plants and 48% of employment. . . . By 1974, the five hundred biggest corporate offices controlled 71% of all manufacturing assets and 76% of the employment." Today, "two-thirds of the *Fortune* 500 . . . headquarters are located in the twenty-five largest metropolitan areas. New York City still contains one out of every seven headquarters, three times more than Chicago, the next largest corporate center" (*Contested City,* 30–31).

15. The reasons for the early decentralization of economic activity in the American metropolis were both technological and social. On the one hand, American industry was far more capital intensive than its European counterparts in the interwar period. Requiring increasing acreage for each employee, modern industries found plentiful cheap land outside the metropolitan areas. On the other hand, since the depression of 1893, labor unrest and militant strikes had moved from smaller towns and outlying areas into the larger cities. There, the numbers and poverty of the immigrant masses nourished in the native middle classes a feeling of besiegement and fear of class warfare. See David M. Gordon, "Capitalist Development and the History of American Cities," in William K. Tabb and Larry Sawers, eds., *Marxism and the Metropolis* (New York: Oxford University Press, 1978), and "Class Struggle and the Stages of American Urban Development," in D. Perry and A. Watkins, eds., *The Rise of Sunbelt Cities* (Beverly Hills, Calif.: Sage, 1977). The classic work on early suburbanization is Sam Bass Warner, *Streetcar Suburbs* (Cambridge, Mass.: M.I.T. Press, 1973).

16. Mollenkopf, *Contested City,* 108. I follow his analysis closely in this section. On suburbanization before World War II, see Lash and Urry, *End of Organized Capitalism,* 116, and Table 4.5. Most industrial plants put up by the federal gov-

ernment in the war years (about twice the volume of what private industry built) were in the suburbs, and they were turned over to the private sector at the war's end. See Patrick J. Ashton, "The Political Economy of Suburban Development," in Tabb and Sawers, *Marxism and the Metropolis,* and Mollenkopf, *Contested City,* 98–109.

17. The most important programs for the cities were the Public Works Administration and the Work Progress Administration, the Housing Authority of the PWA, and the Federal Housing Authority, which, unlike other legislation, was directly designed by deadly foes of public and subsidized housing (representatives of the building industry and of the powerful National Association of Real Estate Boards). See Mollenkopf, *Contested City,* 54ff.

18. Mollenkopf, *Contested City,* 71.

19. Leonardo Benevolo, *History of Modern Architecture,* vol. 2, *The Modern Movement* (Cambridge, Mass.: M.I.T. Press, 1971), 651.

20. Richard Pommer, "The Architecture of Urban Housing in the U.S. in the Early 1930s," *Journal of the Society of Architectural Historians* 37 (1978): 235. Pommer analyzes extensively the projects open to modern influences, some of which were included by Henry Russell Hitchcock and Philip Johnson in the 1932 International Style exhibition. Architectural research groups interested in housing— Buckminster Fuller's group and the Housing Study Guild organized by Lewis Mumford and Henry Wright in New York, the Architectural Research Group organized by Louis Kahn among unemployed architects in Philadelphia—influenced some of the practitioners, among whom were several Europeans (Oskar Stonorov and Alfred Kastner in Philadelphia, William Lescaze in Philadelphia and New York, and Alfred Frey and Albert Mayer in New York). Henry Wright, Clarence Stein, and their associates (like Frederick Ackerman, who became the director of New York City's Housing Authority) had a ubiquitous influence. Pommer believes that Henry Wright was the only one in his generation (he died in 1936) who understood European housing; his efforts to amalgamate it with American design led to his break with Clarence Stein.

21. With her classic book, *Modern Housing* (Boston: Houghton-Mifflin, 1934)— written after her trip to Europe with Mumford in the late 1920s—Catherine Bauer had become an expert in both European and American subsidized and low-cost housing. Lewis Mumford, of course, was widely known both as an independent scholar and as an advocate for affordable and humane housing and democratic urban planning.

22. Vincent Scully comments on the work of Henry Wright and Clarence Stein: "Working in a tradition as much Jeffersonian as picturesque . . . these two most dedicated of American housing experts and planners of the 1920s and 1930s had obviously come to loathe the density of the city and to hate its streets: they clearly used their radial roads to separate the buildings on both sides, not to connect them, as the city street had done, with a common, multiple-use public space." Their urban housing groups also showed "great suburban, perhaps even village charm" (*American Architecture and Urbanism,* rev. ed. [New York: Henry Holt and Co., 1988], 163–64).

23. See Robert Stern, "International Style: The Crimson Connection," *Progressive Architecture,* Feb. 1982. As a young architecture professor, Holmes Perkins

helped Walter Gropius weather his first semester at Harvard. Later, as dean, he transformed the University of Pennsylvania's School of Architecture from a stubborn Beaux-Arts stronghold into a premiere modernist school (interview with the author, 1981).

24. Yet the United States in the 1930s counted with some remarkable architectural achievements in the modern style. Among many other notable buildings, the pioneering work of Frank Lloyd Wright's first Chicago phase had influenced European architects since the beginning of the century. In the 1920s, Rudolph Schindler and Richard Neutra brought modernism of European stamp to the original architecture of the West Coast. In the 1930s, Frank Lloyd Wright added two masterpieces to his opus: the extraordinary buildings for the Johnson Wax Company in Racine, Wisconsin, and the "Falling Water" house at Bear Run, Pennsylvania. In the large cities, says Vincent Scully, "the last of the old" skyscrapers and "the first of the new" appeared: Most notable among the "old" was the Beaux-Arts plan of the Rockefeller Center, built from 1931 to 1939, and the McGraw Hill building by Raymond Hood of 1931. The "new" was the Philadelphia Saving Fund Society building of 1932, designed by George Howe, a Beaux-Arts architect who had chosen modernism and would become dean at Yale, and his Swiss partner William Lescaze. See Scully, *American Architecture,* 151–54ff. The modern style was established enough in 1932 for an important businessman like James Willcox, chairman of PSFS, to be persuaded by Howe and Lescaze's logic, if not quite by the aesthetics of the building. See Robert Stern, "International Style: Immediate Effects," *Progressive Architecture,* Feb. 1982, and *George Howe: Toward a Modern American Architecture* (New Haven: Yale University Press, 1975).

25. The proceedings of the Connecticut General Life Insurance Conference of 1957 on the problems of cities were published by Wilfred Owen under the title *Cities in the Motor Age* (New York: Viking, 1959). See the classic work by Edgar M. Hoover and Raymond Vernon, *Anatomy of a Metropolis* (Cambridge, Mass.: Harvard University Press, 1959), and Raymond Vernon, *The Myth and Reality of Our Urban Problems* (Cambridge, Mass.: M.I.T.-Harvard Joint Center for Urban Studies, 1962).

26. See Barry Checkoway, "Large Builders, Federal Housing, Postwar Suburbanization," in Rachel Bratt, Chester Hartman, and Ann Meyerson, eds., *Critical Perspectives on Housing* (Philadelphia: Temple University Press, 1986), in particular 120–23. I have relied for this section on *Critical Perspectives;* on Gwendolyn Wright, *Building the Dream* (Cambridge, Mass.: M.I.T. Press, 1983); on Bernard J.J. Frieden and Lynne B. Sagalyn, *Downtown, Inc.: How America Rebuilds Cities* (Cambridge, Mass.: M.I.T. Press, 1990); and on Martin Mayer, *The Builders: Houses, Peoples, Neighborhoods, Governments, Money* (New York: Norton, 1978). Federally insured mortgages, repaid over twenty-five years at low interest rates, required only a 10 percent down payment, while veteran mortgages required none and could be repaid over thirty years at 4 percent interest (Frieden and Sagalyn, *Downtown,* 11ff.). Mayer illustrates this with the example of a vet who bought a Levittown house for $8,000 in 1949 and was still paying $38 a month for it in 1977; next door, a Vietnam vet who had just bought the same type of house for $40,000 with a 9 percent thirty-year VA mortgage would have been paying $321 a month (*Builders,* 14).

27. Ashton, "The Political Economy of Suburban Development," 74.

28. The architect-planner Andrés Duany predicted in a 1990 interview on National Public Radio that the more modest suburbs will become "the new slums." On the types of suburbs and the inequality among them, see Logan and Molotch, *Urban Fortunes*, 187–99, and 193–95 on the racial segregation of the suburbs. See also Wright, *Building the Dream*, 248–49, for the endorsement of residential racism by the Federal Housing Authority.

29. Checkoway, "Large Builders," 122–23, and Michael Stone, "Housing and the Dynamics of U.S. Capitalism," in Bratt, Hartman, and Meyerson, *Critical Perspectives*, 51. See also Wright, *Building the Dream*, 242ff.

30. See Benevolo, *History of Modern Architecture*, 2:663ff.

31. The FHA, for one, did not consider that too-modern designs were a sound investment, and it turned down Frank Lloyd Wright's moderate-cost prefabricated "Usonian" houses. From 1941 on, Walter Gropius returned with Konrad Wachsmann to his early interest in prefabrication, in the hope of bringing some sort of order to the suburbs through standardization of parts and inventive planning, but it was never applied (Benevolo, *History of Modern Architecture*, 2:661–62). In the private sector, some builders commissioned prototype designs from architects, notably Joseph Eichler in California. "A typical contract with a builder gave the architect a retainer fee of $1,000 and $100 for each house that was built from his plans. The architectural journals endorsed these collaborations, proudly declaring that the influence of professional architects would be the salvation of mass building" (Wright, *Building the Dream*, 248–53). The influential designs for upscale private houses that became associated with "the California life-style" have practically all been suburban: So were, for example, Neutra's 1920s houses as well as his later work; most of Frank Lloyd Wright's houses—not only the "Usonian" prototypes but his luxurious homes on the West Coast and elsewhere; the Bay Region homes by William Wurster and Joseph Esherick before and after the war; Walter Gropius's and Marcel Breuer's houses in New England after 1938; and the "Case Study Houses" commissioned by the magazine *Arts and Architecture* between 1945 and 1966 in southern California (from architects Charles Eames, Craig Ellwood, Quincy Jones, Pierre Koenig, Richard Neutra, Raphael Soriano, and Eero Saarinen, among others). See Elizabeth A. T. Smith, ed., *Blueprints for Modern Living: History and Legacy of the Case Study Houses* (Cambridge, Mass.: M.I.T. Press, 1990).

32. Mayer, *Builders*, 32–33.

33. Ashton, "The Political Economy of Suburban Development," 72ff. During the 1960s, central cities lost, on the whole, 9 percent of their white population, while the black population grew by about 40 percent. "By 1980, 55 percent of blacks versus 24 percent of whites lived in central cities, and almost one-third of the entire central city population was black or Hispanic. During a period (1969–76) in which government-defined poverty dropped for the United States, it increased 6 percent in central cities and 16 percent in those larger than one million" (Susan Fainstein and Norman Fainstein, "Economic Change, National Policy, and the System of Cities," in Susan S. Fainstein et al., *Restructuring the City* [New York: Longman, 1983], 4).

34. At the end of the 1970s, industrial employment in the larger cities was down to 25 percent (compared to 75 percent in 1930), while the proportion of suburban

commuters to center city started to dwindle. See Lash and Urry, *End of Organized Capitalism*, 116–18.

35. Housing Advisory Committee, quoted in Mollenkopf, *Contested City*, 115. Of the committee's twenty-three members, "ten were bankers and lenders, seven were in real estate, architecture and building supply." A lawyer, a conservative economist, two officials of building trade unions, a Republican Housing Authority director from Cleveland, and the chairman—the new appointee to the head of the Home and Housing Financing Authority—completed the list. The new coalitions are described in *Contested City*, 77, 118–19ff., and in Frieden and Sagalyn, *Downtown*, 17–19.

36. Frieden and Sagalyn, *Downtown*, 16, 19.

37. Frieden and Sagalyn, *Downtown*, 44.

38. Scully, *American Architecture*, 167–69.

39. These apt words are William H. Jordy's. See his *American Buildings and Their Architects*, vol. 4, *The Impact of European Modernism in the Mid-Twentieth Century* (Garden City, N.Y.: Anchor/Doubleday, 1976). For Vincent Scully, Mies taught architects what was lost in the essentially graphic architecture of Gropius and Breuer: how to build "properly firm, permanent urban structures once again." Large bureaucratic firms (in particular the multicity firm of Skidmore Owings and Merrill) attained real excellence in following Mies's models closely. See Scully, *American Architecture*, 184ff.

40. Jordy, *American Buildings*, 4:249–51.

41. The literature on this brutal destruction of human lives is large. Jane Jacobs's *The Death and Life of Great American Cities* (New York, Random House, 1961) is perhaps the classic critique of urban renewal. A sensitive ethnographic account is Herbert Gans, *The Urban Villagers* (New York: Free Press, 1962). Robert Caro, *The Power Broker: Robert Moses and the Fall of New York* (New York: Knopf, 1974), offers a complete analysis of the renovation of New York and a powerful portrait of the man who became the emblem of cities killed by highways. Frieden and Sagalyn, *Downtown*, Chap. 2, provide a summary and an extensive bibliography. They report that 63 percent of all the families displaced from 1949 through 1963 whose race was reported were nonwhite (p. 28). By 1978, the residents of public housing were over 60 percent nonwhite, against 26 percent in 1944 and 39 percent in 1951. See Rachel G. Bratt, "Public Housing: The Controversy and Contribution," in Bratt, Hartman, and Meyerson, *Critical Perspectives*, 339. The production of public housing peaked in 1971, with 91,000 units. The private sector had become involved from 1959 on, in direct competition with public housing. The "turnkey" form of subsidized housing—important for architects—was introduced in 1965 (a developer's team competes to enter into a contract with a local housing authority, to which the developer then sells the finished project at a stipulated price; Bratt, "Public Housing," 341–42).

42. See Mollenkopf, *Contested City*, Chaps. 2 and 3. On the relation between urban renewal and ghetto revolts, see Roger Friedland, *Power and Crisis in the City* (London: Macmillan and Co., 1982).

43. Frieden and Sagalyn, *Downtown*, 266.

44. This was the conclusion drawn from survey data on the preferences of suburban and urban residents. See William Michelson, "Most People Don't Want What Architects Want" *Trans-action* 5, no. 8 (July–Aug. 1968): 37–43.

45. For a thorough comparison of Northeast and Southwest cities, see Mollenkopf, *Contested City,* Chap. 6.

46. Mollenkopf, *Contested City,* 131, and Bratt, "Public Housing," 341. The percentage of architect-designed housing is reputedly negligible (there are no precise figures; estimates vary from 5 to 20 percent), but it is presumably stable, and it constitutes a very large part of what smaller firms design. The fluctuations of the construction industry and of real estate investment affect architectural practice in complex ways: For many architects, the loss of commissions for the commercial and institutional facilities required by large-scale new housing developments (the only kind that has an effect on statistics) has much graver consequences than the decline of housing starts in itself. Smaller firms, on the other hand, may benefit if strong demand, coupled with increases in the price of new housing, results in more rehabilitation and renovation of older structures. See Larson et al., "The Professional Supply of Design." However, in a recession, all investments decline; the fall in housing starts is just a sensitive indicator of the economic cycle because of the direct and symbiotic association of real estate with capital markets. For the period before the deregulation of the savings and loans, see Mayer, *Builders,* 353–415.

47. Mollenkopf reports that if the CDBG allocation formula "had not been amended in 1977 . . . New England would have lost 37% of its funds while the West South Central region would have increased 203%. The share of funds going to large central cities would have dropped from 71.8% of HUD grants to 42.2%. . . . Between 1971 and 1974, for example, grants to Dallas increased tenfold, Houston fourfold, Phoenix fourfold and Birmingham fivefold, while most northeastern cities made little gains" (*Contested City,* 134–35).

48. Michael Pagano and Richard Moore, *Cities and Fiscal Choices* (Durham, N.C.: Duke University Press, 1985), quoted in Adams, *Politics of Capital Investment,* 140.

49. Richard Child Hill, "Crisis in the Motor City: The Politics of Economic Development in Detroit," in Fainstein et al., *Restructuring the City,* 105.

50. In Philadelphia, for instance, city-wide projects *not* located downtown (such as a stadium, two airports, the gas works, an ill-planned convention center, the now defunct municipal hospital, and, in particular, federally mandated improvements to the city's waste-water treatment plants) increased at the expense of neighborhood capital investments far more than did downtown projects from the mid-1960s to the 1980s (Adams, *Politics of Capital Investment,* 129–34).

51. For a detailed description of how low-income housing was pushed out of Battery Park City, see Rosalyn Deutsche, "Uneven Development: Public Art in New York City," in Diane Ghirardo, ed., *Out of Site: A Social Criticism of Architecture* (Seattle: Bay Press, 1991).

52. These techniques included "revenue bonds, tax-increment bonds, hotel or other special use taxes, loans from city agencies, and cash advances from developers" (Frieden and Sagalyn, *Downtown,* 156). About tax-increment financing, the one technique invented to finance private developments, see pp. 97–99, and about its dangers, pp. 248–252.

53. Frieden and Sagalyn, *Downtown,* 314–15 (emphasis added).

54. From 1972 to 1982, architectural receipts for "public and institutional facilities" decreased 10 percentage points (from 36 to 26.6 percent of total receipts,

with the *entire* decline concentrated in the last five years); the receipts for "single-family dwellings" remained about the same (4.2 and 4.7 percent), while "multifamily dwellings" declined from 13.4 to 9.2 percent. During this time, "commercial buildings" receipts went from 30.9 to 32.9 percent in 1977, to 44.5 percent in 1982 (see Gutman, *Architectural Practice,* Table 4, 119).

55. Deutsche, "Uneven Development," 165.

56. David Harvey, *The Condition of Postmodernity* (Oxford: Basil Blackwell, 1989), 91.

57. The innovative reuse of old industrial buildings for specialty shopping malls had started in the 1960s in San Francisco with Wurster, Bernardi, and Emmons's redesign of an old chocolate factory into the enormously successful Ghirardelli Square, followed by Joseph Esherick and Associates' remodeling of The Cannery. Small local entrepreneurs, not professional retail developers like Rouse, financed these smaller projects (see Frieden and Sagalyn, *Downtown,* 74–75; on James Rouse, see 204–5). On Portman and the hotel boom, which, from 1960 to 1982, gave more than 7,000 rooms each to New York, Chicago, Washington, D.C., New Orleans, and Atlanta and over 3,000 to Boston, Philadelphia, San Francisco, Seattle, St. Louis, and seven more cities, see pp. 267–68.

58. Jameson, "Postmodernism, or the Cultural Logic of Late Capitalism," 65–66.

59. Former Mayor Ed Koch is notorious, among other things, for urging "the public" not to give in to panhandlers and for his running battle against homeless loiterers who compromise the image of "ascendant New York." Deutsche analyzes at length his answer to a question at the 1988 convention of the American Institute of Architects about the landmark Grand Central Terminal: "These homeless people . . . they're sitting on the floor, occasionally defecating, urinating, talking to themselves—many, not all, but many—occasionally panhandling. We thought it would be reasonable for the authorities to say 'You can't stay here unless you're here for transportation.' Reasonable, rational people would come to that conclusion, right? Not the Court of Appeals" (quoted in Deutsche, "Uneven Development," 159ff).

60. Frieden and Sagalyn, *Downtown,* 265–66.

61. See Anthony Downs, *The Revolution in Real Estate Finance* (Washington, D.C.: The Brookings Institution, 1985), and Ann Meyerson, "Deregulation and the Restructuring of the Housing Finance System," in Bratt, Hartman, and Meyerson, *Critical Perspectives.*

62. An instructive contrast occurs in an interview Peter Eisenman conducted with Gerald Hines, a developer known for his patronage of elite architects (especially Philip Johnson). Eisenman mentions Berlin, where developers apparently cannot "afford to build office buildings" because the subsidies go to housing. Hines answers: "There are no problems in creating tax incentives; it is a simple matter of legislative lobbying. . . . At present there is a big incentive in building depreciation; you can depreciate any new building in fifteen years. . . . It will bring a lot of speculators into the building industry, which will lead to deterioration in the quality of our building stock" ("Interview: Gerald Hines and Peter Eisenman," *Skyline,* Oct. 1982, 21).

63. Downs, *Revolution,* 108.

64. Quoted by Joseph Giovannini, "The Grand Reach of Corporate Architecture," *New York Times,* Jan. 20, 1985, sec. 3, 28.

65. "Interview: Gerald Hines and Peter Eisenman," 18.

66. Hines' Pennzoil building rented at $3–4 more than the going rate in 1982 and at $2 more in the depressed Houston market of 1985. His Republic Bank (a Dutch-gabled neo-Gothic design by Johnson Burgee) also enjoyed a $1–2 premium per square foot; moreover, it was 90 percent rented (Giovannini "Grand Reach," 28).

67. Scully, *American Architecture,* 290 (emphasis added).

68. First-time home buyers suffered; yet they do tend to have higher than average incomes—their median income was 47 percent higher in 1977 and 52 percent higher in 1979 than that of all households, and 152 percent higher in 1979 than the median income of all renters.

69. The percentage shares of cash family incomes that went to each fifth of families with children was as follows in some crucial years (percentages are rounded off to nearest decimal):

	Lowest	Second	Third	Fourth	Highest	Total
1968	7.4	14.8	19.5	24.5	33.8	100
1978	6.1	13.7	19.5	25.4	35.4	100
1980	5.6	13.3	19.5	25.5	36.1	100
1981	5.4	13.0	19.4	25.8	36.5	100
1983	4.8	12.3	18.9	26.0	38.1	100

From 1978 to 1986, the percentages of households in various income categories varied as follows: below poverty line ($11,000): from 14.2 to 15.1 percent; from $11,000 to 18,900: 14.2 to 18.5 percent; from $18,900 to $46,800 (high budget): 52.3 to 44.3 percent; above $46,800: 19.3 to 22.1 percent. The shrinking of the middle class is visible in these figures. In 1983, the sharpest divergences of median income between metropolitan areas over one million and their suburbs were in the Northeast ($11,900), followed by the South ($9,800), the Midwest ($9,600), and finally by the West ($5,100). At a rate almost half the above, the Northeast and Midwest also led in the differences between smaller cities and their suburbs (adapted from Stephen J. Rose, *The American Profile Poster* [New York: Pantheon, 1986], 11, Table 5; 8, Table 4; and 26, Table 25).

70. See Neil Smith, "Gentrification, the Frontier, and the Restructuring of Urban Space," in Neil Smith and Peter Williams, eds., *Gentrification of the City* (Boston: Allen and Unwin, 1986).

71. I follow here the most recent analysis by Erik O. Wright and Bill Martin, "The Transformation of the American Class Structure, 1960–1980," *American Journal of Sociology* 93 (1987): 1–29, in which the authors revise an earlier study by Wright and Joachim Singelmann. While the category of "experts" replaces the earlier denomination of "semi-autonomous employees," the definitions remain essentially the same. "Petty bourgeois" and "small employers" (which do not concern us here) are either self-employed or own a substantial part of their businesses. "Managers" are employees who make "policy decisions about the operation of the organization in which they work," while "supervisors" have no decision-making power but supervise other workers. "Experts" are employees in professional, technical, and managerial occupations who cannot be classified in any of the other categories, while "workers" are a residual category with lower skills than experts and probably no credentials ("Transformation," 9).

72. Wright and Martin, "Transformation," 16, Table 3, 13, and 19.

73. Frieden and Sagalyn, *Downtown,* 202–3. See also Louise B. Russell, *The Baby Boom Generation and the Economy* (Washington, D.C.: The Brookings Institution, 1982).

74. See Gutman, *Architectural Practice,* 9ff. In the 1960 census, 30,531 persons reported their occupation as architects (an increase of 20.4 percent relative to 1950); 53,670 in 1970 (an increase of 75.8 percent); and 107,693—a 100.7 percent increase—in 1980. Compared to the architects' rate of growth (75.8 in 1960–70 and 252.7 percent in 1960–80), engineers of all categories increased, respectively, by 41.2 and 60.8 percent; civil engineers by 10.8 and 29.1 percent; accountants and auditors by 43.7 and 104.3 percent; lawyers and judges by 25.3 and 142.7 percent; and physicians by 21 and 86.1 percent (Roger Montgomery, "The Rapid Recent Expansion of American Architecture Employment," University of California, Berkeley, Architecture Employment Project Working Paper no. 85–1, June 1985, Tables 1 and 2). I had observed the same exceptional rate of growth in the 1960s, but the recession of the 1970s had led me to expect a decline in the next decade, which simply did not take place (see Larson et al., "The Professional Supply of Design," 252–53).

75. Robert Beauregard, *Gentrification, Strategic Initiatives, and the Left* (Philadelphia: Analysis and Policy Press, n.d.), 5. I have borrowed from his analysis of gentrifiers, pp. 3–5. See also Neil Smith, "Of Yuppies and Housing: Gentrification, Social Restructuring, and the Urban Dream," *Environment and Planning D* 5, no. 2 (June 1987): 151–72. Peter Marcuse has estimated that from 1970 to 1980 gentrification by homeowners helped to displace between 10,000 and 40,000 households in New York City, adding them to the 30,000 to 60,000 displaced by developers and government action ("Abandonment, Gentrification, and Displacement: The Linkages in New York City," in Smith and Williams, *Gentrification of the City*).

76. For architects' residence in cities, see Larson et al., "The Professional Supply of Design," and *Progressive Architecture,* June 1990, 63–64. Fifty-six percent of the readers who responded to the magazine's poll on architects' life-styles preferred to live in cities: 30 percent specified in the "city itself," 19 percent in the suburbs. For young designers' practices, see Alex Cohen, "The Road to Independence," *Progressive Architecture,* July 1990, 100–101. Judith Blau's evidence is in *Architects and Firms* (Cambridge, Mass.: M.I.T. Press, 1987), 120ff.

77. Harvey, *Condition of Postmodernity,* 98.

78. Michael Jager, "Class Definitions and the Aesthetics of Gentrification: Victoriana in Melbourne," in Smith and Williams, *Gentrification of the City.*

79. Sharon Zukin, *Loft Living: Culture and Capital in Urban Change* (New Brunswick, N.J.: Rutgers University Press, 1989).

80. The Canadian private corporation Olympia and York developed the two central office towers, designed by architect Cesar Pelli, while the total plan for Battery Park City was the work of the firm of Alexander Cooper and Stanton Eckstutt (both of whom had been leaders of Mayor John Lindsay's Urban Design Group). See Deutsche, "Uneven Development," 197–98, and note 50, above.

81. See Diana Crane, *The Transformation of the Avant-Garde* (Chicago: University of Chicago Press, 1987), 6 and 2–9, and Zukin, *Loft Living,* 96–110.

82. On community art centers, see Crane, *Transformation,* 9. One hundred three community art centers had been established by the WPA in the 1930s; inter-

estingly, this was the first time that artists were recognized as bona fide members of the labor force during the depression (Zukin, *Loft Living,* 82–83; see also 98–99). On the careers of the average recipient of a Master of Fine Arts degree, see Donald Eckardt, "The Politics of the Avant-Garde: A Sociological Analysis of a Generation of Artists" (Ph.D. diss., Temple University, 1991).

83. Susan Sontag, "One Culture and the New Sensibility," in *Against Interpretation and Other Essays* (New York: Dell, 1966), 299, 302–4.

84. Zukin, *Loft Living,* 199.

85. See Marcuse, "Abandonment, Gentrification, and Displacement." See also Kim Hopper and Jill Hamberg, "The Making of America's Homeless: From Skid Row to the New Poor, 1945–1984," in Bratt, Hartman, and Meyerson, *Critical Perspectives.*

86. See Fred Block's admirable effort to outline the potential of the new phase in *Postindustrial Possibilities.*

87. Lionel Trilling, "The Fate of Pleasure: Wordsworth to Dostoevsky," *Partisan Review* 30 (1963): 178.

CHAPTER 4

1. Gerald Hines, quoted by Joseph Giovannini, "The Grand Reach of Corporate Architecture," *New York Times,* Jan. 20, 1985, sec. 3. Prominent developers like Gerald Hines or Olympia and York also "capitalize on the names of the prestigious corporations that will occupy them . . . giv[ing] the impression that the lead corporations headquartered there own them—as Mr. Hines has done with Pennzoil Place in Houston."

2. "Interview: Gerald Hines and Peter Eisenman," *Skyline,* Oct. 1982, 18 (emphasis added).

3. See Niels L. Prak, *Architects: The Noted and the Ignored* (New York: Wiley, 1984), 19–22.

4. See Robert Gutman's excellent discussion in *Architectural Practice: A Critical View* (New York: Princeton Architectural Press, 1988), 56–60. Even Burgee Johnson, favorites of Gerald Hines (for whom they have designed fourteen towers), have not been able to buck the trend. Burgee says: "Gerry has always insisted on putting a Houston architect on the job with us. My agreement with Gerry is 'anything you can see, *I* do the working drawings for.' All the underground and internal stuff, the elevators and things like that that you can't see, they do the working drawings for" (interview with the author).

5. Suzanne Stephens, "SOM at Midlife," *Progressive Architecture,* May 1981, 138.

6. In 1981, none other than Nathaniel Owings observed: "SOM is taking orders, not creating new ideas. We are putting up office building after office building. Until recently, the firm was praised for its quality. I don't know if we still have that quality" (quoted by Stephens, "SOM," 141). Owings is the retired founder of SOM.

7. Gutman, *Architectural Practice,* 22. See also Judith Blau, *Architects and Firms* (Cambridge, Mass.: M.I.T. Press, 1984).

8. In 1982, architectural firms with over fifty employees represented 1.9 percent of the whole but garnered 29.9 percent of all receipts; firms with twenty to forty-

nine employees were 5.1 percent of the whole and earned 19.1 percent of the receipts; firms smaller than nineteen were 93 percent of the total, with 51 percent of the earnings (Gutman, *Architectural Practice*, Tables 1 and 2, 115–16).

9. Weld Coxe et al., "Charting Your Course," *Architectural Technology*, May–June 1986, 53.

10. The sample was a stratified snowball, formed by selecting U.S. architects from the encyclopedia *Contemporary Architects*, 2d ed. (Chicago: St. James Press, 1987), and by consulting experts. I asked the latter which architects they considered either important in the passage from modernism to postmodernism or now "rising." Especially if the architect I had planned to interview was unavailable, I also used published materials. From 1988 to 1990, I conducted extensive (and, in the case of Philip Johnson, repeated) interviews with twenty-nine architects, eight of whom were partners in very large strong-service firms in Chicago and New York. One of them, Richard Roth of Emory Roth and Sons, is principal in a large strong-delivery firm that makes production drawings in association with design architects of the first rank. Five architects have very small firms: Among these, Julie Eizenberg's husband–wife firm, Koenig Eizenberg in Santa Monica, was the only one just beginning, although it had received much attention since getting the First Design Award of *Progressive Architecture* in 1986. Craig Hodgetts of Hodgetts and Fung in Santa Monica and Stuart Cohen of Chicago had had national reputations but worked only locally, except for their academic commitments. Since I interviewed William Rawn in Boston in 1990, his outstanding work in affordable housing has been receiving national attention from the AIA and from the general press. The other firms range in size from Rob Quigley's (eleven persons) and Morphosis (which goes from thirteen to twenty) to the modal category hovering between sixty and eighty to the very large office of SOM-Chicago. I interviewed Vittorio Gregotti, principal of Gregotti Associates, Milan, at the end of 1990. I was privileged to attend a Research Roundtable organized by the Graduate School of Fine Arts of the University of Pennsylvania, the American Institute of Architects, and the Coxe Group of Philadelphia in April 1989. It was attended by both design and managing partners from firms that have received the AIA national award for design excellence *for the firm's* body of work as a whole. I shall indicate the source as Roundtable when I quote from my notes of the debates.

Except where the information given to me in interview was confidential, I mention the source. To avoid cumbersome footnotes, in this and the following chapters I do not give any other reference for the interviews I conducted myself.

11. This roster of international architectural celebrities, known outside architecture for their personas as much as for their work, is created by the critics, the media, and the architects themselves, with more than a little push from their clients. The "stars" have devoted their lives to architecture and deserve to be considered elite designers. Yet, in an outgrowth of architecture's charismatic tradition, the consuming need that the publicity apparatus has for image, has grabbed the (not unsuspecting) architects. They seem to bask somewhat uncomfortably in the limelight, believing, or affecting to believe, that it will help publicize not only their own careers but the profession as a whole. Steven M. Aronson has described the star system in amusing vignettes; centering the system on Philip Johnson, he builds his celebrity status up. See *Hype!* (New York: William Morrow, 1983). See also Denise

Scott Brown's feminist account of what it means to be married to an architectural "guru" (one's own work becomes invisible in a star system that has no place for women): "Room at the Top? Sexism and the Star System in Architecture," in Ellen P. Berkeley and Matilda McQuaid, eds., *Architecture: A Place for Women* (Washington, D.C.: Smithsonian Institution Press, 1989).

12. The most effective makers of design reputations in New York (and celebrities in their own right) are: Philip Johnson, since the early days of his association with the Museum of Modern Art and the International Style. Robert Stern, who, according to Johnson, "is the one who has really followed—or tried to—the model of my career," doubles his reputation as a postmodernist architect with his academic and scholarly reputation, his writings, the exhibitions he has organized, and the popular series on American architecture for public television. Peter Eisenman, as founder and director of the Institute for Architecture and Urban Affairs, dispensed avant-garde recognition internationally until the institute's demise in 1978.

13. See Hélène Lipstadt, ed., *The Experimental Tradition* (New York: Princeton Architectural Press, 1988).

14. Roundtable, 1989.

15. For a "how to" book full of insight, see Weld Coxe, *Marketing Architectural and Engineering Services,* 2d ed. (New York: Van Nostrand Reinhold, 1982).

16. A common factor—which cannot be taken as representative—is that twenty-four of the twenty-seven elite designers I interviewed have either attended (as undergraduates or graduate students or both) or have taught at elite Eastern schools. Leading in numbers here are Harvard, the University of Pennsylvania, Cornell, and Yale.

17. This comment is by Warren Cox of Hartman Cox in Washington, D.C., winner of the AIA firm award for excellence in design. Like all the other elite designers present at the AIA Research Roundtable, Cox believes that the ideal is to bill the client "on time card" (time spent set at a fixed percentage or multiple) and to move away from both lump sum fees and fees based on a percentage of construction costs, neither of which pays for the time actually spent in design (Roundtable, 1989).

18. John Hejduk, in Barbaralee Diamonstein, *American Architecture Now II,* (New York: Rizzoli, 1985), 129, 133.

19. For evidence about the importance of spouses' incomes for artists, see Donald Eckardt, "Assessing the Avant-Garde: A Sociological Analysis of a Generation of Artists" (Ph.D. diss., Temple University, 1991).

20. Bourdieu's concept of symbolic capital *within a specific field* is different from the more diffuse notion of "cultural capital" and most clear with reference to science. See "The Specificity of the Scientific Field and the Social Conditions of the Progress of Reason," *Social Science Information* 14, no. 6 (1975): 19–47. See also the excerpt "Cultural Reproduction and Social Reproduction," in J. Karabel and A. H. Halsey, eds., *Power and Ideology in Education* (New York: Oxford University Press, 1975).

21. I am grateful to Barbara Czarniawska-Joerges and Kerstin Sahlins-Andersson for having brought this point to my attention.

22. In the depressed real estate market of the early 1990s, SOM has laid off 200 people in six months in its Chicago and New York offices and lost over $100

million in project volume since 1989. KPF has lost about a dozen large projects, and it laid off 9 percent of its permanent staff at the beginning of 1991 ("Back to the Drawing Board," *Newsweek,* April 8, 1991, 60).

23. Known as "the Silver Fox" (for his white hair) in the profession, Kohn is a master of the process of selection by interview. Peter Linneman of the Wharton School's Real Estate Institute observes that Kohn knows how to speak to real estate executives "like one of them, and yet with great authority." Some of Kohn's guidelines: "Don't sketch out the design: you could draw the wrong one, and besides, you make the creative process look too casual. But just as important, try to be the last one interviewed and hope the decision is made right away" (quoted by Suzanne Stephens, "The Selling of the Architect, 1988," *Avenue,* Nov. 1988, 102). After ABC, KPF almost miraculously beat such huge and experienced firms as SOM-Chicago, Philadelphia's Vincent Kling, Helmut Obata Kassabaum of St. Louis, and Caudill Rowlett Scott of Houston for the design of a 437,000 square-foot headquarters building in Kentucky. After that KPF got a job for Motorola through a contact of Kohn's: "Somebody knew of us and recommended that we be interviewed, even though we were new." In three months, a small firm of five people was doing three enormous jobs, which proves they can be done with a small staff!

24. Bunshaft designed the Lever House and the Chase Manhattan buildings in New York, the Beinecke Rare Books Library at Yale, the airport at Mecca, and many other important buildings. His adverse influence on Robert Venturi's career is common knowledge in the profession: Through his position in the Washington, D.C., Fine Arts Commission, Bunshaft engineered a veto of the project by Venturi and Rauch, which had won the competition for Transportation Square.

25. See Pierre Bourdieu, *Distinction: A Social Critique of the Judgment of Taste,* trans. Richard Nice (Cambridge, Mass.: Harvard University Press, 1984), 365.

26. These observations are based on the Roundtable discussions, 1989. For a careful analysis of how size and bureaucratic rules balance each other to produce design recognized in professional awards, see Blau, *Architects and Firms.*

27. Reinforcing Stern's point, the careers of Gropius and Breuer's brilliant students at Harvard in the 1940s (Edward L. Barnes, John Johansen, Philip Johnson, Ioh Ming Pei, Pei's partners Henry Cobb and Araldo Cossutta, Paul Rudolph, Ulrich Franzen, Victor Lundy, and Gropius's partners in the Architects Collaborative, John Harkness and Louis McMillen) basically followed the same pattern: Except for Pei, Harkness, and McMillen, "all began their building careers with suburban houses for the Eastern establishment in New England, New York, and Florida. (Pei was hired right out of Harvard by William Zeckendorf, the legendary urban developer and speculator of the fifties and sixties, to work on schemes in Denver and other cities). . . . Their practice progressed . . . from private house clients to institutional clients who then commissioned schools, campus buildings and housing, theaters, and churches. Few examples of office buildings, other commercial structures, or public and speculative housing are to be found among their commissions of the fifties and sixties. Only beginning in the seventies, in the wake of the urban renewal boom . . . has their work become urban in locale and large in scale" (Klaus Herdeg, *The Decorated Diagram* [Cambridge, Mass.: M.I.T. Press, 1983], 12).

28. Robert Gutman points out that the Hillier Group of Princeton "ranked twentieth in business volume in the list of architectural giants compiled by *Cor-*

porate Design and Realty for 1986, but not until it appointed [Alan] Chimacoff [as director of design] did it begin to be short-listed in major national design competitions" (*Architectural Practice*, 18).

29. Gutman, *Architectural Practice*, 56.

30. Coxe et al., *Marketing*, 84.

31. Here, for instance, is a telling account, again by Michael Graves: "I can't take the guilt of somebody [in the office] saying to me, when I leave at one o'clock in the morning, 'Can't you help me with this? Will you be here tomorrow morning?' No. I will be going to Sarah Lawrence to present our project to the faculty. And I'll go again to present it to the students. And . . . they introduced me yesterday saying 'Michael is here for the fifth or sixth time and the only other famous architect we have ever had is Philip Johnson and we don't think he *ever* came.' But Michael is going, he is showing it to the trustees, he is showing it to the faculty today and he will show it to the students and to the community. . . . If it means a dozen meetings, if it means community work every night . . . just to get some buildings up, I'll do it. And clients *know* that."

32. The involvement of clients who think of themselves as patrons can be cumbersome and is always time-consuming. Frank Gehry's managing partner David Denton thinks that the real patrons are clients who get a sense of personal fulfillment from participating in the process of design; they provide a small percentage of the firm's economic volume ("Actually, they expect a reduction in fees!"; Roundtable, 1989). Robert Stern echoes this: "Houses are marvelous," he says, "they give you a chance for aesthetic expression. . . . But, on the other hand, house clients are not professionals at being clients. . . . [They] are very demanding, the personal contact is wonderful, but it can also be straining."

33. His firm's solution is to base its survival on major interior projects: "300,000 square feet, at least two a year" (Roundtable, 1989).

34. Roundtable, 1989 (emphasis added).

35. Gutman, *Architectural Practice*, 88. See tables at 86 and 119.

36. Large train stations, like Union Station in Washington, D.C., or Grand Central in New York are renovated into upscale shopping malls and "privatized" to the detriment of homeless dwellers.

37. Myers was trained at the University of Pennsylvania when Edward Bacon, by whom he was influenced, was director of planning in Philadelphia. He had then a brilliant but also frustrating career in architecture and urban design in Toronto and practices now in Los Angeles.

38. "Interview: Gerald Hines and Peter Eisenman," 20.

39. DPZ's attacks against the suburbs (a temple to the automobile, isolation, sprawling malls, and office parks), long visible in architectural circles, are getting much attention from the general press. Visibility has gained for DPZ some significant public commissions, such as the twenty-year master plan for Trenton, New Jersey. Duany told a graduate seminar at the Harvard School of Design that the effects of his approach to planning are more likely to shape the future than reform the past: "Our revolution is taking over the codes. . . . Most of my time is not spent designing, but writing codes" (*Philadelphia Inquirer*, Oct. 29, 1990, 10A).

40. Thus, Graham Gund, whose firm won the American Institute of Architects' award for excellence in design, laments that the psychological satisfaction he gets

from designing a house does not seem worth the time it takes from the firm's point of view: "We have too many $5 million projects; the 40 million one makes more sense" (Roundtable, 1989). In a much smaller firm than SOM, Gund echoes Diane Legge's statement of unresolved tension at the beginning of this section.

41. Vincent Scully, *American Architecture and Urbanism*, rev. ed. (New York: Henry Holt, 1988), 280. For an idea of how the mass press presented the skyscrapers of the building boom and their architects, see *Newsweek*, Nov. 8, 1982, 67–76.

42. Firms that have opted *not* to work for speculative clients, firms such as Morphosis or, for a time, Friday Architects, accept limitations that are bound to affect their prospects and those of their employees. A potentially significant phenomenon and career alternative is for architects to turn developers. I do not deal with it here, for only two of the architects I interviewed had acted as developers at the beginning of their independent practice, only in California (taking advantage of runaway real estate inflation) and only on a very small scale. The model that is always cited is the spectacular success of John Portman's design-development firm in conjunction with the Hyatt Hotels chain. See John Portman and Jonathan Barnett, *The Architect as Developer* (New York: McGraw Hill, 1976).

43. *Progressive Architecture*, June 1991, 114. See also the remarkable book by the Egyptian architect Hassan Fathy, *Architecture for the Poor* (Chicago: University of Chicago Press, 1973).

44. Stanley Tigerman says: "The reason architecture does so well here is that it is an autistic event: You don't have to talk. . . . There is the Midwestern antagonism to intellectuals, to talking. This place actually builds. It takes some care and joy in actually detailing and making things well."

45. In many other countries, the architect is not responsible for the working drawings: In Japan, the contractor has full responsibility; it is usual for the architect to have a small field office on the works to follow the execution of the project. In Italy, as in France, the separation between architect and contractor is mediated by a third party, the construction manager, who insures the coherence between the project and its realization. The maturity of segments of the building industry in the United States has made it possible to go directly from the architect's working drawings to execution. Except in the United Kingdom, it is also unusual for architects to *choose* contractors or engineering and other consultants. (I am grateful to Vittorio Gregotti for these details.)

46. Giovannini, "Grand Reach," 27.

47. See Alan Colquhoun's introduction to *Essays in Architectural Criticism* (Cambridge, Mass.: M.I.T. Press, 1985).

48. I borrow from the typology in Coxe et al., "Charting Your Course."

49. Cesar Pelli, who went from Eero Saarinen's "elite" office to head the small design department of a large architectural engineering firm (Daniel Mann Johnson Mendehall in Los Angeles) and from there to Gruen Associates, seems to have been one of the few exceptions. In fact, the awards Pelli won while at DMJM were not sufficient to bring "architectural" commissions to a firm that had no reputation for design. Working within Gruen's large commercial practice offered Pelli (though not Frank Gehry, who for years waited in vain at Gruen's to be promoted to associate) the opportunity to make a name for himself through such buildings as the 1973 Commons and Courthouse Center in Columbus, Indiana, and the Pacific Design

Center in Los Angeles. In 1977, Pelli's reputation gained him the prestigious dean-ship at Yale's School of Architecture. It is not indifferent that Pelli had maintained through teaching and visits the relationship with Yale that he first formed as project captain for Eero Saarinen's Yale buildings. The small practice Pelli started "on the side" with his wife, Diana Balmori, and Fred Clarke of Gruen's had mushroomed into an office of over 100 people by 1989.

50. Architects converted into media stars can be used to sell *any* product, like Michael Graves praising Dexter Shoes in a much-quoted *New York Times* 1987 ad, or the much-less-known but handsome couple of Todd Williams and Billie Tsien in The Gap's shirt ads.

51. No one knows the problem of succession better than John Burgee. In 1968, he and Philip Johnson started a practice that soon specialized in large-scale work for speculative clients, something to which Johnson (though not Burgee) was entirely new. The partnership has become "John Burgee, Architects," a firm for which the eighty-four-year-old Johnson is design consultant, and Burgee has another partner, whose name is not yet publicized. Burgee says "My name *is not* known as Philip's, even though it has been on the firm for twenty years." His strategy is essentially to "focus more on the firm—that is, a group of individuals, not a single person—and to stress more and more the quality that this group of experienced individuals can bring."

For this reason, Burgee wants to keep the office around sixty people, "the size where I am personally involved in each project and [yet] we can do the very big ones." To surmount the problem of succession, Burgee is working to develop another "hybrid," a medium-sized commercial practice of international scope that operates as an all-around service firm. The main difference with the "two-lives hybrid" is Burgee's (not always successful) struggle to keep the working drawings in house. It is possible that Burgee's practice will increasingly resemble the more traditional type of elite architectural firm, once the very high profile due to Philip Johnson's name and to the patronage of Hines Interests dissipates. (The extremely damaging outcome of a 1991 suit by a former partner has forced Burgee to file for Chapter 11 bankruptcy and may well have finished the firm.)

52. Some of the examples I feel bound to name belong to architects already included in the encyclopedia *Contemporary Architects:* the Cannery and Monter-ey's Aquarium by Esherick Homsey Dodge Davis; Tent City and the Transportation Building by Goody and Clancy of Boston; the Loyola Law School or the Hollywood Library by Frank Gehry (before the Pritzker Prize and his international fame); the Anti-Cruelty Society building and the Library for the Blind by Stanley Tigerman in Chicago; Franklin Court by Venturi and Rauch in Philadelphia; Gerald Horn's addi-tion to Northwestern University's Law School for Holabird and Root. Some others belong to architects who are younger and should some day deserve to be included: the Lombard Street Community Center by Friday Architects in Philadelphia; Rob Quigley's Public Library and the Baltic Inn for the homeless in San Diego; Mor-phosis's Outpatient Cancer Unit at Mount Sinai Hospital in Los Angeles; Koning and Eizenberg's affordable housing in Santa Monica; William Rawn's two housing projects for the Bricklayers Union in Boston.

53. Even Bruce Graham, who did not need a career alternative and who com-plains bitterly about the state of architectural education, serves on the board of the

University of Pennsylvania's School of Fine Arts and is the moving force behind SOM's Foundation for Architecture.

54. The Baltic Inn has assuaged the neighborhood's fears so well that Quigley is now designing an upscale SRO for the "higher end of the low-rent market" and several others throughout the city. In Los Angeles, Koning and Eizenberg are designing "the first new SRO hotel in three decades" for a nonprofit developer. See *Progressive Architecture,* June 1991, 104–5.

CHAPTER 5

1. See Anita Jacobson-Widding, ed., *Body and Space: Symbolic Models of Unity and Division in African Cosmology and Experience* (Uppsala: Acta Universitatis Upsaliensis, 1991).

2. Reyner Banham, "A Black Box: The Secret Profession of Architecture," *New Statesman,* Oct. 12, 1990, 23.

3. David Watkin, *Morality and Architecture* (Oxford: Clarendon Press, 1977), 2.

4. "Interview: Henry Cobb and Peter Eisenman," *Skyline,* June 1982, 14. Needless to say, theoretically oriented architects differ sharply about what architectural theory should be. Julie Eizenberg, for instance, talks at length about her and Hans Koning's analysis of the formal architectural grammar of Frank Lloyd Wright's houses. She calls "architectural" the links between spaces, independent of the built elements that express them. Of Eisenman's rotations of basic geometrical forms, she says, "he has made a mystery out of just cutting up a building, putting it back together, and saying it is something very special. . . . Once you have done that . . . someone [still] has got to say this is a good space or it is not."

5. "Interview: Gerald Hines and Peter Eisenman," *Skyline,* Oct. 1982, 21.

6. Michel Foucault, "Space, Knowledge, and Power" [Interview with Paul Rabinow], *Skyline,* March 1982, 20.

7. "Interview: Henry Cobb and Peter Eisenman," 12.

8. Le Corbusier, *Towards a New Architecture,* transl. by Frederick Etchells (1927; reprint, New York: Praeger, 1970), 7.

9. See Banham, "A Black Box," 23.

10. Louis Kahn, quoted by William Jordy, *American Buildings and Their Architects,* vol. 4, *The Impact of European Modernism in the Mid-Twentieth Century* (Garden City, N.Y.: Doubleday/Anchor, 1976), 372. On the Beaux-Arts influence, see 382–92.

11. Le Corbusier, *Towards a New Architecture,* 8–9.

12. Alan Lipman, "The Architectural Belief System and Social Behaviour," *British Journal of Sociology* 20 (1969): 193, 195.

13. Richard Meier, in Barbaralee Diamonstein, *American Architecture Now II* (New York: Rizzoli, 1985), 168.

14. Mary McLeod, "Architecture," in Stanley Trachtenberg, ed., *The Postmodern Moment* (Westport, Conn.: Greenwood Press, 1985), 26ff. I might note in passing the irony that postmodern architects properly called attempt to "speak" the humanist premodern language that their counterparts in other disciplines are busy denouncing and "deconstructing."

15. Watkin, *Morality and Architecture*, 2. For Watkin, the three most persistent "external" explanations of architecture from the nineteenth century on were: (1) religion, sociology, or politics (roughly, a British tradition identified with Ruskin and Pugin); (2) the *Zeitgeist* (a German tradition, echoing romanticism and Alois Riegl's notion that the *telos* of art takes over the artist's individual will); and (3) a rational and technical justification (the French tradition of Viollet-le-Duc and the great Beaux-Arts teachers, in particular Julien Guadet).

16. The search for ennobling affinities (in this case with the Russian avant-garde of 1918–24 and with the philosopher Jacques Derrida *via* his fame in American departments of English) was particularly obvious in the so-called deconstructivist show at the Museum of Modern Art. See the catalog by Philip Johnson and Mark Wigley, *Deconstructivist Architecture* (New York: Museum of Modern Art, 1988).

17. Herdeg, *Decorated Diagram* (Cambridge, Mass.: M.I.T. Press, 1983), 5.

18. Robert Venturi, *Complexity and Contradiction in Architecture* (New York: Museum of Modern Art, 1966), 23.

19. See Robert Stern, "The Doubles of Postmodern," *Harvard Architecture Review* 1 (1980): 76, 82, and Charles Jencks, *The Language of Post-Modern Architecture* (New York: Rizzoli, 1977), 80.

20. Peter Eisenman, "Recent Projects" in *Reconstruction-Deconstruction*, special issue of *Architectural Design* (London) (1989): 29.

21. Elite architects provide further confirmation of what Harrison White has established for industrial markets. In sociological theory, "markets are self-reproducing social structures among specific cliques of firms and other actors who evolve roles from observations of each other's behavior. . . . The key fact is that *producers watch each other* within a market. . . . What a firm does in a market is to watch the competition in terms of observables." See "Where Do Markets Come From?" *American Journal of Sociology* 87 (1981): 518.

22. In Diamonstein, *American Architecture Now II*, 50.

23. Alan Colquhoun, "On Graves," *Oppositions* 12 (1978): 18, 2.

24. See the perceptive analysis by Craig Calhoun, "Imagined Communities, Indirect Relationships, and Postmodernism: Technology, Large-Scale Social Integration, and the Transformation of Everyday Life," paper presented at the Conference of Social Theory and Emerging Issues in a Changing Society, University of Chicago, April 1989.

25. Vincent Scully, "Animal Spirits," *Progressive Architecture*, Oct. 1990, 90, 91. See the whole issue, in particular Mark Alden Branch, "Why (and How) Does Disney Do It?" The $375 million hotel and convention complex includes projects by Graves, Robert Stern, Antoine Predok, and lesser known local architects for the moderately priced hotels. The Dolphin and the Swan, with 2,300 rooms, form the largest convention hotel complex in the Southeast. The $2.3 billion Euro-Disney amusement park (on a site plan developed by Stern Associates, Venturi Rauch Scott Brown, and Tigerman McCurry) includes theme hotels by Stern, Graves, the self-proclaimed "cosmic modernist" Predok, and the French architect Antoine Grumbach as well as an "Entertainment Center" by Frank Gehry. Graves, Stern, Gehry, the Japanese "star" Arata Isozaki, as well as New York's Gwathmey Siegel are working for Disney on other projects and locations, from Isozaki's headquarters in Orlando to Graves's in Burbank. Disney does not spend *outside* the theme park the

millions that it spends inside (the attractions, unlike the hotels, guarantee enormous returns). The client is tough. The CEO, Michael Eisner, asserts that the key to quality is not cost but imagination. Completing the assimilation of his world-famous architects to his prodigiously imaginative designers of park attractions, Eisner asks for "entertainment architecture"—that is, fantasy at the controlled price of an ordinary Sheraton. See Pilar Viladas, "Mickey the Talent Scout," *Progressive Architecture*, June 1988, 104–5.

26. See Charles Moore, "You Have to Pay for the Public Life," *Perspecta* 9–10 (1965): 58–87. Paul Goldberger suggests that Michael Eisner's recourse to famous architects is part of an upgrading effort to reach "yuppie" consumers; see "And Now, an Architectural Kingdom," *New York Times Magazine*, April 8, 1990, 23–24.

27. Walter Benjamin, "The Work of Art in the Age of Mechanical Reproduction," in *Illuminations* (New York: Schocken, 1969), 238–240. The essay was originally published in 1936. Vincent Pecora notes that Benjamin, despairing of the opposition to Hitler, clung to the positive hope that "the right of ordinary people to touch, to use, and yes, perhaps even to throw away when no longer of service" could dispel "all regressive worship from afar," including that of the Führer. See his "Towers of Babel," in Diane Ghirardo, ed., *Out of Site* (Seattle: Bay Press, 1991), 74. For the opposite views of Theodor Adorno and Max Horkheimer, see the excerpt, "The Culture Industry: Enlightenment as Mass Deception," in James Curran, Michael Gurevitch, and Janet Woollacott, eds., *Mass Communication and Society* (Beverly Hills, Calif.: Sage, 1979).

28. Mark Girouard, quoted in Watkin, *Morality and Architecture*, 12.

29. William Pedersen, "Intentions," in *Kohn Pedersen Fox: Buildings and Projects* (New York: Rizzoli, 1987), 302–3 (emphasis added).

30. Joan Goody, in Diamonstein, *American Architecture Now II*, 117.

31. Magali Sarfatti Larson, *The Rise of Professionalism* (Berkeley: University of California Press, 1977), 56–63.

32. Paul Tillich, quoted in Barbara Miller Lane, "Architects in Power: Politics and Ideology in the Work of Ernst May and Albert Speer," *Journal of Interdisciplinary History* 17 (1986): 290.

33. Sir Henry Wotton, quoted in Lipman, "Architectural Belief System," 196.

CHAPTER 6

1. Reyner Banham, "A Black Box: The Secret Profession of Architecture," *New Statesman*, Oct. 12, 1990, 25.

2. Schön identifies twelve normative design domains, which "contain the names of elements, features, relations and actions, and of norms used to evaluate problems, consequences and implications." They are: Program/Use; Siting; Building Elements; Organization of Space; Form; Structure/Technology; Scale; Cost; Building Character; Precedent; Representation; Explanation (Donald Schön, *The Reflective Practitioner: How Professionals Think in Action* [New York: Basic Books, 1984], 95–97).

3. Here, for instance, is an account of the postindustrial reorganization of production in Germany: "Complex products are increasingly conceptualized as systems

of subsystems, or modules. Instead of developing each subsystem itself, *the final producer defines the characteristics of the product as a whole and the functional relations between the different modules of which it is composed.* Whenever possible, each of these is then developed in collaboration with a system supplier who possesses the relevant technical expertise and know-how. Final assembly, however, remains the responsibility of the final producer" (Horst Kern and Charles Sabel, "Trade Unions and Decentralized Production: A Sketch of Strategic Problems in the West German Labor Movement," *Politics and Society* 19 [1991]: 378, [emphasis added]).

4. David Greenspan, "A Conversation at Hammond Beeby and Babka," *Inland Architect*, Nov.–Dec. 1985, 30.

5. Schön, *Reflective Practitioner*, 101.

6. William Pedersen, in Barbaralee Diamonstein, *American Architecture Now II* (New York: Rizzoli, 1985), 179–80 (emphasis added).

7. Cesar Pelli, "Transparency—Physical and Perceptual," *A & U* (Tokyo), Special issue, (1976): 78–79. Of course, Pelli can be much more technical than this. See, for instance, his interview in *Skyline*, May 1982, 23–24. I quote Pelli's more articulate statement in *A & U* rather than his more fluid comments to me in an interview conducted in Spanish.

8. It is hard to find fault with Graham's opinion that "nobody ever thought, 'well, maybe Scandinavians can live in towers, but *can* black people?' They never thought about the segregation they were creating, they actually thought they were doing good."

9. Stanley Tigerman, in Diamonstein, *American Architecture Now II*, 230.

10. Tom Wolfe, *From Bauhaus to Our House* (New York: Farrar Straus Giroux, 1981), Chap. 4.

11. The architectural critic Charles Jencks made a different connection, putting the symbolic death of modernism at July 15, 1972, at 3:32 P.M.—the time at which the slabs of Pruitt-Igoe, Minoru Yamasaki's award-winning project of 1955, were dynamited in St. Louis.

12. Among the most interesting projects were Robert Stern's "Subway Suburb," an ideal plan for an abandoned and burned-out site in the East New York part of Brooklyn; St. Joseph's Village for the elderly (a competition entry); and his unbuilt winning competition for 1,000 units on Roosevelt Island in New York City. Stern's analysis of the social potential of the suburb (in which he acknowledges Stein and Henry Wright's "middle city suburbs" of Sunnyside and Forrest Hills) is extremely interesting; see Barbaralee Diamonstein, *American Architecture Now* (New York: Rizzoli, 1980), 245–48.

13. Kenneth Frampton's critique, "America 1960–1970: Notes on Urban Images and Theory," appeared in *Casabella*, Dec. 1971, 24–38. Denise Scott Brown, "Pop Off: Reply to Kenneth Frampton," 35, 37, and see also Scott Brown, "Learning from Pop," and Robert Venturi, "Learning the Right Lessons from the Beaux-Arts," all in Robert Venturi and Denise Scott Brown, *A View from the Campidoglio: Selected Essays 1953–1984* (New York: Harper and Row, 1984). The reference to "taste culture" (or publics) is from Herbert Gans, who had a profound influence on Scott Brown and Venturi. See his *Popular Culture and High Culture: An Analysis and Evaluation of Taste* (New York: Basic Books, 1974). The criticism

of the Venturis is from Andreas Huyssen, *After the Great Divide* (Bloomington: University of Indiana Press, 1986), 187.

14. Kenneth Frampton, "Towards a Critical Regionalism: Six Points for an Architecture of Resistance," in Hal Foster, ed., *The Anti-Aesthetic: Essays on Postmodern Culture* (Port Townsend, Wash.: Bay Press, 1983), 26, 21, 28.

15. Today, Krier is Prince Charles's favorite architect and architectural adviser in the hoped-for reconstruction of a "Victorian" city.

16. The project had a very limited budget and mostly black tenants. It consisted of several building types (a wall of row houses, three duplexes and one single-story apartment, a four-story apartment building for elderly tenants, and a small community center) on "twenty-five acres of cleared, hilly land located next to a commuter railroad station and a major suburban highway." The exchange took place at the symposium "Beyond the Modern Movement," organized in 1977 by the *Harvard Architecture Review*. See the Spring 1980 issue. Quotations on 207, 215, 216 (emphasis added).

17. Robert Venturi, *Complexity and Contradiction in Architecture*, 2d ed. (New York: Museum of Modern Art, 1977), 14.

18. Robert Stern, in Diamonstein, *American Architecture Now*, 237.

19. This is not quite true. But when I mentioned Mies van der Rohe's still-standing, still-inhabited, still-decent 1920s housing on Berlin's Afrikaner Strasse, Johnson reemphasized form: "Oh, but that was almost *retardataire!*"

20. Philip Johnson, "Reflections: On Style and the International Style; On Postmodernism; On Architecture," *Oppositions* 10 (1977): 18.

21. In the late 1980s, Johnson was sponsoring the "deconstructive" trend. He stressed the pervasive influence of painting: Picasso and cubism inspired Le Corbusier's purism directly; passing through Malevitch's painting and Tatlin's architecture in Russia, then turning West again after "constructivism failed as a formal movement," cubism also inspired the German architects.

22. The broad view is taken from architectural historians before Pevsner's and Giedion's apologias for the Modern Movement. See Robert Stern, "The Doubles of Postmodern," *Harvard Architecture Review* 1 (1980): 75–87. Paradoxically, Peter Eisenman also sees all "humanist" Western architecture as *theoretically* continuous. In "Post-Functionalism," *Oppositions* 7 (1976): n.p., he relies on Levi-Strauss and Foucault to define modernism as "a sensibility based on the fundamental displacement of man." For Eisenman, architecture *needs* the humanist fiction of a central subject to unify, within the subject's single experience, function, and form, "a concern for internal accommodation" and "a concern for articulation of ideal themes in form." Eisenman sees modernism as two *formal* tendencies in dialectical tension: form as the transformation of simpler geometric ideas or Platonic solids, and form as fragments abstracted "from some pre-existent set of non-specific spatial entities" (which presumably exist in nature, the built environment, or history). Few practicing architects can follow Eisenman's theoretical sophistication, nor does he use these terms except in writing, although his abstract analysis takes in much that elite architects say in tangible form. For a cogent critique of the analogy between architecture and linguistics, see Mary McLeod, "Architecture," in Stanley Trachtenberg, ed., *The Postmodern Moment: A Handbook of Contemporary Innovation in the Arts* (Westport, Conn.: Greenwood Press, 1985).

23. Johnson, "Reflections," 18. See Robert Venturi, "A Definition of Architecture as Shelter with Decoration on It, and Another Plea for Symbolism of the Ordinary in Architecture," in Venturi and Scott Brown, *View from the Campidoglio,* 62–67.

24. Vincent Scully, *American Architecture and Urbanism,* new rev. ed. (New York: Henry Holt, 1988), 171.

25. Quoted in Tim Loughran, "Looking at a Dixie Cup Skyline," *Crain's New York Business,* Oct. 17, 1988, 47.

26. Robert Venturi, "Diversity, Relevance, and Representation in Historicism, or *Plus Ça Change,* . . ." in Venturi and Scott Brown, *View from the Campidoglio,* 109, 113, 114 (emphasis added).

27. Cesar Pelli, interviewed by Mark Alden Branch, *Art New England,* April 1990, 13.

CHAPTER 7

1. Some of the most important prizes are awarded by independent institutions interested in the advance of a discipline or an art. Precisely because they are interested in the field as defined by its eminent practitioners, these institutions always delegate their choices to highly regarded representatives. Each year the American Academy of Arts and Letters presents an American architect with the Arnold Brunner Memorial Prize and with a gold medal in architecture. The Pritzker Prize, given annually by the Hyatt Foundation, is an international architecture award modeled on the Nobel Prize. The American Institute of Architects gives each year a gold medal, the highest award within the U.S. profession. It also bestows awards to local AIA chapters and regional and national awards to completed buildings. To recognize the collective nature of architectural work, the AIA also grants an annual award for design excellence to *a firm.*

2. On the mystification by architectural "glossies," see Robert Gutman, *Architectural Practice: A Critical View* (New York: Princeton Architectural Press, 1988), 58–59.

3. The magazine was born in 1920 as *Pencil Points.* It aimed for the audience of draftsmen and apprentices in architectural offices, to whom it offered more than just picture plates—it contained articles on educational and technical services and emphasized draftsmanship and rendering. According to the editor of *Progressive Architecture,* John Morris Dixon, the subscription list was around 73,000 in 1987, plus direct sales. The magazine sold from 11,000 to 12,000 pages of paid advertisements per year.

4. *Progressive Architecture* (hereafter, *PA*), Jan. 1984, 85.

5. *PA,* Jan. 1967, 144.

6. *PA,* Jan. 1988, 76.

7. *PA,* Feb. 1980, 23.

8. *PA,* June 1973, 86. In 1966, when Pelli received *PA*'s First Award, he was still the relatively unknown chief of design for DMJM (Daniel Mann Johnson Mendenhall) of Los Angeles, a huge architectural-engineering firm known for highly competent comprehensive services (and very large projects)—not for originality or excellence in architectural design.

9. *PA*, Jan. 1988, 76. According to a 1973 survey, "almost 75% of the projects awarded . . . are built [and] almost 90% of the projects built are built without changes" (*PA*, June 1973, 86).

10. John Morris Dixon, interview with the author. May 6, 1988.

11. Suzanne Stephens, personal communication to the author, March 1989.

12. John Morris Dixon, "Editorial," *PA*, June 1973, 85. In 1957, the Museum of Modern Art recorded the establishment's acceptance of the International Style in its exhibition "Buildings for Business and Government." Arthur Drexler, the Museum's influential director of Architecture and Design, considered it both a signpost for architectural historians and a factor in the further acceptance of the modernist canon (personal communication of Mr. Stuart Wrede, Mr. Drexler's successor as director of the Architecture and Design Department of the Museum of Modern Art, Sept. 1987).

13. Thomas Creighton, quoted in Wolf von Eckardt, "The First Twenty Years," *PA*, June 1973, 89.

14. John Morris Dixon, "Editorial," *PA*, June 1973: 85 (emphasis added).

15. Rowan, in *PA*, Jan. 1966, 117.

16. *PA*, Jan. 1966, 160.

17. *PA*, Jan. 1966, 162.

18. *PA*, Jan. 1966, 160.

19. *PA*, Jan. 1966, 128–33.

20. *PA*, Jan. 1966, 161.

21. *PA*, Jan. 1966, 162.

22. See Joan Campbell, *The German Werkbund: The Politics of Reform in the Applied Arts* (Princeton: Princeton University Press, 1978), 57–68 in particular.

23. See Vincent Scully, *American Architecture and Urbanism*, new rev. ed. (New York: Henry Holt, 1988), 226–27 and 245–55.

24. The architectural design jury included John Dinkeloo (Kevin Roche's partner) and Sarah Harkness (founding partner of The Architects Collaborative with Walter Gropius) on the side of modernism and large-scale practice. On the side of revisionism, both judges were convinced partisans of a modernist architectural *language*. The two younger men were Charles Gwathmey, one of the New York Five who recognizes to this day Le Corbusier and Louis Kahn as main sources of inspiration, and Craig Hodgetts, winner of two *PA* First Awards, particularly interested in innovative constructional solutions and in a "technological" aesthetics.

25. *PA*, Jan. 1977, 49 (emphasis added).

26. In my study of AIA member firms in 1977, residential commissions represented the second largest type in these firms' average practice. The mean percentage was 26.3 percent for commercial, office, and retail, followed by 21.5 percent residential and, more distantly, by 15.5 percent educational buildings. See Magali Sarfatti Larson, George Leon, and Jay Bolick, "The Professional Supply of Design," in Judith R. Blau, Mark La Gory, and John S. Pipkin, eds., *Professionals and Urban Form* (Albany, State University of New York Press, 1983), 269.

27. See Vincent Pecora's trenchant analysis, "Towers of Babel," in Diane Ghirardo, ed., *Out of Site: A Social Criticism of Architecture* (Seattle: Bay Press, 1991), in particular 67–69.

28. *PA*, Jan. 1967, 167 (emphasis added).

29. *PA,* Jan. 1968, 131–32. The First and Second Awards were conferred, respectively, to extremely cheap public housing in a relocation project by Jan Wampler in San Juan, Puerto Rico, and to Robert Oxman's two prototype fishing villages for the Land Administration of Puerto Rico.

30. *PA,* Jan. 1968, 132.

31. *PA,* Jan. 1970, 107 (emphasis added).

32. Richard Pommer, "The New Architectural Supremacists," *Artforum,* Oct. 1976.

33. *PA,* Jan. 1975, 45.

34. *PA,* Jan. 1982, 131.

35. *PA,* Jan. 1976, 55 (emphasis added).

36. *PA,* Jan. 1976, 74, 56. Raquel Ramati is wrong: Half of the developers of multifamily housing use architects employed in-house (therefore "invisible") for most of their projects. So do many owners of motel and hotel chains (though not one of the largest, the Marriott Corporation; see *PA,* June 1988, 96). See Gutman, *Architectural Practice,* 10–11.

37. *PA,* Jan. 1969, 136.

38. Imagery may be more important in natural than in urban settings since the visual integrity of landscape is easier to invade, even by a house, than the city's patchwork. The 1971 jury relied on this belief to allay its familiar misgivings about conferring the First Award to a private house (for only the second time since 1954). The judges were: Edward Barnes, Yale's adviser for architecture and planning, and Ulrich Franzen—both New York architects known for corporate and institutional work; Barnard College historian John Kouvenhoven; Ezra Ehrenkrantz, specialist in systems construction, member from 1966 to 1968 of various national task forces on cities; and Myron Goldsmith, partner at SOM-Chicago. The following exchange is worth quoting:

KOUVENHOVEN: Aren't we, by picking the Sun Valley house and throwing out all the urban planning things, saying that architects aren't sociologists?

FRANZEN: I think that any architect who thinks he's a sociologist ought to be locked up.

BARNES: One of the intriguing things about this First Award is that it slants down the hill the way the hill does, but also that it does really involve itself very much with itself. . . . The way it would mate with the hill, the snow—you could ski right down it. . . . I wonder why there weren't more people doing anonymous houses, *houses camouflaged in some way so that we don't mess up nature.* (*PA,* Jan. 1971, 61 [emphasis added])

As Ezra Ehrenkrantz judiciously observed, neither this mountain house nor an even more minimalist project left nature untouched; they just used "a different kind of imagery" (*PA,* Jan. 1971, 84).

39. De Blois and Moore, in *PA,* Jan. 1978, 68.

CHAPTER 8

1. The crisis in architectural standards at this point evokes (even if faintly) Thomas Kuhn's account of a science nearing paradigmatic change. The modernist

paradigm had been central for over a decade, even if it never produced the massive dogmatism of scientific work. See Thomas Kuhn, *The Structure of Scientific Revolutions,* rev. ed. (Chicago: University of Chicago Press, 1970).

2. *Progressive Architecture* (hereafter, *PA*), Jan. 1967, 168.

3. *PA,* Jan. 1969, 141, 140, 104 (emphasis added).

4. *PA,* Jan. 1969, 146–47 (emphasis added).

5. Robert Gutman, *Architectural Practice: A Critical View* (New York: Princeton Architectural Press, 1988), 35.

6. *PA,* Jan. 1972, 58.

7. Alexander Tzonis and Liane Lefaivre, "The Architecture of Narcissism," *Harvard Architecture Review* 1 (1980): 54.

8. Tzonis and Lefaivre, "Architecture of Narcissism," 55.

9. See in this regard Göran Wallén's instructive paper on Swedish architecture, "The Scientification of Architecture," in Gernot Böhme and Nico Stehr, eds., *The Knowledge Society: The Growing Impact of Scientific Knowledge on Social Relations* (Dordrecht and Boston: D. Reidel, 1986).

10. *PA,* Jan. 1967, 144.

11. *PA,* Jan. 1970, 79 (emphasis added).

12. *PA,* Jan. 1970, 134–35 (emphasis added).

13. Ulrich Franzen, *PA,* Jan. 1971, 71 (emphasis added).

14. Louis Sauer, *PA,* Jan. 1972, 59 (emphasis added).

15. Moshe Safdie, *PA,* Jan. 1972, 58–59.

16. John Johansen, *PA,* Jan. 1973, 93.

17. *PA,* Jan. 1971, 71ff.

18. *PA,* Jan. 1972, 58.

19. Don Stull and Hugh Hardy, *PA,* Jan. 1973, 92 (emphasis added).

20. *PA,* Jan. 1974, 55.

21. *PA,* Jan. 1974, 55. "It's all this damn mechanical aesthetic," said Denise Scott Brown of "The Machines." Commenting on the best example, she said: "It's a shame to spend all that money making a new old barn, why do you need that sophistication?" And Herb Greene, architect and professor at the University of Kentucky, commented that "Le's Maisons" were "degrading to Le Corbusier," in whose work "things happen not just *around* the building, but *in* the content of the forms. These people have . . . absorbed [the schema] only by taking planes and right angles." Robertson knowingly explained to the others that "It's really more Cornell than Yale. It's Colin Rowe through Peter Eisenman, and then transferred to the less polemical members of the group" Ibid, (67–68).

22. *PA,* Jan. 1974, 52.

23. *PA,* Jan. 1975, 55 (emphasis added).

24. *PA,* Jan. 1975, 46 (emphasis added). When completed, the house was widely published nationally and internationally, launching Arquitectonica, the firm founded in 1977 by Spear, Bernardo Fort-Brescia, and other young architects, to rapid success.

25. On the changing sociological content of the avant-garde see Diana Crane, *The Transformation of the Avant-Garde* (Chicago: University of Chicago Press, 1987), in particular 9–15.

26. Tzonis and Lefaivre, "Architecture of Narcissism," 57.

27. Peter Eisenman, *House X* (New York: Rizzoli, 1982), 38, 36. With *House X*, Eisenman moved toward "decomposition," "deconstruction," *and meaning:* "House X is strongly colored by metaphoric ideas of ruin, decay, and falling to pieces, but it attempts to use these ideas in a totally different fashion from the postmodernists. . . . The imagery of House X is rooted in a pervasive and explicit ideological concern with a cultural condition, namely, the apparent inability of modern man to sustain any longer a belief in his own rationality and perfectability" (34).

28. Vincent Pecora, "Towers of Babel," in Diane Ghirardo, ed., *Out of Site: A Social Criticism of Architecture* (Seattle: Bay Press, 1991), 55.

29. Indeed, in these ten years, the juries conferred a First Award only in 1977, 1979, 1980, and 1985. As in all their awards and citations, the divided jury of 1977 managed to agree on a First Award for different reasons, picking a residence for twenty-four Buddhists in the coastal mountains of California, by Bernard Maquet. In 1979, the First Award went to a remarkable and very beautiful engineering feat: the Ruck-a-Chucky Bridge in Auburn, California. T. Y. Lin International were the structural engineers, with Hanson Engineers, Inc., as consultants; Myron Goldsmith of SOM-Chicago was in charge of architectural design. In 1980, two young Argentinian architects and educators, Rodolfo Machado and Jorge Silvetti, won the award for an urban design that connected two levels of the Rhode Island School of Design by a system of steps and walks. In 1985, Silvetti received an award for an architectural intervention that visually linked four public squares in the Sicilian town of Leonforte. The fact that the bridge was exceptional in the history of the awards and that the same architect received two First Awards out of four given suggests that "events" (as the judges called the bridge) and consistent excellence are recognized even in the absence of clearly spelled-out criteria of evaluation.

30. Henry Cobb, "Forum on the Beaux-Arts Exhibition," *Oppositions* 8 (1977): 174.

31. A visible effect of this limitation is illustrated in this rhetorical question by Natalie de Blois about a "developer's" building: "Why is so much attention lavished on making the exterior as urban and varied as possible, and yet, when one goes inside, the space is all equivalent?" *PA*, Jan. 1978, 79.

32. *PA*, Jan. 1977, 49 (emphasis added).

33. *PA*, Jan. 1977, 61.

34. *PA*, Jan. 1978, 65–66 (emphasis added).

35. None of the 1979 jurors was a celebrity or a flamboyant revisionist. They were Fred S. Dubin, president of Dubin Bloome Associates of New York and Hartford; Barry Elbasani, vice president of Elbasani Logan Severin Freeman of Berkeley; Anthony Lumsden, former collaborator of Cesar Pelli, still at DMJM as vice president and director for design; and Werner Seligmann, formerly of Cornell, dean of the School of Architecture at Syracuse University. The quotation is from Elbasani, *PA*, Jan. 1979, 69.

36. For the distinction between "postmodernism" and "schismatic modernism" see chapter 2 and Robert Stern, "The Doubles of Postmodern," *Harvard Architecture Review* 1 (1980): 75–87. When I interviewed Hodgetts, Gehry, and Thom Mayne in 1989, they were all quick to pick up (while asking me for a sociological explanation) what was by then a cliché—namely that historicist postmodernism, in particular the work of Michael Graves, was the architecture "of the age of Reagan."

See Mary McLeod's perceptive analysis, "Architecture and Politics in the Reagan Era: From Postmodernism to Deconstructivism," *Assemblage* 8 (1989): 23–59.

37. *PA*, Jan. 1983, 84, 96.

38. As we have seen, when Eisenman argues for architecture's "ideological" capacity to project a different vision of the world, his primary concern is the discipline's exploration of its own language and problems. He is concerned neither with the social conditions under which architecture is practiced nor even with who, besides some chosen architects and critics, receives the projected message.

39. Eisenman, *House X*, 34.

40. At forty, Helmut Jahn was already at the top of a firm known for its very large projects. He was to buy it in 1982. Coming from Germany to Chicago in 1966, Jahn was soon taken under the wing of Gene Summers, formerly Mies's close collaborator; he moved to Murphy Associates with Summers and remained when Summers left. Although his international fame was yet to come, his Monroe Center project had been cited by *PA* in 1978, and the Rust-Oleum corporate headquarters in Illinois had been much noticed. The other jurors participated in the heated final debates, without being able to modify their outcome. For urban design, they were: John Kriken, director of urban design and planning at SOM-San Francisco, and Blanche Lemco van Ginkel, director of the School of Architecture at the University of Toronto and partner in van Ginkel Associates. For research: Wolfgang Preiser, partner in Architectural Research Consultants and codirector of the Institute for Environmental Education of the University of New Mexico, and Francis Ventre, chief of the Environmental Design Research Division at the National Bureau of Standards.

41. Even the larger projects were not that large. They included, besides the First Award to Machado and Silvetti's urban design for the Rhode Island School of Design: Arquitectonica's apartment house in Miami, Backen Arrigoni and Ross's condominium in San Francisco, a Public Works Service Center in Evanston, Illinois, by Sisco Lubotsky with Stuart Cohen, a YWCA in Houston by Taft Architects, and the literal historicism of renovations and additions to a hospital in Bayonne, New Jersey, by John Blatteau for a large Philadelphia firm.

42. See John Dixon's thoughtful editorial "Modernism Fights Back" (*PA*, March 1980). The choice of readers' "Views" in February and March of 1980 is extensive but sanitized, no doubt, for the sake of advertising income. The two most frequent complaints were the abandonment of pluralism and . . . Michael Graves. The only supporting letter published came from William Conklin. The most surprising came from Charles Gwathmey, award winner in 1973, juror in 1977: "The PA Design Awards program has become a self-serving and a predictable insidious recurrence. For many years it was Moore and clones, now it is Graves and clones, with the ethic clearly being the more eclectic, decorative and unbuildable, the better" (April 1980, 4). One reader summarized the two feelings: "Rogers, Stern, Gehry and Jahn have arrived at a consensus which eliminates the many directions of thought prevalent in recent years to state in unmistakable terms that the future of architectural design is 'Gravely Obfuscated Embellishism.' *Gravely* because it is a narrow genre of design principally initiated by Michael Graves, although obliquely assisted by Meier, Venturi and, most recently, Tigerman." Another connected it to the types of commissions: "The opportunity to pursue [this] kind of architecture . . . is available only

to those who dabble with the personal statements associated with custom-built houses out in the country. Even at that, I would seriously question the livability of some of these stylistic *tours de force*" (March 1980, 14).

43. *PA*, Jan. 1980, 98, 105 (emphasis added).

44. *PA*, Jan. 1980, 88 (emphasis added).

45. The classic theory of status groups, which derive status honor from a specific style of life and protect it through restrictions on social intercourse, is based on Max Weber. See "Class, Status, Party," in Hans Gerth and C. W. Mills, eds., *From Max Weber* (New York: Oxford University Press, 1967). The most comprehensive modern adaptation is Pierre Bourdieu, *Distinction: A Social Critique of the Judgment of Taste* (Cambridge, Mass.: Harvard University Press, 1984).

46. A now classic philosophical statement on the colonization of aesthetics is Jean Baudrillard's *For a Critique of the Political Economy of the Sign*, trans. Charles Levin (St. Louis: Telos Press, 1981). Two interesting sociological analyses are Craig Calhoun, "The Infrastructure of Modernity: Indirect Relationships, Information Technology and Social Integration," in Hans Haferkamp and Neil J. Smelser, eds., *Social Change and Modernity* (Berkeley: University of California Press, 1990), and David Harvey, *The Condition of Postmodernity* (Oxford: Basil Blackwell, 1989), especially Chaps. 4 and 17. Stuart Ewen's *All Consuming Images* (New York: Basic Books, 1988), though not a theoretical analysis, offers a rich and somewhat rambling description of the consumption of style in contemporary culture. See, in particular, his discussion of architectural form, pp. 199–232.

47. In their famous essay, "The Culture Industry: Enlightenment as Mass Deception," Max Horkheimer and Theodor Adorno commented on the manipulation of fragments and detail for effect (and for profit): "When the detail won its freedom, it became rebellious and, in the period from Romanticism to Expressionism, asserted itself as free expression, as a vehicle of protest against the organization. . . . The totality of the culture industry has put an end to this. Though concerned exclusively with effects, it crushes their insubordination and makes them subserve the formula, which replaces the work. The same fate is inflicted on whole and parts alike. . . . *The so-called dominant idea is like a file which ensures order and no coherence.* The whole and the parts are alike. . . . Their prearranged harmony is a mockery of what had to be striven after in the great bourgeois works of art" (*Dialectic of Enlightenment*, trans. John Cumming (New York: Continuum, 1989), 125–26.

48. *PA*, Jan. 1983, 84.

49. The judges were all fellows of the AIA: Richard Stein of New York, past chairman of the AIA energy task force; Robert Frasca, design partner of the large firm Zimmer Gunsul Frasca of Portland, Oregon; George Hartman of Hartman and Cox in Washington, D.C.; and Romualdo Giurgola, 1980 winner of the competition for the most important government building of the postwar period, the Australian Parliament in Canberra.

50. *PA*, Jan. 1981, 119 (emphasis added).

51. *PA*, Jan. 1981, 119 (emphasis added).

52. See William Pedersen and Elizabeth Plater-Zyberk, *PA*, Jan. 1985, 84, and James Polshek, *PA*, Jan. 1984, 87.

53. *PA*, Jan. 1984, 86–87 (emphasis added).

54. *PA,* Jan. 1985, 85.

55. Kenneth Frampton, "Towards a Critical Regionalism," in Hal Foster, ed., *The Anti-Aesthetic* (Port Townsend, Wash.: Bay Press, 1983), 20, 21. See also chapter 6 above.

56. For Eisenman, *commercial* practice, motivated by the market and the pure benefit of the client, differs from *professional* practice, in which "designing the most square feet for the least cost is mediated by a concern for society at large." Professional practice, when "mediated through a set of a priori forms that are thought to have a quality unto themselves" becomes *artistic* or *aesthetic.* But *ideological* practice is motivated by ideals, "a position on what *should be* the case, as opposed to what *is,* in terms of society, of building, of symbolism" ("Interview: Cesar Pelli and Peter Eisenman," *Skyline,* May 1982, 23).

57. Vincent Scully, "Theory and Delight," *PA,* Oct. 1989, 87.

58. *PA,* Jan. 1985, 85 (emphasis added).

59. *PA,* Jan. 1984, 87 (emphasis added).

60. *PA,* Jan. 1982, 110. Beeby's observation is supported by sociological research. Blau's study of New York architects during 1974–79 showed that the small and flexible entrepreneurial offices fared better in times of crisis than the large firms with corporate clients. Moreover, looking at the awards received by the firms, Blau established that those few small firms that had acquired characteristics of rational organization and management typical of larger and more bureaucratic firms were more likely to do exceptionally good work than the latter (Judith Blau, *Architects and Firms* (Cambridge, Mass.: M.I.T. Press, 1984), Chap. 5.

61. This interpretation is congruent with Ann Swidler's two models for the study of culture, settled and unsettled. See her "Culture in Action," *American Sociological Review* 51 (1986): 273–86.

62. Architectural elites, however, seem much more doubtful about the merit of faithful historical imitations than their most famous advocate, Prince Charles of Britain (advised in architectural matters by Leon Krier).

63. *PA,* Jan. 1987, 86–90.

CHAPTER 9

1. My empirical study supports Andreas Huyssen's argument: "A crucial question . . . concerns the extent to which modernism and the avant-garde as forms of an adversary culture were nevertheless conceptually and practically bound up with capitalist modernization and/or with communist vanguardism, modernization's twin brother. . . . Postmodernism's critical dimension lies precisely in the radical questioning which linked modernism and the avant-garde to the mindset of modernization" ("Mapping the Postmodern," in *After the Great Divide* [Bloomington: University of Indiana Press, 1986], 183). See also Kenneth Frampton's similar approach in "Towards a Critical Regionalism: Six Points for an Architecture of Resistance," in Hal Foster, ed., *The Anti-Aesthetic: Essays on Postmodern Culture* (Port Townsend, Wash.: Bay Press, 1983), 20.

2. Scott Lash's sociological approach to modernism/postmodernism in both architecture and cities admits that it is confusing and ambiguous to take the latter

as cultural objects (*Sociology of Postmodernism* [London and New York: Routledge, 1990], 31; see in particular 31–36 and Chap. 8).

3. Lash takes as a criterion of modernity Weber's central concept about the "self-legislation" of each sphere of culture (the attempt by social actors within each sphere to develop their own conventions and mode of valuation; *Sociology of Postmodernism*, 9). See Max Weber, "Religious Rejections of the World and Their Directions," in Hans Gerth and C. W. Mills, eds., *From Max Weber* (New York: Oxford University Press, 1958).

4. European postmodernism, for instance, started earlier. In part, the reconstruction of ancient urban centers compelled architects to contextualize buildings within both a spatial environment and a historical tradition. From the practice of a few noted firms (notably the Milanese firm of Belgioioso Peressutti and Rogers with their "medieval" skyscraper, the Velasca Tower), which the CIAM congresses brought together up to 1960, to a variety of theoretical articulations, the movement was rapid. See Heinrich Klotz, *The History of Postmodern Architecture* (Cambridge, Mass.: M.I.T. Press, 1988), in particular 83–111. In 1966 Aldo Rossi developed his approach to architecture as the historical, hence specific, elaboration of archetypal geometric forms. See his *The Architecture of the City* (Cambridge, Mass.: M.I.T. Press, 1982), and Klotz, *History of Postmodern Architecture*, 238ff.

5. In architecture, furthermore, the critique of the global ahistoricism of modernism dictated deliberate efforts toward new forms of regionalism. There is no reason that regionalism should be fitting for the headquarters of transnational corporations; and, appropriately, not many headquarters in Asian or Latin American capitals pretend to be "regional." But then the calls for regionalism seldom ask, "Regionalism *for what*?"

6. M. J. Mulkay and B. S. Turner, "Over-production of Personnel and Innovation in Three Social Settings," *Sociology* 5 (1971): 47–61.

7. A note against the *retrospective* attribution of cultural coherence to the varied struggles of the 1960s: The specialized fields of cultural production were affected directly by younger cohorts, who denounced universities, professions, even the political parties of the Left, as arms or accomplices of the state. The struggles of colonized minorities within the United States and the wars waged on colonized peoples without lent gravity to the New Left's distrust of political representation and to the countercultural emphasis on "liberated" social spaces. Because the civil rights struggle and Vietnam infused the whole period with tremendous political intensity, each group of dissenters could interpret its own circumscribed challenge against a particular status quo as a revolutionary effort. Moreover, television news and the newspapers, forcing a synchronic existence on different and only symbolically related events, amplified this illusion. In art-related fields, the residual power of avant-gardist metaphors colored the rhetoric of dissent. As both the student movement and the broader political struggles abated, narrow conflicts remained as metonymies for the wider ones, partial combats that were never as radical in content and significance as their memory. We may also ask if, without Nazi and Stalinist repression, without the bloodbath of war, this would not have happened as well to the art avant-gardes of the revolutionary 1920s and 1930s.

8. This sketch is based on Paul M. Hirsch's work "Processing Fads and Fashions: An Organization-Set Analysis of Cultural Industry Systems," *American Journal of*

Sociology 77 (1972): 639–59. For a full indictment, see the classic text by Theodor Adorno and Max Horkheimer, "The Culture Industry: Enlightenment as Mass Deception," in *Dialectic of Enlightenment*, trans. John Cumming (New York: Continuum, 1989).

9. As Thomas Fisher notes in a recent *Progressive Architecture* editorial, small firms remain numerous, but "the 5% of firms with 20 or more employees now handle 50% of the billings and their economic dominance seems destined to grow as architectural practice becomes increasingly international and—because of computers—more and more capital intensive" (*Progressive Architecture,* Dec. 1991, 7).

10. Hirsch, "Processing Fads," 649.

11. The literature on postmodernism is enormous. Raymond Williams discusses structures of feeling in *Marxism and Literature* (New York and Oxford: Oxford University Press, 1977), 128–35. Some of the important works, many of which I have already quoted: Jürgen Habermas, "Modernity vs. Postmodernity," *New German Critique* 22 (Winter 1981): 3–14; "The French Path to Postmodernity," *New German Critique* 33 (Fall 1984): 79–102; "Psychic Thermidor and the Rebirth of Rebellious Subjectivity" and "Neoconservative Culture Criticism in the United States and West Germany," in Richard Bernstein, ed., *Habermas and Modernity* (Cambridge, Mass.: M.I.T. Press, 1985); "Modern and Postmodern Architecture," in John Forester, ed., *Critical Theory and Public Life* (Cambridge, Mass.: M.I.T. Press, 1985); Jean-François Lyotard, *The Postmodern Condition: A Report on Knowledge,* trans. Geoff Bennington and Brian Massumi (Minneapolis: University of Minnesota Press, 1989), and "Defining the Postmodern," in *ICA Documents 4: Postmodernism* (London: Institute of Contemporary Art, 1986), 6–8; Richard Rorty, "Habermas and Lyotard on Postmodernity," in Bernstein, ed., *Habermas.* David Harvey, *The Condition of Postmodernity* (Oxford: Basil Blackwell, 1989), Fredric Jameson, "Postmodernism, or the Cultural Logic of Late Capitalism," *New Left Review* 146 (July–Aug. 1987): 53–92, and Scott Lash, *The Sociology of Postmodernism* have been quoted either here or in previous chapters. I have found the following helpful: Seyla Benhabib, "Epistemologies of Postmodernism," *New German Critique* 33 (Fall 1984): 103–26, and the entire issue; Charles Bernstein, "Centering the Postmodern," *Socialist Review* 96 (Nov.–Dec. 1987): 45–56; Dick Hebdige, "Staking out the Posts," in *Hiding in the Light* (New York and London: Routledge, 1988); Huyssen, *After the Great Divide;* Fred Pfeil, "Postmodernism as a Structure of Feeling," in Cary Nelson and Lawrence Grossberg, eds., *Marxism and the Interpretation of Culture* (Urbana: University of Illinois Press, 1988); and Andrew Ross, ed., *Universal Abandon? The Politics of Postmodernism* (Minneapolis: University of Minnesota Press, 1988). On the visual arts see *ICA Documents 4: Postmodernism* and Craig Owens, "The Allegorical Impulse: Toward a Theory of Postmodernism," *October* 12 (Spring 1980): 67–86 and 13 (Summer 1980): 59–80. The best critique and the best bibliographic source for architecture is Mary McLeod "Architecture," in Stanley Trachtenberg, ed., *The Postmodern Moment: A Handbook of Contemporary Innovation in the Arts* (Westport, Conn.: Greenwood Press, 1985), and "Architecture and Politics in the Reagan Era: From Postmodernism to Deconstructivism," *Assemblage* 8 (1989): 23–59.

12. Charles Bernstein's critique of Jameson—that he collapses the specific history of each medium and all postmodern manifestations to derive a "dominant," as

if all techniques in every medium were only symptoms of the same disease—applies to much of this pseudo-theorizing. Besides contesting Jameson's specific readings, Bernstein points out that the premise Jameson posits for the postmodern shift (the complete absorption and co-optation of modernism within establishment culture) is false. He accuses Jameson of following for modernism the same faulty procedure he followed to construct postmodernism—collapsing together different art media and different manifestations within each medium. See Bernstein, "Centering the Postmodern."

13. Lyotard, "Defining the Postmodern," 6.

14. Lyotard, *Postmodern Condition*, xxiv and ff.

15. Habermas, "Modern and Postmodern Architecture," 318–19, 322.

16. For an example, see Mark Wigley, "Introduction," in *Deconstructivist Architecture*, Catalog of the Exhibition (New York: Museum of Modern Art, 1988).

17. Jameson gives a striking analysis of John Portman's Bonaventura Hotel in Los Angeles, but he ignores the fact that Portman, being his own developer, is one of the least "alienated" designers one can find in contemporary architecture. Portman goes for success on a broad scale, and his hotels are enormously successful with customers and public. See Jameson, "Postmodernism," 81–83.

18. Walter Benjamin, "The Work of Art in the Age of Mechanical Reproduction," in *Illuminations*, trans. Harry Zohn (New York: Schocken, 1969), 239–41.

19. I am alluding to Walter Benjamin's seventh thesis on the philosophy of history: "Without exception the cultural treasures [a historical materialist] surveys have an origin which he cannot contemplate without horror. They owe their existence not only to the efforts of the great minds and talents who have created them, but also to the anonymous toil of their contemporaries. There is no document of civilization which is not at the same time a document of barbarism" (*Illuminations*, 256).

APPENDIX

1. The simple rank-order coefficients that measure association between ordinal scales, Spearman's r_s and Kendall's tau, show a weak association between the ranking of entries and that of winners from highest to lowest number. These coefficients vary from $+1.0$ when the two rankings are in perfect agreement to -1.0 (perfect disagreement), with 0 showing no relationship whatsoever. Here, the value of Spearman's coefficient is 0.1712 and that of Kendall's 0.1368, relationships that are significant at the 0.051 and the 0.067 levels respectively.

2. See Department of Commerce, Bureau of the Census, *Construction Report*, Series C-30.

3. In private nonresidential construction, the following categories would be most relevant: office buildings; hotels and motels; other commercial; religious; educational; hospital and institutional; miscellaneous nonresidential. Private nonresidential construction as a whole includes categories such as manufacturing facilities, railroads, public utilities, petroleum pipelines, farm structures, and miscellaneous structures that would involve architects only exceptionally and, even then, would most probably involve large architectural-engineering firms, which seldom empha-

size design. For this reason I have considered selected categories, even though the census did not provide broken-down series in every year.

4. Private nonresidential construction as a whole shows a nonnegligible decline of 7.8 percent in 1966–67 (for which broken-down categories are not available) and again in 1969–70 (the decline is 5.7 percent in the categories I have been considering): in both years, the number of submissions to *PA* declined relative to the previous year, while the percentage of winners increased.

Index

Compositor: Impressions

Text: 10/13 Caledonia

Display: Bodoni

Printer and Binder: Edwards Brothers